THE WOMEN'S RIGHTS MOVEMENT SINCE 1945

Recent Titles in the Guides to Historic Events in America
Randall M. Miller, Series Editor

Lincoln, the Rise of the Republicans, and the Coming of the Civil War: A Reference Guide
Kerry Walters

America in the Cold War: A Reference Guide
William T. Walker

Andrew Jackson and the Rise of the Democrats: A Reference Guide
Mark R. Cheathem

The Progressive Era: A Reference Guide
Francis J. Sicius

Reconstruction: A Reference Guide
Paul E. Teed and Melissa Ladd Teed

The War for American Independence: A Reference Guide
Mark Edward Lender

The Constitutional Convention of 1787: A Reference Guide
Stuart Leibiger

The Civil Rights Movement: A Reference Guide
Peter B. Levy

The Immigration and Nationality Act of 1965: A Reference Guide
Michael C. LeMay

The Watergate Crisis: A Reference Guide
Michael A. Genovese

Votes for Women! The American Woman Suffrage Movement and the Nineteenth Amendment: A Reference Guide
Marion W. Roydhouse

The 1960s Cultural Revolution: A Reference Guide
John C. McWilliams

The Reagan Revolution and the Rise of the New Right: A Reference Guide
Kenneth J. Heineman

The Women's Rights Movement since 1945

A Reference Guide

Christina G. Larocco

Guides to Historic Events in America
Randall M. Miller

BLOOMSBURY ACADEMIC
NEW YORK · LONDON · OXFORD · NEW DELHI · SYDNEY

BLOOMSBURY ACADEMIC
Bloomsbury Publishing Inc, 1359 Broadway, 12th Floor, New York, NY 10018, USA
Bloomsbury Publishing Plc, 50 Bedford Square, London, WC1B 3DP, UK
Bloomsbury Publishing Ireland, 29 Earlsfort Terrace, Dublin 2, D02 AY28, Ireland

BLOOMSBURY, BLOOMSBURY ACADEMIC and the Diana logo
are trademarks of Bloomsbury Publishing Plc

First published in the United States of America by ABC-CLIO 2023
Paperback edition published by Bloomsbury Academic 2025

Cover Photo: Pro-choice, women's rights, Planned Parenthood rally and protest
in Washington, D.C, April 24, 2004. (Philip Scalia/Alamy Stock Photo)

Library of Congress Cataloging-in-Publication Data
Names: Larocco, Christina G., author.
Title: The women's rights movement since 1945 : a reference guide / Christina G. Larocco.
Description: Santa Barbara, California : ABC-CLIO, LLC, [2023] | Series: Guides to historic
events in America, Randall M. Miller | Includes bibliographical references and index.
Identifiers: LCCN 2022026260 | ISBN 9781440869075 (hardcover) |
ISBN 9781440869082 (ebook)
Subjects: LCSH: Women's rights—United States—History—20th century. |
Women's rights—United States—History—21st century. | Feminism—United States—
History—20th century. | Feminism—United States—History—21st century.
Classification: LCC HQ1236.5.U6 L37 2023 | DDC 305.42097309/04—dc23/eng/20220707
LC record available at https://lccn.loc.gov/2022026260

ISBN: HB: 978-1-4408-6907-5
PB: 979-8-2163-9234-7
ePDF: 978-1-4408-6908-2
eBook: 979-8-2161-8281-8

Series: Guides to Historic Events in America

For product safety related questions contact productsafety@bloomsbury.com.

To find out more about our authors and books visit www.bloomsbury.com
and sign up for our newsletters.

CONTENTS

SERIES FOREWORD

Perhaps no people have been more difficult to comprehend than the Americans. As J. Hector St. Jean de Crèvecoeur asked during the American Revolution, countless others have echoed ever after— "What then is this American, this new man?" What, indeed? Americans then and after have been, and remain, a people in the process of becoming. They have been, and are, a people in motion, whether coming from a distant shore, crossing the mighty Mississippi, or packing off to the suburbs, and all the while following the promise of an American dream of realizing life, liberty, and happiness. The directions of such movement have changed, and sometimes the trajectory has taken a downward arc in terms of civil war and economic depression, but always the process has continued.

Making sense of that American experience demands attention to critical moments—events—that reflected and affected American ideas and identities. Although Americans have constructed an almost linear narrative of progress from the days of George Washington to today in relating their common history, they also have marked that history by recognizing particular events as pivotal in explaining who and why they believed and acted as they did at particular times and over time. Such events have forced Americans to consider closely their true interests. They also have challenged their commitment to professed beliefs of freedom and liberty, equality and opportunity, tolerance and generosity. Whether fighting for independence or empire, drafting and implementing a frame of government, reconstructing a nation divided by civil war, struggling for basic rights and the franchise, creating a mass-mediated culture, standing up for capitalism and democracy and against communism, to name several critical developments, Americans have understood that historic events are more than just moments. They are processes of change made clear through particular events but not bound to a single moment or instance. Such thinking about the character and consequence of American history informs this new series of Guides to Historic Events in America.

Drawing on the latest and best literature, and bringing together narrative overviews and critical chapters of important historic events, the books in the series function as both reference guides and informed analyses to critical events that have shaped American life, culture, society, economy, and politics and fixed America's place in the world. The books do not promise a comprehensive reading and rendering of American history. Such is not yet, if ever, possible for any single work or series. Nor do they chart a single interpretive line, though they share common concerns and methods of inquiry. Each book stands alone, resting on the expertise of the author and the strength of the evidence. At the same time, taken together, the books in this new series will provide a dynamic portrait of that ongoing work in progress, America itself.

Each book follows a common format, with a chronology, historical overview, topical chapters on aspects of the historical event under examination, a set of biographies of key figures, selected essential primary documents, and an annotated bibliography. As such, each book holds many uses for students, teachers, and the general public wanting and needing to know the principal issues and the pertinent arguments and evidence on significant events in American history. The combination of historical description and analysis, biographies, and primary documents also moves readers to approach each critical event from multiple perspectives and with a critical eye. Each book, in its structure and content, invites students and teachers, in and out of the classroom, to consider and debate the character and consequence(s) of the historic event in question. Such debate invariably will bring readers back to that most critical and never-ending question of what was/is "the American" and what does, and must, "America" mean.

Randall M. Miller
Saint Joseph's University, Philadelphia

Preface and Acknowledgments

L ike millions of others, both in the United States and worldwide, I attended a Women's March in January 2017. My experience of the event itself was underwhelming: downtown Washington, DC, was so packed that I couldn't get close enough to hear the speakers. The signs—clever, heartbroken, full of righteous anger—were the best part. Yet I was happy to have played a small part in signaling to the new administration how many people take women's rights very seriously.

Several years on, the feeling of solidarity that briefly emerged in that moment seems naive. Even before it occurred, the Women's March had become part of a broader debate about race, gender, and voting behavior, as cultural commentators struggled to understand how white women could have voted for Donald Trump. It seemed clear to many that these women had chosen to retain the privileges gained from systemic racism rather than challenge the drawbacks of sexism. This criticism extended beyond conservative white women. A slew of think pieces—and eventually books—took on the history of white feminism, arguing that its adherents had often advanced their own interests at the expense of other women.

I was and am enormously sympathetic to this perspective, which is inarguably true. But I was also, I confess, surprised by its sudden ubiquity in cultural discourse. Didn't everyone know this already? Wasn't it common knowledge, for example, that Betty Friedan's exhortations to women to escape the prison of domesticity ignored the fact that domesticity had never been an option for working-class women, poor women, and women of color?

It's not, of course. The intertwined history of race and gender in the women's movement—like so much else about it—is not common knowledge after all. This book exists for that reason. It distills what I have learned about this history in the past two decades, from primary sources, other historians, and witnessing a series of twenty-first-century reckonings over women, gender, and feminism. As readers will find, the Women's March was, in many ways, a microcosm for the post–World War II women's rights movement: at each juncture, the movement struggled both with external opponents and within itself. Though I endeavor to analyze these events within their historical context, I also hope that the following chapters will help readers understand one part of how we got to where we are today.

When Randall Miller asked me to write this book in 2018, I could not have begun to imagine all the ways the world would change in the intervening three years, from upheaval in my personal life and changes in my professional responsibilities to political instability and a global pandemic. Even in retrospect, I do not really have the words to describe what we have all been through. I must first, therefore, thank my colleagues, including Randall and my editors at ABC-CLIO, not only for the opportunity but also for their tremendous patience as I coped—often badly, occasionally, slightly better—with our new reality. Randall gave me the freedom to write the book I wanted to write and the wise guidance to make it better. I am also grateful to my colleagues at the Historical Society of Pennsylvania (HSP), who generously allowed me to use images from HSP's collections without paying permissions fees. In my personal life, my COVID bubble/Philadelphia family, especially Josh T. Landow, helped keep me sane. If telling Josh about this book on our first date impressed him enough to help me secure a second, then I'm grateful for that too. My family provided crucial support, undiminished by our reliance on Zoom and other technologies. Finally, this book is for my grandmothers, Gisela Jako Jost (1916–2014) and Katherine McCloskey Larocco (1921–2015), feminists in spirit, if not in name. To paraphrase the late Supreme Court justice Ruth Bader Ginsburg, I hope I am even a fraction of what they could have been had they lived in a time more like mine.

INTRODUCTION

I t would be difficult to overestimate how much American women's lives have changed between 1945 and today. In the mid-twentieth century, several states had "head and master" laws that formally subjected women to their husbands. Women were legally obligated to raise children and perform domestic labor, but they had no right to any of their husband's earnings or property. In many states, married women were legally required to change their last names and could be penalized if they did not. Professional and graduate schools regularly set quotas for how many women they would admit, often 5–10 percent or less of admitted students. It was perfectly legal to pay women less for doing the same job as a man or to fire, refuse to hire, or refuse to promote someone for being a woman. Sexual harassment, rape, and domestic violence were "private" issues that women had to endure, with authorities like courts and the police often unwilling to provide recourse. Nowhere in the United States was marital rape recognized as a crime. Abortion was illegal in most cases (and often deadly), and though the first birth control pill was approved in 1960, access to it was not legally guaranteed. But such conditions and restrictions were not immutable. Through the concerted action of several generations of activists, many women's lives improved. Those women activists and their work are the subjects of this volume.

Traditionally, feminist scholarship has divided the feminist movement into three "waves": first-wave feminism, which dated from the mid-nineteenth century through 1920 and concerned itself primarily with women's property and citizenship rights, especially the right to vote; second-wave feminism, which lasted from the mid-1960s through the mid-1980s and worked to eliminate both legal and social barriers to women's full and equal participation in American life; and third-wave feminism, which emerged in the 1990s and attempted to make feminism more inclusive both in subject matter and relevance to different groups of women.

This framework fails to capture the full history of the women's rights movement in a number of ways. First, it posits a singular feminism, ignoring the different sites and strategies that have ebbed and flowed over the course of the past 150 years. Often, this singular definition of feminism has focused on the activism of middle-class white women to the exclusion of other groups. As historian Julie Gallagher puts it, "[T]he wave metaphor highlights periods when middle-class white women were most active in the public sphere."[1] A narrative that focuses on working-class women or immigrant women or Black women may look very different. For many working-class women, developments in the 1930s such as the Wagner Act, which granted federal protection to unions, and the emergence of the CIO, may have been just as significant as suffrage. For Black women, the Great Migration was arguably more transformative than the Nineteenth Amendment. These women's focus and forms of activism were not precursors to or variations on white middle-class feminism, but rather, powerful movements with their own histories, dynamics, and trajectories. So too does the wave metaphor often substitute activism on the coasts for activism across the nation, positing it as something that began on the East and West Coasts and then crested across the nation, when in truth, different geographies also followed different trajectories, with grassroots feminism springing out of local conditions.

The wave metaphor also downplays the crucial activism that took place between the waves. Most crucially for this volume, the wave metaphor in its most stringent application suggests that there was no feminism between the ratification of the Nineteenth Amendment in 1920 and the publication of *The Feminine Mystique* in 1963 (again, both events that primarily benefited or spoke to white women). In the face of overwhelming evidence to the contrary, even restricting oneself to the postwar era, this claim appears laughably myopic. Through unions and the federal Women's Bureau of the Department of Labor, women fought for and often won paid maternity leave, equal pay for equal work, and other benefits. Long before she became famous for instigating the Montgomery Bus Boycott,

Rosa Parks traveled across the South investigating instances of rape and sexual assault against Black women and seeking justice for survivors. In 1955, women in Los Angeles founded the Daughters of Bilitis (DOB), which became the nation's first lesbian rights group. The postwar era was far from quiet.

Relatedly, the wave metaphor fails to account for the connections between and among these different eras. Alice Paul and the National Woman's Party (NWP) breathed new life into the suffrage movement in the second decade of the twentieth century, crucially pushing for a federal amendment while other organizations remained focused on state-by-state battles. By this measure, Paul and her allies were exemplary first-wave feminists. But she was also the architect of the Equal Rights Amendment (ERA), one of the key demands of the second-wave feminist movement. Paul herself continued to advocate for the measure until shortly before her death in 1977. To what wave, then, do Paul and the ERA belong?

Yet the persistence of the wave metaphor is not entirely baseless. First, it is absolutely true that powerful forces limited feminism's efficacy in certain time periods, including the 1950s and '80s; to suggest otherwise does a disservice to activists' perseverance. Ironically, however, feminists and their opponents have unintentionally collaborated to perpetuate this narrative. As chapter 1 of this volume recounts, the political exigencies of the Cold War necessitated downplaying one's pre- and early postwar feminist commitments. In order to avoid red-baiting, activists such as Betty Friedan argued inaccurately that she had been content in domesticity for many years, never questioning women's roles until she found that many of her classmates from Smith College were unhappy. Her experiences, she insisted, were not unique; American women had drifted along for decades without challenging the status quo. For many years, women's historians were content to retell the Betty Friedan version of the story. Conservatives, by contrast, have often painted the 1950s as a golden era of peace and prosperity, free from the discord of the next decade—especially the social upheavals of the civil rights, feminist, and gay and lesbian liberation movements. On the eve of the 2016 election, for example, 74 percent of white evangelical Protestants indicated nostalgia for the 1950s.[2] Though the political goals differ, both visions depend upon the same myth: there was no feminism in the 1950s. (A concomitant, equally insidious myth is that no women worked for wages in the 1950s.)

Some intrepid historians have begun to suggest alternatives to the wave metaphor, including streams, rivers, or groundswells. Members of different generations, however, continue to *self-identify* with these terms. "Third-wave feminist," for example, was a self-conscious identity from its inception, usually used to differentiate oneself from earlier feminist itera- tions. "Second-wave feminists" have followed suit, often using the term to defend their legacy from younger women.

For this reason, this study does employ the concepts of second- and third-wave feminism, though recognizing that they more accurately re- flect the *identities* of some (especially white, middle class) activists than they do the *reality* of the women's rights movement. At the same time, as Dorothy Sue Cobble, author of the hugely influential *The Other Women's Movement*, points out, scholars of women's movements may have been entirely too literal in transmuting the concept of waves from the natural world into the historical one:

> The homogeneous, univocal wave does not exist in nature. Up close, the ocean is full of cross-currents and eddies. Up close, it is hard to separate one wave from another, to see where one begins and another ends. Waves overlap, their currents mostly submerged, one spilling into another. They are continuous and multiple. There are little waves within big waves, and waves within troughs as well as within crests. Indeed, out on the sea of women's reform, there is little still water in sight.[3]

Another issue concerns the terms "feminist" and "feminism" themselves. The history of the women's rights movement comprises much more than the actions of self-identified feminists. In many cases, fierce advocates of women's rights have—often for very good reasons—rejected the feminist label. (Less commonly, self-identified feminists have advocated positions that seem at odds with much of the movement's history.) Starting in the 1920s, the term became more and more exclusively associated with the NWP, which meant that women's rights advocates who opposed the ERA were often reluctant to call themselves feminists, which they associ- ated with a dangerous individualism. Many Black women, working-class women, and such Progressive allies as Eleanor Roosevelt belonged to this group. For reasons of race, class, and political priorities, some of the mid- twentieth century's most indefatigable champions of women's rights did not call themselves feminists.

Other groups of women have also perceived feminism as white and middle class. Frances Beal, the author of *Double Jeopardy: To Be Black and Female* and a founder, in 1968, of the Third World Women's Alliance (TWWA), recalled that women in her activist cohort "did not like" the term "feminism," "because at that time it came to mean women who put female first and that was the only thing, you know, it was a very narrow perception. And what we were trying to deal with was the integration of race, gender, class, in consciousness, and not like put one above the other, because we didn't think it actually operated as one is more important than another, but that there was actually an integration of that."[4] Middle-class white feminists' tendency to focus on such issues as access to abortion and the professions—to the exclusion of equally important issues, including forced sterilization and workplace exploitation—contributed to this alienation. In the 1980s and '90s, backlash had so tarnished the term that many young women were reluctant to claim it, fearing that they would be seen as man-hating. As college student Linn Thomas told *Time* magazine in 1992, "I picture a feminist as someone who is masculine and who doesn't shave her legs and is doing everything she can to deny that she is feminine."[5] Today, the many failures of white feminism continue to hinder the relevance of the term.

At the dawn of the post–World War II era, when the main narrative of this book opens, women's rights activists had reason to be hopeful. True, the immediate post-suffrage era had been a disappointment. The Nineteenth Amendment generated some momentum for furthering women's rights, but these gains were temporary and/or mixed. In the wake of its ratification, Congress decided that it made sense to alter the rules governing women's citizenship; the 1922 Cable Act was intended to do just this. Before 1922, a married woman's citizenship was derivative—that is, it followed her husband's. As a result, if a woman who was a U.S. citizen married a man who was not one, she lost her U.S. citizenship. Harriot Stanton Blatch, a prominent suffragist and the daughter of Elizabeth Cady Stanton, had experienced this fate when she married an Englishman. The Cable Act granted women independent citizenship unless they married a man who was racially ineligible for citizenship—most importantly, men of Asian descent.

The previous year, Progressives had secured a political victory with the passage of the Sheppard-Towner Act, which for the first time allocated federal funds for maternal and infant health. However, many members of Congress voted for it not because they supported the program but rather because they feared that newly enfranchised women would vote as a bloc, punishing those who did not support the measure. When it became clear that this was not happening, congressional support waned, and the program was allowed to expire.

In general, women's activism became more difficult after World War I and into the 1920s. Disappointment that contributions to the war effort had not led to full citizenship rights, the Black civil rights movement embraced Black nationalism and martial masculinity. This reorientation attenuated the efficacy of women's claims on leadership, which often rested on respectability and morality. Additionally, during the war, patriotic groups had painted women's peace activism as un-American. In its wake, a red scare led to the fear of left and labor activism and contributed to a return to the free market ideologies of the Gilded Age, placing Progressivism on the defensive. In this context, the Supreme Court was much less sympathetic to protective labor legislation. A law banning child labor was found unconstitutional, and an amendment intended to replace it passed Congress but failed to be ratified. In *Adkins v. Children's Hospital* (1923), the court—with crucial aid from the NWP—struck down a Washington, DC, minimum wage law for women.

Both women and men turned to disarmament (and sometimes a concomitant isolationism) in the wake of World War I. But disarmament was not the same as pacifism, and women were more successful than men in building a broad-based international peace movement. Founded in 1915, the U.S. branch of the Women's International League for Peace and Freedom (WILPF) grew out of the Woman's Peace Party, established by Carrie Chapman Catt, Jane Addams, and others. WILPF members also included Jeannette Rankin, the first woman elected to Congress. In the 1920s, the U.S. branch of WILPF argued for disarmament, recognition of the Soviet Union, peaceful mediation, and other causes.

In the context of the red scare, however, many saw pacifists as disloyal and subversive. Army officers denounced WILPF by name, and the so-called spiderweb chart significantly damaged the women's movement. Originating in the office of Brigadier-General Amos A. Fries of the Chemical Warfare Service, the spiderweb chart purported to show connections between feminist, pacifist, and progressive organizations with

Other groups of women have also perceived feminism as white and middle class. Frances Beal, the author of *Double Jeopardy: To Be Black and Female* and a founder, in 1968, of the Third World Women's Alliance (TWWA), recalled that women in her activist cohort "did not like" the term "feminism," "because at that time it came to mean women who put female first and that was the only thing, you know, it was a very narrow perception. And what we were trying to deal with was the integration of race, gender, class, in consciousness, and not like put one above the other, because we didn't think it actually operated as one is more important than another, but that there was actually an integration of that."[4] Middle-class white feminists' tendency to focus on such issues as access to abortion and the professions—to the exclusion of equally important issues, including forced sterilization and workplace exploitation—contributed to this alienation. In the 1980s and '90s, backlash had so tarnished the term that many young women were reluctant to claim it, fearing that they would be seen as man-hating. As college student Linn Thomas told *Time* magazine in 1992, "I picture a feminist as someone who is masculine and who doesn't shave her legs and is doing everything she can to deny that she is feminine."[5] Today, the many failures of white feminism continue to hinder the relevance of the term.

At the dawn of the post–World War II era, when the main narrative of this book opens, women's rights activists had reason to be hopeful. True, the immediate post-suffrage era had been a disappointment. The Nineteenth Amendment generated some momentum for furthering women's rights, but these gains were temporary and/or mixed. In the wake of its ratification, Congress decided that it made sense to alter the rules governing women's citizenship; the 1922 Cable Act was intended to do just this. Before 1922, a married woman's citizenship was derivative—that is, it followed her husband's. As a result, if a woman who was a U.S. citizen married a man who was not one, she lost her U.S. citizenship. Harriot Stanton Blatch, a prominent suffragist and the daughter of Elizabeth Cady Stanton, had experienced this fate when she married an Englishman. The Cable Act granted women independent citizenship unless they married a man who was racially ineligible for citizenship—most importantly, men of Asian descent.

The previous year, Progressives had secured a political victory with the passage of the Sheppard-Towner Act, which for the first time allocated federal funds for maternal and infant health. However, many members of Congress voted for it not because they supported the program but rather because they feared that newly enfranchised women would vote as a bloc, punishing those who did not support the measure. When it became clear that this was not happening, congressional support waned, and the program was allowed to expire.

In general, women's activism became more difficult after World War I and into the 1920s. Disappointment that contributions to the war effort had not led to full citizenship rights, the Black civil rights movement embraced Black nationalism and martial masculinity. This reorientation attenuated the efficacy of women's claims on leadership, which often rested on respectability and morality. Additionally, during the war, patriotic groups had painted women's peace activism as un-American. In its wake, a red scare led to the fear of left and labor activism and contributed to a return to the free market ideologies of the Gilded Age, placing Progressivism on the defensive. In this context, the Supreme Court was much less sympathetic to protective labor legislation. A law banning child labor was found unconstitutional, and an amendment intended to replace it passed Congress but failed to be ratified. In *Adkins v. Children's Hospital* (1923), the court—with crucial aid from the NWP—struck down a Washington, DC, minimum wage law for women.

Both women and men turned to disarmament (and sometimes a concomitant isolationism) in the wake of World War I. But disarmament was not the same as pacifism, and women were more successful than men in building a broad-based international peace movement. Founded in 1915, the U.S. branch of the Women's International League for Peace and Freedom (WILPF) grew out of the Woman's Peace Party, established by Carrie Chapman Catt, Jane Addams, and others. WILPF members also included Jeannette Rankin, the first woman elected to Congress. In the 1920s, the U.S. branch of WILPF argued for disarmament, recognition of the Soviet Union, peaceful mediation, and other causes.

In the context of the red scare, however, many saw pacifists as disloyal and subversive. Army officers denounced WILPF by name, and the so-called spiderweb chart significantly damaged the women's movement. Originating in the office of Brigadier-General Amos A. Fries of the Chemical Warfare Service, the spiderweb chart purported to show connections between feminist, pacifist, and progressive organizations with socialist and communist groups around the world, painting all three as un-American. The chart spread quickly to people like J. Edgar Hoover at the FBI and Henry Ford of the Ford Motor Company, and such groups as the Daughters of the American Revolution (DAR) eagerly took up the call. From there, it was easy for right-wing groups to argue that *all* women's organizations were subversive. The newspaper *Woman Patriot*, for example, insisted that the NWP was made up of "soviets" and argued that "like the Communists, the Woman's Party seeks first equality, and then dictatorship—and largely by similar tactics and organization!"[6] No matter that, in the United States, NWP members and communists were fundamentally at odds with each other—in this view, feminism, pacifism, and socialism were inextricably intertwined. Among those most affected by this discourse was reformer Jane Addams, whose reputation never fully recovered during her lifetime.

The suffrage coalition, meanwhile, had disintegrated, primarily over the issue of the ERA. Until 1920, suffrage provided a goal around which feminists of many different stripes could rally, even if they disagreed on nearly everything else. But after the Nineteenth Amendment was ratified, activists were divided: should they continue to work on suffrage, which racist state laws still denied Black women in the South? Or should they turn to the myriad other ways women (specifically, in their case, professional white women) were discriminated against? The NWP chose the latter course.

Even before the Nineteenth Amendment was ratified, NWP members had begun to think about ways to bring about "full legal equality" for women—something they knew suffrage, while a monumental victory, did not even come close to securing. The law still considered women, in many ways, the property of their husbands, if married, and their fathers, if not. They were unlikely to be granted custody of their children in divorce cases and were barred from serving on juries. As noted above, their citizenship was still considered derivative. They did not have equal access to education or the professions, and their remuneration lagged far behind that of men's. While the NWP drafted and lobbied for legislation addressing all these individual issues, their main legislative priority was the ERA, which would have done away with all gender-based discrimination in one fell swoop. First drafted by NWP founder Alice Paul in 1923, its original language insisted that "[m]en and women shall have equal rights throughout the United States and every place subject to its jurisdiction." The more familiar wording, "Equality of rights under the law shall not be denied or abridged by the United States or by any state on account of sex," was introduced in 1943. Paul brought the ERA to the 1923 meeting of the NWP Executive Committee, and it was first introduced in Congress that December. However, when Congress held hearings on the matter two years later, the NWP was shocked to discover that they were the only women's group committed to the amendment.[7]

The reasons for this split lay in the broader historical context of the final push for suffrage, which paved the way for very different understandings of "equality." Many suffragists were also active in the Progressive movement, in which middle-class reformers and their allies in the labor movement and elsewhere attempted to rein in the excesses of the unfettered free market capitalism that had characterized the Gilded Age. Workers, many of them women, put in long hours in factories for little pay and under dangerous conditions. Progressives argued that it was the proper role of the government to protect people from workplace exploitation. Unfortunately, the courts rarely agreed, regularly striking down state laws that mandated minimum pay or maximum hours as violations of "freedom of contract."

Women reformers, however, found a way to break through this hostility by arguing for women's-only protective legislation. In *Muller v. Oregon* (1908), the Supreme Court validated this strategy, and the next several years were characterized by a proliferation of state and local laws mandating women-only minimum wages and maximum hours and preventing women from working at night or under conditions considered especially dangerous. Many of the women involved in crafting this legislation, including future first lady Eleanor Roosevelt and future secretary of labor Frances Perkins, went on to be among the most vocal opponents of the ERA into the postwar era.

The Great Depression brought Progressive policies back into fashion. Progressive women gained unprecedented access to government during the New Deal, in part due to the influence of First Lady Eleanor Roosevelt, herself a longtime reformer who often pushed her husband to listen to her friends in labor, Progressive, and feminist circles. Most obviously, Frances Perkins became the first woman to hold a cabinet-level position when she became secretary of labor in 1933. Within the Department of

Labor, Mary Anderson, originally a bootmaker, continued to serve as head of the Women's Bureau, a post she had held since 1920. Mary McLeod Bethune, founder of the National Council of Negro Women (NCNW), brought her savvy pocketbook politics to both her formal role as director of the Negro Division of the National Youth Administration (NYA) and her informal role at the center of the president's "Black Cabinet." Both Perkins and Anderson—along with such women as Molly Dewson, head of the Women's Division of the Democratic Party—in turn provided opportunities to scores of other women. Beyond the Women's Bureau, New Deal agencies, especially the National Labor Relations Board (NLRB), which oversaw the negotiation and implementation of union workplace contracts, and the Social Security Board (SSB), which administered the 1935 Social Security Act's old-age pensions, disability benefits, and Aid to Dependent Children (ADC), provided women with unprecedented opportunities for professional employment and leadership and decision-making positions.

Perkins brought to her post decades of experience with the Women's Trade Union League (WTUL)—the same organization that Eleanor Roosevelt belonged to—and a commitment to improving conditions and opportunities for women workers, which she came to through firsthand contact with women labor activists. In the wake of the 1911 Triangle Shirtwaist Factory fire, which killed 146 workers, many of them young immigrant women, New York State established a Factory Investigating Commission to document working conditions and prevent future tragedies. On this commission, Perkins served alongside longtime labor activists Rose Schneiderman and Pauline Newman. Later, Perkins attributed to Schneiderman her commitment to working women. Not incidentally, she also met through the commission future senator Robert F. Wagner, sponsor of the Wagner Act, and FDR himself, then a young state senator.

Through both his political commitments and his wife's activism, then, FDR was exposed to feminist and Progressive politics long before he served as either governor or president. In 1926, Eleanor even invited Schneiderman and her partner, Maud Swartz, to their home. FDR, Schneiderman, and Swartz got along famously, talking for hours. As his own political star rose, he continued to rely on these women for staffing and solutions.

The power of Black and working-class women in the New Deal was circumscribed, as only Anderson held real power. Even Perkins was unable to prevent the significant gender disparities in New Deal legislation. But this generation of women was absolutely crucial both for what its members accomplished in their own right and also for the link they provided between early twentieth-century Progressivism and the feminist debates of the early postwar era.

The effects of World War II itself on women's rights are widely known yet often misunderstood. The majority of women who worked for wages during the war had done so before it began, often in low-wage, pink-collar jobs like waitressing and domestic service. They gained access to industrial jobs during the war, which paid far better—especially since the National War Labor Board mandated equal pay for equal work—and granted unprecedented access to unions.

These developments proceeded unevenly. Although FDR's Executive Order 8802 banned racial discrimination in the defense industries, white men and women continued to discriminate against their African American counterparts. Unions were inconsistent allies to Black women. When a UAW local in Detroit voted to integrate, white women protested. "I don't think we should bring the problem of negro women into this meeting," one insisted. "I don't think we should consider bringing them into the shops—if we bring them in even in this crisis we'd always have them to contend with. And you know what that means—we'd be working right beside them, we'd be using the same rest rooms, etc. I'm against it." Employers used this reluctance as an excuse not to hire African American women, arguing that it would slow production and impede the war effort.[8]

Still, World War II was a boon for Black women workers, who used the Fair Employment Practices Commission (FEPC), United Auto Workers (UAW), National Association for the Advancement of Colored People (NAACP), and Urban League to demand access to defense jobs. The UAW, for example, supported a group of Black women who stormed the employment office at Ford's Willow Run plant in Detroit after being denied entrance at the hiring gate. As a result, the company started working with the UAW to establish a program for hiring Black women. The UAW also intervened at the behest of four Black women when white women initiated a hate strike at a Detroit Chrysler plant. Through their own persistence, Black women gained access to well-paying industrial jobs and were able to move out of domestic service in large numbers for the first time. As Fanny Hill joked, "Hitler was the one that got us out of

An African American woman works in World War II–era industry. Many American women worked for wages before the war, but the conflict gave them opportunities to move into better-paid, often unionized positions. (Library of Congress, Prints & Photographs Division, FSA/OWI Collection, LC-USW33-028625-C)

the White folks' kitchen."[9] Women flocked to unions in the 1940s and '50s, from which they demanded many of the rights that characterized the better-known feminism of the 1960s and '70s.

To previous generations of historians, 1945 may seem an inauspicious year to begin a narrative of the women's rights movement; the end of World War II supposedly marked the beginning of a conservative era in which women's lives were primarily defined by domesticity. More recently, however, historians have uncovered an unbroken history of women's activism, one in which the years immediately after World War II provided much of the intellectual groundwork for the feminist revolution of the 1960s, '70s, and beyond. Popular Front women, including those in the orbit of the Communist Party, developed a sophisticated, intersectional feminist critique ready in the second half of the 1940s to burst into the mainstream. Like many Americans, Popular Front feminists hoped and expected that the end of World War II would bring about a renewed focus on Progressive reform. Though the Cold War disrupted this movement's efficacy, it persisted in places like the labor, Black freedom, and pacifist movements.

This volume thus emphasizes continuities, both between feminist "waves" and between periods of supposed quiet and visible revolution. The persistence of women's activism does not mean that the movement did not change over time or that its adherents were unified at any chronological point. If continuity of activism represents one major theme of this volume, diversity, conflict, and compromise within the feminist movement—especially along lines of race, class, and sexuality—represent the second. Nor does this volume downplay the opposition the women's rights movement has faced. From Vice President Richard Nixon's 1959 insistence that women's domesticity proved American superiority in the Cold War to Rush Limbaugh's "feminazis," opponents have characterized feminism as a threat to home, family, and nation. This volume is particularly interested in, and pays special attention to, the women who opposed feminism. It takes them seriously as sophisticated political actors who for various reasons felt that feminism posed a threat to them.

This volume will chart through eight thematic chapters the ways that the women's rights movement changed the political, economic, legal, social, and cultural landscape of the United States. It starts with a challenge to rethink the place of feminism in the early Cold War, emphasizing its awareness of intersectionality and pointing to connections between this era and the feminist revolution of the 1960s and '70s. Feminisms flourished in this era; though divided by identity and strategy, it wrought tremendous changes in women's and others' lives, changing their relationships to family, work, education, government, sexuality, and more. Feminists in the 1980s and '90s learned, however, that such changes were not irreversible. This lesson seems particularly relevant today.

NOTES

1. Julie Gallagher, "Revisiting Constructs and Their Tyrannical Inclinations," in Kathleen A. Laughlin et al., "Is It Time to Jump Ship? Historians Rethink the Waves Metaphor," *Feminist Formations* 22, no. 1 (2010): 82.

2. Betsy Cooper et al., "The Divide over America's Future: 1950 or 2050? Findings from the 2016 American Values Survey," Public Religion Research Institute, Oct. 25, 2016, https://www.prri.org/research/poll-1950s-2050-divided -nations-direction-post-election/.

3. Dorothy Sue Cobble, "The Long History of Women's Freedom Struggles," in Laughlin et al., "Is It Time to Jump Ship?" 87.

4. Frances Beal interview with Loretta J. Ross, Voices of Feminism Oral History Project, Sophia Smith Collection, Smith College, Northampton, MA, Mar. 18, 2005, p. 43, https://www.smith.edu/libraries/libs/ssc/vof/transcripts/Beal.pdf.

5. Linn Thomas, quoted in Claudia Wallis, "Onward, Women!" *Time* magazine, Dec. 4, 1989, 81.

6. *Woman Patriot*, quoted in Nancy F. Cott, *The Grounding of Modern Feminism* (New Haven, CT: Yale University Press, 1987), 261.

7. Christine Lunardini, *From Equal Suffrage to Equal Rights: Alice Paul and the National Woman's Party, 1912–1928* (New York: New York University Press, 1986).

8. Megan Taylor Shockley, "Working for Democracy: Working: Class African-American Women, Citizenship, and Civil Rights in Detroit, 1940–1954," *Michigan Historical Review* 29, no. 2 (2003): 135.

9. Ibid., 127, 141; Fanny Christina Hill, "Hitler Was the One That Got Us Out of the White Folks' Kitchen," in *The Columbia Documentary History of America since 1941*, ed. Harriet Sigerman (New York: Columbia University Press, 2003), 39.

CHRONOLOGY

1892	Ida B. Wells publishes *Southern Horrors: Lynch Law in All Its Phases*, challenging myths about Black sexuality and informing Black women's later struggles for bodily autonomy.
1896	Mary Church Terrell, Anna Julia Cooper, and others establish the National Association of Colored Women (NACW); its motto is "[L]ifting as we climb."
1908	In *Muller v. Oregon*, the Supreme Court upholds an Oregon law establishing maximum working hours for women.
1911	In the wake of the Triangle Shirtwaist Factory Fire, New York State establishes a Factory Investigating Committee, bringing together Frances Perkins, Robert F. Wagner, and Franklin D. Roosevelt.
1915	The Women's International League for Peace and Freedom (WILPF) is founded.
1916	October 16: Margaret Sanger opens a clinic to provide women with information about birth control; for doing so, she and her sister are arrested, tried, and sentenced to thirty days in prison.
	Jeannette Rankin, Republican from Montana, becomes the first woman elected to Congress.

1917	The United States formally enters World War I, sowing division among both suffragists and pacifists.
1918	The Woman in Industry Service is founded to coordinate women's wartime labor.
1919	The First Red Scare tarnishes the reputations of feminists, pacifists, and progressives.
	Post–World War I racial violence leads to the emergence of the New Negro movement.
1920	The Woman in Industry Service becomes the Women's Bureau of the Department of Labor.
	Mary Anderson is appointed head.
	The Nineteenth Amendment is ratified, making it illegal to deny citizens the right to vote "on account of sex."
1921	The Sheppard-Towner Act becomes law, for the first time allocating federal funds for maternal and infant care.
	National Woman's Party members and others found the Women's Committee for World Disarmament.
1922	The Cable Act provides for independent citizenship for many married women.
1923	In *Adkins v. Children's Hospital*, the Supreme Court strikes down a Washington, DC, minimum wage law for women.
	December: The Equal Rights Amendment (ERA) is first introduced into Congress.
1927	In *Buck v. Bell* (1927), the Supreme Court upholds a Virginia law allowing forced sterilization.
1930	Black women found Housewives' Leagues to advance the principle of "Don't buy where you can't work."
	The Supreme Court finds in *Youngs Rubber Corporation v. C.I. Lee & Co., et al.* that condoms (and, by extension, other forms of birth control) can be sold legally for other purposes.
1933	President Franklin D. Roosevelt appoints Frances Perkins secretary of labor, making her the first woman to hold a cabinet-level position.

1935   The National Labor Relations Act (Wagner Act) becomes law, providing legal protection for unions.

The Congress of Industrial Organizations (CIO) is founded, paving the way for the unionization of workers excluded from the American Federation of Labor (AFL), including millions of women.

Mary McLeod Bethune founds the National Council of Negro Women (NCNW).

Aid to Dependent Children is established as part of the Social Security Act.

1936   *United States v. One Package of Japanese Pessaries* decision makes it legal for doctors to send and receive contraceptive devices and information.

1937   The American Medical Association (AMA) lifts its ban on doctors prescribing birth control.

1938   Mary McLeod Bethune becomes director of the Division of Negro Affairs within the National Youth Administration (NYA).

1939   Mary Inman publishes *In Woman's Defense*.

1940   The Smith Act, later used to prosecute communists, makes it illegal to "teach, advocate, or encourage the overthrow" of the government "by force or violence" or associate with any group that did so.

1941   June 25: President Roosevelt issues Executive Order 8802, banning racial discrimination in the war industries and establishing the Fair Employment Practices Commission (FEPC).

December 7: The United States formally enters World War II.

The Community Facilities Act (Lanham Act) provides funds for community centers; two years later, funds are appropriated for childcare facilities.

1942   September: The National War Labor Board dictates that "rates for women shall be set in accordance with the principle of equal pay for comparable quantity and quality of work on comparable operations."

	Suspected of communist influence, economist Mary Dublin Keyserling first comes under investigation as a possible security threat.
	The FBI begins investigating Claudia Jones for her membership in the Communist Party.
1943	Susan B. Anthony II publishes *Out of the Kitchen, into the War*.
1944	Frieda Miller becomes head of the Women's Bureau.
	Rosa Parks investigates the rape of Recy Taylor in Abbeville, Alabama.
1945	January 3: The House Un-American Activities Committee (HUAC) becomes a permanent committee.
	August: With the end of World War II, the mandates of Executive Order 8802 and the National War Labor Board expire.
1946	The ERA is reported out of committee for the first time.
	Feminists in the United Auto Workers (UAW) establish a women's bureau within the union; the next year it becomes the UAW Women's Department.
	The Congress of American Women (CAW) is founded as the U.S. branch of the Women's International Democratic Federation.
1947	ERA opponents propose the Women's Status Bill, which would have maintained certain sex-based protections and established a presidential Commission on the Status of Women.
	President Harry Truman creates the Federal Employee Loyalty Program.
1948	The Communist Party of the United States of America (CPUSA) recognizes gender inequality as a problem separate from the class struggle.
	Mary Dublin Keyserling is investigated for possible communist sympathies by both the FBI and the Commerce Department.
1949	Claudia Jones publishes "An End to the Neglect of the Problems of the Negro Woman."

Eleven CPUSA leaders are convicted under the Smith Act.

1950   January: The Justice Department demands that CAW officers register themselves as foreign agents.

February 9: Senator Joseph McCarthy claims to have the names of over two hundred communists working for the State Department.

The ERA passes the Senate with the Hayden rider, which would have maintained sex-based protections.

Congress passes the McCarran Internal Security Act over President Truman's veto.

Claudia Jones gives "International Women's Day and the Struggle for Peace" speech, leading to her arrest the next year.

1951   The Supreme Court upholds Smith Act convictions in *Dennis v. United States.*

Claudia Jones, Elizabeth Gurley Flynn, and fifteen other communists are arrested.

Sojourners for Truth and Justice issues its founding manifesto calling for an end to racialized sexual violence.

1952   Betty Friedan writes *UE Fights for Women Workers.*

Senate Internal Security Subcommittee investigates Mary Dublin Keyserling for possible communist influence.

Esther Peterson is first investigated by the FBI for potential communist sympathies.

1953   January: Claudia Jones is convicted of conspiring to violate the Smith Act and sentenced to a year and a day in prison.

The ERA again passes the Senate with the Hayden rider, the last time the amendment is seriously considered until 1971.

French feminist and existentialist Simone de Beauvoir's *The Second Sex* is published in English.

December: Amid a State Department loyalty investigation, Frieda Miller resigns as Women's Bureau chief.

1954	*Brown v. Board of Education* overturns the doctrine of "separate but equal"; NAACP lawyers use essay that Pauli Murray wrote in law school.
	Jo Ann Robinson of the Montgomery, Alabama, Women's Political Council (WPC) proposes a boycott of the city's bus system.
1955	March 2: Montgomery, Alabama, teenager Claudette Colvin is arrested for refusing to give up her seat on a bus.
	The Daughters of Bilitis, which becomes the nation's first lesbian rights group, is founded in Los Angeles.
	The AFL and CIO combine to form the AFL-CIO.
	December 2: Rosa Parks refuses to give up her seat on a bus in Montgomery, Alabama, setting off the Montgomery Bus Boycott.
	December 9: Claudia Jones is deported to Great Britain.
1957	Betty Friedan begins working on *The Feminine Mystique.*
	September 4: Members of the Little Rock Nine enter Central High School, mentored by local activist Daisy Bates.
1958	Esther Peterson becomes the AFL-CIO's first female lobbyist.
1959	In his "kitchen debate" with Soviet premier Nikita Khrushchev, Vice President Richard Nixon posits American consumer culture and women's domesticity as the source of American superiority over the Soviet Union.
1960	February 1: The sit-in movement begins at the Woolworth's counter in Greensboro, North Carolina.
	April A meeting at Shaw University inspires the formation of the Student Nonviolent Coordinating Committee (SNCC).
	Students for a Democratic Society (SDS) is founded.
	The U.S. Food and Drug Administration (FDA) approves of Enovid, the first birth control pill.
1961	Esther Peterson becomes head of the Women's Bureau.

Estelle Griswold, president of the Planned Parenthood Federation of Connecticut, is arrested for providing a married couple with birth control instruction.

SNCC takes over Freedom Rides, establishing its reputation as the "shock troops" of the movement.

December 14: President Kennedy issues Executive Order 10980, establishing the President's Commission on the Status of Women (PCSW).

1962 The Javits Bill allocates federal funds for childcare.

1963 January 14: Alabama governor George Wallace pledges his commitment to "segregation now, segregation tomorrow, segregation forever."

February 19: Betty Friedan publishes *The Feminine Mystique*.

May 3: Birmingham, Alabama, police commissioner "Bull" Connor orders the use of police dogs and fire hoses on peaceful protestors.

June 10: The Equal Pay Act becomes law, barring wage differentials in situations where women performed the same work as men.

June 11: Governor Wallace stands in the schoolhouse door to prevent two Black students from entering the University of Alabama.

June 11: President John F. Kennedy pledges his full support to civil rights.

June 12: Civil rights leader Medgar Evers is murdered in his Jackson, Mississippi, driveway.

September 15: Ku Klux Klan members bomb the Birmingham Sixteenth Street Baptist Church, killing four young girls.

September: SDS begins community-organizing work through Economic Research and Action Project (ERAP).

October 11: The PCSW releases its final report, *American Women*.

November 2–4: Eighty-three thousand Black Mississippians participate in Freedom Vote.

1964   Mary Dublin Keyserling becomes head of the Women's
                Bureau.

                February: Virginia representative Howard Smith,
                staunch segregationist and longtime ERA supporter,
                proposes adding "sex" to Title VII of the Civil Rights
                Bill.

                June: Freedom Summer brings thousands of white
                volunteers to work on Black voter registration in
                Mississippi.

June 21   James Chaney, Andrew Goodman, and Michael Schw-
                erner are murdered by KKK members in Philadelphia,
                Mississippi.

                July 2: President Lyndon B. Johnson signs the Civil
                Rights Act into law, banning several forms of discrimi-
                nation and establishing the Equal Employment Oppor-
                tunity Commission (EEOC).

                August: Fannie Lou Hamer and other Mississippi Free-
                dom Democratic Party (MFDP) delegates testify before
                the credentials committee at the Democratic National
                Convention in Atlantic City, New Jersey.

                Arizona senator Barry Goldwater wins the Repub-
                lican presidential nomination with the support of
                the National Federation of Republican Women;
                Mothers for a Moral America forms to support his
                campaign.

                November: White women in SNCC circulate position
                paper on the status of women in the organization.

1965   February: President Johnson orders the bombing of
                North Vietnam.

                April: President Johnson expands the draft, leading to
                intensified anti-war movement.

                Pauli Murray and Mary Eastwood write "Jane Crow
                and the Law."

                Daniel Patrick Moynihan publishes *The Negro Family:
                The Case for National Action* (Moynihan Report).

                June 7: The Supreme Court rules in *Griswold v. Con-
                necticut* that states cannot deny married couples access

to birth control, arguing that marriage constitutes a "zone of privacy."

November: Mary King and Casey Hayden write "A Kind of Memo," detailing their frustrations as women in SDS.

December: At "rethinking conference" in Champaign-Urbana, Illinois, SDS women meet by themselves to discuss their role in the movement.

By the end of the year, most ERAP sites shut down.

1966 The Black Panther Party (BPP) is founded in Oakland, California.

The Black Women's Liberation Group of Mount Vernon/New Rochelle, New York, is founded; its members criticize the reproductive politics of the Black Power movement.

Welfare rights activists form the City-Wide Coordinating Committee of Welfare Groups in New York City.

At Third National Conference of Commissions on the Status of Women, conflict breaks out over Title VII of the Civil Rights Act, leading to the founding of the National Organization for Women (NOW).

July 28: Stokely Carmichael (Kwame Ture) popularizes the term "Black Power" with a speech in Greenwood, Mississippi.

August: Westside group becomes the nation's first white women's liberation group.

New York Radical Women is founded.

December: SNCC votes to become an all-Black organization.

1967 The National Welfare Rights Organization (NWRO) is founded.

1968 Frances Beal, author of "Double Jeopardy: To Be Black and Female," and others found the Third World Women's Alliance (TWWA).

September 7: Feminists protest the Miss America pageant in Atlantic City.

Cell 16 is founded in Boston.

The EEOC rules that sex-segregated help-wanted ads violate Title VII of the Civil Rights Act.

Women's Equity Action League (WEAL) founded to fight discrimination against women in education and employment.

November: Shirley Chisholm becomes the first Black woman elected to Congress.

The National Conference of Catholic Bishops founds the National Right to Life Committee (NRLC).

1969   January: Crowds verbally attack Marilyn Salzman Webb and Shulamith Firestone at a National Mobilization–sponsored anti-war protest when the two identify women as an oppressed group.

February: Carol Hanisch writes "The Personal Is Political."

Robin Morgan publishes edited collection *Sisterhood Is Powerful: An Anthology of Writings from the Women's Liberation Movement*.

Bread and Roses is founded in Boston.

New York Radical Feminists is founded.

Redstockings is founded in New York City.

Chicago Women's Liberation Union (CWLU) is founded.

CWLU-affiliated Jane Collective begins referring women to abortion providers; some members learn how to perform abortions themselves.

Ana Nieto-Gómez and Leticia Hernández found La Hijas de Cuauhtémoc (the Daughters of Cuauhtémoc), one of the first Chicana feminist groups.

Alice Peurala wins sex discrimination suit against U.S. Steel, paving the way for a series of victories in the steel industry.

1970   Robin Morgan writes "Goodbye to All That."

Toni Cade Bambara publishes the edited collection *The Black Woman*.

Boston Women's Health Book Collective publishes *Our Bodies, Ourselves*.

March: Hawaii becomes the first state to legalize abortion.

March: Over two hundred women take over the main office of the *Ladies' Home Journal.*

May 1: Radicalesbians interrupt a meeting of the Second Congress to Unite Women in New York City.

May: NWRO activists take over the Department of Health, Education, and Welfare (HEW) headquarters.

July 1: Abortion becomes legal in New York State.

October: The Comisión Femenil Mexicana (CFM, Mexican Women's Commission) is founded.

Chicana feminist group Concilio Mujeres (CM) is founded.

1971   The Indochinese Women's Conference (IWC) is held in Toronto and Vancouver.

The Furies is founded in Washington, DC.

Women's Advocates, the first center for women who had experienced domestic abuse, is founded in Saint Paul, Minnesota.

May: The Houston YWCA hosts the Conferencia de Mujeres por la Raza, the first national conference of Chicana feminists.

May 25: Black Panther Ericka Huggins is acquitted of her role in the murder of Alex Rackley and is released after two years in jail.

The National Women's Political Caucus (NWPC) is founded in Washington, DC, with the goal of supporting women candidates and women's interests.

President Nixon vetoes the Comprehensive Childcare Development Act.

1972   January 25: Shirley Chisholm announces her candidacy for the Democratic nomination for president, becoming the first woman and the first African American to run for a major party's presidential nomination.

February: Phyllis Schlafly publishes "What's Wrong with 'Equal Rights' for Women?" in *The Phyllis Schlafly Report.*

March: The ERA passes both houses of Congress and heads to the states for ratification.

March 22: In *Eisenstadt v. Baird*, the Supreme Court extends *Griswold* protections to unmarried couples.

Spring *Ms.* magazine first appears; the inaugural issue includes Johnnie Tillmon's "Welfare Is a Women's Issue."

September: Schlafly founds STOP ERA (Stop Taking Our Privileges).

Congress adopts Title IX of the Higher Education Act, barring sex discrimination in educational institutions receiving federal funds.

Women in the Midwest Council of La Raza (MWCLR) form a Women's Caucus and a new organization, the Mid-West Mujeres de la Raza (Women of la Raza).

Ruth Bader Ginsburg and Eleanor Holmes Norton found the American Civil Liberties Union (ACLU) Women's Rights Project.

Feminists in Washington, DC, found the nation's first rape crisis hotline.

Former NOW members found anti-abortion Feminists for Life.

1973   January 22: *Roe v. Wade* overturns state laws banning abortion.

Under pressure from the EEOC, AT&T vows to change hiring practices and provide back pay to women and minorities.

Conservative think tank the Heritage Foundation is founded.

The forced sterilization of twelve-year-old Minnie Lee Relf in Montgomery brings national attention to the issue.

Frustrated members of NOW found the National Black Feminist Organization (NBFO).

1974   Nellie Gray founds the March for Life in Washington, DC.

Joan Little is charged with first-degree murder in the death of Clarence Alligood, who raped her while in prison; her case attracts the attention of feminists and civil rights activists.

Radical Black feminist group the Combahee River Collective is founded.

Elaine Brown becomes chairperson of the BPP.

Coalition of Labor Union Women (CLUW) founded to represent the interests of union women.

9to5 founded to represent clerical workers; the group inspires a 1980 film of the same name.

Congress passes the Women's Education Equity Act and the Equal Credit Opportunity Act.

Women of All Red Nations (WARN) is founded as a feminist offshoot of the American Indian Movement (AIM).

Reproductive rights activists found the Committee to End Sterilization Abuse (CESA) in New York City.

Jane Alpert publishes *Mother Right: A New Feminist Theory*, a founding text of cultural feminism.

1975   Susan Brownmiller publishes *Against Our Will: Men, Women, and Rape*.

Nebraska becomes the first state to outlaw marital rape.

1976   Former California governor Ronald Reagan challenges President Gerald Ford for the Republican presidential nomination.

The Hyde Amendment makes it illegal to use Medicaid funds for abortions except in cases of rape or incest.

Eleven Chicana women sue the Los Angeles Medical Center of the University of Southern California for allegedly sterilizing them without their consent.

Dr. Constance Redbird Pinkerton-Uri prompts a government investigation into sterilization abuse against Native American women.

Anita Bryant founds Save Our Children (later, Protect America's Children) in Dade County, Florida, to fight against a new ordinance banning discrimination against gay men and lesbians.

1977	Libertarian Cato Institute is founded.
	Conference for International Women's Year (IWY) is held in Houston, Texas.
	Lottie Beth Hobbs, founder of the Pro-Family Forum, organizes conservative counterrally against the IWY conference.
	Reproductive rights activists found the Committee for Abortion Rights and against Sterilization Abuse (CARASA).
1978	Women employed by the *New York Times* win a class-action sex discrimination lawsuit.
	The Pregnancy Discrimination Act amends the Civil Rights Act to make pregnancy a protected category.
1979	Judge rules that EEOC can force Sears Roebuck & Company to adhere to the company's own affirmative action policies; EEOC goes on to file a sex discrimination lawsuit against the company.
	Television preacher Jerry Falwell founds the Moral Majority.
	Beverly LaHaye founds Concerned Women for America (CWA) in San Diego, California.
	Feminist theologian Mary Daly publishes *Gyn/Ecology*.
	Women against Pornography (WAP) becomes the face of the feminist anti-pornography movement.
1980	Ronald Reagan wins the Republican presidential nomination and the presidency; his party removes its support from the ERA.
1981	Sandra Day O'Connor becomes the first woman to serve on the Supreme Court.
	Andrea Dworkin publishes *Pornography: Men Possessing Women*.
1982	The ERA expires, three states short of ratification.
1983	June 18: Astronaut Sally Ride becomes the first American woman in space.
	Indianapolis city council passes an anti-pornography law with the support of both anti-pornography feminists and Christian conservatives.

1984	Geraldine Ferraro becomes the first woman to appear on a major party's presidential ticket, as Democrat Walter Mondale's running mate.
1985	The Supreme Court rules that workplace sexual harassment violates workers' civil rights.
	The government takes on obscenity in congressional hearings on "porn rock" and Attorney General Edwin Meese's commission on pornography.
1986	EEOC loses its sex discrimination case against Sears.
	Terry Randall and other anti-abortion activists found Operation Rescue.
	The Supreme Court overturns the Indianapolis anti-pornography statute.
1987	Andrea Dworkin publishes *Intercourse*.
1991	July 1: Clarence Thomas is nominated to the Supreme Court, igniting controversy over his alleged sexual harassment of lawyer Anita Hill.
	October 3: Bill Clinton announces his candidacy for the 1992 Democratic presidential nomination; his wife, Hillary Rodham Clinton, becomes a lightning rod for controversy over gender roles.
1992	January/February: Rebecca Walker publishes "Becoming the Third Wave" in *Ms.* magazine, announcing the arrival of a new generation of feminists.
	June 29: In *Planned Parenthood of Southeastern Pennsylvania v. Casey*, the Supreme Court approves of new state-level restrictions on abortion but declines to overturn *Roe v. Wade*.
	November: "Year of the Woman"; Carol Moseley-Braun becomes the first Black woman elected to the Senate.
1993	February 3: President Bill Clinton signs the Family and Medical Leave Act (FMLA) into law.
	June 22: Ruth Bader Ginsburg is nominated to the Supreme Court.
	Rachel MacNair, former president of Feminists for Life, founds the Susan B. Anthony List, which funds pro-life political candidates.

1995   The United Nations' Fourth World Conference on
            Women endorses a comprehensive plan to achieve
            global gender equality.

1996   August 22: President Bill Clinton signs the Personal
            Responsibility and Work Opportunity Reconciliation
            Act (PRWORA) into law, eliminating Aid to Fami-
            lies with Dependent Children (AFDC, formerly ADC)
            and replacing it with Temporary Aid to Needy Fami-
            lies (TANF).

1998   January: News breaks that President Bill Clinton
            engaged in an affair with former White House intern
            Monica Lewinsky.
            June 25: The Supreme Court rules against the "NEA
            Four" in obscenity case.

2000   Jennifer Baumgardner and Amy Richards, both born
            in 1970, publish *Manifesta: Young Women, Feminism,
            and the Future*, arguing that rumors about feminism's
            death are greatly exaggerated.

2001   November 17: First Lady Laura Bush declares that the
            "the fight against terrorism is also a fight for the rights
            and dignity of women."

2003   November 5: President George W. Bush signs into law
            a ban on late-term abortions.

2008   Sarah Palin becomes the second woman to appear on
            a major party's presidential ticket, as Republican John
            McCain's running mate.
            Barack Obama is elected president, the first Black per-
            son elected to the office.
            December 18: The George W. Bush administration's
            Rule on Provider Conscience (popularly called "con-
            science clauses") allows medical practitioners to decline
            to provide treatments to which they object.

2009   Abortion provider Dr. George Tiller is murdered while
            serving as an usher in his church.

2010   March 23: President Barack Obama signs the Afford-
            able Care Act into law, igniting a series of controver-
            sies over coverage for birth control and abortion.

2011	The Supreme Court rules in a 5-4 decision that the 1.5 million women suing Walmart for sex-based employment discrimination do not constitute a class.
2013	Facebook chief operation officer Sheryl Sandberg publishes *Lean In: Women, Work, and the Will to Lead*.
2014	June 30: In *Burwell v. Hobby Lobby Stores, Inc.*, the Supreme Court exempts "closely held" companies from the ACA birth control mandate if their owners object to it on religious grounds.
	August 24: Pop star Beyoncé appears at the MTV Video Music Awards with "FEMINIST" emblazoned on the wall behind her, ushering in an era of "marketplace feminism."
2016	July 26: Hillary Rodham Clinton officially becomes the first woman to win a major party's presidential nomination.
	October 7: The *Access Hollywood* tape emerges, seemingly dooming Republican presidential nominee Donald Trump's campaign.
	November 8: Donald Trump wins the presidential election despite losing the popular vote.
2017	January 21: More than 470,000 people descend on Washington, DC, for the inaugural women's March on Washington; across the country, as many as five million participate.
	October: The #MeToo movement, founded in 2006 by Tarana Burke, becomes a cultural and political force in the wake of allegations against Harvey Weinstein and others.
2018	July 9: Brett Kavanaugh is nominated to the Supreme Court; controversy erupts over his alleged past sexual assaults.
2020	The COVID-19 pandemic exposes and intensifies women's dual burden as caregivers and breadwinners.
	September: Supreme Court justice and feminist stalwart Ruth Bader Ginsburg dies, setting up a struggle about Supreme Court appointments in an election year.

November: Senator Kamala Harris is elected vice president of the United States.

2021   Texas Senate Bill 8 bans nearly all abortions in the state; the Supreme Court declines to block the law.

2022   June 24: In *Dobbs v. Jackson Women's Health* Organization, the Supreme Court upholds a Mississippi law banning abortions after fifteen weeks and overturns *Roe v. Wade.*

CHAPTER 1

LEFT AND LABOR
FEMINISM IN THE
COLD WAR

INTRODUCTION: POSTWAR DOMESTICITY REVISITED

According to popular perception, the years after World War II were a time of conformity in which women had little choice but to devote themselves to home and family. This was certainly the image that Betty Friedan presented in her landmark feminist manifesto, *The Feminine Mystique* (1963). "In the fifteen years after World War II," she wrote, the "mystique of feminine fulfillment [in the home] became the cherished and self-perpetuating core of contemporary American culture." Girls and women "learned that truly feminine women do not want careers, higher education, political rights—the independence and the opportunities that the old-fashioned feminists fought for. Some women, in their forties and fifties, still remembered painfully giving up those dreams, but most of the younger women no longer even thought about them."[1] For decades, Friedan's argument led historians and others to assume there was little to no feminism between the end of World War II and the early to mid-1960s.

In many ways, of course, the postwar era was conservative when it came to gender, as marriage and family became more central to Americans' lives. After World War II, people married earlier and had more children, decisions that many had delayed or avoided during two decades of depression and war. The average marriage age after World War II was twenty-two for men and twenty for women, and more children were born between 1948 and 1953 than had been born in the previous thirty years.

Some cultural messages did emphasize domesticity. Psychiatrists Marynia Farnham and Ferdinand Lundberg denounced modern women as the "lost sex," arguing that women who were unhappy with domesticity were mentally ill and that women who worked outside the home would lose their femininity. Women who did voice discontent were often diagnosed as mentally ill, and many were prescribed tranquilizers or committed to psychiatric institutions.

The emerging Cold War further emphasized the importance of family. As the threat of nuclear war with the Soviet Union loomed, domesticity, family, and the home—and women in it—appeared to be the only safe havens. Within this safe haven, gender roles were to be strictly maintained. Government pamphlets told women that the surest way to stay safe in the face of a nuclear attack was to keep their houses as clean as possible; if they did not do so, experts incorrectly insisted, their families would be more likely to die in the attack.

George Kennan's foreign policy of containment, in which communists were contained within a well-defined "sphere of influence," had its analog in unofficial domestic policy: "subversive" individuals needed to be contained so they would not contaminate the rest of society. This logic associated gender and sexual subversion with communism, charges men and women could hope to avoid only if they enacted their gender in the "right" way. As early as 1942, author Philip Wylie wrote in his book *Generation of Vipers* that overbearing mothers were to blame for raising weak sons and producing America's inability to stand up to communists. In 1960, undersecretary of labor James O'Connel argued that "when a woman comes to be viewed first as a source of manpower, second as a mother, then I think we are losing much that supposedly separates us from the Communist world. The highest calling of a woman's sex is the home."[2]

Similar logic appeared in the kitchen debate between Vice President Richard Nixon and Soviet premier Nikita Khrushchev. In 1959, Nixon traveled to the Soviet Union, where he engaged in a heated debate with Khrushchev at the opening of the American National Exhibition in Moscow. Standing before a model American kitchen, Nixon attributed the superiority of the American way of life lay to the availability of consumer goods, especially household appliances. Thanks to the advances of consumer capitalism, he argued, American women did not have to work as hard as their Soviet counterparts.

The ideology of domesticity was real, but it was just that: an ideology. In reality, the majority of the women who worked for wages during World War II had done so before the war and continued to do so afterward. Women in the paid workforce were pushed *down*—from well-paid, often unionized, manufacturing jobs to pink-collar, service, and domestic work—but not *out of* the labor market. Even in 1947, the lowest point of postwar women's paid employment, more women were working for wages than in 1940. By the mid-1950s, the number of employed women surpassed the height of wartime employment. This trend continued for the remainder of the 1950s, with paid employment, especially among married women, increasing dramatically. The proportion of wives who worked for wages doubled from 15 percent in 1940 to 30 percent in 1960; in the same period, the number of mothers who worked for wages leaped 400 percent (from 1.5 million to 6.6 million). By 1960, twice as many women were employed as in 1940, and 40 percent of women over sixteen had a paid job.

There were several reasons for this growth. Many families, especially minority families, had never been able to survive on a single income. The kinds of work people were doing also changed in the 1950s as the United States shifted from a manufacturing-based economy to a service-based economy. Positions including sales personnel, telephone operators, and clerical workers also proliferated, and many of these new jobs were held by women. Most families could also not afford to participate in the so-called affluent society on a single income, and a wife's paycheck could facilitate participation in the middle-class consumer economy. The ideology of domesticity thus competed against the fact that women's paid employment was desperately needed by both an expanding economy and individual families hoping to enjoy the perks of middle-class living.

Domesticity was also a far less pervasive ideology than later political commentators—feminists and right-wing pundits alike—have claimed. As historian Joanne Meyerowitz has shown, mainstream publications were far less united in their messages toward women than Friedan claimed; they were as likely to celebrate women's accomplishments as women's domestic lives. Historians have also uncovered sites in which feminist activism persisted in this era. Cold War–era feminisms both drew on earlier forms of activism, including suffrage and Progressivism, and fed into the more visible activism of the 1960s and '70s. Understanding the feminist

activism of the 1940s and '50s—and the challenges it faced—is necessary to seeing the shape and trajectory of the twentieth-century women's
movement.

COMPETING FEMINISMS IN POSTWAR AMERICA

One reason why this era in women's activism has been overlooked is that
radical women in the 1930s, '40s, and '50s rarely called themselves feminists. Historians, however, have identified two overlapping ideological and
activist strands: left feminists and labor feminists. Neither formal designa-
tions nor official organizations, the terms describe women who advocated
gender equality but opposed the Equal Rights Amendment (ERA). Their
work revolved around three loci: radical groups such as the Communist
Party and its feminist offshoot, the Congress of American Women; labor
unions; and the federal government. Almost all the women discussed here
were involved at one point or another with at least two of these institutions, along with educational institutions and the left and labor press.
These overlapping circles were made possible by a broad left-liberal coalition in the 1930s and the first half of the 1940s, which allowed for a cross-
fertilization of ideas and activism from the New Deal to the Communist
Party. Liberals and the left were not nearly as divided as they would be
later. Still, some historians have found it useful to distinguish between
left feminists and Popular Front feminists, a term that generally implies
proximity to the Communist Party.

Historian Dorothy Sue Cobble has identified an ethos of "labor feminism" whose adherents "recognized that women suffer disadvantages
due to their sex and because they sought to eliminate sex-based disadvantages" and that "put the needs of working class women at its core."
Philosophically opposed to the individualism of the NWP, an interracial,
cross-class group of labor feminists primarily made unions (and, to a lesser
extent, government appointments) the vehicles to attain "full industrial
citizenship," which required removing barriers *and* erecting supports to
allow women to combine paid work with family life. Their specific goals
included "an end to unfair sex discrimination, equal pay for comparable
work, a family or living wage for women and men, the revaluing of the
skills in 'women's jobs,' [and] economic security and social supports from
the state and from employers for child-bearing and child rearing." They

were flexible in their deployment of "sameness" and "difference" rhetoric, arguing for whichever would produce the greatest *equity* in a given situation. Labor feminists made their biggest impact in the 1960s, when they served on presidential commissions, shaped legislation, and contributed directly to the founding of the National Organization for Women (NOW), the premiere organization of the liberal feminist movement.[3] Before that could happen, however, some of the more radical elements of labor feminism—as well as left and Popular Front feminism—would be filtered out by the anti-communist crusade against feminism.

Left and labor feminists faced a committed antagonist in the National Woman's Party (NWP), which pursued the ERA with singled-minded focus. By the postwar years, the NWP comprised mostly older, white, educated, middle- or upper-class women. It was a small organization, with four thousand members in 1945—a number that inched up into the early 1950s before plummeting. The NWP, however, had new, powerful allies. Both the Chamber of Commerce and the National Association of Manufacturers (NAM), consistent opponents of organized labor, backed the ERA, seeing in it a way to get around women-only wages and hours laws. Combined with the fact that the NWP rarely supported gender-blind protective legislation or legislation that would strengthen collective bargaining rights, labor feminists saw this alliance as proof that the NWP's professed belief in market-based equality was in truth just an excuse to wage war on working people. Abstract equality was meaningless, they argued, if such policies would make it easier for employers to exploit their workers, as they felt the ERA would do.

For these reasons, Left, labor, and civil rights groups opposed the amendment. "Plain words like 'free,' 'open,' 'equal,' have clear meanings to honest people," wrote communist and labor activist Elizabeth Gurley Flynn, "but in the mouths of employers and politicians they become double talk, like free enterprise, open shop, equal rights."[4] Black women, the most likely American women to combine wage work with family responsibilities, were particularly wary of the amendment's effects. Women in the National Council of Negro Women, for example, opposed the amendment "because in their view it simply confirms rights they already possess and places in jeopardy protections won only after years of hard work."[5] The AFL-CIO and Women's Bureau in the Department of Labor also went on record in opposition.

National Woman's Party members gather in Washington, DC, to advocate for the ERA before the House Judiciary Committee, 1948. Future chair Emma Guffey Miller is third from left. (Group of some of the speakers before the House Judiciary Subcommittee at a hearing in Washington, DC, on the proposed Equal Rights Amendment now before Congress, March 10, 1946. Caroline Katzenstein papers [Am.8996], Historical Society of Pennsylvania. Reproduced with permission from the Historical Society of Pennsylvania.)

With the backing of the Chamber of Commerce, NAM, and mainstream members of both political parties, the ERA was reported out of committee for the first time in 1946. The following year, its opponents proposed the Women's Status Bill, which would have gotten rid of discriminatory sex-based legislation but kept protections in place—as an alternative to the ERA. The bill also included a recommendation for a presidential commission on the status of women—realized in 1961—modeled after Truman's commission on civil rights. Initially supported by congresswomen allied with organized labor, the bill soon attracted the attention of such male progressives as Emanuel Celler. The main group lobbying for the bill was the National Committee on the Status of Women, chaired by Women's Bureau chief Mary Anderson. Though the bill was reintroduced every year until 1954, it quickly disappeared after that.

After 1954, progressive women supported a version of the ERA with an amendment known as the Hayden rider. Introduced by Carl Hayden, Democratic senator from Arizona, the Hayden rider held that the ERA "shall not impair any rights, benefits, or exemptions now or hereafter conferred by law" on women—an attempt to reconcile the ERA with women-only protective legislation. The NWP refused to support this version, putting them in the awkward position of opposing their own bill. As its members saw it, the Hayden rider was "a studied effort to cement into the Constitution the very discrimination the Resolution was designed to eliminate."[6] Katharine St. George, NWP member and Republican representative from New York, had cosponsored the bill in the House, but she, too, withdrew her support. "Who determines what 'rights, benefits, or exemptions' include?" she queried the next year. "I think it is my right to work all night on a job and get the extra pay."[7] St. George exemplified the kind of professional white women who tended to support the ERA. The ERA passed the Senate with the Hayden rider in 1950 and 1953, and the bill was considered again in 1956. But none of these bills became law, and Congress did not seriously consider the amendment again until 1971.

New histories will need to reintegrate the NWP into the broader history of postwar feminism in order to explain how the goal of a tiny, fringe group of mostly wealthy, older, white women increasingly became one of the central demands of feminism over the course of the 1960s and '70s. Though not specifically tied to the trajectory of feminism, historian Jefferson Cowie has hinted at one intriguing answer. The middle decades of the twentieth century, he argues, constituted a "great exception" in U.S. history, the one time in the nation's development that Americans seriously considered, and sometimes even implemented, collective solutions to social problems. As the decades wore on, however, individual solutions increasingly replaced collective ones. Labor historian Nelson Lichtenstein earlier located this shift in the nearly thirty years between the 1935 Wagner Act, which protected and empowered workers as a group, and the 1964 Civil Rights Act, which did the same for individuals.[8] The classically liberal ERA may thus have benefited from changing ideas of rights and the subjects to whom they attached.

WOMEN IN THE POSTWAR LABOR MOVEMENT

If there was a mass movement for women's rights in the immediate post-war era, it was located in unions. This was where women argued for, and sometimes won, maternity leave, equal pay, and other benefits that allowed them to lead fuller, richer lives both in and out of the workplace. By the early 1950s, three million women were union members, with another two million in women's auxiliaries that often echoed feminist demands. As women's membership in unions increased, union leadership was forced to pay more attention to women's needs. Both the AFL and the CIO worked for improvements in day-care facilities. The AFL called for a special focus on organizing women workers and providing aid to workers trying to secure equal pay provisions in contract negotiations. The CIO went further, calling for, among other changes, legal and contractual guarantees of equal pay; seniority lists that protected women workers, including those who took maternity leave; and access to adequate childcare and rest facilities and leadership training. The CIO also worked closely with the Women's Bureau of the Department of Labor, sending it papers for criticism and comment.

In some unions, starting with the UAW, women were able to pressure male leadership to establish their own women's bureaus. Feminists in the UAW established a women's bureau at the union's national convention in 1946; the next year it became the UAW Women's Department. Mildred Jeffrey, who was educated at Bryn Mawr and the University of Minnesota and worked for the federal government during World War II, became its first director. Dorothy Haener (1918–2001), later a member of the President's Commission on the Status of Women and one of the founders of the National Organization for Women, was involved in the UAW Women's Department from the beginning, and Caroline Davis served as director from 1948 until her retirement in 1973. The Women's Department used the union grievance filing system to protest unfair hiring and promotion practices. It was also instrumental in the unanimous 1955 passage of a new resolution reaffirming the "democratic principle that all members shall be guaranteed full protection without discrimination based on sex or marital status."[9]

Beyond merely joining unions in large numbers in the 1940s, women were increasingly taking on leadership roles in these unions. Like earlier generations of leaders, these women often came from female-dominated trades. They were, however, more diverse in terms of race, ethnicity, and industry. They tended to be second-generation immigrants or from families with a longer history in the United States. Some were active in the AFL, and some held positions in CIO unions where there was more communist influence, like the United Electrical Workers. Most, however, were concentrated in CIO unions with close ties to the Democratic Party and a strong left-liberal anti-communist agenda.

United Packinghouse Workers of America (UPWA) activist Addie Wyatt is representative of this group in many ways. Like many other African American women, Wyatt first gained access to a union during the war. Seventeen in 1941, with five younger brothers and sisters to support, she went to work at Chicago's Armour meatpacking plant. She filed her first workplace grievance when the plant foreman gave her job to a newly hired white woman and moved her to a less desirable position. She did not fully appreciate the importance of unions until she got pregnant, however: her local had won the right for its members to take an entire year off and have their job held until they returned. In 1952, she was elected vice president of her local, using this and later positions to advance the rights of women and minorities.

Women in the UPWA, including Wyatt, were at the forefront of fighting racial and gender discrimination in the workplace. The Packinghouse Workers union was 30 percent Black, but African Americans were restricted to the dirtiest, lowest prestige jobs in the plant. While white women trimmed, weighed, sliced, and wrapped meat, Black women were often restricted to the offal department, where they flushed worms and feces from animals' intestines. An interracial group of UPWA women set up special grievance departments for complaints of racial discrimination and tested companies' hiring procedures. They separately sent groups of Black and white women to apply for jobs, documenting instances when Black women were turned down and white women were hired automatically. Their activism won recognition from government arbitrators, who forced companies to hire Black women in more desirable positions. The UPWA also teamed up with groups, including the NAACP to boycott retail establishments that did not serve African Americans. Along with other CIO unions, it pursued such legislative changes as the creation of a permanent FEPC, an end to racial discrimination in the armed forces, and the abolition of the poll tax.

The 1940s' labor movement also attracted middle-class, college-educated women. Despite their training and education, they were shut out of many prestigious jobs, and they saw union work as a way to put their educations to use in research, education, and legislation. Labor feminism thus comprised a cross-class coalition.

No one was more important in this regard than Esther Peterson (1906–97). Born in Utah, she received her BA from Brigham Young University in 1927 and then moved to New York to attend Columbia Teachers College. Her husband, a socialist, introduced her to prominent labor figures and encouraged her to teach night classes to women workers at the local Young Men's Christian Association (YMCA). She spent the summers of 1932–39 teaching at the Bryn Mawr Summer School for Women Workers. Her union positions included a year as a paid organizer for the American Federation of Teachers (AFT) and then a staff position in the education department of the Amalgamated Clothing Workers of America (ACWA). She went on in 1958 to become the AFL-CIO's first female lobbyist and the highest-ranking woman in the Kennedy administration, from which she served as vice chair of the President's Commission on the Status of Women.

Peterson did not think of her work as feminist, but she consistently advocated for women. "I didn't think of the Bryn Mawr Summer School for Working Women as 'feminist,'" she later said. "We didn't think in those terms in those days. I didn't, anyway. But I remember the woman's focus. I just thought of them as strong women." She found it unfair that the ACWA executive board was almost entirely men when "women were the largest part of the union. They were the backbone of the union and did all of the work. But all the unions were dominated by men." She and other women who worked for the union tried to organize themselves, only to be disbanded by ACWA president Sidney Hillman.[10]

In government, the Women's Bureau in the Department of Labor proved the staunchest ally to labor feminists. Founded during World War I to oversee women's work in the defense industries, it expanded to investigate and advocate for all aspects of women's labor, including the ability to combine paid labor with family life. In doing so, the Women's Bureau provided a vital link between Progressive Era women's activism and

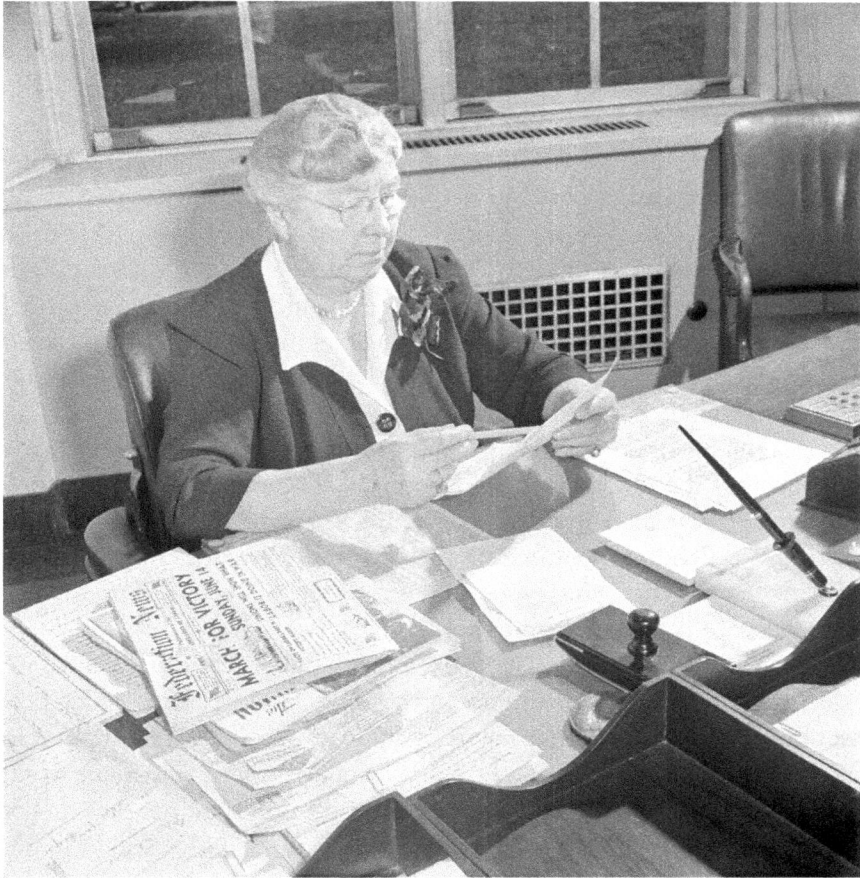

Head of the Women's Bureau of the Department of Labor Mary Anderson in Washington, DC. Anderson served in this position from the bureau's founding in 1920 until 1944. (Library of Congress, Prints & Photographs Division, FSA/OWI Collection, LC-DIG-fsa-8d21272)

second-wave feminism. Its head from 1944 to 1953, Frieda Miller (1890–1973), had been active in labor and consumer politics since the 1910s.

Born in La Crosse, Wisconsin, Miller graduated from Downer College in Milwaukee in 1911. She spent four years pursuing graduate work in economics, sociology, political science, and law at the University of Chicago and then took a position as a research assistant at Bryn Mawr College. From 1917 to 1923 she was secretary of the Philadelphia Trade Union's

League. "Disgusted with academic life," she "wanted to do something more socially beneficial than writing a dissertation." The WTUL fit the bill. Through the WTUL she met Pauline Newman, a fellow activist who became Miller's lifelong partner, their relationship cemented by Newman's care for Miller when she fell ill in the flu epidemic of 1918. Miller and Newman together raised Miller's daughter. Miller participated in the founding of the Workers' Education Bureau of America, a clearinghouse for college- and union-based worker education programs, and the Bryn Mawr Summer School for Women Workers. Miller and Newman settled in New York, where they gained access to Franklin and Eleanor Roosevelt and the Democratic Party apparatus. In 1938, New York governor Herbert H. Lehman made her the state's second woman (after Frances Perkins) to serve as commissioner of labor. In this position, she oversaw (among many other issues) the enforcement of Roosevelt's executive order mandating equal pay for women working in defense industries during World War II. In 1944, Perkins appointed her head of the Women's Bureau. During Miller's tenure, the bureau established a Labor Advisory Committee to help generate policy ideas and priorities.[11]

Through unions and the Women's Bureau, labor feminists worked for sweeping changes both in and out of the workplace. These included protections for vulnerable groups of women; an end to sex discrimination in hiring, layoffs, promotions, and transfers; equal pay for comparable work; and policies to support combining wage work and child-rearing. Labor feminists did not win many of their demands in the 1940s and '50s, but their policy initiatives—and their relationships with politicians in the Democratic Party—came to fruition in the 1960s. Elsewhere, another group of women was developing the intellectual basis for the coming feminist revolution.

POPULAR FRONT FEMINISM

In 1948, the CPUSA formally recognized gender inequality as a problem unto itself, but only after more than a decade of concerted activism by women members. Mary Inman, who published *In Woman's Defense* serially in 1939 and as a book the following year, was one of the first to do so. Among Inman's readers was Susan B. Anthony II. Susan B. Anthony II (1916–91) was born in Easton, Pennsylvania, the granddaughter of the famous suffragist's younger brother. She graduated from the University of Rochester in 1938. As a student, she became involved in the peace movement, though she also called for lifting the arms embargo to anti-fascist forces in the Spanish Civil War. After graduating, she moved to Washington, DC, where she worked as a research assistant in the National Youth Administration. She also worked with the National Negro Congress, a CP-affiliated civil rights organization founded at Howard University. She completed a master's degree in political science at American University in 1941.

Despite her great-aunt's example and several years of involvement in progressive causes, Anthony had not thought much about the problems women faced as women. Reading *In Woman's Defense* set her on a life path that these other experiences did not. The book had come at the perfect time, Anthony wrote in an admiring letter to Inman in December 1940. "I had been married only a few months and was getting restive under the role that even my very progressive husband expected of women—that of the docile servant of detail, whose main thoughts should be concentrated on buying a new chair cover and fascinating menus."[12] Anthony was married to Henry Hill Collins Jr., a CP member who worked in several New Deal–era agencies, from 1940 until the two divorced in 1948.

Anthony and Inman became friends and formed tentative plans for a progressive women's group that could serve as a counterweight to the individualistic NWP, though U.S. entry into World War II halted these plans. Anthony spent the war working as a journalist. In addition to her position as city desk editor at the *Washington Star*, she contributed articles to the *New York Times Magazine*, *Christian Science Monitor*, and others. Often inspired by research she conducted on women's lives during and after the war, much of her work dealt with women's labor and immigration issues. A book, *Out of the Kitchen, into the War*, was published in 1943. In 1946, she hosted a radio program, "This Woman's World," quickly canceled for being too radical.

The war crystallized Anthony's feminist politics. In 1941, she interviewed a number of famous women activists, including Carrie Chapman Catt, Eleanor Roosevelt, and Margaret Mead, on what American women needed. All of them agreed with her that, while tremendous progress had been made in the hundred years since an organized women's movement emerged, many barriers to equality still existed. Taking a job as a mechanic-learner at the Washington Navy Yard, she began to formulate a concrete plan for action.

The majority of the women who worked at the plant were mothers balancing paid work and domestic responsibilities, including housework and childcare. What was needed, she argued, was a comprehensive set of policies and practices that would facilitate these dual roles. Anthony's argument was neither new nor unique, though she developed it through a specific set of circumstances: the political exigencies of wartime, especially a war fought against fascism. Nazi ideology identified women's place as "Kinder, Küche, Kirche" (children, kitchen, church). Anthony noted, "[T]he fascist concept of woman is that her life's work is to breed and feed. She breeds a dozen years and feeds for a lifetime. After breeding— after having fulfilled her biological function—she is then, according to the fascists, only useful to brood over the kitchen stove. The boundary for women, under fascism, is the home; and beyond that boundary she must not go."[13] Democracy, by contrast, must embrace more expansive roles for women. For women who came of age in the 1930s and '40s, the specter of fascist gender norms was never far away. Their antipathy to domesticity and emphasis on work as the key to liberation, blind though it often was to race and class differences, must be understood in this context.

When the war ended, Anthony again turned her attention to the idea of a progressive women's group, drawing heavily on Inman's work. The resulting group, the Congress of American Women (CAW), was founded in 1946 as the U.S. branch of the Women's International Democratic Federation (WIDF). WIDF had been founded the previous year by communist resistance leaders in Paris. In addition to Anthony, CAW's founders included reformer Mary van Kleeck; Elizabeth Gurley Flynn; and Nora Stanton Barney, Elizabeth Cady Stanton's granddaughter. Though openly tied to the CP, CAW's constituency was ideologically diverse, including a good number of former suffragists, middle-class liberals, Progressive reformers, and trade unionists.

CAW promoted international peace, child welfare, and women's advancement. As head of the organization's Commission on the Status of Women, Anthony deserves much of the credit for developing the organization's feminist demands. In her "Report of the Commission on the Status of Women," Anthony outlined the ways that social and economic policies kept women from claiming their proper position. The government should promote women's formal entry into politics, equal pay for equal or similar work, an end to discrimination in education and the workplace, the expansion of unions and New Deal protections, federally funded childcare, a national housing project, and communal cooking and cleaning resources. Like other left feminist groups, CAW members rejected the ERA as detrimental to working-class women. Instead, they promoted Anthony's "Women's Status Bill," which ended discrimination while maintaining protective legislation.

In 1948, Anthony left CAW to become the WIDF representative at the UN. Replacing Anthony as head of the Commission on the Status of Women, Betty Millard (1911–2010) continued the group's feminist agenda. A keen student of women's history, she made sure all CAW chapters knew of the upcoming hundredth anniversary of the 1848 Seneca Falls convention, which she and fifty other women commemorated with a rally at Elizabeth Cady Stanton's grave. She is best known for her pamphlet "Woman against Myth," which argued that feminism and socialism were inherently connected.

In the 1930s and '40s, the CP was also the most radical anti-racist organization in the United States. American communists were relatively sympathetic to the issues faced by Black women. White men and women alike in the party recognized Black women's "triple oppressed" status, and they launched educational discussions about this status. During World War II, they emphasized to employers and the government the importance of industrial jobs and unions to Black women's economic security.

White CAW members recognized that Black women faced additional discrimination, and the organization counted several Black women among its leaders. It supported some important civil rights initiatives, including a national campaign to end lynching in the South and another to defend Rosa Lee Ingram. A poor sharecropper in Ellaville, Georgia, Ingram and her two sons were sentenced to death for accidentally killing the white farmer who tried to rape her.

When white American communists talked about Black women, however, they tended to tack these discussions onto those addressing the "general" problems American women faced. In 1949, Claudia Jones published "An End to the Neglect of the Problems of the Negro Woman," partly in response to the fact that even otherwise sensitive analyses of race by white men and women had blind spots.

Born Claudia Vera Cumberbatch in Trinidad, then a British possession, Claudia Jones (1915–64) immigrated to the United States with her family in 1923. They settled in Harlem, a mecca of the Black diaspora. While a student at Wadleigh High School in New York, she participated in the junior NAACP. She began her work as a journalist in 1935–36, when she wrote a weekly column, "Claudia's Comments," for a Black newspaper in Harlem. She started writing for the publication of the Young Communist League (YCL), *Weekly Review*, upon joining both the CP and YCL in 1936, eventually becoming editor in chief of the organization and national chairperson of the YCL. Jones became secretary of the CP's National Women's Commission in 1947, and she was the only Black woman on the party's central committee. As an organizer, she traveled across the country to recruit new party members. She also served as an editor of "negro affairs" for the *Daily Worker*. In the early 1950s, Jones wrote a weekly column, "Half the World," for the "Woman Today" section of the Sunday *Daily Worker*. She was CAW's most important intellectual, developing ideas that, among their other contributions, became the basis of Black feminist thought in the 1960s and '70s.

In "An End to the Neglect of the Problems of the Negro Woman," Jones recognized Black women's paradoxical position in American society generally and the left specifically: exploited economically, politically, and culturally by mainstream society, Black women provided the most consistent, often most militant grassroots support for progressive organizations working for peace, civil rights, and economic justice. Yet the left often ignored the concerns of this most committed constituency and excluded them from leadership roles. Jones linked Black women's roles as workers, mothers, and Black Americans, anticipating the later development of intersectionality theory.

The most concrete way in which Black women were exploited was economically. Many Black men faced low pay and inconsistent employment; as a result, Black women engaged in paid labor at higher rates than any other group of American women. In many cases, they were the main breadwinners for their families. But Black women were excluded from most jobs, consigned to those with the lowest pay and the most minimal labor protections. Jones's mother, for example, worked in the garment industry, where she suffered from the effects of overwork and died at age thirty-seven. "The conditions of non-union organization, of that day, of

speed up, plus the lot of working women, who are mothers and undoubtedly the weight of immigration to a new land where conditions were far
from as promised or anticipated, contributed to her early death," Jones
wrote.[14]

As the backbone of movements for peace and economic and social
justice, Black women by all rights should have been leaders in the global
anti-imperialist movement. But progressive white men and women and
Black men marginalized them, re-creating the conditions of mainstream
society. It was to these groups, in fact, that the neglect of the title primarily referred. "This neglect," she wrote, "[had] too long permeated the
ranks of the labor movement generally, of Left-progressives, and also of
the Communist Party." White and Black men bore some responsibility
for this neglect, but no one had failed Black women more than progressive white women. As a fellow oppressed group, Jones argued, they should
have known better.[15]

More than perhaps any other twentieth-century feminist, Betty Friedan
has been excoriated for ignoring the intersectionality that Jones emphasized. She has come to represent a white, middle-class feminism blind to
the realities of race and class. Yet the *Feminine Mystique* author's politics
matured in milieus similar to CAW. She was, without a doubt, a Popular
Front feminist.

Born Bettye Goldstein in Peoria, Illinois, in 1921, Friedan entered
Smith College in 1938. She wrote for and eventually edited the school's
student newspaper, penning articles about fascism, labor rights, women's
equality, and other political issues. She also learned about the history of
radicalism, most importantly from economics professor Dorothy Wolff
Douglas. From Wolff Douglas, Friedan learned about the connections
between women and social and economic organization, especially Nazi
Germany's relegation of women to home, church, and family. With anti-
Semitism on the rise both at home and abroad, the specter of fascism was
especially frightening to the Jewish Friedan. Wolff Douglas also encouraged Friedan to spend the summer of 1941 at Highlander Folk School in
Tennessee, which trained labor and civil rights leaders. There, she took
writing workshops and learned about union organizing, and she began to
understand anti-Semitism within the broader context of racism.

After a year pursuing graduate work in psychology at the University
of California at Berkeley, Friedan took a job with *Federated Press*, a labor

news service in New York. From 1943 to 1946, she wrote articles on such issues as unfairly low wages among factory workers, unsafe and unsanitary conditions in segregated schools, and the need to oppose fascism both at home and abroad. She also praised the work of CAW, which gave her hope that the end of the war might usher in a more progressive era.

Friedan lost her job with *Federated Press* in 1946, an event that would later factor heavily in her personal mythology. Later that year, she became a staff writer for *UE News*, where she stayed until 1952. *UE News* was published by the United Electrical, Radio and Machine Workers of America, a radical union in the CIO. With strikes at Westinghouse and GE plants across North America in 1946, UE helped to usher in a new era of labor militancy and widespread strikes. As a result, the union also found itself a major target of McCarthyism.

At *UE News*, Friedan took on such issues as employer greed, anti-Semitism, and the growing power of the House Un-American Activities Committee (HUAC). Yet her most important work for UE focused on women, including a thirty-nine-page pamphlet titled *UE Fights for Women Workers*, which the union published in 1952. In its recognition of the intersections of gender, race, and class in women's lives—as well as age, marital status, family responsibilities, and other factors—*UE Fights for Women Workers* is a remarkable document; that Friedan wrote it makes it even more remarkable in the history of American feminism.

Friedan lost her job with UE in 1952. As with her departure from *Federated Press*, the reasons behind the layoff were complex. Gender issues were at play, but so were political exigencies. Facing criticism from anti-communist UAW president Walter Reuther, *Federated Press* pushed out its most radical staff members, including Friedan. While it is true that UE laid off the two women on the publication staff and kept the two men, the union was also in crisis at the time. Expelled from the CIO along with ten other unions in the wake of the 1948 election, UE found its membership and coffers decimated. In 1946, when Friedan went to work for UE, the union had six hundred thousand members; by 1950, this number was seventy thousand. Continued staff support at the same level was impossible.

McCarthyism thus changed the trajectory of Friedan's professional life. It also affected her personal life, as almost every organization and cause—and many people—with which she had been affiliated with faced scrutiny. Dorothy Wolff Douglas was targeted by HUAC, fellow Smith professor

James Gibson by the FBI. Segregationists red-baited Martin Luther King Jr. and others who had spent time at Highlander, which opponents called a "communist training school." Her Berkeley mentor, Ralph Gundlach, lost his tenure at the University of Washington because of his political commitments; other Berkeley professors with whom she studied were fired for refusing to sign the state of California's loyalty oath. David Bohm, her boyfriend at Berkeley, was called to testify in front of HUAC, and his academic career in the United States was ruined. *Federated Press* was so weakened by McCarthyism that it closed its doors in 1956. Reactionary forces were circling close, and Friedan knew that she, too, could be a target. Understandably, then, she took refuge in the suburbs. Later in life, she never mentioned her more radical past, claiming that she had never thought about women's issues until she was preparing to write *The Feminine Mystique*. Only later did historians uncover how fundamentally McCarthyism had affected her life—and, more broadly, the history of American feminism.

THE ANTI-COMMUNIST CRUSADE AGAINST FEMINISM

It was never illegal in the United States to belong to the Communist Party. Yet in the 1940s and '50s, an overlapping set of new agencies, laws, and hearings regularly deprived suspected communists of their right to earn a living and even subjected them to prison or deportation.[16] The 1940 Smith Act made it illegal to "teach, advocate, or encourage the overthrow" of the government "by force or violence" or associate with any group that did so. It was under this act that, in 1949, eleven Communist Party leaders were tried, convicted, and imprisoned for as long as five years, although they had not committed any crimes. In 1951, the Supreme Court upheld their convictions in *Dennis v. United States*. The majority acknowledged that the convictions were due solely to beliefs, not actions, but argued that the defendants represented a "clear and present danger" that overrode their First Amendment rights.

In 1947, President Harry Truman created the Federal Employee Loyalty Program, which gave government security officials authorization to screen two million federal government employees for "political deviance" and authorized the attorney general to draw up a list of "totalitarian, fascist, or subversive organizations." Membership, affiliation, or even sympathy with these groups was enough to determine disloyalty. For example, people who had belonged to the Soviet-American Friendship Society during World War II (when the United States and the Soviet Union were allies) were considered potentially disloyal.

Passed over Truman's veto in 1950, the McCarran Internal Security Act required communists to register with the government and revoked the passports of those suspected of communist sympathies, including the performer and civil rights activist Paul Robeson. It also established provisions for setting up concentration camps for subversives in the event of a national emergency as well as the detention of dangerous, disloyal, or subversive persons.

First established as the Dies Committee in 1938, HUAC became a standing organization after World War II. HUAC called in for questioning individuals who may have belonged to organizations on the attorney general's list. If witnesses acknowledged membership in these groups, they were asked to "name names" of others who had been in these groups with them. If they refused to do so, they could be held in contempt of court and subject to federal prosecution. If they refused to answer any questions, committee members assumed they were communists who did not want to reveal their past associations.

The man whose name is often used synonymously with this era—Republican senator Joseph McCarthy of Wisconsin—was only one piece of this broader anti-communist infrastructure. In a 1950 speech in Wheeling, West Virginia, McCarthy announced that he had a list of over two hundred communists working for the State Department. When pressed for specifics, McCarthy changed the numbers and charges around. Sometimes he claimed to have fifty-seven names, sometimes eighty-one. Sometimes the individuals included were actual Communist Party members, sometimes they were potential "loyalty risks" or people with communist connections. McCarthy never produced any evidence, but he spent four years using his Senate subcommittee to accuse government agencies, federal employees, members of the news media, and finally, the army of being under communist influence.

In the 1930s and '40s, under the auspices of the New Deal, progressive women and men flocked to serve in precisely the government agencies that McCarthy and his cohort despised. For professional women in particular, who had fewer opportunities in the private sector, civil service was often the best option to use their skills and education. By the 1930s, white women had access to some of the nation's top law schools, but they often had difficulty securing jobs afterward. If a woman scored well on the civil service exam, however, it was difficult to reject her because she was a woman. Many lawyers and academics thus found their way into government service. Of the New Deal agencies, the National Labor Relations Board (NLRB) and the Social Security Board (SSB) were particularly receptive to women. In 1930, women were 15 percent of all federal employees; by 1947, they were 24 percent of federal employees nationwide and 45 percent in Washington, DC.

Of a slightly different cast from the first generation of female New Dealers, Frances Perkins most notably, members of this generation of progressive female civil servants were more likely than their forebears to argue for sexual emancipation, less likely to advocate maternalism, and more likely to marry and have children. Though still predominantly white and middle- to upper-class, they were somewhat more diverse and significantly more likely to actively oppose racial discrimination. Civil rights movement leaders Ella Baker and Pauli Murray, both of whom worked for the Workers Education Project, were among this cohort.

Many of these women (and men) were the children of radicals from the 1910s who had embraced suffrage and other aspects of gender egalitarianism. A significant number cut their political teeth in the 1930s' student movement, helping to organize workers and visiting the Soviet Union. Many of the women and men in this second generation of New Dealers were married to each other, which caused problems for employment and made women susceptible to firing later on. The married women in this group often chose to keep their own last name, and all had high expectations of their male counterparts.

Historians have long recognized that the Cold War presented conservatives with an opportunity to rein in what they saw as the unrestrained growth of government under the New Deal. But this attack on government agencies was also an attack on perceived gender transgression. To conservatives, civil service was a place where gender roles ran amuck, populated by effeminate, nonproductive (because of employment by the federal government) men and unduly powerful women.

By the late 1930s, these men were already attacking the New Deal as communist infiltrated. They were particularly concerned with the

influence of feminist consumer groups—most notably, the League of
Women Shoppers (LWS)—over the NLRB, where a significant number
of its members were employed. Founded in 1935, the LWS encouraged
women to "use their buying power for social justice, so that the fair price
which they pay as consumers will also include an American standard of
living for those who make and market the goods they buy." Though similar to the Progressive Era's National Consumers League (NCL), the LWS
focused more on unionization than on wages and hours laws, as the older
group had done. When LWS investigations contributed to a pro-labor
NLRB ruling in 1936, congressman Martin Dies (soon to head the Dies
Committee, the precursor to HUAC) began investigating communist influence in both groups. In the wake of more intense investigations after
1947, the national LWS disbanded in 1949.[17]

In 1939, congressional conservatives established the Smith Committee, chaired by Virginia Democrat Howard Smith, to investigate communist influence in the NLRB. A segregationist, ERA supporter, and rabid
anti-communist (the Alien Registration—or Smith—Act that passed the
next year was his brainchild), Smith was a tailor-made opponent for left
feminists and vice versa. Indeed, the committee sought to delegitimize
the agency by exaggerating women's influence and emphasizing their
youth, relative inexperience, and supposed incompetence. Congressmen
attacked female civil servants in the NLRB for neglecting domestic work
and for daring to write opinions that affected men, and they implied that
women were naive and susceptible to communist blackmail (an attack
that was also leveled against gay men in government). Like many organizations of its time, the NLRB's left-liberal spectrum included some communists, but their presence in no way constituted an infiltration.[18]

The NLRB survived the Smith Committee's investigation, but it was
left weakened, on the defensive, and less able to defend its employees.
Many left feminists within the agency left for the Office of Price Administration (OPA), especially its consumer division, which was headed by
political scientist and labor activist Harriet Elliott and her deputy, Caroline Ware. But the Smith Committee turned its attentions to the OPA as
well, making it clear that the agency had been singled out in part because
of perceived gender transgressions. According to one congressman, for
example, the social scientists who populated the OPA's ranks were "short-
haired women and long haired men."[19]

The attacks on the OPA mirrored the more general attacks on women in government. The right argued that women in government positions were trying to act like men; they were simultaneously unnatural, incompetent, and susceptible to communist influence. Single women with prominent jobs were attacked as lesbians; married women were accused of taking jobs away from men. Ware, Mary Dublin Keyserling, Frieda Miller, and Esther Peterson all faced allegations that affected their careers.

Investigations were quick to point out the ways in which their subjects defied gender conventions. Ware, one investigator noted, "uses single name yet has been married for several years"; she was "known to defy conventions." The University of Wyoming had previously broken Ware's contract when they discovered she was married. Dublin Keyserling was "a queer woman [who] used her maiden name and didn't want to be blamed for her husband's mistakes."[20] Women in Congress were affected too. In 1950, California representative Helen Gahagan Douglas lost her Senate bid when her opponent, Richard M. Nixon, red-baited her. She was, he insisted, "pink right down to her underwear."[21]

The several investigations of Mary Dublin Keyserling demonstrate many of these trends. Born in 1910 in New York City, Dublin Keyserling was the daughter of Russian Jewish immigrants. Her father was a public health expert, and her mother was a settlement house worker. She too developed an interest in these issues at a young age; her thesis at Barnard explored how the industrial revolution affected women in New England. She worked on plans for public health insurance in the early 1930s and then pursued graduate studies at the London School of Economics and Columbia. Returning to the United States, she taught at Sarah Lawrence College from 1933 to 1938, during which time she had students investigate housing conditions in slums and design family budgets. In 1938, she became the head of the NCL, leading the organization's campaigns for the Fair Labor Standards Act (FLSA), against weakening the National Labor Relations Act (NLRA), for labor standards for domestic workers, and for national health insurance.

Mary Dublin married lawyer and economist Leon Keyserling in 1940, and both went on to hold prominent government positions in the Roosevelt and Truman administrations. Like others, the Keyserlings faced multiple investigations, which started as early as 1942. Mary, however, was the main target of these investigations. Because both spouses worked for the federal government, she was seen as a parasite who had taken a job that rightfully belonged to a man. In 1948, J. Edgar Hoover launched a full-scale investigation into Mary's background, which was also the subject of a Commerce Department loyalty board investigation. Mary denied all the charges against her and was cleared. Three years later, a separate investigation by the Senate Internal Security Subcommittee (SISS) cleared Mary on loyalty but not security grounds, and both she and Leon resigned.

In front of the SISS, the Keyserlings painted themselves as liberal anti-communists, a strategy that allowed them to survive the 1950s. They joined the liberal Americans for Democratic Action and became active in centrist Democratic politics. As president, Lyndon B. Johnson appointed Mary to head the Women's Bureau. Loyalty investigations had pushed left feminists to adopt liberal (accommodationist, capitalist, and Democratic) positions. When a more radical feminism reemerged in the late 1960s, those who had survived the McCarthy era and reinvented themselves in its wake appeared to younger women to be relics of the establishment.

Labor feminists, too, were red-baited. In 1949, the State Department loyalty board turned its attention to Esther Peterson's husband, Oliver, who worked there as a labor advisor. In 1952, he was called to testify in front of McCarthy's Senate committee. The FBI launched an investigation into Esther's activities too. Esther believed the investigations were punishment for their labor activism and friendship with figures in the civil rights movement, including actor Paul Robeson. She also felt that the government hoped to use her against her husband. Oliver was cleared in 1953—and then again, after subsequent investigations, in 1955 and 1962. In the midst of these accusations, Esther burnished her anti-communist credentials, volunteering for the anti-communist International Confederation of Free Trade Unions and writing a pamphlet against communist influence in the labor movement, *Women, It's Your Fight Too*. Esther's career survived these allegations, and she became hugely influential as President Kennedy's director of the Women's Bureau. But the investigations took their toll, especially on Oliver's health. "We paid a big price for what we believed in the labor movement," Esther later recalled.[22]

Women's Bureau chief Frieda Miller was also investigated several times. This was not the first time in her long career that Miller had faced red-baiting. During the First Red Scare, after World War I, several Philadelphia women's groups threatened to withdraw financial support of the

WTUL if the organization did not moderate its pro-labor rhetoric. After World War II, she was first investigated for her involvement in the American Society for the Protection of the Foreign-Born and the LWS. She was cleared in 1949 but faced new allegations or investigations in 1950, 1953, and 1955. She resigned her position in December 1953, when a State Department loyalty investigation was still pending.

The government meted out the harshest punishment to women who were involved in or close to the Communist Party, including leaders of CAW. According to HUAC, the organization's purpose was not to advance women, but rather, "to serve as a specialized arm of Soviet political warfare in the current 'peace' campaign to disarm and demobilize the United States and democratic nations generally, in order to render them helpless in the face of the Communist drive for world conquest." It was, committee members argued, a "Communist hoax specifically designed to ensnare idealistically minded but politically gullible women" into acting against the United States. CAW disaffiliated from WIDF in December 1949, but in January 1950, the Justice Department demanded that its officers and board members register themselves as foreign agents. Members chose to disband rather than face imprisonment.[23]

As an African American, woman, immigrant, and communist, Claudia Jones threatened conservatives in Congress and elsewhere as no one else did. As Jones put it in 1956,

> I was deported from the U.S.A. because as a Negro woman Communist of West Indian descent, I was a thorn in their side in my opposition to Jim Crow racist discrimination against 16 million Negro Americans in the United States, in my work for redress of these grievances, for unity of Negro and White workers, for women's rights and my general political activity urging the American people to help by their struggles to change the present foreign and domestic policy of the United States.[24]

The FBI began surveilling Jones in 1942. Her file eventually ran to almost one thousand pages, much of it citing her writings about racial and gender equality. Jones was arrested and briefly jailed in 1948 and 1950, but her most significant run-in with the law came in June 1951, when she and sixteen other communists—including longtime feminist and labor activist Elizabeth Gurley Flynn—were arrested just days after the Supreme Court upheld the first set of Smith Act convictions. The recent ruling validated the government's strategy in such prosecutions: it was not necessary to prove that a defendant had taken action against the government to secure a conviction under the Smith Act. Prosecutors only needed to prove that the defendant had expressed ideas that could be interpreted as advocating such actions. In Jones's case, the inciting spark was a 1950 speech titled "International Women's Day and the Struggle for Peace," which the indictment claimed was "in further pursuance of said conspiracy [to overthrow the government] and to effect the objects thereof." Convicted with eleven others of conspiring to violate the Smith Act, Jones was sentenced in January 1953 to serve a year and a day in prison. The defendants pursued the appeals process for two years, but in January 1955, Jones entered the Women's Penitentiary in Alderson, West Virginia. Her health had suffered during the trial, and it continued to deteriorate in prison. In October her sentence was commuted for good behavior. She was released to stay with her father only to suffer a heart attack, which doctors attributed in part to her imprisonment. In November, Jones voluntarily agreed to leave for Great Britain. Her deportation order came on December 5, and she sailed for London four days later. As just one measure of the complicated nature of this era, December 5, 1955, was also the first day of the Montgomery Bus Boycott.[25]

CONCLUSION

By the mid-1950s, a cogent, intersectional feminist analysis was ready to burst forth and change the contours of American society. At the same time, proponents realized that this view was not politically viable in conservative postwar America, where McCarthyism ruined the lives of many Popular Front feminists and others. They were investigated (Mary Dublin Keyserling), fired (Caroline Ware), imprisoned (Elizabeth Gurley Flynn), and/or deported (Claudia Jones). Some groups, like the pacifist Women Strike for Peace, adopted traditional motherhood as a tactic to survive the era's anti-communist hysteria, even bringing their young children to hearings in front of HUAC. And some activists, like Friedan, chose to lie low until times evolved. Though anti-communist hysteria had abated somewhat by the time Friedan published The Feminine Mystique in 1963, continued fears of red-baiting may have made her wary of looking beyond the concerns of middle-class white women.

One of the hallmarks of late twentieth-century white, liberal feminism—getting women out of the home and into the workplace—thus had its roots in a midcentury interracial coalition of anti-fascist radicals. The very real specter of fascism to a generation that survived World War II pushed the threat of fascist gender norms—"Kinder, Küche, Kirche"—to the front of women's minds. They further saw the economic exploitation of women and people of color as a weapon that was used against all working people. But when strained through the forces of McCarthyism and contracting political possibilities, what remained part of mainstream discourse was a weakened, much more moderate call for workplace equality, especially for professional white women.

NOTES

1. Betty Friedan, *The Feminine Mystique* (New York: W. W. Norton & Company Inc., 1963), 16, 18.

2. James O'Connel, quoted in Susan M. Hartmann, "Women's Employment and the Domestic Ideal in the Early Cold War Years," in *Not June Cleaver: Women and Gender in Postwar America, 1945–1960*, ed. Joanne Meyerowitz (Philadelphia: Temple University Press, 1994), 86.

3. Dorothy Sue Cobble, *The Other Women's Movement: Workplace Justice and Social Rights in Modern America* (Princeton, NJ: Princeton University Press, 2005), 3–4, 5–6.

4. Elizabeth Gurley Flynn, "Life of the Party," *Daily Worker*, Mar. 9, 1950.

5. Statement of Patricia Harris, National Council of Negro Women, in *Equal Rights: Hearings before a Subcommittee of the Committee on the Judiciary, United States Senate, Eighty-Fourth Congress, Second Session, on S. J. Res. 39, Proposing an Amendment to the Constitution of the United States Relative to Equal Rights for Men and Women, April 11 and 18, 1956* (Washington, DC: Government Printing Office, 1956), 52.

6. Helen Elizabeth Brown, "Broken Pledges Damage Nation's Prestige," *Equal Rights*, Oct. 1954, 7.

7. Katharine St. George, quoted in National Woman's Party, "The Truth about the Hayden Rider," Mar. 1958, box 1, folder 9, Katzenstein Papers, HSP.

8. See Jefferson Cowie, *The Great Exception: The New Deal and the Limits of American Politics* (Princeton, NJ: Princeton University Press, 2016), and Nelson

Lichtenstein, *State of the Union: A Century of American Labor* (Princeton, NJ: Princeton University Press, 2000).

9. Kathleen A. Laughlin, *Women's Work and Public Policy: A History of the Women's Bureau, U.S. Department of Labor, 1945–1970* (Boston: Northeastern University Press, 2000), 27; Brigid O'Farrell and Felicia L. Kornbluh, *Rocking the Boat: Union Women's Voices, 1915–1975* (New Brunswick, NJ: Rutgers University Press, 1996), 174–75; Cobble, *The Other Women's Movement*, 39, 73–74 (quote on 73).

10. Esther Peterson, "You Can't Giddyup by Saying Whoa: Esther Peterson, Amalgamated Clothing Workers of America (1906–)," in O'Farrell and Kornbluh, *Rocking the Boat*, 64, 68–69, 79.

11. "Frieda S. Miller, Labor Official for the State and Nation, Dead," *New York Times*, Jul. 22, 1973; Annelise Orleck, *Common Sense and a Little Fire: Women and Working-Class Politics in the United States, 1900–1965* (Chapel Hill: University of North Carolina Press, 1995), 123, 136–37 (Miller quote on 136), 144–45, 147–50, 167; Cobble, *The Other Women's Movement*, 52.

12. Susan B. Anthony II, quoted in Kate Weigand, *Red Feminism: American Communism and the Making of Women's Liberation* (Baltimore: Johns Hopkins University Press, 2001), 51.

13. "Susan B. Anthony II on Women's Rights in the Postwar World, 1943," in *World War II: The Definitive Encyclopedia and Document Collection*, vol. 5: *Documents*, ed. Spencer C. Tucker (Santa Barbara, CA: ABC-CLIO, 2016), 2221.

14. Claudia Jones, "An End to the Neglect of the Problems of the Negro Woman," in *Let Nobody Turn Us Around: Voices of Resistance, Reform, and Renewal: An African American Anthology*, 2nd ed., ed. Manning Marable and Leith Mullings (Lanham, MD: Rowman & Littlefield Publishers Inc., 2009), 318, 320, 321; Carol Boyce Davies, *Left of Karl Marx: The Political Life of Black Communist Claudia Jones* (Durham, NC: Duke University Press, 2008), 35, 199 (quote).

15. Jones, "An End to the Neglect of the Problems," 316, 319, 323, 324.

16. For an overview of this era, see Ellen Schrecker, *Many Are the Crimes: McCarthyism in America* (Princeton, NJ: Princeton University Press, 1998).

17. Landon Storrs, *The Second Red Scare and the Unmaking of the New Deal Left* (Princeton, NJ: Princeton University Press, 2012), 51, 54 (quote), 55–56, 75.

18. Ibid., 61–65.

19. Ibid., 67, 76, 78–80, 81 (quote).

20. Ibid., 44–45, 88, 90 (quotes), 100.

21. Ibid., 88; Richard Nixon, quoted in Greg Mitchell, *Tricky Dick and the Pink Lady: Richard Nixon vs. Helen Gahagan Douglas: Sexual Politics and the Red Scare, 1950* (New York: Random House, 1998), 183–85.

22. Storrs, *The Second Red Scare*, 229–31; Peterson, "You Can't Giddyup by Saying Whoa," 77–78.

23. *Report on the Congress of American Women, October 23, 1949* (Washington, DC: Committee on Un-American Activities, U.S. House of Representatives, 1949), 1, 3; Weigand, *Red Feminism*, 63–64.

24. Jones, quoted in Davies, *Left of Karl Marx*, 205.

25. Davies, *Left of Karl Marx*, 194, 200–201, xxv; "Text of Indictment of 21 Communist Leaders on Conspiracy Charges," *New York Times*, Jun. 21, 1951; "Red Agrees to Leave Country," *New York Times*, Nov. 18, 1955.

CHAPTER 2

WOMEN IN THE CIVIL RIGHTS MOVEMENT

INTRODUCTION: WOMEN'S RIGHTS AND BLACK CIVIL RIGHTS

In 1951, the founding manifesto of a new group, Sojourners for Truth and Justice, deplored the history of racialized sexual violence in the United States. "We have seen our daughters raped and degraded," the founders argued in "A Call to Negro Women." Many of the group's members had been involved in defending Rosa Lee Ingram, so they knew how sexual violence threatened Black women's dignity and lives.[1]

One hundred thirty-two women attended the Sojourners' first meeting. Brought together by their work on the Ingram case and inspired by the writing of Claudia Jones and poet Beulah Richardson, Sojourners was the only radical left group led by, and focused solely on, the needs of Black women. Over the course of the next year, participants met (or tried to meet with) officials in the White House, Justice Department, and Pentagon to protest government inaction against racism; mounted a campaign protesting the murders of Florida NAACP leader Harry Moore and his wife, Harriet; and called for five thousand women to march on Washington, DC, in a day of mourning for Harriet.

In 1952, however, the group dissolved. The Communist Party USA, with which many Sojourners were affiliated, was less inclined to support a group led by Black women than it was to support the Congress of American Women or male-led civil rights groups. At the same time, McCarthyism pushed mainstream civil rights groups to the right. The FBI surveilled the Sojourners for the entirety of its existence, accumulating over 450 pages of information in a single year and concluding that the organization was a communist front. After the Sojourners' demise, "no other African American women's group until the late 1960s formulated an explicitly left-wing, transnational program like that of the Sojourners." In 1968 and 1974, respectively, the mantle would be taken up by the Third World Women's Alliance and the Combahee River Collective, with whom the Sojourners shared a titular nod to abolitionist women.[2]

Yet in various ways, the better-known civil rights activism of the 1950s and '60s kept alive the spirit and goals of the Sojourners. The same focus on protecting Black women's bodies animated the activism of Rosa Parks, Jo Ann Robinson, Daisy Bates, and Fannie Lou Hamer. It would be incorrect to separate these women out from feminist history and understand them only within the confines of civil rights movement history. While the towering figures of men such as Martin Luther King Jr.—men who sometimes had trouble recognizing women's contributions—can make it difficult to see, Parks, Pauli Murray, and Ella Baker understood that, for Black women, civil rights and women's rights could not be separated. As Sojourner Beulah Richardson noted in her 1951 poem "A Black Woman Speaks," Black and white women experienced patriarchy in different but fundamentally intertwined ways. As wives or chattel, both were beholden to white men in a form of slavery. Rather than using these related experiences as a springboard to solidarity, however, white women turned to racism as a form of compensation for their own oppression. Black women's voices thus played a unique and necessary role in pointing out and challenging these interlocking power systems. Bearing in mind the ways that activists like Richardson navigated their identities as both African Americans and women, historians should follow their lead in seeing connections between these movements.

It is well known that the civil rights movement inspired the feminist movement of the 1960s and '70s, providing much of the language, organizational know-how, and grassroots infrastructure necessary for women to pursue their rights. Perhaps equally well known are the ways in which male leaders of the civil rights movement frustrated their female counterparts by failing to appreciate women's contributions to the movement and see the connections between race and gender.

It would not be correct, however, to say that the arrow of influence between the civil rights movement and the women's rights movement only went in one direction. Nor was it merely the case that women were the unsung grassroots backbone of the movement, playing central but unappreciated roles in its most visible and successful actions (though they were). Beyond these roles, women were often willing to go further in their pursuit of racial equality than men were. Lawyer and activist Pauli Murray, for example, pushed for an end to segregation while Thurgood Marshall and the NAACP were still arguing merely to mitigate its effects. Overall, the arguments, strategies, and organizations Black women developed to protect themselves as not only African Americans but also *as women* provided the modern civil rights movement with much of its shape and many of its most visible successes. They also anticipated—in some cases, by decades—similar arguments made by white women about sexual and bodily autonomy. According to historian Danielle McGuire,

> [D]ecades before radical feminists in the women's movement urged rape survivors to "speak out," African-American women's public protests galvanized local, national, and even international outrage and sparked larger campaigns for racial justice and human dignity. . . . Civil rights campaigns [across the South] . . . had roots in organized resistance to sexual violence and appeals for protection of black womanhood.[3]

WOMEN IN THE CIVIL RIGHTS MOVEMENT BEFORE WORLD WAR II

The struggle for racial justice long predated the well-known civil rights movement of the 1950s and '60s. In the decades after emancipation, women played key roles in this movement, developing many of the tactics and some of the rhetoric their successors would use later. Through churches; schools; the vast network of women's clubs; and direct, individual action, women were the backbone of the struggle for racial justice in the late nineteenth and early twentieth centuries, sometimes, by virtue of being women, able to do what their male counterparts could not.

The decades after the Civil War saw an expansion of the rights of African Americans followed by a swift and dramatic contraction. The Thirteenth Amendment (1865) abolished slavery, the Fourteenth Amendment (1868) established equal citizenship rights, and the Fifteenth Amendment (1870) extended the franchise to Black men. Freed people eagerly reestablished families; sought economic stability and independence; developed their own institutions, especially churches and mutual aid societies; and participated in politics, voting, and running for office. Overwhelmingly loyal Republicans, Black men were elected to both state and national legislatures. Many, however, found themselves trapped within the system of sharecropping, which often left them working for their former owners on the same land they had worked while enslaved. Further, sharecropping contracts required that tenants turn over an agreed-upon portion of their crops at the end of the season as "payment" for the use of the land and to compensate landowners for seeds and other materials, with sharecroppers keeping what remained as their due for the year's labor. When the market value of the sharecropper's portion of the crop failed to provide enough return to pay off debts to the landowner or the merchant at the local country store that had provided credit for goods during the course of the year, often at very high interest rates, the sharecropper fell into a system of debt peonage that was almost impossible to escape.

Moreover, the political rights freed people won during Reconstruction (1865–77) were attacked by resentful whites. Southern whites worked assiduously to disenfranchise the Black men who had recently won the right to vote through intimidation and violence at the polls and by enacting literacy tests, poll taxes, and grandfather clauses that effectively eliminated Black voting across the South by the end of the nineteenth century. Some states required potential voters to analyze obscure passages of the state constitution, which most laypeople did not have the skills to do. By the early twentieth century, state-mandated racial segregation became legal policy, with southern states enforcing the practice in every type of public facility, including public transportation, schools, hotels, and restaurants. Collectively, these policies were known as Jim Crow laws. Finally, racial terrorism—most visibly in the emergence of the Ku Klux Klan (KKK) and the rise of lynching and extralegal mob killings, most commonly of Black men—became widespread.

Lynching was both deeply entrenched in intersections of race, gender, and sexuality and an impetus to women's activism. White southerners—men and women alike—insisted that lynching was justified as punishment for supposedly hypersexual Black men who raped white women, whom they saw as pure. Cultural representations of this myth, which persisted throughout the Jim Crow era, include D. W. Griffith's popular film *The Birth of a Nation* (1915), which portrays the KKK as the heroes of Reconstruction and the defenders of pure white woman-hood, and Harper Lee's 1960 novel, *To Kill a Mockingbird*, in which Atticus Finch defends Tom Robinson, a Black man whom Mayella Ewell, a white woman, has accused of trying to rape her. When Tom is shot and killed trying to escape from prison after his conviction, Scout, the young narrator, understands that "Tom was a dead man the minute Mayella Ewell opened her mouth and screamed."[4] In the Jim Crow South, even the most disreputable white woman would be believed over a Black man even if he had physical limitations that made it impossible for him to have assaulted her.

Activist Ida B. Wells (1862–1931) knew that the argument used to justify lynching was a lie. Born a slave in Mississippi, Wells came from a family involved in the leadership of Black communities; the securing of civil rights; and the betterment of political, economic, and social conditions in the decades after emancipation. Over seventy years before Claudette Colvin, Rosa Parks, and others protested segregation on Montgomery, Alabama, buses, Wells challenged segregated seating on Tennessee trains. In 1884, she was forcibly moved from a train for taking a seat in the ladies' car, the section of the train where no smoking was allowed. As an African American, authorities considered her outside the category of "lady." She sued the railroad company and won, although the Tennessee Supreme Court later overturned the decision on appeal. Demoralized by the decision, Wells nonetheless redoubled her commitment to anti-racist activism. In 1889, she became part owner of a Memphis newspaper, *Free Speech and Headlight*, which she used to publicize crimes committed against African Americans.

In 1892, she turned her attention to anti-lynching activism. Wells had long known that the purported reason for lynching—that Black men raped white women—was a lie. The issue became personal that year, when three of her friends—Thomas Moss, William Stewart, and Calvin McDowell—were lynched. Moss owned the People's Grocery Store in Memphis, and Stewart and McDowell were his employees. Located across the street from a white-owned and white-operated grocery store, Moss's business provided unwelcome competition to the nearby white establishment. Wells concluded that lynching was a punishment for African Americans who stepped outside their "proper" sphere economically, socially, or politically. She wrote and spoke widely on the issue, earning the opprobrium of whites. When they burned down her newspaper office, she left Memphis for good.

Less confrontational than Wells were the overlapping constituencies of the Black women's club movement and the Black church, many of whom came from W. E. B. Du Bois's "talented tenth." In his 1903 book *The Souls of Black Folk*, Du Bois defined this group as the best and brightest in African American society. Educated by universities, these individuals were to instruct other members of the race and advance civil rights. Many members of this group, especially women, trained to become teachers, a profession that often also encompassed aspects of social work.

Formal education was important to this group, but so, too, was the broader doctrine of respectability, of which education was a part. By adhering to middle-class white norms of respectability—including thrift, sexual decorum, traditional family structure, piety, and hard work—talented tenth members hoped to earn a measure of respect in the eyes of white Americans. They believed in the philosophy of racial uplift and worked hard to encourage lower-class African Americans to conform to these behaviors as well.

The Black women's club movement exemplified these beliefs. Founded in 1896 as an umbrella group to oversee all Black women's clubs, the National Association of Colored Women (NACW) had as its motto "[L]ifting as we climb." Its founders, including Mary Church Terrell and Anna Julia Cooper, believed that women had a special duty and mission to uplift the race. She wrote:

> In the era about to dawn, her [woman's] sentiments must strike the keynote and give the dominant tone. And this because of the nature of her contribution to the world. . . . Her kingdom is not over physical forces. Not by might, nor by power can she prevail. Her position must ever be inferior where strength of muscle creates leadership. If she follows the instincts of her nature, however, she must always stand for the conservation of those deeper moral forces which make for the happiness of homes and the righteousness of the country. In a reign of moral ideas she is easily queen.[5]

While critical of Black men, clubwomen also realized that the omnipresent threat of lynching made it more difficult to engage in the political work that women could undertake without being seen as threatening.

This work included not only respectability focused initiatives to encourage personal hygiene and moral improvement but also classes on economic advancement and job placement; founding kindergartens, scholarships, and orphanages; and such explicitly political work as lectures advocating woman suffrage and lobbying against lynching and segregation and for the restoration of Black men's voting rights, greater access to utilities, and more police protection in Black neighborhoods.

Many of these same women used the Black church, especially the Baptist church, to effect change. Though unable to become pastors, women filled many behind-the-scenes leadership roles while simultaneously developing a feminist theology through which they argued for greater authority and respect within the church structure. Additionally, they created schools, nurseries, hospitals, orphanages, and old folks' homes; fought for social reforms, including temperance, literacy and education, and suffrage; battled segregation laws; and petitioned the government for social and economic equality.

While the power of respectability waned amid the emergence of the New Negro movement, which emphasized Black nationalism and martial masculinity, after World War I—and, with it, women's ability to take on leadership roles in civil rights organizing—its continuing relevance in the mid-twentieth century is a central reason why the Montgomery Bus Boycott centered around Rosa Parks, not any of the myriad other women who had taken similar actions. Its long history also highlights what a radical break from tradition such groups as the Student Nonviolent Coordinating Committee (SNCC), and particularly, the ideologies of its members' most important mentor, Ella Baker, represented. Finally, the historical role of women in the Black church paved the way for gender-inflected conflicts between grassroots leaders, including Baker, and such charismatic men as Martin Luther King Jr.

In the 1930s, women again rose to positions of prominence within the civil rights movement, taking on secondary leadership roles in the New Deal infrastructure and founding their own grassroots organizations. In both arenas, the inimitable Mary McLeod Bethune led the way. Born in South Carolina in 1875, Bethune's parents were former slaves. She founded a school that became the prestigious Bethune-Cookman College, and in 1924, she was elected president of the NACW (beating out Ida B. Wells in the process). Under her presidency, the NACW focused on obtaining a federal anti-lynching bill, helping rural women and women in industry, training clerks and typists, and raising the status of women in the Philippines, Puerto Rico, Haiti, and Africa. The group also raised the funds to buy a home to serve as its first national headquarters during her tenure.

In 1929, Bethune concluded that a new Black women's group was necessary. Six years later, her vision resulted in the National Council of Negro Women (NCNW). As an insider to the NACW, Bethune knew all too well that the older group had become anachronistic. Amid the economic upheaval of the Great Depression, many Black women were more concerned with their status as workers than their identity as moral arbiters. African Americans were particularly hard hit by the Depression, with unemployment reaching 50 percent in some Black communities. In New York City, women domestic workers were forced to try to find work in the city's "slave market," lining up each morning on the street waiting for prospective employers to hire them. Since work was so scarce, women—many of them the sole breadwinners in their families—had to constantly underbid one another. A young Ella Baker, discussed below, wrote an article condemning this practice.

For these reasons, Bethune and others came to see economic power as the key to racial progress. In the pages of the NAACP magazine *The Crisis*, W. E. B. Du Bois discussed economic cooperatives and the power of consumers. In New York, Baker cofounded the Young Negroes' Cooperative League (YNCL) in 1930 with the goal of organizing the buying power of young Black men and women. Across the country, Black women formed Housewives' Leagues to advance the principle of "Don't buy where you can't work." Fannie B. Peck, founder in 1930 of the Housewives' League in Detroit, hoped to "stabilize the economic status of the Negro through directed spending." The Detroit league became the model for the national Housewives' League, which boasted ten thousand members by 1935.[6]

The focus on economic power suited both Bethune and the tenor of the times perfectly, for it also informed many New Deal programs. Aided by her friendship with Eleanor Roosevelt, Bethune was at the center of the president's "Black Cabinet." Her official position was director of the Negro Division of the National Youth Administration (NYA), which involved finding employment for sixteen- through twenty-one-year-olds.

Bethune's material concerns also help to illuminate differences between the NCNW and its predecessor, the NACW. For Bethune, the inclusion of the term "Negro" in the new group's title was quite intentional and significant. In part, it reflected the increased racial pride growing out of the New Negro movement. But since "colored" was the preferred term among light-skinned and affluent African Americans, the term was also a rejection of the "lifting as we climb" ideology, which held that the Talented Tenth, as they rose through the ranks of society, would bring the less fortunate with them, in part, by teaching them the norms of respectability. Bethune was far less interested in women's morality than she was in getting money in their pockets.

These competing priorities reflected the different backgrounds of NACW founder Mary Church Terrell and Bethune. Terrell was born into a Talented Tenth family and was raised to be a model and leader of the race. Bethune, by contrast, was raised by a family of hardworking farmers, who scrimped and saved to get by. As a result, she was not interested in grand declarations on men's and women's differences. She was interested in practical politics and material improvements in Black people's—especially women's—lives.

In the decades after World War II, the strategies that Black Americans had been developing for decades started to bear fruit. A war fought against white supremacism provided the civil rights movement with rhetorical ammunition, and a generation of Black veterans was even less willing than before to accept the racial status quo. The Second Great Migration gave African Americans more access to good jobs and voting rights, which made them a powerful new constituency for politicians to deal with. The onset of the Cold War and the need to present the United States as a place of liberty and equality also made some mainstream, liberal politicians—including Truman, Eisenhower, and Kennedy—more inclined to support modest civil rights gains. Additionally, the growth of the media provided new attention to both long-standing activist strategies, like boycotts and challenges to segregation, and violent repercussions. Inspired by leaders like Wells, Bethune, and others, women played key roles in this revitalized struggle, as they had in the past. Their predecessors had instilled in succeeding generations of Black children a racial pride that would make putting up with the daily humiliations of segregation inconceivable.

DEVELOPING A LEGAL STRATEGY FOR EQUALITY:
BROWN V. BOARD OF EDUCATION OF TOPEKA

In the 1940s and '50s, such established organizations as the NAACP started to make real progress in their challenges to the legal underpinnings of segregation. Important cases either struck down or chipped away at segregation in primary elections (*Smith v. Alright*, 1944), housing (*Shelley v. Kramer*, 1948), and higher education (*Sweatt v. Painter*, 1950). None was more consequential than *Brown v. Board of Education of Topeka* (1954).

At the center of this case was a young woman named Linda Brown, a third grader in Topeka, Kansas, who had to walk a mile to the bus stop, where she caught a bus to the Black elementary school. The walk was a difficult one; in particular, Brown had to go through a dangerous, isolated railroad switch. Moreover, there was a white elementary school only a few blocks away from her home. Her father, Oliver Brown, tried to enroll her in the white school. Turned away, he sued, eventually taking his daughter's case all the way to the Supreme Court, where it was combined with four other cases on segregation in public schools to form the basis of the *Brown* decision.

Lawyer Thurgood Marshall, who in 1967 became the first African American to sit on the Supreme Court, led the NAACP legal team. Their case focused on the psychological effects of segregation. Drawing on the research of psychologist Kenneth Clark, who had shown that Black children educated in segregated schools developed a negative self-image, Marshall argued that segregation inevitably created low self-esteem and a permanent sense of inferiority in Black children. In contrast, the opposing legal team focused solely on legal precedent, arguing that psychological studies did not matter.

Divided, the justices asked for rearguments based on the relationship of the case to the Fourteenth Amendment. Fate intervened when Chief Justice Fred Vinson died suddenly and Earl Warren joined the court. As attorney general of California during World War II, Warren had actively participated in the internment of Japanese Americans. He came to regret this and spent much of his time on the Supreme Court trying to remedy inequalities in American life. Under Warren's leadership, the Supreme Court unanimously found that "separate but equal" violated the Fourteenth Amendment.

Lawyer and activist Pauli Murray. Murray developed creative legal strategies to challenge both racial and gender discrimination, the combination of which she termed "Jane Crow." (Library of Congress, Prints and Photographs Division, NYWT&S Collection, LC-USZ62-109644)

Marshall's contributions to the civil rights movement are rightfully celebrated. Less well known is the woman who pushed him to challenge segregation head-on. One of the preeminent legal minds of the civil rights and feminist movements, Pauli Murray was born in Baltimore in 1910 before spending most of her early life in Durham, North Carolina. While a student at Hunter College in New York City in the late 1920s and early '30s, she lived at the Harlem Young Women's Christian Association (YWCA), which put her in the center of the cultural and political flowering of the Harlem Renaissance. There, she became friends with Dorothy Height, who worked for the YWCA director and later became president of the NCNW, and Ella Baker, who lived nearby. She also had the opportunity to hear such speakers as Langston Hughes, Countee Cullen, W. E. B. Du Bois, Paul Robeson, A. Philip Randolph, Mary Church Terrell, and Mary McLeod Bethune.

After college, Murray held a number of jobs, including working with Baker in the Workers Education Project of the Works Progress Administration (WPA), which sent her to Harlem and the Lower East Side to teach classes on labor issues to Black workers. Though an intellectual who read voraciously in this era about communism; socialism; and sex, gender, and sexuality, she also put herself on the front lines of civil rights activism, which led to her arrest in Petersburg, Virginia, for resisting bus segregation. After criticizing the Roosevelt administration's timorous response to racism, she struck up a friendship with Eleanor Roosevelt, which lasted until the former first lady's death in 1962. As a field secretary for the Workers Defense League, she collected money for the defense of a Black sharecropper accused of killing a white landowner, and in 1942, at the behest of A. Phillip Randolph, she helped organize a march to protest his execution.

She also hoped to further her education. She was rejected from the University of North Carolina twice, first from its sociology department and second from its law school. At least, the first rejection was explicitly due to her race. Murray publicized this unfair treatment through newspaper articles, and she even considered suing the school until Thurgood Marshall dissuaded her.

Finally admitted to Howard University Law School, Murray met friends and mentors who pushed her thinking on the interrelatedness of race and gender. In her second year in the program, she became friends with Caroline Ware, who had just been hired by the history department. Ware and NWP member Betsy Graves Reyneau, who arrived at Howard in 1943, taught Murray about the history of the women's rights movement. Based in part on these influences, Murray started formulating a legal strategy for overcoming discrimination based on both race and gender using the Thirteenth and Fourteenth Amendments. Later, NAACP lawyers used an essay she wrote in law school to build their case in *Brown*.

After a brief stint in California, where she studied at Berkeley and became the first African American to hold the position of deputy attorney general in the state, she returned to New York. She thought about looking for a job in the federal government, but her allies there—like Ware—were under attack. Instead, she found work as a research assistant for Alexander Pekelis of the American Jewish Congress, who was currently preparing an amicus brief for *Mendez v. Westminster* (1947), then pending in the Ninth

Circuit Court of Appeals. Murray drew on her considerable knowledge and experience to craft a thorough research-based report in favor of the plaintiffs, who argued that California's practice of segregating Mexican American children into separate schools violated the constitution. The court ruled in their favor, establishing an important legal precedent.

Murray's work relied on social scientific evidence to wage an all-out attack on *Plessy v. Ferguson*, presaging Marshall's work on *Brown* and other cases. Murray and others had convinced him that it was time to start arguing not for better segregated facilities but for an end to segregation itself.

NOT SO OLD AND TIRED: ROSA PARKS, JO ANN ROBINSON, AND THE MONTGOMERY BUS BOYCOTT

Coming on the heels of *Brown v. Board*, the Montgomery Bus Boycott provided an early example of successful direct action. On December 1, 1955, spry forty-two-year-old Rosa Parks refused to give up her seat to a white passenger on a bus in Montgomery, Alabama. A longtime activist, Parks had been a member of the NAACP for fifteen years and had recently spent time at Highlander Folk School in Tennessee, receiving training in nonviolent civil disobedience.

Parks's action was not premeditated, but E. D. Nixon, the president of the Alabama NAACP and the head of a local chapter of the Brotherhood of Sleeping Car Porters, and his cohorts had been looking for a figure around whom they could rally to challenge segregation and sadistic treatment from white drivers on city buses. Earlier in 1955, teenager Claudette Colvin had anticipated Parks's refusal. But Colvin was pregnant and unmarried, and in the wake of *Brown v. Board*, white supremacists had raised fears of sexual impropriety among African Americans and between African Americans and whites to a fever pitch. In this context, civil rights activists had little choice but to embrace respectability. A long-married, economically stable, outwardly unimposing member of the community, Parks's respectability was unimpeachable. When Nixon heard Parks had been arrested, he felt almost gleeful: the Montgomery police, he knew, had no idea whom they were dealing with or what hay activists could make with the arrest.

The previous year, Jo Ann Robinson, an English professor at nearby Alabama State College and president of the Women's Political Council

(WPC), had proposed a boycott of the city bus system, but the movement's male leaders resisted until Parks's arrest. That same night, Robinson and other WPC members worked through the night copying and distributing thousands of flyers announcing that a boycott would begin the next day. Nixon, too, sprang into action, calling all the contacts he had assembled over his more than a decade of activism. The following evening, the boycott was formally organized, and the Montgomery Improvement Association (MIA) was founded shortly thereafter. Members selected twenty-six-year-old Martin Luther King Jr., who had recently moved to Montgomery, to head the organization. For 381 days, African Americans carpooled or walked miles to and from work, bringing the bus company and several downtown stores to the brink of bankruptcy. In November 1956, the Supreme Court declared segregation on buses unconstitutional.

The boycott catapulted King to fame, but Parks is remembered largely as a symbol. Parks's history as a gritty and fearless activist has been lost. As McGuire puts it,

> [T]he presentation of Parks as a woman worthy of protection enabled African-American ministers and male leaders, most of whom had been reluctant to the WPC's calls for a boycott, to take credit for and assume leadership of the boycott. By stepping forward, they could fulfill their manly duty to defend black womanhood, a role that white supremacy had denied them for centuries.[7]

Lost, too, in this flattening of Parks's legacy is the centrality—indeed, the indispensability—of Black women's decades-long attempts to protect themselves from rape and sexual assault to the success of the modern civil rights movement.

Parks herself was a product of rape; several of her ancestors had been conceived out of relationships between white masters and their female slaves. As a young activist in the 1930s, she was aware of how both the rape of Black women and false accusations of rape against Black men maintained unequal race relations. She followed such cases as that of twelve-year-old Birmingham, Alabama, resident Murdus Dixon, who was raped at gunpoint by her employer, a white man whom police refused to arrest. She and her husband also raised money and held meetings to help the defense of the "Scottsboro boys."

Parks joined the Montgomery NAACP in 1943 and was immediately elected branch secretary, which meant that she traveled around the area collecting evidence of discrimination. She quickly gained a reputation as someone that victims of racial violence, including sexual violence, could talk to. It is not surprising, then, that Nixon sent Parks to her hometown of Abbeville, Alabama, to investigate a rape.

In September 1944, six white men kidnapped and raped twenty-four-year-old Recy Taylor, who was walking home from church. After spending time in Abbeville, Parks returned to Montgomery, where she and other supporters founded the Alabama Committee for Equal Justice for Mrs. Recy Taylor. The case generated national attention, becoming a cause célèbre around which civil rights activists rallied, publishing articles, raising money, and signing petitions. Nonetheless, two separate grand juries refused to hand down indictments, though Taylor's attackers were well known and her story corroborated. Yet the activism the case generated bore fruit. Shortly after the organization was founded in Alabama, there were Committee for Equal Justice branches in sixteen states and Washington, DC, contributing to a national network of activists. The original Alabama branch eventually became the MIA. Thus, the attempt to secure justice for Taylor and, more broadly, to protect Black women's bodies provided the infrastructure for successful direct action a decade later.

Robinson, the woman most responsible for success of the boycott, has not received even the symbolic esteem in which Parks is held. Born in Georgia as the youngest of twelve children, Robinson received a BS from Georgia State College and an MA from Alabama State College. She taught in public schools and colleges, joining the faculty of Alabama State College in 1949. She joined the WPC that same year, later becoming its president. Robinson later recalled that "we [the WPC] were 'woman power,' organized to cope with any injustice, no matter what, against the darker sect." And these injustices were legion. As the WPC became better known in the community, people began approaching its members with complaints, many of them about buses. By December 1955, the WPC had been calling for a boycott—and for full integration—for years, but they faced resistance from men, both the white politicians with whom they had formed working relationships and the Black ministers who held moral sway over their communities. In contrast to her indefatigable behind-the-scenes work, Robinson kept a low profile during the boycott itself because

she did not want to adversely affect her college. This decision likely affected her legacy. Still, Robinson was among those leaders arrested on
February 21, 1956, and tried under Alabama's anti-boycott law. In her
mug shot, her face bears a small, proud smile.[8]

What even Robinson may not have known, however, is that in the
years before she joined the group, WPC was committed to seeking justice
for survivors of sexual violence in ways that anticipated the Montgomery
Bus Boycott. Indeed, one of the organization's early goals was to "come
to the defense of women who had been victimized by rape and other
physical assaults." In the 1940s and '50s, this violence—including sexual
violence—was often linked to access to public transportation. In 1942,
Ella Ree Jones, a student at Alabama State Teachers College in Montgomery, was pulled off a bus, beaten by police officers, arrested, and fined
when she refused to give up her seat. Three years later, two Black female
army privates were attacked and sexually harassed for doing the same. In
1946, a Montgomery police officer raped the sixteen-year-old daughter of
a woman who refused to give up her seat; local law enforcement let him
slip out of town without being fired or arrested. Through these and other
cases, WPC members and other activists learned that putting pressure
on the justice system rarely worked. Economic pressure, however, proved
more effective. In 1951, Sam E. Green, a white man, raped Flossie Hardman, a fifteen-year-old Black girl whom he employed, in his car. Hardman
and her parents sued, but the jury exonerated Green after only five minutes of deliberation. In response, the NAACP, WPC, and other groups
decided to boycott Green's store. Within weeks, his business was on the
brink of failure. Montgomery activists would not soon forget that boycotts
could be a powerful tool for providing justice.[9]

DAISY BATES AND THE LITTLE ROCK NINE

Attacks on women's bodies motivated activists in Little Rock, Arkansas,
too. After the *Brown* decision, the NAACP attempted to register Black
students in previously all-white schools in cities throughout the South.
The Little Rock school board agreed to comply with the high court's ruling, and in 1957, the NAACP registered nine Black students to attend the
previously all-white Little Rock Central High School. The students met
with so much resistance—including from arch-segregationist governor

Orval Faubus, who dispatched the National Guard to try to prevent the students' entrance—that President Eisenhower federalized the National Guard to protect the students.

The summer before they enrolled in Central High School, members of the Little Rock Nine prepared with local NAACP leaders, including Daisy Bates. Born Daisy Lee Gatson in Hutting, Arkansas, in 1914, Daisy's parents tried to shield her from the realities of racism. When she was eight, however, she learned of the traumatic events at the center of her family history. When she was a baby, three white men raped and killed her biological mother, dumping her body in a river. Bereft, Daisy's biological father left her with his two best friends.

When eight-year-old Daisy confronted her adoptive father with what she knew, he explained to her the pattern of which her mother's rape and murder was a part. "He told me of the timeworn lust of the white man for the Negro woman—which strikes at the heart of every Negro man in the South," she later recalled.[10] The anger she felt at these men motivated her lifelong activism.

In 1941, Daisy and her husband, L. C. Bates, moved to Little Rock, where they founded a newspaper, the *State Press*, which they used to bring attention to injustices committed against African Americans. She became a leader in the Little Rock and statewide NAACP and, like Parks in Montgomery, a go-to person for survivors of racial and sexual violence. She and L. C. publicized these crimes in the *State Press* and were sometimes able to help secure trials and, occasionally, even convictions.

ELLA BAKER AND THE STUDENT NONVIOLENT COORDINATING COMMITTEE

The modern civil rights movement comprised a number of different leadership styles that reflected different strategies and goals. To understand the role of women in the civil rights movement and the relationship between this activism and the women's rights movement, two are especially important.

The first strategy, the top-down leadership tradition, was the most visible and is the best known today. Exemplified by men like King and organizations like the Southern Christian Leadership Conference (SCLC), which King founded after the success of the Montgomery Bus Boycott, and the NAACP, this strategy focused on large-scale, national events. This tradition reflected the assumption that well-educated members of the clergy and other national leaders—almost, if not entirely, all men—influenced the masses.

The 1963 March on Washington exemplified this strategy. Not coincidentally, this event pushed women to the sidelines. Despite the national prominence of women including Rosa Parks, Dorothy Height, Ella Baker, and many others—and despite organizer Bayard Rustin's own experiences with discrimination as a gay Black man—women were nearly invisible at the march. Only one, Daisy Bates (replacing Medgar Evers's widow, Myrlie, who was stuck in traffic), spoke. They did not meet with the president, and they did not march with King and the other male leaders—instead, the movement's most prominent women marched with the wives of their male counterparts.

The second tradition was the grassroots community-organizing tradition, exemplified by women like Ella Baker and Fannie Lou Hamer and men including Baker's protégé, Bob Moses. Reflecting women's unheralded work in the Black church and other institutions, ordinary women were the foot soldiers of this movement, which assumed that, in Baker's words, "strong people don't need strong leaders." In this view, local people knew best how to solve their own problems and end their own oppression, and thus, they—not well-educated, elite outsiders—needed to be the leaders of any movement for social change.

Where this organizing strategy was implemented, leadership was at the local level and often decentralized, with women, the poor, and ordinary citizens playing key roles. These individuals served as the backbone of the movement, composed its rank and file, and carried on the local struggle long after national leaders and organizations left the scene to plan other highly publicized events.

Ella Baker was among the most influential leaders hewing to the second orientation. Born in 1903 in Norfolk, Virginia, Baker developed a sense for social justice early in her life. Growing up in North Carolina, she listened to her grandmother tell stories about slave revolts and her own attempts to exercise autonomy in her life. As a slave, her grandmother was whipped for refusing to marry a man whom her owner had chosen for her. Self-educated and religious, Baker's parents taught her a sense of social responsibility that she would always carry with her. Baker's mother was a

Civil rights activist Ella Baker. An advisor to Martin Luther King Jr. and a mentor to the Student Nonviolent Coordinating Committee, Baker believed that the most marginalized individuals, not the elite, should be the leaders of any social movement. (Library of Congress, Prints and Photographs Division, Visual Materials from the NAACP Records, LC-DIG-ppmsca-38688)

teacher and churchwoman who taught her children the value of proper grammar and deportment and the necessity of helping the less fortunate.

At Shaw University in Raleigh, North Carolina, Baker was a passionate and spirited student. She earned excellent grades and challenged school policies that she thought were unfair. After graduating as class valedictorian in 1927, she moved to New York City, where she involved herself in a number of activist organizations, including the YNCL and the Workers' Education Project of the WPA. She became active with the NAACP in 1940, working as a field secretary and then director of branches from 1943 until 1946. She resigned over differences in leadership styles: she found the leaders elitist and thought the association was not open to dissenting views or to the full participation of local leaders. In 1957, Baker moved to Atlanta to work with SCLC. The organization, however, was a poor fit. King hesitated to hire Baker, a woman, for a permanent position. In the meantime, she disagreed with the organization's policy of promoting strong central leadership over grassroots organization.

Elsewhere, however, a movement that seemed to exemplify her beliefs in local grassroots activism emerged. By 1960, ordinary people all over the country were launching direct action campaigns against Jim Crow and other humiliations. In February that year, four Black college students sat down at the whites-only lunch counter at the Woolworth's in Greensboro, North Carolina. The sit-in movement quickly spread across the South, and Baker convinced King and SCLC to sponsor an April meeting of the sit-in leaders at her alma mater, Shaw University. Attracting over two hundred participants, the meeting inspired the formation of the Student Nonviolent Coordinating Committee (SNCC).

Throughout 1960 and 1961, SNCC staged sit-ins and stand-ins at lunch counters, bus stations, movie theaters, and other public facilities; coordinated boycotts of segregated businesses, and mounted support campaigns for protestors who were arrested. The Freedom Rides, which they took over that year, thrust them into the national spotlight. Initiated by the Congress for Racial Equality (CORE), Freedom Rides involved activists attempting to ride buses all the way from Washington, DC, to New Orleans in a challenge to segregation on public transportation. When CORE abandoned the project due to violence, SNCC took up the cause. The Freedom Rides cemented SNCC's reputation as the "shock troops" of the movement and led the Interstate Commerce Commission to mandate full desegregation of all interstate travel facilities.

With Baker's encouragement, SNCC focused on organizing local communities. Between 1961 and 1964, its members launched dozens of projects in rural and urban communities across the South. In each, SNCC members either worked with existing desegregation, voter registration, and other kinds of campaigns or tried to identify local leaders who could begin these campaigns. SNCC mandated that local people should organize themselves; members—often with more formal education and financial stability and, increasingly, from outside the South—should not impose their own ideas about organizational structure and leadership upon these communities. A direct reflection of Baker's teachings, this orientation also marked a major shift in the way civil rights groups operated in the South. Contra both Du Bois and the early King, in this view, the Black middle class and elite—the Talented Tenth—had no special claims on leadership within the Black community. Rather, leadership should emanate from the bottom of the class hierarchy. Oppressed people knew what they needed better than more privileged outsiders did. This, in a nutshell, was the theory of participatory democracy to which Baker and SNCC hewed and that the white student left and women's liberation movement adopted later in the 1960s.

In fall 1963, SNCC launched an ambitious voter registration drive in Mississippi, the "belly of the beast" of southern racism. Named Freedom Vote, the initiative included a mock election intended to show that, contrary to the insistence of southern whites, southern Blacks *did* want to vote but were kept away by violence and intimidation. The campaign was a great success, with around eighty thousand freedom ballots cast.

But Freedom Vote augured change in SNCC. Organization leaders had allowed Al Lowenstein, a white liberal and academic, to recruit some of his white students from Yale and Stanford universities to work on the campaign. Although some southern whites had worked with SNCC from the beginning, this was the first time that large numbers of white volunteers joined them. The media fixated on these volunteers, which brought attention to the cause. Across the country, Americans witnessed the plight of Black Mississippians nightly on their televisions.

The attention could not have come at a better time; 1963 was a desperately violent year across the South. NAACP organizer and World War II veteran Medgar Evers was murdered in his Jackson, Mississippi, driveway by Byron de la Beckwith, a white supremacist, Klansman, and member of the local white Citizens' Council, just hours after President John F. Kennedy had finally pledged his full support to civil rights. In Birmingham, Alabama, police commissioner "Bull" Connor unleashed police dogs on peaceful protestors, including children. In September in that same city, four Ku Klux Klan members bombed the Sixteenth Street Baptist Church, killing four young girls—Addie Mae Collins, Cynthia Wesley, Carole Robertson, and Carol Denise McNair—all between the ages of eleven and fourteen. Law enforcement in the state had little interest in curbing such atrocities; the state's governor, George Wallace, had pledged his commitment to "segregation now, segregation tomorrow, segregation forever" in his inaugural speech that January, a promise he tried to keep by blocking the entrance to the University of Alabama auditorium to prevent its desegregation (the "stand in the schoolhouse door").

Combined with the media attention granted to white volunteers, this wave of violence against Blacks convinced some SNCC leaders that the presence of white bodies would provide a degree of protection from un-checked violence. This gambit, unfortunately, was unsuccessful. Mere days after the campaign began, three young male volunteers—James Chaney, who was Black, and Andrew Goodman and Michael Schwerner, who were white—were abducted, tortured, and killed by Ku Klux Klan members in Philadelphia, Mississippi. Many members of SNCC, more-over, had never liked the idea of bringing in white volunteers in the first place, and they resented the fact that the media did not pay attention to them until whites were present in large numbers. One of the individuals who hesitated to support this plan was Stokely Carmichael (later Kwame Ture), who was elected chair of SNCC two years later. Carmichael was a media figure, and during his tenure, the organization turned away from community organizing and toward dramatic, public events. With this shift, the position of women in SNCC changed too.

THE POSITION OF WOMEN IN SNCC

Perhaps nowhere else in the twentieth-century United States offered as much gender parity as did SNCC through 1964. In Baker, younger mem-bers saw an alternative model of womanhood, one that, while not ex-plicitly feminist, encouraged faith in their abilities and the possibility of a life that did not revolve around marriage and family. As Baker biogra-pher Barbara Ransby puts it, "[H]er [Baker's] fundamental commitment to a democratic vision and inclusive political practice was not based on a feminist perspective per se, but unconsciously, Baker had laid a founda-tion for subsequent black and White radical feminist work." Still, SNCC presented women with challenges as well as opportunities—challenges that, because the first works to address the relationships between the civil rights movement and the 1960s women's movement were penned by white women, were often misunderstood and exaggerated in early histories.[11]

While men were the most visible leaders of SNCC, women's contri-butions did not go unrecognized. Ruby Doris Smith Robinson—who, sadly, died of leukemia at age twenty-six and was unable to tell her story later—was a respected leader within the organization, eventually becoming its executive secretary. Women directed their own community projects, and they put their lives on the line just as men did. Women, too, were brutalized, arrested, and thrown in jail, and they were at a higher risk of sexual violence than were men. Gwendolyn Zoharah Simmons, a Memphis native and Spelman College student who became a project director in KKK stronghold Laurel, Mississippi, recalled spending three nights in jail, being chased in a car by men with guns, and having the town sheriff point a gun at her. When Diane Nash, SNCC's first female field secretary, faced a two-and-a-half-year prison sentence for her activism, she voluntarily turned herself in rather than fleeing the state even though she was six months pregnant. Half a century later, she remained miffed that so many at the time thought she only did so because her husband made her. After working on a Freedom Vote campaign in Hattiesburg, Mississippi, Jean Smith Young actually volunteered to work in Philadelphia, Mississippi, the town where three SNCC workers had been kidnapped, tortured, and murdered. Dorothy Zellner, a white woman from a family of immigrant Jewish leftists, was hit by high-pressure hoses during a demonstration in Danville, Virginia, where she witnessed others being brutally beaten.

In the early histories of women in SNCC, the racial and sexual politics of Freedom Summer obscure these accomplishments. White women, many of them devout southern Christians like Casey Hayden, were involved in SNCC from the beginning. As Joan Trumpauer Mulholland, a white woman from Virginia, put it, "Both as a Christian and as a southerner, I felt that when I had a chance to do something to change things, I should do it."[12] Others, like Zellner, came from families historically involved in left and labor activism. But the influx of thousands of white volunteers, many of them northerners unfamiliar with the racial and sexual mores of the South, brought tensions over women's roles to the fore.

During Freedom Summer, women learned how to organize, write press releases, run mimeograph machines, mediate conflicts, and think strategically and theoretically. But they often experienced the group's commitment to freedom and egalitarianism as at odds with their reality. New volunteers were rarely sent into the field (to register voters, for example), and women were often expected to take responsibility for domestic tasks and perform secretarial work.

Hayden, Mary King, and other white women hinted at this unequal division of labor in their 1964 SNCC Position Paper, which was anonymously circulated in the group. Enumerating assumptions made within the movement about "women's work," the authors encouraged their readers to see similarities between racism and sexism. "Assumptions of male superiority," they wrote, "are as widespread and deep rooted and every much as crippling to the woman as the assumptions of white supremacy are to the Negro."[13] Historians often frame this document as an important precursor to the women's liberation movement that emerged later in the decade and evidence for the connections between these two movements. Its context is thus particularly important to understand.

Historians have also emphasized the degree to which women in SNCC were relegated to sexual object status. For decades, an offhand comment from Carmichael that "the position of women in SNCC is prone"—implying that they were there only to be willing sexual partners for men—seemed to exemplify women's second-class status within the organization. When asked about it since, however, the women who were present at the time characterized Carmichael's remark as a good-natured joke. Certainly, any milieu that brought together thousands of college students was destined to be sexually fraught, and racial issues—especially around who partnered with whom, and which men found which women to be desirable—heightened these tensions, with Black women often feeling passed over. Simmons recalled that much of her time was taken up "becoming a sexual relations counselor."[14] But it was unequivocally not the case that women were valued only as sexual objects. Decades later, Young tackled this controversy head-on:

> I cannot end without saying something about the controversy over the role of women in SNCC. I never felt discriminated against as a woman in this organization. In fact, I felt and experienced just the opposite. SNCC was a liberating experience for me as a woman. The staff, including Stokely Carmichael, always treated me as an esteemed member of the team and always encouraged me to stretch my wings and fly. In the SNCC that I knew the message was "Do whatever you are big enough to do."[15]

The slow-to-evolve historiography thus seems to reflect white women's (and men's) misunderstanding about their own roles in the organization more than it does reality. Only hubris would make it seem reasonable for newly minted white volunteers to assume leadership of an organization established by and for African Americans, but the northern college students who flocked South in 1964 chafed against their status as foot soldiers. Simmons, for example, ran into trouble getting white men in particular to see her as an authority figure.[16] While it is true that white women in the Freedom Summer class did much clerical work, this was not because they were women per se: it was because they were white women. But white northerners did not understand southern cultural mores—especially those that hinted at sex between Black men and white women. SNCC simply could not send Black men and white women to do field-work together in the rural South. To do so would put everyone's lives even further at risk.

CONCLUSION: WOMEN, THE MISSISSIPPI FREEDOM DEMOCRATIC PARTY, AND THE FATE OF THE COMMUNITY-ORGANIZING TRADITION

In many ways, the summer of 1964 seemed the apogee of the community-organizing tradition—and, with it, women's influence—in the civil rights movement. Thousands of young people descended on Mississippi, where they sought to make Baker's vision of cultivating local leadership a reality. The grassroots movement was so strong that even the federal government was taking note: on July 2, President Lyndon B. Johnson signed the Civil Rights Act (discussed in the next chapter) into law, officially ending the era of legally sanctioned segregation. Then, in August, Fannie Lou Hamer, who had been trained in the community-organizing tradition, addressed a national audience at the Democratic National Convention in Atlantic City, New Jersey. But each of these events heralded change within the movement.

In August 1964, Fannie Lou Hamer spoke to the credentials committee at the Democratic National Convention. She was there representing the Mississippi Freedom Democratic Party (MFDP), which was intended to challenge the official, all-white Mississippi delegation. Born on October 6, 1917, in Montgomery County, Mississippi, she was the granddaughter of a slave and the youngest of twenty children. Her parents were share-croppers, and at age six, Hamer began helping her parents in the cotton fields. By the time she was twelve, she was forced to drop out of school and work full time to help support her family.

Educated by the experiences of her grandmother, her mother, and herself, Hamer learned early on that a "black woman's body was never hers alone." Twenty of her grandmother's twenty-three children were products of rape. Her mother carried a shotgun with her in case she was attacked. Hamer herself had a forced hysterectomy in 1961 when she went to the hospital to have a cyst removed from her stomach. She knew that she risked death if she contacted a lawyer.[17]

Hamer was drawn to SNCC in 1962, although she had previously been active in the NAACP. Fired from her job on a plantation for attempting to register to vote, she began teaching citizenship classes for SCLC, becoming county supervisor for citizenship training and later a field secretary for SNCC. In June 1963, she was jailed, brutally beaten, and sexually abused for her participation in SNCC-related activities, including attempts to register to vote. She almost died as a result of that beating, from which it took her more than a month to recover.

In Atlantic City, Hamer spoke in front of the credentials committee in a televised proceeding that reached millions of viewers. She told the committee how African Americans in many states across the country were prevented from voting through illegal tests, taxes, and intimidation and of her experience with police brutality, discrimination, and sexual abuse.

But Johnson, wary of a wave of public support for the MFDP, preempted Hamer's address by scheduling his own press conference at the same time. The president made a deal with Hubert Humphrey: Humphrey could be his running mate if he offered the MFDP a compromise measure of two at-large, nonvoting seats. Despite the urging of King and others that the organization take the compromise, the MFDP turned it down. Already a break between the civil rights movement and the liberal establishment, the MFDP's decision to support Johnson's candidacy despite his poor treatment of them frustrated many younger activists.

Over the next few years, fallout from Freedom Summer and Atlantic City, dissatisfaction with the liberal establishment, a growing generation gap within the movement, escalation of the war in Vietnam, and other factors affected the civil rights movement's trajectory. By 1966, its new orientation had coalesced around the concept of Black

Power. While the ascendance of Black Power presented women with new challenges, it also fed directly into the reemergence of a distinct, radical Black feminism, earlier embodied by the Sojourners for Truth and Justice.

NOTES

1. Eric S. McDuffie, "A 'New Movement of Negro Women': Sojourning for Truth, Justice, and Human Rights during the Early Cold War," *Radical History Review* 101 (2008): 81–106 (quote on 86–87). See also Danielle McGuire, *At the Dark End of the Street: Black Women, Rape, and Resistance: A New History of the Civil Rights Movement from Rosa Parks to the Rise of Black Power* (New York: Vintage Books, 2010), 79–82.

2. McDuffie, "A 'New Movement of Negro Women,'" 97.

3. McGuire, *At the Dark End of the Street*, xx.

4. Harper Lee, *To Kill a Mockingbird* (1960; repr., New York: Warner Books, 1982), 241.

5. Anna Julia Cooper, *A Voice from the South* (Xenia, OH: Aldine Printing House, 1892), 133.

6. Barbara Ransby, *Ella Baker and the Black Freedom Movement: A Radical Democratic Vision* (Chapel Hill: University of North Carolina Press, 2003), 82–83; Darlene Clark Hine, "The Housewives' League of Detroit: Black Women and Economic Nationalism," in *Visible Women: New Essays on American Activism*, ed. Nancy A. Hewitt and Suzanne Lebsock (Urbana: University of Illinois Press, 1993), 223–41.

7. McGuire, *At the Dark End of the Street*, 108.

8. Jo Ann Gibson Robinson, *The Montgomery Bus Boycott and the Women Who Started It: The Memoir of Jo Ann Gibson Robinson*, ed. David J. Garrow (Knoxville: University of Tennessee Press, 1987), 23.

9. McGuire, *At the Dark End of the Street*, 65.

10. Daisy Bates, *The Long Shadow of Little Rock: A Memoir* (1962; repr., Fayetteville: University of Arkansas Press, 1986), 15.

11. Ransby, *Ella Baker and the Black Freedom Movement*, 298. Baker was married for several years and eventually adopted her niece, but her marriage did not interfere with her activism, and many of her colleagues did not even know about it. The clearest example of this tendency among early histories of the relationship between the civil rights movement and feminism is Sara Evans, *Personal Politics: The Roots of Women's Liberation in the Civil Rights Movement and the New Left* (New York: Vintage Books, 1979); cf. Belinda Robnett, *How Long? How*

Long? African American Women in the Struggle for Civil Rights (New York: Oxford University Press, 1997).

12. Joan Trumpauer Mulholland, "Diary of a Freedom Rider," in *Hands on the Freedom Plow: Personal Accounts by Women in SNCC*, ed. Faith Holsaert et al. (Urbana: University of Illinois Press, 2012), 17. Active in SNCC since 1961, Mulholland served a two-month prison sentence for her participation in the Freedom Rides.

13. Anonymous, "SNCC Position Paper #24," *Women and Social Movements in the United States, 1600–2000*, Nov. 6–12, 1964, http://womhist.alexanderstreet.com/SNCC/doc43.htm.

14. Gwendolyn Zoharah Simmons, "From Little Memphis Girl to Mississippi Amazon," in Holsaert et al., *Hands on the Freedom Plow*, 14.

15. Jean Smith Young, "Do Whatever You Are Big Enough to Do," in Holsaert et al., *Hands on the Freedom Plow*, 30.

16. Simmons, "From Little Memphis Girl to Mississippi Amazon," 15.

17. Ransby, *Ella Baker and the Black Freedom Movement*, 307–8; McGuire, *At the Dark End of the Street*, 192–93.

CHAPTER 3

A Civil Rights Movement for Women

INTRODUCTION

In a fourth-season episode of the acclaimed period drama *Mad Men*, advertising copywriter Peggy Olson vents about the discrimination she faces in the workplace. "I have to say," she tells her future boyfriend Abe, "most of the things Negroes can't do, I can't do either, and nobody seems to care. . . . Half of the meetings take place over golf, tennis, in a bunch of clubs where I'm not allowed to be a member, or even enter. The University Club said the only way I could eat dinner there was if I arrived in a cake." "All right, Peggy," Abe responds sarcastically, "we'll have a civil rights march for women."

The interaction is a joke that reveals several layers of truth about the women's movement in the early 1960s. First and most obvious is Abe's inability to see women as a class of people who are discriminated against; he understands race as a category of analysis, but not sex or gender. For women like Peggy, the civil rights movement provided a language to understand and express their own status, especially in relation to the major institutions of American society. But Peggy and other ambitious professional white women tended to see these identities as parallel, not intersecting, and without an understanding of their own privilege. When Abe points out that Peggy's agency employs no Black copywriters, she responds, "I'm sure they could fight their way in like I did."

Finally, Abe's derision is a joke for the audience, many members of which may know that, a year after the episode takes place, activists launched "an NAACP for women." A movement that brought together frustrated housewives, labor feminists, civil rights movement veterans, and others, liberal feminism made tremendous progress toward legal, economic, and political equality for women.

BETTY FRIEDAN AND *THE FEMININE MYSTIQUE*

By the mid-1950s, Betty Friedan had established herself as a talented freelance writer for mass-circulation women's magazines. In contrast to stories Friedan later told, these magazines regularly highlighted women's achievements outside the home. Friedan herself regularly contributed articles on women's education, neighborhood activism, and career success, celebrating the same accomplishments and condemning the same discourses she would in *The Feminine Mystique*. Friedan's best-known work, then, was a natural outgrowth of, not a reaction against, her earlier life and work.

Friedan began work on *The Feminine Mystique* in 1957. Approaching the fifteenth anniversary of her graduation from Smith, Friedan asked her classmates to complete a survey about their lives and experiences. After several false starts with magazines, she signed a book contract to publish her findings with W. W. Norton. In the meantime, Friedan's initial reporting, which appeared in the *Smith Alumnae Quarterly* in 1961, suggested that her classmates were largely leading happy, fulfilling lives. As professionals, wives, and mothers, or combinations thereof, the article suggested, elite women found meaning in a variety of ways. But when Friedan painted a slightly darker picture of women's lives the following year in *Good Housekeeping*, she was inundated with letters. The article had resonated with readers, many of whom felt unfulfilled and feared that they lacked a sense of self. This second, less positive perspective would be the one Friedan presented in *The Feminine Mystique* in 1963.

Friedan opened her first chapter, "The Problem That Has No Name," with a passage that has become famous:

The problem lay buried, unspoken, for many years in the minds of American women. It was a strange stirring, a sense of dissatisfaction, a yearning that women suffered in the middle of the twentieth century in the United

States. Each suburban wife struggled with it alone. As she made the beds, shopped for groceries, matched slipcover material, ate peanut butter sand-wiches with her children, chauffeured Cub Scouts and Brownies, lay be-side her husband at night—she was afraid to ask even of herself the silent question—"Is this all?"[1]

According to the author, starting in the late 1950s, she gradually became aware of "the problem that has no name," a sense of "quiet desperation" among American housewives, who lacked for nothing material yet felt empty, incomplete, and at times like they did not even exist. "The femi-nine mystique," she wrote, "permits, even encourages, women to ignore the question of their identity." In 1973, Friedan told the *New York Times* that "until I started writing the book, I wasn't even conscious of the woman problem. . . . I, like many other women, thought there was some-thing wrong with *me* because I didn't have an orgasm waxing the kitchen floor." In this version of Friedan's life, the author drifted from career to career "with no particular plan," "no sense of purpose." Eventually, she "married, had children, lived according to the feminine mystique as a sub-urban housewife." Like other women, she supposedly believed that she should find complete fulfillment in her husband and children; as a result, her life had become a monotonous blur of housework and child-rearing. Though many women were dissatisfied with these roles, they often feared the repercussions that could result from sharing their feelings.[2]

The Feminine Mystique reflected aspects of Friedan's activist and intel-lectual history, including her early anti-fascism, her Marxist-inflected critique of consumerism, and her training in psychology. The postwar em-phasis on domesticity, for example, rang uncomfortably close to "Kinder, Küche, Kirche"; she compared the home to a "comfortable concentration camp" and argued that the main function of domesticity was to encour-age women to buy consumer goods to power the postwar economy. But a comparison between early drafts and the eventual published work makes clear that Friedan consciously excised materials on racism, anti-Semitism, and radicalism, thus severing her own proposed solutions from the history of left, labor, and civil rights feminisms.[3]

Left feminist and historian Gerda Lerner noted this weakness. "I have one reservation about your treatment of your subject," she wrote in an otherwise complimentary letter to Friedan,

[Y]ou address yourself solely to the problems of middle-class, college educated women. . . . Working women, especially Negro women, labor not only
under the disadvantages imposed by the feminine mystique, but under the
more pressing disadvantages of economic discrimination. To leave them
out of consideration of the problem or to ignore the contributions they can
make toward its solution, is something we simply cannot afford to do. . . . It
is my belief, that one of the most insidious results of the feminine mystique
is that it led women to believe that their problems could be solved on the
basis of the individual family.[4]

Lerner's critique was apt, though she did not, perhaps, appreciate the
extent to which Friedan's analysis reflected as much as it perpetuated a
culture that privileged individualism. *The Feminine Mystique* was steeped
not only in her formal training in Abraham Maslow's theories of self-actualization but also in the popular psychology of David Riesman, C. Wright
Mills, William H. Whyte, and others—thinkers who would have recognized their own advice to men in Friedan's exhortations that a woman
must "believe that voice inside herself, when it denies the conventional,
accepted truths by which she has been living." Friedan's work applied
to women an already-familiar critique of postwar suburban conformity as
damaging to the self. This familiarity helps to explain why *The Feminine
Mystique*, though neither wholly original nor wholly unique, resonated
with American women. According to biographer Daniel Horowitz, it may
also help to explain why, though she read and appreciated Simone de
Beauvoir's *The Second Sex*, Friedan downplayed her indebtedness to this
earlier work: the book had not been well received by male intellectuals
upon its 1953 English-language publication.[5]

Friedan's message did many women much good. Of the thousands of
letters that Friedan received, many came from women outside of the college-educated classes. "You have just given my [sic] back myself," wrote
one grateful, representative reader. But in making her work palatable to a
white, middle-class audience, Friedan abandoned the structural critiques
of the young labor journalist and Popular Front feminist in favor of a
more individualistic focus on self-actualization—specifically, "the lifelong
commitment to an art or science, to politics or profession." As historian
Stephanie Coontz points out, "*The Feminine Mystique* contained no call
for women to band together to improve their legal and political rights."

Three years after the book's publication, however, Friedan joined together with a group of women who had spent the early 1960s engaged in similar work to found just such an organization.[6]

THE PRESIDENT'S COMMISSION ON THE STATUS OF WOMEN

Longtime labor feminist Esther Peterson found herself frustrated in the late 1950s. "It was the only time that I felt personal discrimination," she later said. As a lobbyist for the AFL-CIO, she discovered that she was being paid less than her male predecessor. When she asked the AFL-CIO treasurer to be paid the same amount, he refused on the basis that she did not need it because her husband made a good living.[7]

But the low esteem in which her colleagues held her at times paid off in unexpected ways. The AFL-CIO paired each lobbyist with a senator or representative whom they kept apprised of labor's positions on legislative issues. Peterson's male colleagues did not trust in her ability to influence legislators. "Oh, give her to [John F.] Kennedy," someone suggested, "he won't amount to much." It was, Peterson remembered, "the best break that I ever had." She found then-representative Kennedy to be confident, inquisitive, and willing to learn. Peterson and Kennedy worked together again when he served on the Senate Labor Committee. She became one of the early supporters of his presidential run, and he looked to her as his point person in the labor movement.[8]

Kennedy won the November 1960 election by a razor-thin margin, in part, due to the support of the AFL-CIO. Eager to acknowledge the importance of organized labor in general and Peterson in particular in securing his victory, Kennedy appointed her head of the Women's Bureau and assistant secretary of labor. Peterson was confirmed easily, but she did face opposition to her nomination to the Women's Bureau from Emma Guffey Miller, head of the NWP, who called her opposition to the ERA "antagonistic to the movement of the freedom of women."[9]

Kennedy's close ties with organized labor thus posed a conundrum for the new president when it came to women's issues, especially since women, too, had helped secure his victory. In the lead-up to the election, NWP members had leveraged its uncertain outcome to win support for the ERA from both parties. Vice President and Republican presidential

candidate Richard Nixon endorsed the measure in a September 2 statement drafted by the NWP itself. Emma Guffey Miller then used her position as Democratic National Committee woman from Pennsylvania
to pressure Kennedy as well. "We Democrats want the credit of giving
women equality under the law through you as president," she wrote, and
"now that Vice President Nixon has endorsed the Amendment, I am ur-
gently requesting you do the same." Taking this step would "silence the
gloating of the Republican women over Nixon's endorsement." Other
Democratic NWP members threatened to withhold their support if Kennedy did not support the amendment. "I am planning not to work for, not
to contribute to campaign funds, and not to vote for any Democratic candidate for the highest office in our land until I am assured that my Party
will actively support the EQUAL RIGHTS AMENDMENT," wrote Caroline Katzenstein. The candidate received the message, and on October
7, he assured Miller that he would "interpret the Democratic platform,
as I know it is intended, to bring about, through concrete actions including the adoption of the Equal Rights for Women Amendment, the full
equality for women which advocates of the equal rights amendment have
always sought." Vice presidential candidate, Lyndon B. Johnson similarly
assured Miller of his support. With these statements in hand, the NWP
expected concrete action from the president and his administration—and
soon. But most of the labor movement still opposed the ERA, and endorsing it risked alienating a crucial constituency within the Democratic
Party.[10]

In truth, the president would have preferred not to enter the ERA fray
at all. Instead of staking out a concrete position, Kennedy embraced a
compromise measure that he hoped would stave off further controversy:
the President's Commission on the Status of Women (PCSW). Reviving
an idea that labor women had first proposed in the 1940s, Peterson suggested the commission to secretary of labor Arthur Goldberg, who encouraged Kennedy to support the measure. Recognizing that "prejudices and
outmoded customs act as barriers to the full realization of women's basic
rights," Kennedy charged the PCSW with "developing recommendations
for overcoming discriminations in government and private employment
on the basis of sex and for developing recommendations for services which
will enable women to continue their roles as wives and mothers while
making a maximum contribution to the world around them."[11]

Labor activist Esther Peterson with President Kennedy, 1961. Peterson served as head of the Women's Bureau and executive vice president of the President's Commission on the Status of Women. (Franklin D. Roosevelt Library)

The twenty-member commission comprised both administration members and outside experts. As head of the Women's Bureau, Peterson became executive vice president of the PCSW, and she convinced Kennedy to appoint Eleanor Roosevelt as chair. Kitty Ellickson left her position with the AFL-CIO to work full time for the commission. Other members included Mary Callahan of the International Union of Electrical Workers (IUE), Dorothy Height of the NCNW, historian Caroline Ware, and Addie Wyatt of the UPWA.

The PCSW spent the next two years researching and compiling its report. In the meantime, Peterson and her allies lobbied Congress for additional measures that would help women combine wage work and domestic responsibilities. Between 1960 and 1966, Congress debated some 432 pieces of legislation related to women's rights. These efforts bore some fruit, including the 1962 Javits Bill, which allocated funds for childcare; an expansion of minimum wage coverage; and the 1963 Equal Pay Act. All were limited—the Equal Pay Act, for example, only applied in cases where women performed exactly the same work as men—but labor women supported them as necessary first steps.

Issued in 1963, the PCSW's report, *American Women*, was as much a Cold War document as it was a feminist one; it framed its calls for greater equality in the mobilization of women's "manpower" as "unused resources" that could increase American productivity and the ability to better reflect American values:

> Respect for the worth and dignity of every individual and conviction that every American should have a chance to achieve the best of which he—or she—is capable are basic to the meaning of both freedom and equality in this democracy. . . . We believe that one of the greatest freedoms of the individual in a democratic society is the freedom to choose among different life patterns. Innumerable private solutions found by different individuals in search of the good life provide society with basic strength far beyond the possibilities of a dictated plan.[12]

It was a savvy strategy, one that—contra the anti-feminist Cold Warriors of the 1950s—claimed for feminism the essential, classically liberal tenets of Americanism. It also demonstrates that some of the most important language of late twentieth-century feminism, including freedom of choice, derived in part from the need to make feminism compatible with this geopolitical struggle.

Like *The Feminine Mystique*, *American Women* called for greater educational and professional opportunities for women. At the time of the commission's work, 80 percent of girls and women could expect to work for wages at some point in their lives, the largest concentration of them in clerical work. Roughly twenty-three million women, approximately 60 percent of whom were married, were in the paid workforce, a number expected to rise to thirty million by 1970. Increases in the numbers and percentages of married women and mothers in the paid workforce were particularly dramatic. These patterns made such factors as employment discrimination, training opportunities, and protective legislation (discussed below) especially pressing.

The PCSW was far more attuned than was Friedan to the needs of working-class and minority women. The commission recognized, for example, the "dual burden" of African American women, who sought paid employment while raising preschool-aged children at twice the rate of their white counterparts. Black women, Native American women, and Latinas were also much more likely to be concentrated in low-paying service occupations. The commission called for an end to discrimination based on race, including the hidden forms of discrimination in supposedly race-blind legislation. As unions were among the most effective means to fair workplace conditions, Wagner Act protections needed to expand to include agricultural and domestic workers, two fields in which women and people of color were concentrated.

For women to take full advantage of expanded educational and professional opportunities necessitated access to affordable, high-quality childcare. Though some 3.5 million women with children under six worked for wages in 1963, licensed day-care facilities offered only 185,000 slots. This situation, commissioners argued, "reflects primarily a lack of community awareness of the realities of modern life." The exigencies of the modern economy demanded a vast expansion of the Javits Bill, as well as the establishment of services at federal, state, and local levels. At the same time, however, the commission "recognize[d] the fundamental responsibility of mothers and homemakers and society's stake in strong family life," and it largely affirmed the existing division of labor within and outside the home. While childcare and domestic labor remained under women's purview, men, the commission argued, "should continue to have primary [financial] responsibility for support of his wife and minor children."[13] This recommendation rested on the assumption that two-parent households were the norm, limiting the report's relevance to single mothers.

The commission exercised caution in its section on gender-specific labor standards, recognizing that federal protections for both men and women were ideal. It found certain restrictions on women's work, including those limiting night work and lifting heavy objects, to do more harm than good, and it recognized that hours limitations hurt professional women, whose advancement often depended on time commitment. Ultimately, however, the commission concluded that "state legislation limiting maximum hours of work for women should be maintained, strengthened, and expanded." Concomitantly, the commission considered but ultimately declined to endorse the ERA, placing its faith instead in the Fourteenth Amendment and selective litigation. As the authors of the report wrote, "[S]ince the Commission is convinced that the U.S. Constitution now embodies equality of rights for men and women, we conclude that a constitutional amendment need not now be sought in order to establish this principle. But judicial clarification is imperative in order that remaining ambiguities with respect to the constitutional protection of women's rights be eliminated."[14]

THE CIVIL RIGHTS ACT OF 1964

On June 11, 1963, the same day that Alabama governor George Wallace attempted to block two Black students from registering for classes at the University of Alabama, President Kennedy addressed the nation, calling for "every American to enjoy the privileges of being American without regard to his race or his color." After two years of only modest support for the civil rights movement, Kennedy endorsed what became the Civil Rights Act of 1964. Kennedy addressed race alone; nothing in his speech suggested that the resulting legislation would become a landmark victory in the fight for women's equality. But as the congressional debate over the law demonstrates, these issues were deeply—though at times counterintuitively—intertwined.

By 1964, Mary Dublin Keyserling had replaced Peterson at the Women's Bureau. Both women actively supported the Civil Rights Bill, which promised to end not only de jure Jim Crow (Title I) but also employment discrimination based on race, ethnicity, religion, and national origin (Title VII). In February, Virginia representative Howard Smith, a staunch segregationist and longtime ERA supporter, proposed adding "sex" to Title VII. Smith had also introduced the 1940 Alien Registration (Smith) Act, part of the anti-communist apparatus that had targeted so many left and labor women. The NWP had long ago won Smith's support by convincing him that protective legislation threatened the profits of Virginia textile mills, which depended on the long hours and low pay of female workers.

Though Smith insisted that his support for women's rights was genuine, his actions—including a mocking speech on the House floor—suggested otherwise. Moreover, the idea for the sex amendment had come not from Smith himself but from Alice Paul and possibly Emma Guffey Miller. The choice of Smith to introduce the amendment was also strategic. Michigan congresswoman and NWP member Martha Griffiths had asked him ahead of time to do so, arguing that he, and not she, could marshal the support of the House's southern bloc.

Motivations within the NWP for taking these actions were likely mixed. Some, including Paul, may have hoped that the bill would accomplish some of their ends through different means (as indeed it did). Others may have been willing to risk the bill's passage if it brought attention to sex discrimination and consequently more support for the ERA. But many, including the "lieutenants" whom Paul deputized to bring the idea to Smith, were openly hostile to the bill and hoped for its defeat. As Paul's lieutenant Nina Horton Avery, a longtime supporter of segregation, confided to Smith, as far as the NWP was concerned, the sex amendment was "merely a tool of strategy to take the pressure of the passage of any CRB." She was grateful to Smith and others "who will use their brains and energies to prevent a mongrel race in the US and who will fight for the rights of white citizens in order that discrimination against them may be stopped."[15]

Even supporters of the bill engaged in open race baiting. Griffiths insisted that, were the bill passed without the sex amendment, "white women will be last at the hiring gate." "Down at the bottom of the list," she continued, "is going to be a white woman with no rights at all." She found it "incredible . . . that white men would be willing to place white women at such a disadvantage . . . a vote against this amendment today by a white man is a vote against his wife, or his widow, or his daughter, or his sister." A letter from Miller, read into the House debate, claimed that past antidiscrimination ordinances had "discriminated against the white, native-born American woman of Christian religion." Labor feminist ally and PCSW member Edith Green was the only congresswoman to oppose the sex amendment.[16]

Most labor feminists, including Peterson, opposed the sex amendment for two reasons. First, they feared that it would jeopardize women-only protective legislation. But in this instance, even that perennial concern was secondary to the worry that the amendment would sink the entire bill. Peterson feared that "the addition of the new provision would defeat the bill. I for one was not willing to risk advancing the rights of all women at the expense of the redress due black men and women." Congresswoman Green agreed, offering on the House floor that "if I have to wait for a few years to end this discrimination against me, and my women friends—then as far as I am concerned I am willing to do that if the rank discrimination against Negroes will finally be ended." As Dorothy Sue Cobble concludes, for labor feminists, "at least in 1964, securing a law banning race discrimination took precedence over legislation banning sex discrimination."[17]

Once the sex amendment passed the House, support for and opposition to the bill curiously realigned. The Johnson administration supported the bill as it was, and most labor feminists followed suit, fearing, as did the president, that reopening debate on the bill was not worth the risk. And in the end, many of the sex amendment's most vocal supporters voted against the bill itself, suggesting that their concern for women's rights was never more than a smoke screen for racism.

Yet this tale of backroom dealings and NWP perfidy must not overshadow the less dramatic but equally important story of how the sex amendment became a part of Title VII. Pauli Murray had recognized for years that sex must be a protected category under any civil rights bill. Without it, she argued, such legislation would fail to protect Black women. Based in part on her background as a civil rights lawyer, Murray developed a trenchant perspective on the ERA debate: attacking sex discrimination through the courts on the basis of the equal protection clause of the Fourteenth Amendment—as the NAACP had done in *Brown* and other cases—was a stronger and more feasible strategy than was fighting for a new amendment. Murray's arguments rested on an understanding of sex and race—and thus sexism and racism—as analogous categories. There was, she argued, a "very close parallel between the status of women and their struggle for equal opportunity and the status of Negroes for the same objective." Just as civil rights lawyers had fought against "Jim Crow," women's rights lawyers must now fight against "Jane Crow."[18]

Developing a legal rationale for this more capacious interpretation of the equal protection clause, Murray looked to *Hernandez v. Texas*, a Supreme Court case decided the same year as *Brown*. *Hernandez* revolved around the legality of barring Americans of Mexican heritage from jury service. Since members of this group were legally white, they were not being discriminated against based on race per se. The court, however, determined that the equal protection clause extended to any groups—or classes—who faced unequal treatment. Observing this case with interest, Murray determined that, if the courts could consider Americans of Mexican heritage a class, the same should apply to women. It was only "the failure of the courts to isolate and analyze the discriminatory aspect of differential treatment based upon sex" that had prevented such rulings thus far.[19]

In 1962, Eleanor Roosevelt appointed her longtime friend to the PCSW in the hopes that Murray's strategy would prove a palatable alternative to both sides of the debate. Murray's approach was controversial, but she was eventually able to use her position within the PCSW's Committee on Civil and Political Rights to convince the majority of commissioners to accept her strategy. The PCSW's reluctance to endorse the ERA, then, was based not on misguided loyalty to an outdated perspective, but rather, on the possibilities opened up by a radical new understanding of the relationship between race and sex.

Murray's particular insights into this relationship became crucial when the civil rights bill moved from the House to the Senate. Minority leader Everett Dirksen, a Republican from Illinois, had promised to marshal his party's support for the bill—but only after his forty demanded changes were met. One of them was the removal of sex from Title VII. Alarmed, feminist supporters of the bill urged Murray to write a memorandum discouraging this change. Put in the awkward position of supporting a measure introduced by a staunch segregationist whose anti-communist crusade had harmed some of her closest friends, Murray nonetheless seized the opportunity. Contrary to what Griffiths and others had argued in the House debate, Murray correctly pointed out that Black women—*not* white women—were most likely to suffer from a version of Title VII without sex. "Since it is exceedingly difficult for a Negro woman to determine whether she is being discriminated against because of race or sex," Murray argued, there was nothing to stop a potential employer from telling a Black, female job candidate that she had been turned down because of sex when truly it was because of race. In the end, Dirksen's proposed change solicited so much opposition—from Murray, the NWP, other women's groups, female senators, and others—that he did not even introduce it.[20]

TITLE VII, THE EEOC, AND THE FOUNDING OF NOW

Male members of Congress had enjoyed the debate over adding the sex amendment to Title VII. Beyond Smith's mocking speech, even liberal congressmen such as Emanuel Celler joined in the fun, insisting that the final words in his marriage were always "yes, dear." Unfortunately, the agency created to enforce Title VII, the Equal Employment Opportunity Commission (EEOC), similarly considered sex discrimination a joke. EEOC director Herman Edelsberg called its inclusion in Title VII "a fluke . . . conceived out of wedlock." When an attendee at the White House Conference on Equal Opportunity speculated that Playboy clubs may now have to employ male bunnies, the media christened Title VII the "Bunny Law." In 1965, the EEOC even ruled that segregated help-wanted ads did not violate the law. "Why should a mischievous joke perpetrated on the floor of the House of Representatives be treated by a responsible administration body with this kind of seriousness?" asked the *New Republic* in defense of the ruling. Section 703(d) of Title VII, which allowed employers to make decisions based on the sex of the applicant in the case of a "bona fide occupational qualification" (BFOQ), provided just the loophole defenders of the status quo needed.[21]

The reality of women's work lives belied legislators' levity. In its first year, the EEOC received nine thousand complaints; nearly one-third of them were from women. In some parts of the country, the fraction of complaints from women rose to nearly half. Many of these complaints came from labor women, including those in the UAW and meatpacking and steel industries. Emboldened by the protection their unions offered, labor women were often justifiably less afraid of employer retaliation than were women workers in other sectors. But with the EEOC underfunded and disinclined and Congress and the president by then distracted by Vietnam, few of these complaints were pursued. Even earnest efforts by the EEOC to grapple with the new law's implications reflected confusion; first asserting in 1965 that protective labor laws did not necessarily violate Title VII, the agency reversed course the following year.

A growing women's network watched these developments with interest. In 1962, Kennedy had authorized state-level women's commissions, many of which were established by 1965. Though labor women served on these commissions, the demands on their time were often greater than those on the business and professional women—including erstwhile left feminist Betty Friedan—who came to dominate these bodies. State commissions thus often comprised different demographics and held different priorities than had the PCSW—priorities that placed equality in hiring and promotions above maintaining protective labor laws.

In the meantime, by 1965, Murray feared that the promise of the Civil Rights Act and her proposed Fourteenth Amendment strategy had failed to garner momentum toward equality. To generate more attention, she coauthored with fellow lawyer Mary Eastwood, whom she knew from the PCSW, an article titled "Jane Crow and the Law." Though much of the article reiterated Murray's Fourteenth Amendment strategy, it also moved toward accepting the fact that Title VII may well mandate changes in protective legislation, which Murray had shied away from during her time with the PCSW. That same year, she sparred publicly with EEOC chair Franklin Roosevelt Jr., an appearance that attracted the attention of, among others, Friedan. Murray introduced Friedan to members of the PCSW circle, including those who were most vocal about the need to push the EEOC to enforce Title VII.

To many longtime labor feminists, including Mary Dublin Keyserling, these changes augured poorly. While also concerned with equality in hiring and promotion, she still believed that state-level protective labor laws were necessary and urged caution in asking the EEOC to pursue sex discrimination claims more actively. But her views no longer reflected a consensus among labor women, and in 1966, Caroline Davis and Dorothy Haener of the UAW informed Peterson and the EEOC of their disagreement. As Haener later put it, Keyserling "was just absolutely deaf to anyone who suggested that the state protective laws didn't protect, that they did discriminate sometimes."[22]

This acrimony came to a head later that year, at the Labor Department–sponsored Third National Conference of Commissions on the Status of Women. As conference chair, Keyserling was quick to stifle debate on the EEOC. That night, a group of women, including Pauli Murray, Davis, and Haener, gathered in Friedan's hotel room and resolved to demand that the conference push the EEOC for its inaction on sex discrimination. The next morning, Keyserling ruled both this resolution and one in support of the ERA out of order. In response, the dissidents planned to create "an NAACP for women," a phrase Haener attributed to activist Dollie Lowther Robinson. In 1963, Barnard professor Phoebe Morrison had alerted Murray to a potential stumbling block to her Fourteenth Amendment strategy: "There is no pressure group like NAACP to press litigation. Or rather . . . there are several women's groups which might— and there is no agreement among them—so that there is lacking the solid front which NAACP managed to present." Murray herself suggested amid her work on Title VII "that we needed a private organization of women to make our point of view felt, something a little more attuned to the Space Age than the NWP, and it may be that the time is nigh." Indeed, it seemed that the time for such an organization had come.[23]

Catherine Conroy, Communications Workers of America leader and member of the Wisconsin Governor's Commission on the Status of Women, described the scene at lunch that day:

> The Women's Bureau had a luncheon, and they had a podium thing that had tiers of people at the head table. The luncheon was the biggie and they had some senators there and they had the head table and the head head table and the head head head table. You never saw so many people at the head table. Anyway, there were twenty-six of us, I think, at two different tables, passing notes around, creating NOW right there in this luncheon in front of these people. I know that Mary Keyserling wondered what in the hell's going on down there at these tables, 'cause we're running around.[24]

Scribbling on a napkin, Friedan gave the new organization a name, the National Organization for Women (NOW), and a goal: "to take the actions needed to bring women into the mainstream of American society, now." NOW was formally organized with Friedan as president, Davis as secretary-treasurer, and Haener as a member of the executive board. Former EEOC commissioner Aileen Hernandez became vice president.[25]

NOW's "Statement of Purpose," the organization's founding document, focused on the need for women to reach "their fullest human potential" and live "in truly equal partnership with men." Equally invested in assuming the "privileges and responsibilities" of citizenship, NOW members sought "equality of opportunity and freedom of choice" for women, possible only "by accepting to the full the challenges and responsibilities they share with all other people in our society, as part of the decision-making mainstream of American political, economic and social life." Practically, this goal mandated "break[ing] through the silken curtain of prejudice and discrimination against women in government, industry, the professions, the churches, the political parties, the judiciary, the labor unions, in education, science, medicine, law, religion and every other field of importance in American society." Reflecting its origins in the feminist split over

Title VII, NOW announced its intention to exert pressure on the EEOC and other levers of governmental power.[26]

The UAW sponsored NOW in its first year, and many of the materials the new organization produced came from the union's Women's Department. The UAW also lent access to copy and mimeograph machines and a WATS phone line, which provided free or cheap phone calls and without which national organization was impossible. This arrangement ended when NOW endorsed the ERA in 1967, but, despite the temporary loss of some labor women, membership in the new organization grew rapidly. As Conroy put it, "NOW grew by itself. It was an idea whose time had come. I couldn't believe it, because here I am trying to organize a union and I'm having a terrible time. . . . I thought, we just have to knock people on the heads to join unions, but NOW—you can't keep them away." The following year, the rift between labor and NOW began to heal when the UAW reversed its position on the ERA, with the AFL-CIO soon following suit. A realignment in American feminist politics had taken place, with a new definition of equality to match.[27]

Until the mid-1960s, the Peterson/Keyserling vision of equality had prevailed among the majority of American feminists. Though recognizing that many differences between men and women were social, not biological, feminists of this stripe nonetheless emphasized these differences when it came to advocating for legislative and other forms of change. Hearkening back to such early twentieth-century activists as Florence Kelley, Peterson, Keyserling, and their allies hoped eventually to see protective labor legislation extended to men, but they were not willing to sacrifice those that existed for women out of an abstract commitment to equal (meaning identical) treatment. Their vision of equality was predicated on difference and protection. By contrast, the vision that emerged from NOW, and that remained the most widely embraced ideology among American feminists for the rest of the twentieth century, privileged the classical liberalism of the American Revolution, positioning women as citizens who deserved the same treatment that men received. Emphasizing what political theorists call "negative liberty," liberal feminists focused on the removal of impediments to women's full participation in established American institutions, including government and the market economy, rather than seeking changes within the institutions themselves (as left and labor feminists had and as radical feminists in different ways would). As Betty Friedan told the *New York Times*, NOW's goal was to allow women to "enjoy the equality of opportunity and freedom of choice which is their right . . . in truly equal partnership with men."[28]

From its de facto headquarters in the New York City apartment that belonged to Betty Friedan, now divorced, to the local chapters that prolif-erated across the country, NOW made equal employment opportunity its first priority. Women's rights, the organization argued in a letter to Presi-dent Johnson, were a natural but overlooked aspect of the Great Society, the Johnson administration's attempt to extend the benefits of the New Deal to those deprived of its benefits:

> As part of the Great Society program, your administration is currently engaged in a massive effort to bring underprivileged groups—victims of discrimination because of poverty, race, or lack of education—into the mainstream of American life. However, no comprehensive effort has yet been made to include women in your Great Society program for the under-privileged and excluded.[29]

In 1967, Johnson agreed to add "sex" to a 1965 executive order that banned racial discrimination among federal contractors. NOW also pres-sured the EEOC to ban sex-segregated help-wanted ads, picketing the *New York Times* and dumping newspapers in front of local EEOC offices to publicize the issue. "Women can think as well as type," read one picket sign at the *New York Times*; outside the New York City EEOC office, one declared that "Title Seven has no teeth, EEOC has no guts." Unmoved, the newspaper defended its policy as legal and helpful to readers. In March 1968, a group of women planned to dress in formal wear; attend an EEOC hearing uninvited; and, with hope, cause enough of a stir to attract media attention. One of them planned to carry a sign showing two secretaries chained to their typewriters. In August 1968, the EEOC finally complied with NOW's demands.[30]

Though primarily concerned with legislative changes enacted through official channels, NOW members also courted media attention through direct action, including in the examples described above. Other actions challenged cultural expectations of women. For example, the organization awarded a "barefoot and pregnant in the kitchen" award for advertisements that portrayed women in discriminatory and/or stereotypical ways. On May 14, 1967—Mother's Day—a group of women dumped a mountain of aprons in front of the White House, in the same spot where suffragists had picketed fifty years earlier. As historian Ruth Rosen notes, "[N]othing reflected the rejection of the fifties housewife more starkly than that trash pile of aprons." Despite its more complicated reality, women's domesticity was a potent symbol for feminists. As part of a planned, national series of "rights, not roses" demonstrations, the Mother's Day protest at the White House also recalled the "bread and roses" demand of early twentieth-century women labor activists, especially those involved in the 1912 Lawrence, Massachusetts, textile strike. Betty Friedan and other activists also sat in or picketed outside restaurants and bars that refused to serve women.[31]

Much of NOW's early activism benefited ordinary working women, not the professional classes with which NOW became—somewhat unfairly—almost exclusively associated in the popular mind. One of its first efforts was a successful campaign against airlines that refused to hire or retain married stewardesses and those above age thirty-one. In addition to being discriminatory, these practices had been a huge windfall for airlines, which constantly cycled through new cohorts of young women whom it could hire at low wages and fire before they became eligible for raises and benefits. NOW also pushed the EEOC to apply Title VII to federal poverty programs, fighting for agencies to pay equal attention to women and allow them to deduct childcare expenses from their taxes. NOW's Legal Defense Fund, which fought discrimination in the courts, supported women who were suing Colgate-Palmolive and Southern Bell Telephone for refusing to hire women to work in their southern factories. NOW also fought for many measures that would make it easier to combine paid work with domestic responsibilities, including maternity leave and childcare centers.

These concerns were reflected in NOW's 1968 Bill of Rights for women, which called for paid maternity leave, tax deductions for working parents, and equality with men in anti-poverty programs, including job training (War on Poverty programs had focused on the importance of men's paid employment). This last set of changes must not interfere with "a parent's right to remain at home to care for his or her children" and must protect "women['s] dignity, privacy and self respect." The new manifesto also called for the immediate passage and ratification of the ERA and an end to laws criminalizing birth control and abortion.[32]

Though evidence of a thoughtful, growing agenda that took into consideration women's changing needs, these expanded goals also reflected NOW's perennial struggle to balance its constituencies. Women like Murray, attuned to the differences among women, had to be constantly vigilant. In 1966, she successfully intervened in the drafting of the organization's Statement of Purpose to make sure it recognized economic justice and the interrelatedness of various struggles for equality. By the following year, however, an influx of NWP members into the new organization (along with other factors) eroded this commitment. NOW's increasing focus on the ERA represented the privileging of abstract equality over economic justice and of white, professional women over, especially, poor and/or Black women. As Murray saw it, the group was asking her to do something she could not do: fragment herself "into Negro at one time, woman at another, or worker at another." Frustrated, she did not play an active role in the organization after this point.[33]

In 1973, Black women in NOW poured their frustrations with NOW's relative neglect of Black and poor women into the founding of the National Black Feminist Organization (NBFO). This new organization attracted women who felt caught between white feminists and the male-led Black civil rights movement. Based on the enthusiastic response to its founding, there were many such women, including such prominent activists as Flo Kennedy, Eleanor Holmes Norton, and NOW president Aileen Hernandez. The summer of its founding, NBFO organizers issued a call for interested women to meet in a New York City church; over one hundred attended. In November, an East Coast regional meeting attracted some five hundred women. By the end of 1974, the NBFO had expanded to ten local chapters, many members of which gathered for a national conference. But personal conflicts among leadership and a lack of resources to devote to NBFO's ambitious "umbrella" policy fed into the group's disintegration over the course of 1975 and 1976. The NBFO continued to be important to Black feminism, not least for two of its splinter groups: the National Alliance of Black Women (NABW), which like NBFO threaded the needle between moderate and radical, and the socialist, decidedly radical Combahee River Collective.

CONCLUSION: THE GROWING GENERATIONAL DIVIDE IN AMERICAN FEMINISM

The major documents of liberal feminism, including *The Feminine Mystique*, *American Women*, and NOW's "Statement of Purpose," emphasized law over culture and women's public lives over their private lives. The authors of these documents understood connections among these areas, acknowledging, for example, the role of cultural expectations that discouraged women from pursuing certain professions and the need for expanded access to childcare. NOW's "Statement of Purpose" called for a more equitable division of domestic responsibilities and an end to deleterious media images of women. In 1968, the organization included reproductive choice in its bill of rights, and three years later, it belatedly recognized lesbian rights. But while these thinkers certainly knew that the personal was political, they believed that the most urgent problems required action elsewhere.

Thus less than a year into the new organization's existence, NOW's strategies and goals appeared stodgy to some younger feminists. "When the young radical kids came into the movement," Friedan remembered in 1973, "they said it was 'boring' or 'reformist' or 'capitalist co-option' to put so much emphasis on jobs and education. But very few women can afford to ignore the elementary economic facts of life." She resented the "manhating sex/class warfare" of younger women. "It seemed to me the women's movement had to get out of sexual politics," she wrote. "I thought it was a joke at first—those strangely humorless papers about clitoral orgasms that would liberate women from sexual dependence on a man's penis, and the 'consciousness-raising' talk that women should insist now on being on top in bed with men." Liberal feminism had its limits, including an unwillingness to question such American institutions as capitalism, representative democracy, and the nuclear family; an inability to recognize the importance of sexual politics; and, in Friedan's case, an open homophobia. Still, Friedan could justifiably have raised an eyebrow at the younger feminists criticizing her focus on jobs and education from the left—after all, she was reiterating a long-held Marxist belief in the centrality of the material conditions of people's lives.[34]

NOTES

1. Friedan, *The Feminine Mystique*, 15.

2. Ibid., 19–21, 70, 71; Friedan, quoted in Stephanie Coontz, *A Strange Stirring: The Feminine Mystique and American Women at the Dawn of the 1960s* (New York: Basic Books, 2011), 103.

3. Daniel Horowitz, *Betty Friedan and the Making of* The Feminine Mystique: *The American Left, the Cold War, and Modern Feminism* (Amherst: University of Massachusetts Press, 1998), 211–13; Friedan, *The Feminine Mystique*, 37, 206–7, 307–9.

4. Letter from Gerda Lerner, Feb. 6, 1963, box 57, folder 715, Betty Friedan Papers, MC575, The Arthur and Elizabeth Schlesinger Library on the History of Women in America, Radcliffe Institute for Advanced Study, Harvard University, Cambridge, MA.

5. Horowitz, *Betty Friedan and the Making of* The Feminine Mystique, 208–9; Friedan, *The Feminine Mystique*, 31; Ruth Rosen, *The World Split Open: How the Modern Women's Movement Changed America* (New York: Penguin Books, 2000), 6.

6. Letter from reader in Suffern, New York, Nov. 8, 1964, Friedan Papers, Schlesinger Library (quote); Friedan, *The Feminine Mystique*, 348; Coontz, *A Strange Stirring*, 33.

7. Peterson, "You Can't Giddyup by Saying Whoa," 78.

8. Ibid., 79–80.

9. Ibid., 80–81; Emma Guffey Miller, quoted in Cobble, *The Other Women's Movement*, 153.

10. Rosen, *The World Split Open*, 64–65; Richard Nixon, "Statement by the Vice President on the Equal Rights Amendment," Sept. 2, 1960, box 1, folder 11; "Statement Prepared for Vice President Nixon to Deliver on August 26," Aug. 20, 1960, box 1, folder 11; Emma Guffey Miller to John F. Kennedy, Sept. 3, 1960, box 1, folder 9; Caroline Katzenstein to Kennedy, Sept. 10, 1960, box 2, folder 4; Kennedy to Miller, Oct. 7, 1960, box 1, folder 9; Lyndon B. Johnson to Miller, Oct. 19, 1960, box 1, folder 9, all in Katzenstein Papers, HSP. The ERA only came up for debate in the Senate once in this election year, in July. Before any discussion took place, Senator Hayden offered his usual amendment, which was agreed to by a voice vote. The measure was then sent back to the Judiciary Committee. Neither Kennedy nor Johnson specified in their correspondence with Miller which version of the bill (S. J. Res. 69) they supported, a technicality that the NWP was content to ignore for the moment.

11. John F. Kennedy, "Executive Order 10980—Establishing the President's Commission on the Status of Women," The American Presidency Project, Dec. 14, 1961, https://www.presidency.ucsb.edu/node/235889; Cobble, *The Other Women's Movement*, 159–60.

12. *American Women: Report of the President's Commission on the Status of Women* (Washington, DC, 1963), 2.

13. Ibid., 19.

14. Ibid., 37, 45.

15. Cobble, *The Other Women's Movement*, 175.

16. 110 Cong. Rec. 2,578–80 (1964) (statement of Rep. Griffiths), 2,582 (1964) (Miller, quoted in statement of Rep. May); ibid., 175–76.

17. Cobble, *The Other Women's Movement*, 176; 110 Cong. Rec. 2,582 (1964) (statement of Rep. Green).

18. Rosalind Rosenberg, *Jane Crow: The Life of Pauli Murray* (New York: Oxford University Press, 2017), 250.

19. Ibid., 254.

20. Ibid., 278.

21. Rosen, *The World Split Open*, 71–73. As chair of the House Judiciary Committee, Celler had added the original version of Title VII to the legislation. Rosenberg, *Jane Crow*, 274–75. With the establishment of the EEOC, Progressives realized the long-sought goal of establishing a permanent version of the wartime Fair Employment Practices Commission (FEPC). Celler's opposition to the sex amendment, which focused on military service and effects on the family, also anticipated later, conservative opposition to the ERA. 110 Cong. Rec. 2,577 (1964) (statement of Rep. Celler).

22. Cobble, *The Other Women's Movement*, 183–84; Dorothy Haener, "Sometimes You Have to Rock the Boat," in O'Farrell and Kornbluh, *Rocking the Boat*, 178. By 1966, amendments to the FLSA eliminated most federal-level distinctions between men and women's work.

23. Rosenberg, *Jane Crow*, 273 (Morrison quote), 279 (Murray quote).

24. Catherine Conroy, "Somebody Has to Have the Guts," in O'Farrell and Kornbluh, *Rocking the Boat*, 246.

25. Rosen, *The World Split Open*, 75.

26. NOW Statement of Purpose, 1966, https://now.org/about/history/statement-of-purpose/.

27. Conroy, "Somebody Has to Have the Guts," 247.

28. Betty Friedan, quoted in Lisa Hammel, "They Meet in Victorian Parlor to Demand 'True Equality' NOW," *New York Times*, Nov. 22, 1966.

29. NOW to Lyndon B. Johnson, quoted in Hammel, "They Meet in Victorian Parlor to Demand 'True Equality NOW."

30. "11 Picket *Times* Classified Office to Protest Male-Female Labels," *New York Times*, Aug. 31, 1967; Marilyn Bender, "The Feminists Are on the March Once More," *New York Times*, Dec. 14, 1967. The August 31, 1967, article went

out of its way to mention NOW's more controversial positions, including support for the ERA and legalized abortion.

31. Rosen, *The World Split Open*, 84.

32. NOW Bill of Rights, 1968, https://350fem.blogs.brynmawr.edu/about/1968 -bill-of-rights/.

33. Rosenberg, *Jane Crow*, 309.

34. Friedan, *The Feminine Mystique*, 385, 388–89.

CHAPTER 4

THE WOMEN'S
LIBERATION
MOVEMENT

INTRODUCTION

In 1969, Robin Morgan began compiling a collection titled *Sisterhood Is Powerful: An Anthology of Writings from the Women's Liberation Movement.* A founding member of New York Radical Women, a white women's liberation group, Morgan was already well known as a former child actor and current media figure. Using her celebrity status and her connections in publishing, she convinced Random House, a mainstream publisher of respectable tomes, to take on a radical text including such essays as "The Politics of Orgasm," "The Hooker," and "Notes of a Radical Lesbian."

Though "no one article is meant to be 'representative' of anything other than some part of all women," Morgan intended the book as a whole to be representative of the women's liberation movement.[1] An edited anthology rather than a single-author monograph seemed to make sense as did profit sharing among various organizations. The collection was intentionally messy, darting between cartoons, manifestoes, and poems in a nonlinear, nonhierarchical way, as women's groups themselves often tried to proceed. In many ways, the topics covered, including work, marriage, motherhood, religion, sexuality, and housework, were also representative of the women's liberation movement's major concerns.

Morgan also knew that the women's liberation movement did not comprise only white women, and she made a conscious effort to include authors from different backgrounds and with diverse, sometimes

contradictory, views. One of them was Frances M. Beal. Born in Bing-
hamton, New York, in 1940 to an African American and Native American father and a mother descended from Russian Jewish immigrants, Beal
spent most of her childhood in Queens, watching her mother participate
in leftist politics and observing with horror the violence enacted against
Black Americans. She became an activist at the University of Wisconsin, later working with SNCC and for the National Council of Negro
Women, where she grew close with Dorothy Height. She is best known as
a founder of the Third World Women's Alliance (TWWA) and particularly for her widely reprinted and anthologized essay, "Double Jeopardy:
To Be Black and Female," which appeared in 1970 in both *Sisterhood Is
Powerful* (in truncated form) and Toni Cade Bambara's anthology *The
Black Woman*. Beal recalled of the essay's origins, "I explicitly wrote it
because I was called by Robin Morgan to say that she was doing *Sisterhood
Is Powerful* and she wanted an essay on black women. And I said I would
take a few of the things I had already started on and pull together kind of
an overview, and that's how 'Double Jeopardy: to be Black and Female'
was born."[2]

In addition to Beal's essay, the collection included contributions by
Eleanor Holmes Norton; the Black Women's Liberation Group of Mount
Vernon, New York; and Florynce Kennedy. In several pieces, Chicana
women documented their experiences. By and large, however, women of
color appeared in separate sections—"Women in the Black Liberation
Movement: Three Views," "Colonized Women: The Chicana"—rather
than in sections dedicated to the "general" concerns of the women's liberation. This organization made sense to Morgan, who identified the wom-
en's liberation movement as the first with "the potential of cutting across
all class, race, age, economic, and geographical barriers—since women in
every group must play essentially the same role, albeit with different sets
of costumes." And, of course, the vast majority of the authors included in
the volume were white women.[3]

This chapter does not primarily address conflicts between or among
feminist groups. Yet Morgan's anthology provides a useful jumping-off
point for rethinking the emergence and trajectory of the women's liberation movement. Historians of the white women's liberation movement
have admirably endeavored to connect this movement to the civil rights
movement, even if the connection was long misunderstood. A vibrant

literature documents and analyzes the Black women's liberation movement, framing it as an outgrowth not only of the male-led civil rights and Black Power movements but also of the earlier activism and thought of such women as Claudia Jones, Rosa Parks, and the members of Sojourners for Truth and Justice. General or comprehensive surveys of the American women's movement have also made diversity a goal. This last group still tends to fall short, however, in prioritizing the white women's liberation movement as one to which Black women and others responded. Standard narratives often present the white women's liberation movement first, using the experiences of other groups as supplements or counterpoints—as did Morgan.

It is true that women of color sometimes blanched at the term "feminism." Women in TWWA, Beal recalled,

> at least in the chapter that I was working with in New York—did not like that term [feminism], because at that time it came to mean women who put female first and that was the only thing, you know, it was a very narrow perception. And what we were trying to deal with was the integration of race, gender, class, in consciousness, and not like put one above the other, because we didn't think it actually operated as one is more important than another, but that there was actually an integration of that. And I'm proud to say, I think that the activists of that period were the first ones to put together this kind of construct about the integration of different things.[4]

As Beal saw it, the term "feminism" could not account for the ways that gender interacted with race, class, and other factors—what we today call intersectionality. Accordingly, it makes more sense to center the experiences of the interracial coalition that developed this key concept.

"DOUBLE JEOPARDY": BLACK AND "THIRD-WORLD" FEMINISMS

Frances Beal was likely not thinking about her connections to Claudia Jones when she sat down to write "Double Jeopardy" in 1969, but she well could have been. In laying bare the multiple, interlocking systems that dehumanized Black women, Beal invoked her predecessor's words from two decades earlier.

Like Jones, Beal dissected the ways in which capitalism and racism colluded to exploit Black people. "The system of capitalism (and its after birth . . . racism) under which we all live, has attempted by many devious ways and means to destroy the humanity of all people, and particularly the humanity of black people."[5] Black men often faced difficulty finding meaningful work, and Black women were kept segregated into low-paid drudgery. These realities coexisted uneasily with mainstream expectations for men and women, and Black men sometimes posited reclaiming their masculinity as the solution. Again, like Jones, Beal recognized that some of the individuals fighting against racist and sexist institutions—namely, Black men and white women—often attempted to do so by ignoring or re-creating the exploitation of Black women.

"Unfortunately," she wrote, "there seems to be some confusion in the Movement today as to who has been oppressing whom. Since the advent of black power, the black male has exerted a more prominent leadership role in our struggle for justice in this country. He sees the system for what it really is for the most part. But . . . certain black men are maintaining that they have been castrated by society but that black women somehow escaped this persecution and even contributed to this emasculation." As a result of this incorrect belief, some Black men were "exerting their 'manhood' by telling black women to step back into a domestic, submissive role"—not only a "counter-revolutionary position" but one that reinforced the status of each Black woman in America as a "slave of a slave."[6]

Chapter 2 of this volume pushed back against the narrative that women were marginalized within the civil rights movement. Indeed, despite very real instances of sexism, participation in this movement was an empowering experience for women—through 1964, SNCC, in particular, was likely one of the most empowering places on the earth, and certainly in midcentury America, for women. How, then, to explain Beal's argument? As 1964 gave way to 1965, the fallout from Freedom Summer and the Atlantic City convention, the continuing intransigence of racism, and the Black student movement's growing disappointment with white liberals and more established Black voices facilitated a new kind of racial consciousness, which activists termed Black Power. On the face of it, Black Power was not about gender. In cultivating a new response to mainstream American racial-gender mores, however, the Black Power movement had a complicated effect on Black women and the Black women's liberation movement. At the same time, the base of operations for the civil rights movement was moving from the rural South, where older Black women held a long-recognized role in the community, to students in northern cities, who were more receptive to Black Power.

These assertions did not emerge from a vacuum. Political context mattered. In the mid-1960s, as SNCC began to pursue a more radical agenda, assistant secretary of labor Daniel Patrick Moynihan prepared what became *The Negro Family: The Case for National Action* (commonly referred to as the "Moynihan Report"). Though a liberal who supported civil rights legislation, Moynihan also advanced the deeply racist idea that African Americans would continue to struggle until they corrected their "pathological" family structure—specifically, one in which, supposedly, Black men had abdicated responsibility and women bore an outsized influence. In Moynihan's view, problems within Black communities derived from the fact that Black women had too much power. In a commencement speech at Howard University just months before Moynihan issued his report, President Johnson anticipated his advisor's argument. Calling for a proactive approach to advancing Black civil rights, he nonetheless laid much of the blame for Black poverty on "the breakdown of the Negro family structure. For this, most of all, white America must accept responsibility. It flows from centuries of oppression and persecution of the Negro man. It flows from the long years of degradation and discrimination, which have attacked his dignity and assaulted his ability to produce for his family."[7] Accordingly, many of Johnson's War on Poverty programs focused on training Black men for jobs that would help restore them to their "proper" place in the family.

Many civil rights leaders recognized that Moynihan's report was hogwash. But in a strange way, his argument coincided with Black Power ideology, and many of those who condemned the report's racism embraced its gendered arguments. As historians Dana Ramey Berry and Kali Nicole Gross point out, many activists believed that "the liberation of Black people rested in the Black man being restored to his rightful place at the head of Black families and of Black social justice movements."[8] Both Black Muslim and nationalist groups advanced this ethos. Activist and scholar Angela Davis, for example,

> became acquainted very early with the widespread presence of an unfortunate syndrome among some Black male activists—namely to confuse their

political activity with an assertion of their maleness. . . . These men view Black women as a threat to their attainment of manhood—especially those Black women who take initiative and work to become leaders in their own right. The constant harangue by the US men was that I needed to redirect my energies and use them to give my man strength and inspiration so that he might more effectively contribute his talents to the struggle for Black liberation.[9]

For Black women, especially those in activist circles, this perspective created a heartbreaking conundrum: If they advanced feminist ideas or even their rights to be leaders in racial justice movements, they risked accusations that they had betrayed Black men. But supporting Black men's uncontested right to lead meant putting aside their own ambitions.

No one understood this tension better than the members of the Combahee River Collective (CRC), who recognized that "accusations that Black feminism divides the Black struggle are powerful deterrents to the growth of an autonomous Black women's movement." A radical Black feminist group founded in 1974, the CRC was named for Harriet Tubman's successful mission to free 750 enslaved people at the Combahee River in 1853. Though many CRC members engaged in such political issues as reproductive rights (both access to abortion and the end of forced sterilization), rape, and other forms of violence against Black women, and welfare and workplace rights, the organization itself became primarily a study group. Its 1977 statement, a classic text in feminist history, laid necessary groundwork for contemporary understandings of intersectionality—what scholar Keeanga-Yamahtta Taylor, in a recent book on the CRC, described as the ways in which "interlocking" or "simultaneous" forms of oppression "[create] *new* measures of oppression and inequality." The CRC statement also includes the first known use of the term "identity politics," which members understood, again according to Taylor, as "an analysis that would validate Black women's experiences while simultaneously creating an opportunity for them to become politically active to fight for the issues most important to them." Long marginalized by both white women and Black men, CRC members believed, quite simply, that their own liberation as Black women was a goal worth working toward. In the end, they argued, Black women's liberation would benefit all people: "If Black women were free," they wrote, "it would mean that everyone else would have to be free since our freedom would necessitate the destruction of all the systems of oppression."[10]

For many historians, the Black Panther Party (BPP), founded in Oakland, California, in 1966 by Huey Newton and Bobby Seale, has exemplified the masculinist cast of the Black Power movement. Though he later repudiated such actions, as a young man, BPP minister of information Eldridge Cleaver delighted in his ability to rape women. Elaine Brown, who served as BPP chairperson from 1974 to 1977, recalled multiple instances of sexual harassment. On one occasion, other men even excused the cruel hours-long beating she received from a male BPP member. The reasoning: "Don't no bitch disrespect me!"[11]

This does not mean that men in the Black Power movement were any more sexist than more moderate Black men, white men, or any other group of men. Rather, as the Moynihan Report makes clear, the Black Power movement reflected the misogyny of mainstream society. Still, women often found purpose, camaraderie, and joy in Black Power organizations, including the BPP. Women made up 60 percent of the group's members, and some even attained leadership roles within the organization, including Brown, Kathleen Cleaver (communications secretary, 1967–71), and Ericka Huggins (Central Committee member, 1977–79). Brown, Cleaver, and Huggins were also leaders in the New Haven, Connecticut, chapter. As in the Washington, DC, area, some chapters actively worked against gender discrimination. Huggins also served as director of the party's Intercommunal Youth Institute/Oakland Community School, founded in 1973 to educate the children of Oakland in both scholastic basics and egalitarian politics. (Three years later, she was the first Black woman elected to serve on the Alameda County Board of Education.) And everywhere, rank-and-file women also established free breakfast programs, food and clothing drives, and medical clinics. Though most Panther women did not call themselves feminists at the time, associating the term with a movement of middle-class white women, the organization offered ample opportunity to implement feminist theories on the ground.

Occasionally, the persecution women faced on behalf of or within the movement could actually foster a greater appreciation for women's contributions. In the second half of the 1960s, FBI surveillance of, and interference with, Black Power movements was widespread. For example, agents cultivated conflict between the BPP and the similarly oriented Us Organization, leading to a violent confrontation in 1969. Two BPP members, including Ericka Huggins's husband, John, were killed. In retaliation, BPP members tortured and murdered nineteen-year-old Alex Rackley, whom they suspected of being an informant. Huggins, whose voice was heard on a recording of the crime, was among those arrested and charged. She was eventually acquitted, but not before spending two years in prison, separated from her infant daughter. In response, even Eldridge Cleaver was forced to admit that "the incarceration and suffering of Sister Ericka should be a stinging rebuke to all manifestations of male chauvinism within our ranks. . . . A woman can be just as revolutionary as a man and . . . we cannot relegate her to an inferior position."[12]

These harrowing experiences also shaped the priorities of the Black women's liberation movement—specifically, their activism on behalf of women who had been wrongfully incarcerated. Ericka Huggins was just one of dozens of Panther women imprisoned in this era, and she recognized the potential of organizing incarcerated women. While in prison, she founded the Sisterlove Collective, which helped newly imprisoned women adjust to life in prison and forged community through the act of hair-braiding. As Huggins recalled, "We braided each other's hair and curled each other's hair and over the hair-doing we had all kinds of conversations about how we wanted the world to work and unfold. It looked so harmless to the prison guards, but it was revolutionary."[13] Other incarcerated Panther women experienced pregnancy and childbirth in prison, and even more experienced sickness and poor health. In part, as a result of these experiences, radical women turned their gaze toward the carceral experiences of regular Black women.

In 1974, Joan Little, a nineteen-year-old Black woman living in North Carolina, was arrested for a series of break-ins. Little's youth and young adulthood had included previous run-ins with law enforcement, and by the early 1970s, she had acquired a reputation. She pled guilty to this latest set of charges and prepared to serve two consecutive seven- to ten-year sentences. But here the real case began. While incarcerated, Little was raped by Clarence Alligood, a sixty-two-year-old white jailer with a history of coercing sexual favors from imprisoned women. Little fought him off, stabbing him eleven times with an ice pick, and escaped. Though physical evidence of the rape abounded and several other women testified to Alligood's previous attacks, a grand jury quickly indicted Little for murder. If convicted, she would face an automatic death sentence. Instead, an interracial coalition of feminists, along with racial justice and anti–death penalty activists, rallied to Little's defense. Among those who did so was Rosa Parks, who continued her decades-long campaign seeking justice for Black women who had experienced sexual violence. The Black women's liberation movement arose as much from this history as it did from the male-led Black Power movement.

Accordingly, though the shift that took place between the end of 1964 and 1966 certainly spurred more feminist organizing, independent Black women's organizations predated this reorientation. As early as circa 1960, Mount Vernon, New York, resident Patricia Robinson became involved in local reproductive politics, founding a group to help pregnant teenagers. Shortly after the assassination of Malcolm X in 1965, Robinson participated in the New York City-based group Black Women Enraged (BWE), founded to aid the slain leader's family. Later, BWE turned its attention to anti-war and anti-draft organizing. Through her work in Planned Parenthood (her father was on the organization's national board), Robinson was also in close contact in the mid- to late 1960s with a number of white feminists, whom she advised as they began founding their own women's liberation groups. Robinson also exchanged ideas with June Jordan, a white feminist in California.

Back in Westchester County, Robinson's cohort had organized a welfare rights organization and a rent strike in 1964. Two years later, they organized a freedom school for local children. Eventually, this group, which became the Black Women's Liberation Group of Mount Vernon/New Rochelle, developed a pointed and self-conscious critique of the gender (particularly, reproductive) politics of middle-class Black radicals.

Part and parcel with Black Power gender ideologies were the beliefs that Black women should bear children for Black men and that birth control constituted Black genocide. In an influential and widely reprinted article primarily written by Robinson, the Mount Vernon/New Rochelle group rejected these arguments. Taking the form of a letter to radical Black men, the piece argued that birth control provided "the freedom to *fight* genocide of black women and children. . . . Poor black women in the United States have to fight back out of our own experience of oppression. Having too many babies stops us from supporting our children, teaching them the truth, or stopping the brainwashing, as you say, and from fighting black men who still want to use and exploit us."[14]

Another early Black women's liberation group, the Third World Women's Alliance (TWWA), emerged directly from SNCC. For Frances M. Beal and other founders, the hypocrisy within the movement became overwhelming: "We're talking in SNCC about freedom and liberation and night-long things about throwing off the shackles of the past . . . we can't talk about freedom and liberation and talk about putting women down."[15] Beal and a group of like-minded women founded the Black women's liberation movement within SNCC; by 1968 TWWA existed independently. Like Robinson and the Mount Vernon/New Rochelle group, TWWA members criticized radical Black men's embrace of middle-class, white gender norms; challenged the idea that their most important role was as "breeders" for the movement; and rejected the idea that birth control and abortion constituted Black genocide. (Beal herself had nearly died from an illegal abortion at age seventeen, and she knew other young women who had not survived.) As in Beal's "Double Jeopardy," members also identified the collusion between capitalism and racism. Their worldview was explicitly intersectional.

TWWA developed these and other theories through a process of consciousness raising, in which a group of women discussed their individual experiences and connected them to broader social and political structures. Beal recalled, "[W]e began to talk about our roles—I'll never forget this, we sort of said 'what does it mean to be a Black woman or a Puerto Rican woman?'"[16] Similar discussions had taken place within SNCC; as Beal recalled in 2005, "[A]s women got together and began talking about their role in the society and their role here, within the organization, some of us began to see it wasn't an individual problem but a social problem."[17] As discussed below, consciousness raising is most commonly associated with the white women's liberation movement, but its importance to TWWA shows that this was yet another technique that white women learned from the examples of the civil rights and Black/Third World women's liberation movements.[18]

By 1970, TWWA had about 200 members, most in the Northeast and on the West Coast. Chapters called for free education, childcare, and health services for women of color, as well as a more robust social safety net for poor families, among other initiatives. Finally, it published a newspaper, *Triple Jeopardy*, which circulated among and influenced the thinking of other women's liberation groups long after most chapters had folded or changed focus by the late 1970s.

So called because it included Black, Puerto Rican, and Asian American women, TWWA advanced an international, anti-imperial stance. Beal had lived for several years in France, and her main work with SNCC was in its International Affairs Commission, which focused especially on decolonization. Accordingly, TWWA members believed that oppressed groups around the world, including Black Americans, were connected by virtue of their colonized status. Black women in the United States, for example, were connected to Vietnamese women fighting American imperialism. In what scholar Judy Wu had termed "radical orientalism," the Asian woman as freedom fighter sometimes became romanticized within U.S. Third World (and white) feminism.[19] A series of articles in *Triple Jeopardy*, for example, praised the revolutionary women of China, North Korea, and the Philippines as potential examples for women in such places as Puerto Rico. Vietnamese women, of course, were the most common example; as an anonymous Panther woman argued in 1969, "We feel that the example given us by the Vietnamese women is a prime example of the role women can play in the revolution. The Vietnamese women are out there fighting with their brothers, fighting against American imperialism, with its advanced technology. They can shoot. They're out there with their babies on their backs, as the case may be, and they're participating in the revolution just as the Vietnamese men are participating in the revolution, in the national liberation struggle."[20]

The experiences of actual women of color in TWWA, however, were multivalent. For Puerto Rican women, for example, the organization's capacious understanding of reproductive rights, which extended beyond abortion to the issue of forced sterilization, was a breath of fresh air. And though restrictive immigration policies meant that the Asian population in the United States—and TWWA—was small, the few Asian American feminists who joined the group found it to be the most appropriate outlet for their politics. For a time the only Asian American in the group, Christine Choy felt more kinship among its Black and Puerto Rican members than she did with other Asian Americans. Born in Shanghai shortly after the Chinese Revolution, Choy moved to the United States as a teenager. She attended Columbia University, where she became involved in

TWWA, eventually serving as art director for *Triple Jeopardy*. TWWA's revolutionary, leftist politics resonated with her much more than did the conservatism of many Chinese immigrants to the United States. Already by the mid-1960s, the perception of Asian Americans as a "model minority" rewarded assimilation and discouraged activism among these groups. For Choy, the existence of a global Third World, and the potential for an international alliance of Third World feminists, held more potential.

As some historians see it, the romanticization of Asian women revolutionaries had its benefits. Judy Tzu-Chun Wu points out that "the hypervisibility of Asian female revolutionaries helped Asian American women to create their own political subjectivity and to subvert their political invisibility. In other words, the political heroism of women in socialist Asia played a central role in creating Third World feminism in the United States."[21] In 1971, this "hypervisibility" inspired the Indochinese Women's Conference (IWC). Held in Toronto and Vancouver, the IWC gave approximately one thousand American and Canadian women—including some 120 women of Asian descent—the opportunity to meet six revolutionary women from Southeast Asia (two from North Vietnam, two from South Vietnam, and two from Laos). Japanese American Pat Sumi, who had traveled to North Korea, North Vietnam, and China the year before with Eldridge Cleaver and Elaine Brown, was among the event's organizers. She was part of a successful effort to schedule a separate (without white women) meeting for women of color with the six visitors, which she and others saw as necessary to foster interracial connections among women of color. Sumi also wrote about her travels for the Chinese American newspaper *Getting Together*, sponsored by the revolutionary socialist organization I Wor Kuen.[22]

Donna Kotake's experiences at the conference were representative of her generation of Asian American feminists. Born to Japanese American parents in San Francisco, in 1971, Kotake was a student at San Jose State University. Attending the conference, she later recalled, not only heightened her pride in being an Asian woman but also fostered connections with other women of color—both in the United States and around the world. Activist Evelyn Yoshimura pointed out that the same logic that subjected women in Southeast Asia to sexual violence and other forms of gendered and racial abuse also informed racism against Asian Americans. According to Yuri Kochiyama, the best-known Asian American woman

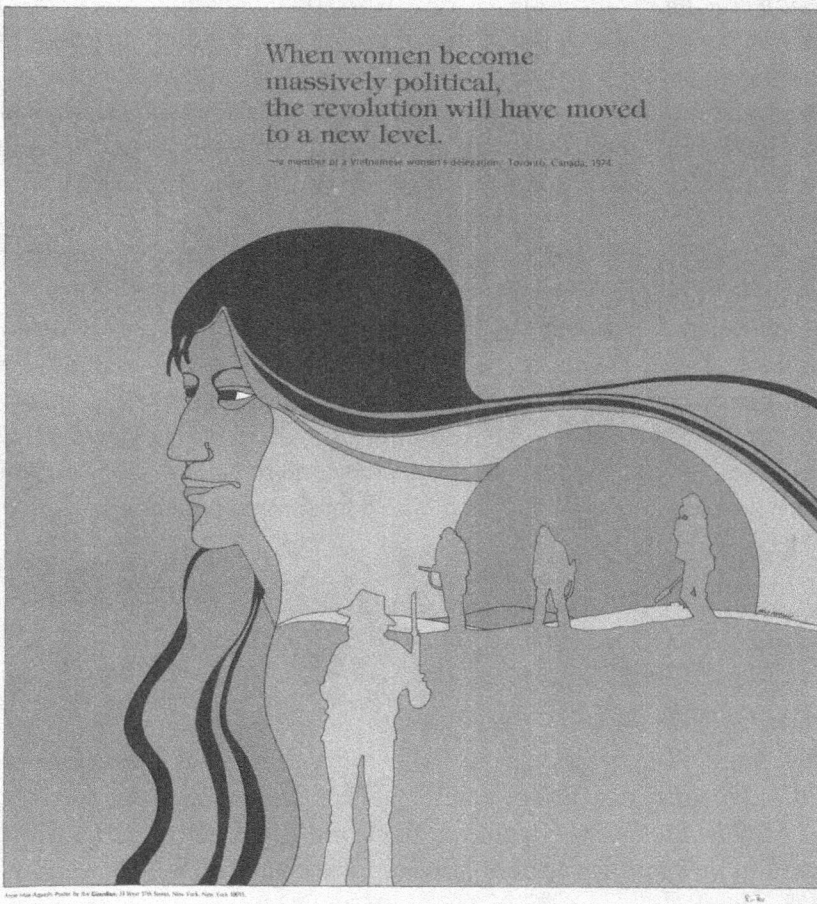

Peg Averill, "When Women Become Massively Political, the Revolution Will Have Moved to a New Level," ca. 1976–80. In the 1970s, the revolutionary women of Vietnam and elsewhere provided inspiration to North American feminists, including those of Asian descent. (Library of Congress, Prints & Photographs Division, LC-DIG-ds-13354)

activist of her generation, "[F]or most North American women who attended [the IWC], it was the most moving event of that time."[23] This was so even for women who could not attend the conference but who could read extensive coverage about it in the journal *Asian Women*, first published that same year.

Chicana feminists also engaged with the emerging Third World feminist perspective. Initially, this orientation posed a conundrum: the Chicano movement had long emphasized cultural nationalism and self-determination as pillars of any anti-colonial movement. Chicana feminists, however, recognized that they shared commonalities with other marginalized groups of women both within and outside the United States. These issues came to a head at the IWC, discussed in depth earlier in this chapter. As Felicitas Nuñez, a student at San Diego State University, reported, "[I]n speech after speech the Historical Presentations made by our Hawaiian, Black, Native American, Indian, Puerto Ricana, Chicana, Philipina, and Indochinese, we saw how the same tactics used to conquer, betray and humiliate us as a people were repeated with others."[24] The IWC thus provided space for Chicanas to discuss and reconcile these competing perspectives. In many ways, the conference was a turning point in the development of U.S. Third World feminism and feminist theory.

"OUR POLITICS BEGIN WITH OUR FEELINGS": THE EMERGENCE OF THE WHITE WOMEN'S LIBERATION MOVEMENT

When asked to envision the American women's movement of the late 1960s and '70s, many people will likely conjure images of an event similar to the 1968 Miss America protest, one of the first major public protests of the women's liberation movement. "Welcome to the Miss America Cattle Auction!" read a sign on the Atlantic City boardwalk on September 7, 1968. One hundred members of the women's liberation movement had gathered to protest the Miss America pageant, which seemed to represent everything the movement had risen up against: sexism, racism, jingoism, and consumerism. Singing and chanting as they marched, demonstrators threw into a Freedom Trash Can (but did not burn, though they had planned to) what they called "woman-garbage," including "bras, girdles, curlers, false eyelashes, wigs, and representative issues of Cosmopolitan, Ladies' Home Journal, Family Circle, etc." A giant puppet with chains attached to her red, white, and blue swimsuit represented "the chains that tie us to these beauty standards against our will."[25]

According to Carol Hanisch, the idea for the protest came from New York Radical Women, the women's liberation group to which she belonged. As Hanisch, Robin Morgan, and other women discussed the Miss America pageant, they developed a set of ten reasons for the protest. First and foremost, they rejected "the degrading Mindless-Boob-Girlie Symbol," the dehumanizing process by which women were judged solely by their looks. They also criticized the pageant's racism, its enthusiastic embrace of consumer capitalism, and its connections to U.S. military involvement in Vietnam. "Last year," demonstrators noted, "she [Miss America] went to Vietnam to pep-talk our husbands, sons, and boyfriends into dying and killing with a better spirit. . . . We refuse to be used as Mascots for Murder."[26]

The Miss America protest holds a unique place in cultural memory, one that has been distorted since the event itself took place. Almost immediately, the media began gleefully reporting that the protestors had burned bras. Despite the fact that the history of feminism includes no recorded examples of bra burning, anti-feminists continue to use the epithet "bra burner" against women's rights advocates.

For the most part, however, historians have been content to repeat the Hanisch/Morgan story of how the protest came to be. According to Alice Echols, Morgan "did the bulk of [the] event's organizing."[27] But Black lawyer and activist Florynce Kennedy was a key organizer of the women's liberation protest. "I was the force of that," she recalled later.[28] Thanks in large part to Kennedy, the women's liberation protest borrowed many tactics from the civil rights and Black Power movements. Most histories of the protest, however, leave her out. The history of the women's liberation movement remains whitewashed in many people's minds.

In truth, the white women who participated in the Miss America protest worked in a tradition that emerged from involvement in civil rights, Black Power, and the male-led white student left in the early and mid-1960s. The experiences of two white women, longtime SNCC activists Mary King and Casey Hayden, begin to demonstrate this point. From Virginia, Mary King followed the example of her minister ancestors to become involved in the YWCA and then SNCC. Born Sandra Cason in Austin, Texas, Casey Hayden's politics crystallized from her early experiences as the daughter of a single mother. As a student at the University of Texas, she too was drawn to the YWCA. She also chose to live in the Christian Faith and Life Community, the only integrated housing on campus. Her work with the YWCA took her to Atlanta, where she worked with Baker to develop workshops on race and racism. As communications assistant to SNCC president Julian Bond and a respected project organizer, respectively, King and Hayden held positions of great responsibility within the organization, developing skills they would bring with them to the feminist movement. They also internalized SNCC's ideology. As historian Ruth Rosen writes, "SNCC's emphasis on community, the redemption of the powerless, and the promotion of self-determination would provide much of the structural and ideological foundation for a new feminist movement." They relied, too, on the analysis they developed from reading and discussing *The Second Sex*, a book that would have a far greater influence on King and Hayden's generation than on Betty Friedan's. King recalled, "Our copy of de Beauvoir's *The Second Sex* was underlined, creased, marked up, and finally coverless from our study of it."[29]

King and Hayden's experiences both were and were not exceptional. As two of just a handful of whites involved in SNCC in its early years—most importantly, pre–Freedom Summer—they had access to leadership positions that newer recruits did not. They had spent their lives in the South and understood the roles that they as white women could and should play in the movement. They also perceived clearly the organization drifting toward a more hierarchical structure after the successes and failures of Freedom Summer, a development that augured poorly for women. The hundreds of white northern women who volunteered in 1964 also learned the skills necessary to mobilize a social movement and imbibed SNCC's radically egalitarian ideology, but they did not see how gender, particularly within the context of southern racial mores, functioned within the organization as clearly as did longer-term members.

By the fall of 1964, it was clear that SNCC was an organization at a turning point—and in need of some soul-searching. At a retreat in Waveland, Mississippi, in November 1964, King, Hayden, and others circulated the anonymous "SNCC Position Paper, Nov. 1964," which documented the discrimination that women faced within the organization. Aspects of this discrimination had always existed—men held most of the formal leadership positions and often expected women to fulfill clerical and/or domestic labor—but as long as the organization was focused primarily on grassroots organizing, fieldwork provided an empowering alternative to this formal imbalance. These possibilities disappeared once the organization began focusing more on large-scale media events centered around individual, compelling personalities. "Whether women held leadership positions didn't matter in actuality prior to this time," Hayden later remembered, "since the participatory, town-hall style, consensus-forming nature of SNCC's operation meant that being on the Executive Committee or a project director didn't carry much weight anyway." King and Hayden thus primarily responded to the organization's growing *hierarchy*, of which gender disparity was a *by-product*.[30]

Nonetheless, the paper was a turning point in the development of an independent women's movement. Beyond cataloging the concrete forms of discrimination women in SNCC faced, it provided a new language for women to talk and think about themselves. In SNCC, women learned to think about Black Americans as a group or class of people, deployed race as a category of analysis (a lens through which to view and understand people's experiences), and discovered how the expectations of the dominant class affected the inner, emotional lives of marginalized groups, limiting not only the concrete opportunities open to them but also the futures they could imagine for themselves. Now, King and Hayden drew an explicit comparison between race and gender to describe their own experiences:

> The average white person finds it difficult to understand why the Negro resents being called "boy," or being thought of as "musical" and "athletic," because the average white person doesn't realize that he assumes he is superior. And naturally he doesn't understand the problem of paternalism. So too the average SNCC worker finds it difficult to discuss the woman problem because of the assumption of male superiority. Assumptions of male superiority are as widespread and deep rooted and every much as crippling to the woman as the assumptions of white supremacy are to the Negro.[31]

This intellectual model obviously has its limitations. Saying that gender is *like* race overlooks the ways in which these categories are mutually constitutive (each creates the other). Even more importantly, it leaves no room for the experiences of Black women. In 1964, however, it was a revolutionary way of thinking about women's status. For better and for worse, this analogy significantly affected the ideology of the white women's movement.

The response to the paper also alienated some women from the civil rights movement itself. After a long day of discussion and debate, several members of the SNCC inner circle, including King, Hayden, and Stokely Carmichael, retreated to a nearby pier to decompress. Known for his irreverent sense of humor, Carmichael began riffing on the day's discussion and movement culture more generally—culminating with his observation that "the position of women in SNCC" was "prone." As noted in chapter 2, the quip produced some hurt feelings, though most in attendance laughed. The problem was that Carmichael fell in love with his own wisecrack, which he repeated at event after event. Severed from the context of a joke among friends, Carmichael's statement seemed proof that women would never be respected within SNCC.

In 1966, SNCC became an all-Black organization, asking white members to leave and organize poor whites. The immediate issue became moot for white women like King and Hayden, but they would bring their experiences to bear on their work in the white student left, where gender dynamics were also fraught.

In the early 1960s, idealistic young people troubled by the discrepancy between American discourses of freedom and equality and American realities of poverty, discrimination, and militarism clamored for a revitalized left. Founded in 1960, Students for a Democratic Society (SDS) quickly became one of the most important organizations in this New Left. Many SDS members also participated in the civil rights movement, where they learned from SNCC the importance of the community-organizing tradition and what they would call participatory democracy. Baker and others had taught these young women and men that the way to build a social movement was to go into local communities and learn from local leaders rather than imposing their own ideas or assuming that they had special knowledge that local people did not. This ethos manifested itself most explicitly in the Economic Research and Action Project (ERAP), the community-organizing wing of the organization created in September 1963 with a grant from the UAW. In such cities as Cleveland, Ohio; Newark, New Jersey; and Chicago, Illinois, SDS members lived in poor communities and tried to reach out to their neighbors, Black and white alike, trying to empower local leaders and encourage the poor to organize themselves.

Local ERAP initiatives met with mixed success. By and large, women were far more successful than men at cultivating relationships with local activists. While SDS men in Chicago became fascinated with and even emulated the working-class white machismo they encountered in pool halls and other spots, SDS women in Cleveland organized mothers waiting in line at local welfare offices. (Not coincidentally, many of the links between SNCC and SDS were women.) And, of course, SDS men and women worked with locals in various cities to secure some notable victories, including having the poor organize a successful national ERAP conference in February 1965, organizing successful rent strikes, and winning representation on local War on Poverty boards. Some years later, SDS women who had been involved in the Newark ERAP initiative founded that city's first women's center.

By the end of 1965, however, most ERAP projects had been shut down. There were a number of reasons for this decision, but the most important by far was the escalation of the war in Vietnam. In February that year, President Lyndon Johnson ordered the bombing of North Vietnam; a few short months later, he instituted the draft for large numbers of young men. Suddenly, the war—and, importantly, the draft—seemed the most urgent issue for the quickly growing organization to address. Most mainstream and countercultural discourse framed the draft as a men's issue—"Girls Say Yes to Boys Who Say No," a popular poster promised.

The escalating war in Vietnam, the organization's growing focus on it, and the resulting end of ERAP thus led to significant losses for women in SDS. These problems did not emerge out of nowhere. While the CP and broader Old Left (however grudgingly) recognized the necessity of addressing the "woman question" (see chapter 1), SDS men scoffed at the question's very existence (or were unaware that previous generations of young leftists had dealt with many of the same issues that they were now attempting to address). The national office of SDS, moreover, had never been particularly friendly to women in leadership roles. But as long as ERAP initiatives existed, there were places where women's voices could be heard and they could continue the community-organizing work of Highlander and SNCC. Certainly leftist women cared about ending the war and did not want to see men they cared about drafted, but they also did not want to abandon the community-organizing tradition to which many of them had now devoted half a decade. "I wanted to organize," recalled Betty Garman, "not engage in verbal debate."[32] To SDS men, however, such issues as the rights of welfare mothers were "soft subjects" compared to discussing the failures of American foreign and economic policy.

It did not help that SDS culture prioritized endless competitive intel-
lectualizing, a discursive model in which most women were not trained.
At meetings, it could be difficult to get a word in edgewise. Women would
patiently wait their turn while one of their male counterparts extempo-
rized on American imperialism or corporate liberalism. But "the men,"
one woman noted, "they never finished." On the rare occasion that a
woman was able to speak, Nancy Hollander remembered, "the men suddenly stretched, and chattered among themselves." Hollander's then-hus-
band, SDS president in 1963, Todd Gitlin, later admitted that SDS was
indeed "a young boys' network" and that movement intellectual culture
exacerbated this problem. Hollander and Gitlin's story, moreover, exem-
plifies one of the few ways women could attain visibility within SDS—a
sexual relationship with a powerful man. Anne Weills, an SDS activist in
the Bay Area, recalled that, no matter how eloquently a woman spoke,
"half the time people would ignore you. I'd think, 'I'm not saying it well.
I'm not saying it loud enough.' Finally I'd get to say something. Complete
silence. A few minutes later, a man would get up and say the same thing.
Suddenly, the room became electrified. Invisibility. That's what was so
painful."[33] Though it was certainly not a conscious strategy, SDS men
seemed determined to alienate women from their own experiences and
emotions—a perception that would fundamentally shape the women's
liberation movement.

Increasingly, women realized that SDS—and the white student left
more generally—was an inadequate vehicle to address their concerns. In
November 1965, almost exactly a year after their SNCC position paper,
King and Hayden addressed "A Kind of Memo" to a group of movement
women. In documenting their frustrations with the left, the paper echoed
much of what they had written the previous year, including the unequal
division of work both within and outside the movement and the analogy between race and gender. "There seem to be many parallels that can
be drawn between treatment of Negroes and treatment of women," they
wrote, and "many people who are very hip to the implications of the racial
caste system, even people in the movement, don't seem to see the sexual
caste system, and if it's raised they respond with: 'That's the way it's supposed to be. There are biological differences.' Or with other statements
that sound like a white segregationist confronted with integration." The
paper also detailed problems women faced in personal relationships; the

negative effects of such cultural institutions and practices as marriage, child-rearing, and women's magazines; and the derision faced when trying to raise these issues.[34]

This paper, however, went further than the SNCC position paper, demonstrating an awareness of what women's liberationists would later term "the personal is political." "We've talked in the movement," King and Hayden wrote,

> about trying to build a society which would see basic human problems, (which are now seen as private troubles), as public problems and would try to shape institutions to meet human needs rather than shaping people to meet the needs of those with power. To raise questions like those above illustrates very directly that society can't deal with real human problems and opens discussion of why that is so. (In one sense, it is a radicalizing question that can take people beyond the legalistic solutions into arenas of personal and institutional change.)[35]

Early on, feminists of King and Hayden's generation and politics announced that they would focus on a different set of problems, and offer a different set of solutions, from those that NOW and other liberal feminist groups prioritized.

The next month, December 1965, SDS members gathered in Champaign-Urbana, Illinois, for a "rethinking conference." Most of the thinking—and talking—centered on King and Hayden's memo. But, for the first time, women refused to let men dominate these discussions. Instead they met alone, hashing out not only the nature of their position in SDS but also—even if they did not know it—their vision for a new feminist movement.

Tensions simmered for the next two years. Then, in August 1967, Black and white activists met in Chicago for the National Conference for New Politics (NCNP), the goal of which was to nominate a Black-led ticket for the 1968 presidential election. Led by longtime activists Jo Freeman and Shulamith Firestone, women introduced a resolution to guarantee women's equal participation in the conference. But men responded with amusement and derision, officially approving of the resolution but refusing to discuss any of the issues it raised. The climax of the confrontation left an indelible image in Jo Freeman's mind: "William

Pepper patted Shulie [Firestone] on the head and said, 'Move on, little girl; we have more important issues to talk about here than women's liberation.'"[36]

The very next week, a group of women that later became the Westside group, the first white women's liberation group in the nation, drafted a letter "To the Women of the Left," which condensed two months of discussion into a brief summary of what the authors had learned about their "colonial status in this society"—a condition that, though it required equal educational, political, and economic opportunities, would not change simply through these measures. Radical changes were also required in areas of reproductive control, relationships with men, and the household division of labor. So, too, were changes in an individual's consciousness: "Women are often their own worst enemies," the authors posited, "because they have been trained to be prejudiced against themselves."[37] An independent women's liberation movement would necessarily address all these issues.

Another incident further demonstrated the futility of continuing to work within the male-led left. In January 1969, the National Mobilization Committee sponsored a protest against both the Vietnam War and Richard Nixon's inauguration, scheduled for the next day. The organizers included among the speakers two women: Marilyn Salzman Webb, who had thus far remained loyal to SDS, and Shulamith Firestone, who was already active in radical feminist organizing in New York. As soon as Webb began her speech declaring women an oppressed group, the crowd grew rowdy. Webb recalled, "[F]ist fights broke out. Men yelled things like 'Fuck her! Take her off the stage! Rape her in a back alley!'"[38] Webb finished her speech, and then the crowd subjected Firestone to the same treatment. On stage, the male organizers did nothing to dissuade the crowd from such behavior. Later, Webb, Firestone, and others debriefed in Webb's apartment. The phone rang, and upon answering, Webb heard a still-unidentified woman say, "If you or anybody like you ever gives a speech like that again, we're going to beat the s— out of you. SDS has a line on women's liberation, and that is *the line*." Hostility had turned into open threats, leading yet more women to decide that autonomous women's groups were the only way forward.

As Robin Morgan documented in "Goodbye to All That," originally published in the underground newspaper *The Rat*, leaving the left was a slow and painful process. In her essay, Morgan took aim at "the friends, brothers, lovers in the counterfeit male-dominated Left. The good guys who think they know what 'Women's Lib,' as they so chummily call it, is all about—and who then proceed to degrade and destroy women by almost everything they say and do." The movement that had promised freedom, she argued, offered only another form of the exploitation women faced in mainstream society: they were useful to men only as long as they were sexually available.[39] (Women who resisted this form of "liberation" were often accused of being uptight or having "hang-ups.") A genuine revolution must not and could not be run by the oppressors (all men); rather, it must emanate from the oppressed ("black, brown, and white *women*"). All women, "no matter how else [they were] oppressed," shared a particular kind of pain, one that derived from "the primary oppression of being female in a patriarchal world." And so it was "the job of revolutionary feminists to build an ever stronger Independent Women's Liberation Movement, so that the Sisters in counterfeit captivity will have somewhere to turn, to use their power and rage and beauty and coolness in their own behalf for once, on their own terms, on their own issues, in their own style—whatever that may be."[40] Morgan's conclusion included a long, raw passage full of anger, sadness—and hope:

Goodbye, goodbye forever, counterfeit Left, counterfeit, male-dominated cracked-glass mirror reflection of the Amerikan Nightmare. Women are the real left. We are rising, powerful in our unclean bodies; bright glowing mad in our inferior brains; wild hair flying, wild eyes staring, wild voices keening: undaunted by blood we who hemorrhage every twenty-eight days; laughing at our own beauty we who have lost our sense of humor; mourning for all each precious one of us might have been in this one living timeplace had she not been born a woman; stuffing fingers into our mouths to stop the screams of fear and hate and pity for men we have loved and love still; tears in our eyes and bitterness in our mouths for children we couldn't have, or couldn't *not* have, or didn't want, or didn't want *yet*, or wanted and had in this time of horror. We are rising with a fury older and potentially greater than any force in history and this time we will be free or no one will survive.[41]

The new women's movement had a lot to live up to.

In cities across the country, women founded such groups as Bread and Roses (Boston, 1969–73), Cell 16 (Boston, 1968–73), the Chicago Women's Liberation Union (1969–77), New York Radical Women (1967–69), New York Radical Feminists (1969–72), and Redstockings (1969–70), embarking on a project of consciousness raising and political activism. In small groups, women discussed issues including sex, the division of labor within the household, beauty culture, and more. Seeing commonalities between their own and other women's experiences, participants realized that their experiences were not just personal or individual but also social, structural—and political. The idea for the protest of the 1968 Miss America pageant came from a consciousness-raising group, as did many other similar actions.

Though many white women's liberationists encountered the theory and practice of consciousness raising in SNCC, the movement's emphasis on this process derived from women's experiences in SDS and the male-led white student left more generally. As Bread and Roses members Linda Gordon and Meredith Tax recognized, the abstract theorizing of leftist men left little room for human experience or emotion. "Sometimes it seems like we all gave up what makes us most human when we went into the movement," they wrote, characterizing discussions within SDS as reflections of "their [men's] competitiveness among themselves; their verbal diarrhea; the way they intellectualize everything and hardly ever say anything that isn't totally abstract; the way they never talk about themselves or their feelings except when under attack."

By contrast, Gordon and Tax argued "that the surest antidote to rhetoric is speaking out of one's experiences."[42] "Our politics begin with our feelings," wrote Joan Jordan of Redstockings, "feelings are a direct response to the events and relationships that we experience; that's how we know what's really going on." In "The Personal Is Political," Carol Hanisch translated this theory into practice. In consciousness-raising groups, women took turns discussing their personal experiences. At the end of each meeting, they identified commonalities and connections among these experiences. It was through this process that the personal became—or rather was recognized as—political. From there, women could plan concrete actions aimed at changing oppressive social structures. As Kathie Sarachild described, "[O]ur feelings will lead us to our theory, our theory to our action." Consciousness raising was not intended to be an end unto itself. Nor did it guarantee, as chapter 6 will explore, that all such discussions would lead to the same theories.[43]

"OUR CULTURE, HELL!": CHICANA FEMINISTS AND THE CULTURE OF MACHISMO

Emerging from the Chicano movement of the late 1960s, an independent Chicana feminist movement began to organize roughly concurrently with the Black and white women's liberation movements. Like these other two movements, the Chicana feminism of the late 1960s and '70s responded most immediately to the masculinist cast of male-led student movements (SNCC, SDS) and (like Black feminism) the charge that women play a supportive role in the revolution lest they be seen as traitors to the cause.

By the second half of the 1960s, younger Chicano activists (as in the Black civil rights movement) had become frustrated with the assimilationist goals of some of their older counterparts. This new orientation emphasized "pride in our heritage, our language, and the humanistic values governing our personal relationships" and pursued a vision of *Chicanismo* (Chicano-ness).[44] By spring 1968, the United Mexican American Students (UMAS), later Movimiento Estudiantil Chicano de Aztlàn (MEChA) / the Chicano Student Movement of Aztlàn, boasted ten chapters at schools in and around Los Angeles. (Aztlàn is the name of the parts of Mexico—now the states of California, Arizona, New Mexico, Colorado, and Texas—taken by the United States between 1845 and 1848.) Unlike Black students, who found community at historically Black colleges and universities (HBCUs), Chicanos had no such infrastructure and were often isolated in majority-white institutions. Chicano groups helped assuage the loneliness and the pressure to fit into white American norms. This was the experience of both Ana Nieto-Gómez and Leticia Hernández, both of whom first encountered UMAS at Long Beach State University and went on to found one of the first Chicana feminist groups, La Hijas de Cuauhtémoc (the Daughters of Cuauhtémoc).

College and political organizing offered a great deal of freedom to young women like Nieto-Gómez and Hernández, many of whom had been more restricted in their childhood and adolescence than their male counterparts. They flocked to the Chicano movement, playing crucial roles in founding and staffing a number of organizations. Yet they began to experience the same contradictions that Frances M. Beal found in SNCC and Mary King and Casey Hayden found in SDS: in a movement dedicated to freedom and equality, women were expected to defer to and support men. In the Chicano movement, this belief derived from both Chicanismo and *carnalismo* (brotherhood). In order to resist white racism and/or assimilation into white society, traditional Chicano culture must be preserved, gender roles and all. Men were to be the public faces of the movement; women were to provide behind-the-scenes support. One student organization actually hid its female leaders from an influential national leader, Rudolfo "Corky" Gonzalez, when he came to campus to speak. In 1969, the Chicano Youth Liberation Conference, attended by as many as fifteen hundred students, even issued a statement claiming that "the Chicana Woman does not want to be liberated."[45]

"OUR CULTURE, HELL!" Chicana feminists responded—though in practice they threaded the needle of cultural preservation with great dexterity.[46] They argued, first, that *machismo* (masculine pride) did not reflect Indigenous Chicano/a culture, but rather, responded to white racism. Carving out a more prominent role for Chicanas would thus strengthen the movement and make it better able to confront white supremacy.

Accordingly, Chicana feminists often highlighted their connections to earlier women's activism. Labor activist Dolores Huerta, for example, inspired many younger women, who borrowed Huerta's concept of family-based politics (essentially, the idea that the family, both biological and sociological, could function as a center of resistance). Reimaging gender roles within the family, then, could be both antipatriarchal and anti-colonial. Chicana feminists also looked further back in their history. Founded in 1969 as a consciousness-raising and Chicana history study group, La Hijas de Cuauhtémoc intentionally named itself after a women's rights group that organized on both sides of the U.S.-Mexico border during the Mexican Revolution. Las Hijas founded and distributed a newspaper of the same name, counseled Chicana students, helped Chicana and Chicano students access federal education programs, developed Chicano studies programs, worked for abortion and welfare rights, and organized a regional conference of Chicana feminists. Not wanting to be seen as separatist, they also continued to participate in and fundraise for campus Chicano groups.

Neither donning the mantle of history nor continuing to support male-led organizations could protect Chicana feminists from the ire of their male counterparts, however. According to Leticia Hernández, a *Las Hijas* article on "Macho Attitudes" particularly incensed men. "We were ridiculed," she remembered, "'all that slop and all that ridiculous feminist b—and ha ha ha . . . oh here come the feminists, they're trying to be white women.' . . . It was hell."[47] When Ana Nieto-Gómez was elected president of Long Beach State MEChA, her defeated male opponent would not let the matter rest. He organized other MEChA members to hang her in effigy, present a theatrical funeral mass, and bury her and two other members of Las Hijas. Though Las Hijas members refused to be daunted by the incident, the group began to disband as founding members moved on to other activist or academic pursuits.

Chicana feminism quickly spread beyond college campuses. In October 1970, a group of women participated in a "Workshop on Women" at the National Mexican American Issues Conference (NMAIC). After discussing such topics as low wages, single motherhood, and the invisibility of women in Chicano history, they issued a resolution that simultaneously condemned the exclusion of women from leadership positions and emphasized the need to continue working with men in the movement, founding the Comisión Femenil Mexicana (CFM, Mexican Women's Commission) as an independent group affiliated with the NMAIC.

One of CFM's founders, Francisca Flores, had also helped found a predecessor group, the League of Mexican American Women, in 1958. In her forties by that point, she had already been active in progressive politics in California for decades. She belonged to several Mexican American rights organizations; vocally opposed segregation; and advocated for organized labor, universal health care, and women's rights.

Spreading throughout California, CFM established a job training and employment opportunity center for Mexican American women; created free twenty-four-hour childcare centers; spread news and information about Chicanas; and spoke out on political issues that affected Chicanas, including their exploitation as workers. It also joined forces with another Chicana feminist group, Concilio Mujeres (CM), founded in 1970 by single mother and longtime activist Dorinda Moreno. Under Moreno's leadership, CM focused on its energies on educating Chicana women and other Americans on that group's history and lived experiences. It encouraged Chicana women to enter higher education and the professions, distributed a journal, sponsored an educational television show, and established a library.

In May 1971, the Houston YWCA hosted the Conferencia de Mujeres por la Raza, the first national conference of Chicana feminists. Attended by as many as six hundred women, the gathering grew out of a series of regional meetings. Echoing earlier Chicana feminist groups, conference goers criticized the sexism of men in the movement. However, it also addressed the personal lives of Chicanas, including sex and marriage. Attendees called for access to free, legal abortion and birth control through community centers run by Chicanas, as well as free twenty-four-hour childcare. Increasingly over the course of the 1970s, Chicana feminists also focused on forced sterilization and welfare rights (see chapter 6).

Nor was the movement restricted to the Southwest, where the nation's largest concentration of Spanish speakers lived, or to such large urban centers as New York City. As they did in these other locations, geographical, demographic, and historical realities shaped the Chicana movement elsewhere. In the Midwest, for example, Chicanas could not claim to be from the ancestral homeland of Aztlàn and thus did not have the same connection to U.S. imperialism. Instead, Chicanas found themselves living within a more diverse Latinx population, including individuals with roots in Mexico, Puerto Rico, South America, Central America, and the Caribbean. As such, it made sense to these activists to organize based on *La Raza*, a flexible term that loosely encompassed the Hispanophone world in the Americas. La Raza Unida Party (RUP), which served as a hub of political organizing in the Southwest, did not have as much leverage in the Midwest both because the population was smaller and because RUP functioned on a state-by-state basis. A regional group, the Midwest Council of La Raza (MWCLR), became the most effective vehicle for organizing Latinx and Chicano/as in that area.

Originally from Muskegon, Michigan, Olga Villa was a founding member, the first secretary, and a crucial organizer for MWCLR. In 1972, at the group's first major event, the Mi Raza Primero conference, Villa (back in her hometown), her friend Jane Gonzalez, a community organizer, and other women challenged the male leadership of the organization. As the historian Leticia Wiggins puts it, they "decried the lack of female voices, macho attitudes, and general inattention to women's issues."[48] Some fifty women formed a Women's Caucus, adopted a set of resolutions, and formed a new organization, the Mid-West Mujeres de la Raza. They also made plans to hold a conference, Adelante Mujer, in South Bend, Indiana, later that year. Chicana or La Raza feminism had officially become a fully articulated movement that was both national and regionally specific with an ideology that was both singular and capacious.

CONCLUSION

In a 1970 leaflet, Bread and Roses asked a difficult question about feminism's future. "Some women," the authors wrote,

> look to the state and federal legislation to give us the unrestricted humanity which has been denied us for so long. They have decided to "work within the system." In other words, they say, "Let us into the world you men live in. Give us your education and your jobs and your public positions. Free us with childcare programs designed in your offices." Is this really what we want? How about female generals in Vietnam? DO WE WANT EQUALITY IN THE MAN'S WORLD, OR DO WE WANT TO MAKE IT A NEW WORLD?[49]

The next section in this volume will explore three different sets of answers to this question: those made by liberal feminists, those made by women's liberationists and radical feminists, and those made by conservative anti-feminists.

NOTES

1. Robin Morgan, "Introduction," in *Sisterhood Is Powerful: An Anthology of Writings from the Women's Liberation Movement*, ed. Morgan (New York: Vintage Books, 1970), xviii.

2. Frances Beal interview with Loretta J. Ross, Voices of Feminism Oral History Project, Sophia Smith Collection, Smith College, Northampton, MA, Mar. 18, 2005, pp. 37–38, https://www.smith.edu/libraries/libs/ssc/vof/transcripts/Beal.pdf.

3. One essay, written by a white woman, addressed the status of women in China. Quote from Morgan, "Introduction," xviii.

4. Beal preferred the term "Black women's liberation." Beal interview, 43.

5. Frances M. Beal, *Double Jeopardy: To Be Black and Female*, 1969, http://www.hartford-hwp.com/archives/45a/196.html.

6. Ibid.

7. Lyndon B. Johnson, Commencement address at Howard University, 1965, https://teachingamericanhistory.org/library/document/commencement-address-at-howard-university-to-fulfill-these-rights/.

8 . Dana Ramey Berry and Kali Nicole Gross, *A Black Women's History of the United States* (Boston: Beacon Press, 2020), 188.

9. Angela Davis, *An Autobiography* (1974; repr., New York: International Publishers, 1988), 161.

10. Keeanga-Yamahtta Taylor, "Introduction," in *How We Get Free: Black Feminism and the Combahee River Collective*, ed. Taylor (Chicago: Haymarket Books, 2017), 4; "The Combahee River Collective Statement," Apr. 1977, in Taylor, *How We Get Free*, 22–23, 24.

11. Elaine Brown, quoted in Berry and Gross, *A Black Women's History of the United States*, 190.

12. Eldridge Cleaver, quoted in Berry and Gross, *A Black Women's History of the United States*, 192.

13. Ericka Huggins, quoted in Mary Phillips, "The Feminist Leadership of Ericka Huggins in the Black Panther Party," *Black Diaspora Review* 4, no. 1 (2014): 192.

14. Black Women's Liberation Group, Mount Vernon, New York, "Statement on Birth Control," in Morgan, *Sisterhood Is Powerful*, 360. This essay also appeared in Toni Cade Bambara, ed., *The Black Woman: An Anthology* (New York: New American Library, 1970).

15. Frances M. Beal, quoted in Benita Roth, *Separate Roads to Feminism: Black, Chicana, and White Feminist Movements in America's Second Wave* (New York: Cambridge University Press, 2004), 90.

16. Beal, quoted in Roth, *Separate Roads to Feminism*, 91.

17. Beal interview, 35.

18. In her introduction to *Sisterhood Is Powerful*, Morgan wrote that "women's liberation is the first radical movement to base its politics—in fact, create its politics—out of concrete personal experiences. We've learned that those experiences are *not* our private hang-ups. They are shared by every woman, and are therefore political. The theory, then, comes out of human feeling, not out of textbook rhetoric. *That's* truly revolutionary, as anyone knows who's ever listened to abstract political speeches" (xvii–xviii).

19. See Judy Wu, *Radicals on the Road: Internationalism, Orientalism, and Feminism during the Vietnam Era* (Ithaca, NY: Cornell University Press, 2013).

20. *Panther Sisters on Women's Liberation*, Sept. 17, 1969, http://revolution .berkeley.edu/assets/deleted_womens-lib-1.pdf.

21. Judy Tzu-Chun Wu, "Asian American Feminisms and Women of Color Feminisms: Radicalism, Liberalism, and Invisibility," in *Asian American Feminisms and Women of Color Politics*, ed. Lynn Fujiwara and Shireen Roshanravan (Seattle: University of Washington Press, 2018), 45.

22. Though not exclusively a feminist organization, I Wor Kuen included many women in leadership roles, and the group injected important Third World feminist tenets into its activism.

23. Yuri Kochiyama, quoted in Wu, "Asian American Feminisms and Women of Color Feminisms," 47–49.

24. Felicitas Nuñez, quoted in Dionne Espinoza, "'La Raza en Canada': San Diego Chicana Activists, the Indochinese Women's Conference of 1971, and Third World Womanism," in *Chicana Movidas: New Narratives of Activism and Feminism in the Movement Era*, ed. Dionne Espinoza, María Eugenia Cotera, and Maylei Blackwell (Austin: University of Texas Press, 2018), 270.

25. New York Radical Women, "No More Miss America!" Aug. 22, 1968, box 8, folder Culture, Rosalynn Baxandall and Linda Gordon Research Files on Women's Liberation, TAM 210, Tamiment Library/Robert F. Wagner Labor Archives, New York University.

26. Ibid.

27. Alice Echols, *Daring to Be Bad: Radical Feminism in America, 1967–1975* (Minneapolis: University of Minnesota Press, 1989).

28. Florynce Kennedy, quoted in Georgia Paige Welch, "'Up against the Wall Miss America': Women's Liberation and Miss Black America in Atlantic City, 1968," *Feminist Formations* 27, no. 2 (2015): 81.

29. Rosen, *The World Split Open*, 106; Mary King, quoted in Rosen, *The World Split Open*, 57.

30. Casey Hayden, quoted in Rosen, *The World Split Open*, 108.

31. [Mary King, Casey Hayden, et al.], SNCC Position Paper, Nov. 1964, https://www.crmvet.org/docs/6411w_us_women.pdf.

32. Betty Garman, quoted in Rosen, *The World Split Open*, 119.

33. All quotes from Rosen, *The World Split Open*, 117, 118.

34. Mary King and Casey Hayden, "A Kind of Memo," Nov. 18, 1965, https:// repository.duke.edu/dc/richardsonjudy/jrpst002017.

35. Ibid.

36. Jo Freeman, quoted in Rosen, *The World Split Open*, 129.

37. SDS women, "To the Women of the Left," 1967, in *Dear Sisters: Dispatches from the Women's Liberation Movement*, ed. Rosalyn Baxandall and Linda Gordon (New York: Basic Books, 2000), 28, 29.

38. Marilyn Salzman Webb, quoted in Rosen, *The World Split Open*, 134.

39. In her essay "The Grand Coolie Dam" (1970), writer Marge Piercy made a similar point about the New Left's re-creation of mainstream gender practices. "My anger," she wrote, "is because they have created in the movement a microcosm of that oppression and are proud of it."

40. Robin Morgan, "Goodbye to All That," 1970, in Baxandall and Gordon, *Dear Sisters*, 53, 56.

41. Ibid., 57.

42. Linda Gordon and Meredith Tax, "Life in the Movement" (Part One), 1970, box 1, folder 6, Women's Liberation Research Files.

43. Linda Gordon and Meredith Tax, "Life in the Movement" (Part One), 1970, box 1, folder 6; Joan Jordan, "Our Politics Begin with Our Feelings," Mar. 21, 1970, box 1, folder 29; Carol Hanisch, "The Personal is Political," undated [1969], box 1, folder 55; Kathie Sarachild, "A Program for Feminist 'Consciousness Raising,'" 1968, box 1, folder 55, all in Women's Liberation Research Files.

44. Rudolph O. de la Garza, quoted in Roth, *Separate Roads to Feminism*, 135.

45. Chicano Youth Liberation Conference, quoted in Roth, *Separate Roads to Feminism*, 134.

46. Francisca Flores, quoted in Roth, *Separate Roads to Feminism*, 138.

47. Leticia Hernández, quoted in Roth, *Separate Roads to Feminism*, 140.

48. Leticia Wiggins, "'Women Need to Find Their Voice': Latinas Speak out in the Midwest, 1972," in Espinoza, Cotera, and Blackwell, *Chicana Movidas*, 80.

49. Bread and Roses, "Outreach Leaflet," 1970, in Baxandall and Gordon, *Dear Sisters*, 35.

CHAPTER 5

SECOND-WAVE FEMINISM AND THE RIGHTS REVOLUTION

INTRODUCTION

Since the 1980s, journalists, activists, and historians have asked whether the second-wave feminist movement succeeded. If the answer is yes, this chapter provides the evidence. By the 1970s, a robust organizational infrastructure made it possible for women to make real changes in their lives. In this decade alone, women gained tremendous access to previously male-dominated professions, educational programs, formal politics, and—through changing laws governing reproductive control—the same kinds of sexual autonomy and agency that men experienced.

But the answer to this perennial question depends on the metric one uses to evaluate it. In the examples provided above, *access* is the key word. To some feminists, equal access to such institutions as the capitalist economy and representative democracy was the goal; recall NOW's goal "to bring women into full participation in the mainstream of American society now." This chapter leaves open for the moment the question of whether second-wave feminists succeeded in changing these institutions themselves.

WORKPLACE JUSTICE

By the late 1960s, the relationship between feminists and the Equal Employment Opportunity Commission (EEOC) had changed, thanks in part to the efforts of agency staffer Aileen Hernandez and legal counsel Sonia Pressman. Both members of NOW (Hernandez was its first president), the two women were instrumental in convincing the EEOC to change its position on sex-segregated help-wanted ads and to maintain a narrow definition of bona fide occupational qualifications (BFOQs). As a child, Pressman and her German Jewish parents had immigrated to the United States in the midst of Hitler's rise to power. This background provided Pressman with an intimate understanding of persecution, and she became a double agent of sorts within an agency originally inclined to be conservative on sex discrimination issues. For her troubles, she earned the reputation of being a "sex maniac."

Once the EEOC declared that organizing job postings into "Help Wanted—Female" and "Help Wanted—Male" categories violated Title VII, feminists were emboldened to tackle other forms of workplace discrimination. Frequently backed by the NOW Legal Defense and Education Fund—inspired by the NAACP body of the same name—these included successful challenges to the steel industry and AT&T, the nation's single largest employer of women. By 1970, it also accounted for fully 7 percent of EEOC complaints. Scared into compliance by twenty-five thousand pages of evidence that the EEOC had compiled against them, by 1973, AT&T had established goals and timetables for hiring women and minorities, and they had provided back pay to thirteen thousand women and two thousand minority men. Women also won changes at retailer Sears Roebuck & Company, the nation's second-largest employer of women, which, in almost all cases, restricted opportunities to earn commissions and advancement to men. In 1978, more than 550 women employed by the New York Times won a class-action sex discrimination lawsuit.

Professional women founded a number of new organizations to investigate and protect themselves from workplace discrimination. In 1968, a group of federal civil servants founded Federally Employed Women, or FEW, which emphasized the group's small numbers. In a three-year period (1968–71), academic women founded some fifty groups aimed at gender discrimination within their disciplines. When Bernice Sandler, who received her doctorate in education from the University of Maryland, could not find a tenure-track position, she sensed a pattern and began to investigate. At her behest, the Women's Equity Action League (WEAL) asked the Department of Labor to assess all federally funded colleges and

Women Protesting Sears, ca. 1968–77. In 1974, the EEOC launched a sex discrimination lawsuit against Sears Roebuck and Company. Though a federal court ruled in favor in Sears twelve years later, negative publicity resulting from the case led the company to increase hiring of women and minorities. (Women Protesting Sears, ca. 1968–77. National Organization for Women. Philadelphia Chapter Records, 1968–1977 [2054], Historical Society of Pennsylvania. Reproduced with permission from the Historical Society of Pennsylvania.)

universities for nondiscrimination compliance. WEAL also charged 250 institutions with specific instances of sex discrimination. In response, colleges and universities reexamined both hiring and admissions practices. Prior to the 1970s, many graduate and professional schools, including law schools and medical schools, had in place quotas and other measures designed to limit how many women could be admitted to the program. Once these limitations were lifted, women's presence in such programs increased rapidly. Only 7.5 percent of medical school graduates in 1969, women composed more than 19 percent of this group just seven years later.

These developments resonated outside the professional sector. Women were increasingly moving into previously male-dominated jobs in the closely guarded segments of labor such as construction, electrical installation and repair, and high-commission sales. In the 1970s and early '80s, women launched a vigorous campaign to gain access to these positions. To feminists, this was a long-overdue corrective and a symbolic compensation to the "Rosies" who had been pushed back into traditionally female jobs after World War II. By 1983, women held some 105,000 of the nation's construction jobs. While this number constituted only 2 percent of the industry's labor force, it was a substantial gain.

Alice Peurala's efforts to open up the steel industry were crucial. Born in 1928 in Saint Louis to Armenian immigrant parents, Peurala absorbed her father's commitment to justice for working people. She first joined a union while working in the service industries as a teenager in the 1940s, during which time she also participated in Congress of Racial Equality–led sit-ins and attended the convention at which the Progressive Party nominated Henry Wallace as its presidential candidate. After moving to Chicago with a friend at age twenty-two, she was fired from her job in an electrical factory over suspicions that she was a communist. In 1953, she began working for the U.S. Steel Corporation at its South Works plant, joining Local 65 of the United Steelworkers of America (USWA). Many of the women who had worked at South Works during World War II had long since been laid off by the time the company hired Peurala as a metallurgical observer, a position she balanced with care for her young daughter, Jami.

When Jami started school, Peurala hoped to exchange her unpredictable schedule for a regular day shift. Routinely rebuffed by her supervisors, she saw men whom she had trained promoted over her. Though Peurala's boss openly confessed to her that the company did not want women in these positions, the official reason was always quite different:

> I had been asking my boss for consideration for one of those jobs [in the metallurgical department]. They kept telling me that there weren't any openings, or that they had other people in mind for them. They never posted any of these jobs. You could never bid on them. You just didn't know about them. All of a sudden, somebody you are working with is moved up. When you inquired, you got pretty vague answers. . . . Then the Civil Rights Act was passed in 1964, and I thought, here's my chance. In the fall of 1967 near the end of that year, a guy that I had broke in, who had about four years of service, was going to move up into the main lab. . . . I

called the man who was in charge of hiring people for that job and asked him if I could be considered. He said, "No, we don't want any women on these jobs." I said, "But it's against the law, you can't keep me from any job because I'm a woman. Would you put that in writing?" He said, "No, I don't think so; I'll have to think about it." A few days later, the boss came over and told me that officially the reason I was not selected for the job was that I did not have the educational background and that I couldn't work overtime, and that there was heavy lifting on the job that I couldn't handle.[1]

Peurala filed a grievance with the union and then an official complaint with the EEOC, which found that the company's reasons for refusing to promote Peurala did not hold water—they either applied equally to her male colleagues or were irrelevant to the position. In 1969, Peurala won her case in court.

After moving into her new, long-sought position as a product tester, Peurala became involved in USWA politics. The union had given her little help during her sex discrimination suit, and in the early 1970s, union leadership seemed divorced from rank-and-file priorities. By the middle of the decade, however, the union became a staunch supporter of gender and racial equality, including the Equal Rights Amendment and affirmative action. Within a two-year period (1977–79), women's employment in the steel industry rose by 20 percent. Peurala was elected to the local's grievance committee, formed a women's committee within the local, and in 1979 was elected president of Local 65—the first woman in the nation to hold such a position in the steel industry. By convincing USWA leadership that opening jobs to women was in the union's best interests, Peurala and others remapped assumptions about men's and women's work.

In 1974, Peurala became a founding member of the Coalition of Labor Union Women (CLUW), a cross-union organization made possible by connections forged in the PCSW, NOW, and other feminist political groups. Though many members knew one another from other kinds of activism, it was rare for an organization to bring together women from different unions *as union members*, and the excitement at the endeavor showed: more than three thousand women attended CLUW's founding meeting. From the beginning, CLUW benefited from the presence of women whose leadership skills had been cultivated over the course of decades; for example, Addie Wyatt, a leader in the meatpackers union and a longtime advocate for workplace justice for Black women, became its vice president. Wyatt and others like her trained a new generation of women leader labors. CLUW's ties to traditional organized labor, however, sometimes hampered its efficacy. More hierarchical than many other feminist organizations, CLUW assiduously avoided the appearance of competition with individual unions, and it did not include unorganized workers.

Also starting in 1974, a group comprising both clerical workers and women's liberation movement veterans pioneered a new labor organization inspired by Saul Alinsky's community-organizing techniques and César Chávez's farmworkers' union. Originally named Women Employed (WE), the group quickly became 9to5, which represented clerical workers across the nation.[2] Borrowing the techniques of the women's liberation movement, 9to5 used consciousness raising and widely distributed questionnaires to identify patterns in how women were treated in the workplace, later publicizing information about unequal pay; barriers to advancement; and other problems through press releases, flyers, and protests. They also brought suit against a number of major companies. In 1980, the experiences of actual 9to5 members informed a film of the same name. Jane Fonda, who starred in the film alongside Dolly Parton and Lily Tomlin, knew one of the group's early members through her anti-war work and arranged for women clerical workers to teach the film's writers and cast about their lives. Though exaggerated for comedic effect, the film reflected the real experiences of female clerical workers.

These experiences included rampant workplace objectification and sexual harassment. Feminist groups protested this treatment, including a successful challenge to weight requirements for airline stewardesses. Routinely fired when they reached a certain age, married, or gained weight, stewardesses were also required to wear demeaning "fly me" buttons. NOW lobbied the Federal Communications Commission (FCC) to deny licenses to television stations that denigrated women, taking aim not just at the fact that producers, directors, and editors were overwhelmingly men but also the high beauty standards for women, even in serious places such as the news. In 1973, the organization launched a public service ad campaign satirizing the frequency with which women were hired (or not hired) based on their looks. In it, a man in business attire lifts his pant legs to reveal shapely calves. "Hire him. He's got great legs," the caption reads.

If applying this standard to men seemed absurd, the ad implied, applying it to women was equally so.[3]

Beyond affecting hiring practices, the objectification of women in the workplace contributed to a culture in which sexual harassment was, if not actively encouraged, at least tacitly accepted. Eleanor Holmes Norton, Washington, DC, delegate to Congress, and Supreme Court justice Ruth Bader Ginsburg developed ingenious legal rationales against this practice. A former SNCC activist who had traveled to Atlantic City with the Mississippi Freedom Democratic Party (MFDP) in 1964, Norton was a protégé of Pauli Murray, Yale Law School graduate, cofounder of the National Black Feminist Organization, and cofounder (with Ginsburg) of the ACLU Women's Rights Project. While at the ACLU, she represented women pursuing a class-action lawsuit against *Newsweek*. Irritated when the magazine hired the wife of a senior editor rather than a female staff member to write an article on women's liberation, female staffers soon recognized a pattern in their exclusion from staff writer positions. With the help of Norton, the ACLU, and the EEOC, women at *Newsweek* won important changes. Norton's work with the ACLU thus flowed seamlessly into her tenure as head of the EEOC (1977–81), where she pushed the agency to greater efforts on behalf of women and minorities and established guidelines against sexual harassment in the workplace.

Continuing on at the ACLU Women's Rights Project, Ginsburg pursued other means of tearing down the legal underpinnings of sex discrimination. Her own knowledge of these practices was hard-won. As a student at Harvard Law School, the dean made Ginsburg and the eight other women in the class describe to faculty members what they were going to do with their degrees that would justify taking spots that would otherwise go to men. Then, despite graduating at the top of her class and serving on the law review at both Harvard and Columbia, she graduated without a single job offer. When she finally did find a job, she found that she was being left out of important meetings held at men-only clubs. After she read Simone de Beauvior's *The Second Sex* and began teaching classes on women and the law, Ginsburg "caught fire."[4]

Ginsburg's legal practice focused on several different aspects of sex discrimination. Her first case for the ACLU challenged a state law mandating the firing of any public school teacher who became pregnant. Again, this case grew out of her personal experience—her employer had demoted her as a result of her first pregnancy, and she carefully hid her second. Along with other cases, her work contributed to the passage of the 1978 Pregnancy Discrimination Act, which amended the Civil Rights Act to make pregnancy a protected category. She also argued that sex discrimination and stereotypes hurt everyone, men and women alike. To make this point, she chose her cases carefully, taking on, for example, the case of a widower who had been denied his wife's social security benefits. Finally, like Norton, Ginsburg contributed significantly to Americans' understanding of sexual harassment, arguing in several cases that it constituted a form of sex discrimination and thus violated Title VII. Norton and Ginsburg's activism on this subject paid off in 1985, when the Supreme Court ruled that sexual harassment did indeed violate workers' civil rights.

LEGISLATIVE AND ELECTORAL POLITICS

In the late 1960s, and especially the '70s, second-wave feminism and the rights revolution propelled women into formal electoral politics as never before. Fannie Lou Hamer, who had been poorly treated at the 1964 Democratic National Convention, was a keynote speaker four years later. In 1971, she and some three hundred other women gathered in Washington, DC, to found the National Women's Political Caucus (NWPC). NWPC membership represented an interracial, cross-class coalition. In addition to Hamer, it included Betty Friedan; Ms. magazine cofounder Gloria Steinem; congresswomen Bella Abzug and Shirley Chisolm; LaDonna Harris, a leader in the Native American movement; civil rights activist Myrlie Evers; NCNW president Dorothy Height; Olga Madar, UAW leader and later a founding member of CLUW; and NWRO vice president Beulah Sanders.

With a goal to "end racism, sexism, institutional violence and poverty through the election and appointment of women to public office, party reform, and the support of women's issues and feminist candidates across party lines," the NWPC sought early on to increase women's presence at each party's nominating convention in 1972. Its success in this endeavor was significant: female delegates to the Republican convention rose from 15 to 30 percent and to the Democratic convention from 13 to 40 percent. Democratic candidate George McGovern was particularly receptive to the NWPC, which meant that women attained visibility and influence within his campaign.

More significant than women's participation in McGovern's campaign, however, was NWPC member Shirley Chisholm's own presidential run. In 1968, after serving for three years in the New York State Assembly, Chisholm became the first Black woman elected to Congress. There, she supported such programs as Head Start, school lunches, and food stamps, and she belonged to the Congressional Black Caucus and the Congressional Women's Caucus from their founding. She also vocally opposed the Vietnam War. In 1972, she became the first woman and the first African American to run for the nomination of a major party.

Born in Brooklyn to Barbadian immigrant parents, Chisholm spent her childhood going back and forth between these locales. When she was three years old, in 1928, her parents sent Chisholm and her two younger sisters to live with her grandmother in Barbados, hoping to save enough money to provide stable futures for their daughters in the United States. Despite unpropitious times, the girls returned to Brooklyn six years later, in the midst of the Great Depression. The family's Brownsville neighborhood was mostly white and Jewish, a group that decades later would make up a substantial portion of Chisholm's constituency in New York's Twelfth Congressional District. Her father was a devoted Garveyite, and he and his friends would stay up late into the night discussing racial and labor politics (Chisholm's father was a proud member of the Confectionery and Bakers International Union). When he was not working or politicking, he instilled in Chisholm and her sisters a rigorous work ethic, especially regarding their educations. In 1936, the family moved to Bedford-Stuyvestant, where a bigger apartment could better accommodate their growing daughters. But the Depression ground on, and a new job did not provide Chisholm's father with the additional income he had hoped for. Her mother was forced to find work as a domestic for white families. In the meantime, though Bed-Stuy was approximately 50 percent Black (including growing numbers of migrants from the South, who according to Chisholm demonstrated disappointingly little racial consciousness), the neighborhood was riven with racial conflict in a way that Brownsville had not been.

Still, Chisholm excelled in the face of hardship, garnering honors of many kinds at Girls High, from which she graduated in 1942, and receiving scholarship offers from Vassar, Oberlin, and other colleges. Concerned about the cost of room and board, however, she enrolled that fall at Brooklyn College, where she planned to study teaching, one of the few paths open to educated Black women. Writing about these years in 1970, Chisholm revealed the continuing influence of her Garveyite father: "If I had gone to Vassar," she recalled, "the rest of my life might have been different. Would I have become one of the pseudo-white upper-middle-class black women professionals, or a doctor's wife with furs, limousines, clubs, and airs? I can't believe that would have happened, but one never knows."[5] Brooklyn College was mostly white, but its campus hummed with political activity, and professors and fellow students alike encouraged Chisholm to get involved. After graduating cum laude in 1946, she started attending the meetings of a city Democratic Club, often challenging unwritten mores of race, gender, and bossism. She demanded the right to speak and the right to ask questions about issues that were important to her. For a time she worked with Wesley McD. (Mac) Holder, a Guianian immigrant, former newspaper editor, and political insurgent. Holder founded the Bedford-Stuyvesant Political League (BSPL) with the goal of electing Black candidates, and until she challenged his leadership, Chisholm was his trusted lieutenant. In 1960, the Unity Democratic Club took over the BSPL's mission, and four years later, it nominated Chisholm as its candidate for the New York State Assembly.

Between on-the-ground organizing and office holding, Chisholm had spent over twenty years in politics by 1972. In January that year, Chisholm announced her presidential campaign in Brooklyn, New York, parts of which she represented in Congress. Addressing a national audience, she highlighted her universal appeal: "I am not the candidate of black American, although I am black and proud. I am not the candidate of the women's movement of this country, although I am a woman and I'm equally proud of that. . . . I am the candidate of the people of America." Yet she was unafraid to stake out controversial positions, criticizing, among other ills, the war in Vietnam, environmental destruction, the undue influence of the elite on politics, and the amorality of the Nixon administration. She especially encouraged greater plurality in American politics: "[We must] open our societies to the energies and abilities of countless new kinds of groups of Americans—women, blacks, browns, Indians, Orientals, and youth, so that they can develop their own full potential and thereby participate equally and enthusiastically in building a strong and just society." She believed that the country was ready for a president who was not necessarily white and male.[6]

Chisholm's candidacy, however, faced opposition from both expected and unexpected sources. As campaign worker Robert Gottlieb recalled, he arrived at his very first campaign stop in North Carolina to find his luggage defaced with the message "go home, n—r." Chisholm received support from Black women and students, but white feminists rallied around McGovern, as did Black men, including such prominent national figures as Jesse Jackson, John Conyers Jr., and Julian Bond. In the end, Chisholm's candidacy garnered only 152 delegates at the Democratic National Convention. McGovern's delegate count, by contrast, was overwhelming enough that he did not have to make any concessions to Chisholm—such as a Black running mate or a woman in the Cabinet—in exchange for her delegates.[7]

But to Chisholm, failure to secure the nomination did not define her legacy. As she put it less than a year before her death in 2005, "I want history to remember me not just as the first black woman to be elected to Congress, not as the first black woman to have made a bid for the presidency of the United States, but as a black woman who lived in the 20th century and dared to be herself. I want to be remembered as a catalyst for change in America."[8]

Her actions after 1972 bore this perspective out. Though Chisholm was disappointed that so few NWPC members offered anything but symbolic support for her presidential campaign, she was still on hand to help organize the group's founding convention in Houston, Texas, in 1973. Few commentators failed to notice the striking diversity of the 1,500 women gathered. "We were struck by the astonishing diversity of the crowd," wrote an attendee from Minnesota, "and to be in the midst of it was a kaleidoscopic delight."[9] While these different constituencies sometimes butted heads over procedure and representation, their presence also generated real results. The NWPC established permanent minority caucuses for Black, Latina, and Native American women, with guaranteed representation on the National Steering Committee. Later, permanent caucuses represented Asian Americans, lesbians, and others. "The air is shivery with possibilities," observed writer Toni Morrison of this diverse gathering of women.[10] Later that year, Black women from NOW and the

NWPC founded the National Black Feminist Organization (NBFO), discussed in the next chapter.

THE EQUAL RIGHTS AMENDMENT

In 1969, the EEOC ruled that women-only protective legislation violated Title VII of the Civil Rights Act, ending a nearly fifty-year rift in the feminist movement and encouraging it to rally around the ERA. Between 1970 and 1972, women's groups including the NWPC mounted a massive campaign in support of the measure, generating more mail on Capitol Hill than the Vietnam War. The Nixon administration technically supported the ERA, appointing in 1970 a Task Force on Women's Rights and Responsibilities. But the administration quickly suppressed the resulting report, *A Matter of Simple Justice*, until Women's Bureau head Elizabeth Koonz secured its publication some months later. Far beyond endorsing the ERA, the report urged a much more active role for government in securing equality.

In the meantime, grassroots activists demanded immediate action, as twenty Pittsburgh NOW members interrupted a congressional hearing. Longtime ERA supporter and congresswoman Martha Griffiths heeded their call, working to secure enough signatures from her colleagues to allow the ERA to bypass a committee vote in the House. The ERA passed both houses of Congress in March 1972, forty-nine years after it was first introduced.

Later that year, in expansive planks calling for greater rights for women, both party platforms endorsed ratification. By the end of 1972, twenty-two of the necessary thirty-five states had done so. Reflecting on the passage of not only the ERA but also Title IX, the expansion of the EEOC's mandate, and tax exemptions for working parents, Bella Abzug noted that 1972 was "a watershed year. We put sex discrimination provisions into everything. There was no opposition. Who'd be against equal rights for women? So we just kept passing women's rights legislation."[11] That same year, feminist policymakers and activists began advocating, researching, and drafting versions of the Women's Education Equity Act, which tackled both material and cultural biases in the educational system, and the Equal Credit Opportunity Act, which officially ended common discriminatory practices against women in the credit industry, which regularly

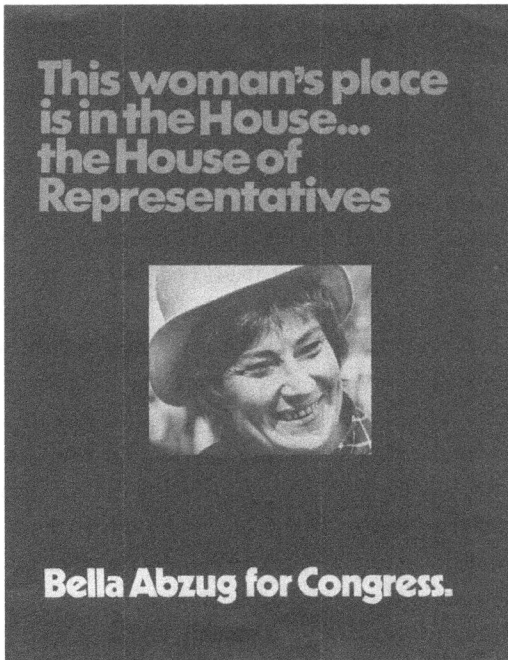

This woman's place
is in the House...
the House of
Representatives

Bella Abzug for Congress.

Campaign flier for Congresswoman Bella Abzug, Democratic representative from New York from 1971 until 1977. A frequent sponsor of feminist legislation, Abzug launched her first congressional campaign with a cheeky nod to domesticity. (Collection of the U.S. House of Representatives)

denied them access to consumer credit and often refused to consider their income in mortgage applications. Both policies became law in 1974.

TITLE IX

In 1972, the same year that Congress passed the ERA, it adopted Title IX of the Higher Education Act. It read: "No person in the United States shall, on the basis of sex, be excluded from participation in, be denied the benefits of, or be subjected to discrimination under any educational program or activity receiving federal financial assistance." In recent years, Title IX has become an important tool in the fight against on-campus sexual assault. Before that, it was best known for its effects on women's athletic participation. In 1971, a year before Title IX became law, girls and women made up only 7 percent of high school athletes and 2 percent of college athletes. By 2001, those numbers had changed to 41.5 percent and 43 percent, respectively.

The provision's key architects, however, had not really had either issue in mind. Rather, they were focused on such discriminatory practices as the higher grade point averages required of women for admission to some state universities and caps on enrollment in graduate and professional schools, none of which the Civil Rights Act had addressed (see chapter 3). After Bernice Sandler finished her PhD, a friend told her of the difficulties finding a job came from the fact that she "[came] on too strong for a woman." One potential employer told her that he would not hire women because they took too many absences to care for their children; another told her that she was "not really a professional[,] just a housewife who went back to school." These and other similar practices had been well documented in both 1970 and 1971, when representative Edith Green of Oregon, who first introduced a version of the bill, held hearings on discrimination against women in educational institutions. As representative Patsy Mink of Hawaii recalled amid the bill's thirtieth anniversary in 2002, "When it [Title IX] was proposed, we had no idea that its most visible impact would be in athletics. I had been paying attention to the academic issue. I had been excluded from medical school because I was female." Sports barely featured in hearings or debates about the bill.[12]

At first glance, this absence makes sense: college sports were not federally funded. But the law applied to *all* parts of institutions that received *any* federal funding, not just the programs that this funding targeted. At many schools, sports—often exemplified by football—were a glaringly obvious site of discriminatory spending. (Opponents of Title IX have often claimed that football revenue pays for other athletic programs, but the vast majority of football programs do not even break even.)

In 1979, the Department of Health, Education, and Welfare (HEW) circulated three-pronged guidelines for implementation. To safeguard funding, schools had to demonstrate compliance with at least one of these prongs:

1. Is athletic participation *proportional* to the general student population?
2. Does the school consistently attempt to develop programming to meet the *interests* of the underrepresented sex?
3. Do the school's current programs meet the *interests* of the underrepresented sex?

Since its passage, opponents of Title IX have insisted that women are simply less interested in sports. The second and third prongs of the HEW guidelines address this argument. Women's sports leaders have developed what became known as the *Field of Dreams* rationale: "If you build it [women's athletic programs], they will come." Courts, too, have been reluctant to see women's supposed lack of interest as justification for flouting Title IX. As a federal appeals court put it in 1996, "To assert that Title IX permits institutions to provide fewer athletics opportunities for women than for men, based on the premise that women are less interested in sports than men, is (among other things) to ignore the fact that Title IX was enacted in order to remedy discrimination that results from stereotyped notions of women's interests and abilities."[13]

Such stereotypes had a long history. Though girls found opportunities for exercise in schools, YWCAs, and settlement houses, vigorous exercise and notions of white, middle-class, heterosexual adult femininity coexisted uneasily. As Bil Gilbert and Nancy Williamson put it in a *Sports Illustrated* article in 1973, women who persisted in their athletic pursuits were "apt to be subjected to social and psychological pressures, the effect of which is to cast doubts on her morals, sanity and womanhood." Individual sports including figure skating, tennis, and golf—largely the province of elite white women—have received more cultural approbation than have team sports like softball and basketball. Many women, too, shied away from sports in response to homophobic associations between women athletes and lesbians. As recently as 1971, the year before Title IX was implemented, a Connecticut judge justified banning girls from a high school track team on the basis that "athletic competition builds character in our boys. We do not need that kind of character in our girls, the women of tomorrow."[14]

Women's sports would have grown without Title IX. As Cold War competition fueled the growth—and growing importance—of the Olympics, women's athletics took on a political cast. The growing women's movement challenged stereotypes about the female body, insisting that it was not merely decorative. In 1973, for example, tennis player Billie Jean King's famous "Battle of the Sexes" victory over self-avowed chauvinist Bobby Riggs became a media spectacle, drawing new attention to these changing ideas about women's bodies.

Though Title IX brought much more visibility to women's sports, it also threatened the autonomy and even viability of independent women's

Tennis player Billie Jean King. One year after the implementation of Title IX, King brought greater attention to women's sports with her victory over Bobby Riggs. King continues to advocate for equality for female athletes today. (Jerry Coli | Dreamstime.com)

sports organizations. In response to these changes, in 1966 women's sports leaders founded the Commission on Intercollegiate Athletics for Women (CIAW) to expand opportunities for women college athletes. In 1972, the Association for Intercollegiate Athletics for Women (AIAW) expanded the group's mission as a national membership organization. The National Collegiate Athletic Association (NCAA) had opposed Title IX from the start, arguing first for the exclusion of sports in general and then at least of revenue-generating sports. But when its implementation became inevitable, NCAA leaders decided that they might as well try to harness the moneymaking potential of women's sports for themselves. The CIAW, and then the AIAW, had begun holding a series of national championships for women's sports in the late 1970s. The NCAA began holding a series of competing tournaments at the same time, offering financial incentives that the women's organizations could not match. By 1982, the AIAW had closed its doors, and with it went the opportunity for a different ethos of collegiate athletic competition.

REPRODUCTIVE RIGHTS AND THE BODY

Feminists of all stripes were also determined to gain more control over their bodies, as access to birth control and safe, legal abortion became important priorities. Illegal abortions were dangerous and expensive, and women could only obtain legal abortions by giving a humiliating testimony in front of doctors and hospital administrators to prove why the pregnancy was a threat to their health. Judicious estimates suggested that between five hundred and one thousand women died from illegal abortions per year in the early to mid-1960s, the majority of them women of color. And at this time, even access to birth control was not guaranteed in many states.

In the early twentieth century, distributing birth control was illegal under obscenity laws. Though most pre–World War I American feminists believed that birth control was central to their cause, Margaret Sanger took up the issue with unmatched vigor, focus, and longevity. Like Alice Paul with suffrage and, later, the ERA, Sanger was largely a one-issue activist.

Born in 1879, Sanger was drawn to birth control through both her training as a nurse and her personal background; she believed that her mother's life had been shortened by the constant cycle of pregnancy and childhood. Sanger argued instead for the importance of voluntary motherhood, the idea that women should be able to choose when, if, how many, and under what circumstances they had children. This was not a new idea—important nineteenth-century proponents included reformer Mary Gove Nichols—but it became much more prominent through Sanger's advocacy.

After moving to New York City in 1911, Sanger became involved in socialist and feminist circles. In 1912, she published a series of articles in *Call* magazine titled "What Every Girl Should Know." Articles discussed male and female physiology in depth; described sex as natural, clean, and healthy; and educated readers on venereal diseases. The U.S. Post Office declared the last article unmailable under the Comstock law, and a frustrated Sanger left for Paris. There, she was exposed to the widespread efficacy of birth control in France, and she studied with the radical sexologist Havelock Ellis, who believed, among other tenets, that homosexuality should not be considered deviant.

Back in New York, Sanger broke with the Socialist Party and began an independent paper, *The Woman Rebel*. It appeared seven times in 1914 before being suppressed by the Post Office. She then wrote a pamphlet titled *Family Limitation*, one hundred thousand copies of which were printed and distributed by the Industrial Workers of the World (IWW), a radical labor organization. In it, she recommended and explained a variety of contraceptive methods (of varying efficacy), including douches, condoms, pessaries, sponges, and suppositories. While promising that birth control would make abortion unnecessary, she nonetheless defended women's right to have abortions (a position she later reversed), even recommending an abortifacient. She presented birth control in terms of class struggle, writing that "the working class can use direct action by refusing to supply the market with children to be exploited, by refusing to populate the world with slaves." This economic argument resonated deeply later, amid the Great Depression of the 1930s.

In 1916, Sanger organized a clinic in the Brownsville section of Brooklyn, then an extremely poor Jewish and Italian immigrant neighborhood. She distributed to every family in the district a handbill printed in English, Yiddish, and Italian. The clinic did not provide women with contraceptives; rather, it provided patients with the principles of contraception and showed them a cervical pessary. Still, women lined up outside when the clinic opened on October 16, and after nine days, the staff had collected case histories of 464 women. Unfortunately, one patient turned out to be a policewoman, who confiscated all the clinic's equipment and case histories. Sanger and her sister, Rose Byrne, were tried separately and each sentenced to thirty days on Blackwell's Island.

After World War I, Sanger became much more conservative. She realized that she needed to appeal to the middle class, and she increasingly emphasized the importance of experts and, at times, even advocated eugenics. As the eugenics movement grew in popularity, she saw in its emphasis on family limitation a way to further her own cause. Her embrace of pseudoscience was thus in large part opportunistic, not ideological, though it still led her to advocate some seriously inhumane policies, such as forced sterilization and immigration restriction. This complicated figure went on to play a key role in the development of the birth control pill, perhaps the most important twentieth-century scientific advancement for women.

It was in this broader historical context that Estelle Griswold, executive director of the Planned Parenthood Federation of Connecticut, was arrested in 1961 for providing a married couple with birth control instruction in violation of an 1879 state law forbidding any aid given "for the purpose of preventing contraception." Connecticut's "Barnum law"—named for its champion, circus promoter, and Connecticut state lawmaker P. T. Barnum—went further than the federal Comstock law, which banned sending birth control through the mails. Despite yearly pleas from birth control advocates, the legislature refused to change the law, often citing specious or nonexistent evidence to support this decision. As recently as 1955, a Hartford doctor testified to the legislature that "psychiatrists have noted that the problem child's behavior can be traced to the emotionally unstable and sexually frustrated mother using birth control measures."[15] Intransigent lawmakers prompted Griswold to found a referral service that arranged for and provided transportation to neighboring states with less draconian restrictions.

An unsuccessful challenge to the law in 1943 nonetheless suggested that the courts might provide a way forward. One doctor challenged the law on the basis that it restricted his ability to practice medicine. The Supreme Court rejected this argument, noting that the law posed no challenge to *his* rights. The decision left open the possibility, however, that the law might in fact limit patients' constitutional rights. Bearing this precedent in mind, Griswold and her allies gathered a group of four women (along with, in three cases, their husbands) to challenge the law. But in *Poe v. Ullman* (1961), the Supreme Court sidestepped the question of the actual law, finding in a five-to-four decision that the plaintiffs had no case because Connecticut had never prosecuted women under its auspices. Then, borrowing a page from Sanger's playbook, Griswold opened a Planned Parenthood League in New Haven. As she had hoped, two police officers showed up within four days.

Both Griswold's actions and the swift legal retribution she received suggest that much had remained the same between 1916 and 1961. But much had also changed—legally, scientifically, and culturally. A series of Supreme Court cases had chipped away at the legal mechanisms barring the dissemination of birth control (or information about it), and more liberal attitudes toward sexuality had developed. In 1930, the court found in *Youngs Rubber Corporation v. C.I. Lee & Co.*, *et al.*, which dealt with a trademark infringement case between two condom companies, that condoms (and, by extension, other forms of birth control) could be sold legally for other purposes. This decision led to a mass market for birth control products euphemistically marketed as health or hygiene products. In 1936, the *United States v. One Package of Japanese Pessaries* decision made it legal for doctors to send and receive contraceptive devices and information, effectively invalidating the long reach of the Comstock law. The following year, 1937, the American Medical Association (AMA) lifted its ban on doctors prescribing birth control.

The availability of condoms in drugstores and birth control prescriptions from private doctors made remaining restrictions seem hypocritical and arbitrary. In 1960, the FDA approved the first birth control pill, Enovid, which provided women with a convenient, reliable way to prevent pregnancy without having to insert a diaphragm or rely on men to use condoms. Then, too, despite the progress that the Equal Pay Act and Civil Rights Act represented, it remained legal to discriminate against pregnant workers—including by firing them—until 1978. Pregnancy thus meant the possibility of lost income.

Though Griswold and her colleague were initially found guilty, Griswold and her lawyers, Tom Emerson and Catherine Roraback, took the case all the way to the Supreme Court. A lifelong defender of civil liberties, Roraback had defended members of the Communist Party in the Smith Act trials of the previous decade and would defend members of the Black Panther Party in the next. Emerson, a law professor, argued in court that the state must respect the private, personal nature of a married couple's home life. In 1965, seven of the court's nine justices accepted this argument, determining in *Griswold v. Connecticut* that marriage constituted a "zone of privacy" into which the government could not incur. Though the Constitution did not explicitly protect privacy, some fifty years of legal precedent had found it in the fifth and fourteenth amendments. In 1972, the court's *Eisenstadt v. Baird* decision extended this right to unmarried (heterosexual) couples. "If the right of privacy means anything," liberal justice William Brennan argued in *Eisenstadt*, "it is the right of the individual, married or single, to be free from unwarranted governmental intrusion into matters so fundamentally affecting a person as the decision whether to bear or beget a child."[16]

Eight years after *Griswold* and one year after *Eisenstadt*, the concept of privacy determined the outcome of *Roe v. Wade*, which overturned state laws banning abortion. Jane Roe was the pseudonym of Norma McCorvey, an unmarried pregnant woman whose name headed up a class-action lawsuit challenging an 1879 Texas law criminalizing abortion. McCorvey was represented in front of the Supreme Court by Sarah Weddington, a twenty-five-year-old lawyer who had herself experienced hardship finding a safe and legal way to have an abortion. In fall 1969, Weddington, then a recent law school graduate, was among the founders of a group that focused on referring women to doctors who performed abortions.[17] By 1973, the group had referred more than six thousand women. Its members also began to think about challenging the legal restrictions on abortion. In Texas, it was illegal even in cases of rape and incest. But Weddington and others felt that, outside the state, legal precedent might offer some hope.

By the late 1960s, a loosely connected, somewhat surprising network of activists ranging from established feminist groups to women's liberationists to liberal clergy members had formed to challenge restrictions on abortion. In San Francisco, Patricia Maginnis helped found the Society for Humane Abortion, which fought against abortion laws and referred women to doctors who performed the procedure. In Chicago, college student Heather Booth, who eventually founded the abortion rights group Jane, began performing similar referral work in 1965. In 1970, members of Jane began performing abortions themselves. Their safety record over the next three years matched what doctors attained in legal procedures. The Clergy Consultation Service on Abortion, founded in New York City in 1967, also provided referrals. Though initially reluctant to embrace the issue, NOW included an abortion plank in its 1968 Bill of Rights. Betty Friedan, who eventually supported this inclusion, also participated in early discussions toward what in 1969 became the National Association for the Repeal of Abortion Laws (NARAL), of which Shirley Chisholm became honorary president.

In the mid-1960s, the unexpected intervened in the form of a rubella outbreak, which caused serious birth defects in many cases. As state lawmakers debated easing abortion restrictions in such cases, the topic became a matter of public discourse. In March 1970, Hawaii became the first state to legalize abortion.

A more dramatic contest over repealing New York's 1830 law outlawing abortion began that same month. The previous year, in 1969, a group of women interrupted the proceedings of a New York legislative committee hearing about abortion. Those invited to testify included fourteen men and one woman, a nun. Refused the opportunity to speak, the women then held a public "speak-out" on the topic, sharing their own stories and transforming their abortions from secrets they had learned to be ashamed of into collective political experiences. Within the legislative chamber, Republican assemblywoman Constance Cook had for years spearheaded efforts to repeal the state law, cultivating relationships with and support from experts and activists. Born in Ohio in 1919, Cook received her undergraduate and law degrees from Cornell University. She worked for a private law firm and then as legal assistant to assemblyman Ray S. Ashberry. Upon his 1962 retirement, she ran successfully for his seat. Later in the 1970s, Cook took on the cause of women's ordination, successfully representing Rev. Betty Bone Schiess to the EEOC.

As one of only four women in the state legislature and the repeal bill's author and sponsor, Cook confronted the task of convincing her male colleagues to support the measure. After hours of debate, one unsuccessful vote, and a second that also seemed to fail, Democratic assemblyman George M. Michaels tearfully asked to change his vote, knowing that it augured the end of his political career. Abortion officially became legal in New York State on July 1, 1970.

Though Roe v. Wade took the issue out of states' hands three years later, these early contests remain significant. In the New York legislature as in the nation, views on abortion did not break along party lines. Many Republicans supported reform, and many Democrats did not. In New York, Republican governor Nelson Rockefeller made it clear from the beginning that he supported repeal, as did Perry Duryea Jr., the Republican speaker of the assembly (who eventually cast the deciding vote in that body). Especially among Catholics, religion determined an individual's views on abortion much more than party did. Over the course of the next decade, these alignments would shift amid a resurgent conservative movement, most notably the rise of the Religious Right.

Seeds of this shift appeared early on. Preparing for his reelection campaign in 1972, President Richard Nixon and his advisors saw an opportunity to peel the votes of conservative Catholics away from the Democratic Party. In a letter to Cardinal Terence Cooke, the Catholic archbishop of New York, Nixon inveighed against the new state law and praised the Right to Life movement that had emerged in response and of which Cooke was a leader. Shortly thereafter, the state legislature voted to repeal the law, replacing it with one that allowed abortions only if a woman's life were in danger. Incensed, Rockefeller vetoed the bill, as he had promised. But Nixon, more than Rockefeller, represented the changing face of the Republican Party: more focused than before on social issues, especially those in which gender, sexuality, and religion collided.

Many state legislatures, of course, had no intention of repealing or reforming their abortion laws. But abortion rights advocates had another tool at their disposal: the courts. In 1969, the California Supreme Court declared the state's anti-abortion law unconstitutional. Two months later, a federal judge in Washington, DC, also declared the District of Columbia's anti-abortion law unconstitutional. In Texas, two young lawyers—Weddington and her University of Texas law school classmate Linda Coffee—watched these developments with interest. As two of only five women in a class of over one hundred, the two had become friends. In the two years since Weddington's own abortion, for which she spent her entire savings and traveled to Mexico, she had begun helping women in Austin secure contraception and safe abortions. One of the women she met in this capacity first suggested that Weddington should challenge Texas's anti-abortion law in court. In Dallas, Coffee had also been researching this possibility. The two began searching for a test case.

In fall 1969, twenty-two-year-old Dallas resident Norma McCorvey realized she was pregnant. It was her third pregnancy: she had signed legal rights to her first child over to her mother, and she gave the second up for adoption. She did not want to pursue either of these options the third time and instead pursued a friend's suggestion to try to secure an abortion. But she could not find a doctor to do so in Dallas, and she lacked the funds to travel to California or Mexico. Eventually, a lawyer put her in touch with Coffee, who on March 3, 1970, filed two federal lawsuits: one on behalf of McCorvey (Jane Roe) and one on behalf of David and Marsha King (John and Mary Doe). Marsha had a medical condition that made pregnancy inadvisable, but the pill's side effects were too severe for her. She had traveled to Mexico for an abortion in 1968 or 1969.

After nearly two years working its way through the federal court system, *Roe v. Wade* appeared before the Supreme Court at the end of 1971, with Sarah Weddington presenting oral arguments, alongside a similar case out of Georgia, *Doe v. Bolton*. After a confusing debate that left the justices' opinions unclear, Chief Justice Warren Burger asked Justice Harry Blackmun, appointed three years earlier by Richard Nixon, to draft the court's opinion. He did not relish this task and was unsure of how to proceed. Ultimately, his uncertainty—along with the fact that Nixon had recently appointed two new justices—led him to ask that the case be reargued.

The second hearing in front of the court took place in September 1972. Much had changed in a year. Weddington had prepared for the questions she had not expected the first time. Blackmun, meanwhile, had spent the interim researching the history of abortion. He had been surprised to learn that for much of human history, and until the mid-nineteenth century in the United States, there was little, if any, moral or legal opposition to the procedure. Outside of the court, states continued to repeal their own anti-abortion laws, and public opinion had rapidly shifted in favor of legalization. A 1972 Gallup poll found that 64 percent of respondents, including a majority of Catholics, believed that the decision should be left to a woman and her doctor (up from less than 15 percent four years earlier). Finally, Congress had passed the ERA in March, indicating the growing strength of the feminist movement and signaling a broader shift in attitudes toward women's rights.

In November, Blackmun circulated a fifty-page draft opinion to his fellow justices. After a long history of abortion and its relationship to the medical profession, Blackmun announced his decision: "[T]his right of privacy . . . is broad enough to encompass a woman's decision whether or not to terminate her pregnancy." He also found, however, that this right was not absolute, recognizing "the state's important and legitimate interest in potential life" after the first trimester. In the second trimester, regulations that "reasonably relate to the preservation and protection of maternal health" were allowed, and at viability the states may issue restrictions "except when it is necessary to preserve the life of the mother." The decision, moreover, was left to doctors, not to women. It was "inherently, and primarily, a medical decision and basic responsibility for it must rest with the physician." The final vote was seven to two, with only Byron White and future chief justice William Rehnquist dissenting.

By granting legal protection to reproductive choice, *Roe* made abortion much safer. The language of the decision, however, suggested the strategy that oppositional forces would deploy. While many called for *Roe* to be overturned, more successful early challenges focused on restriction. In the years and decades to come, methods by which abortions could be paid for, the point at which the state's interest in the fetus kicked in (especially the concept of viability), the conditions under which doctors could perform this procedure, and ultimately the fate of *Roe* itself became flashpoints in a series of all-out abortion wars.

Feminists' interests in bodily autonomy extended beyond the issues of birth control and abortion. Like Jane, members of the women's health movement believed that women should have knowledge of and authority over their own bodies and health. Fed up with the condescending treatment women received from doctors and other health-care providers, members of the Boston Women's Health Book Collective educated themselves on all aspects of women's health, including but not limited to sexuality and reproduction. The book that resulted from these studies, *Our Bodies, Ourselves*, was first published in 1970 and is still in print. Across the nation, feminists practiced "self-help gynecology," encouraging women to study and observe their own bodies and question doctors' authority if their advice did not ring true.

Women's liberationists and liberal feminists alike established grassroots support systems for women who had experienced rape or domestic abuse. In 1971, members of a Saint Paul, Minnesota, consciousness-raising group established the first center for women who had experienced domestic abuse. Called Women's Advocates, the organization provided a telephone hotline, legal advice, and emergency housing. Within a few years, local institutional networks coalesced into the National Coalition against Domestic Violence; by 1982, three hundred shelters and forty-eight state coalitions served women who had experienced intimate partner violence.

Women's liberationists and liberal feminists alike established grassroots support systems for women who had experienced rape or domestic abuse. Two years after the abortion speak-out, in 1971, members of New York Radical Feminists organized a similar demonstration about the issue of rape. In 1972, feminists in Washington, DC, founded the nation's first rape crisis hotline. From there, rape crisis centers proliferated quickly across the nation, offering counseling, legal advice, and other services. Feminists also pressured police departments, health-care providers, and legislatures to treat rape victims with respect. Until the 1970s, criminal proceedings for rape required two witnesses (a tall order considering the nature of the crime), and defense attorneys regularly admitted a woman's past sexual experiences into evidence. By the early 1990s, these and many other practices had changed.

More slowly, states began revising laws on marital rape. Before 1975, marital rape was legal in every state in the United States. In the eyes of the law, in fact, marital rape was an impossibility: a husband could not rape his wife because marriage itself constituted consent, forever and under all circumstances. As California state senator Bob Wilson "joked" in 1979, "If you can't rape your wife, who can you rape?"[18] Diana Russell, author of The Politics of Rape (1975), and Laura X, founder of the Berkeley Women's History Library, began a campaign to raise public awareness of and change laws around this issue. Many Americans first heard the term "marital rape" in the 1978 trial of John Rideout in Salem, Oregon. Rideout was acquitted of beating and raping his wife, but the case garnered a storm of media attention and spurred a national debate. By 1993, every state had outlawed marital rape.

Though its origins remain unclear, Take Back the Night has become a visible symbol of movements against rape and sexual assault, especially on college campuses starting in the 1980s. Often occurring annually, local iterations of the protest have included candlelight vigils; survivor testimony; and most famously, marches through parts of cities where women have been taught to feel unsafe. Over the years, the movement has changed to better reflect the reality of rape and sexual assault (women are more likely to know their assailant), women's different relationships to public space based on race and class, and the need for inclusivity.[19]

CONCLUSION

One of the indelible images of the second-wave feminist movement comes from the 1977 National Women's Conference in Houston, Texas. In it, well-known feminists Billie Jean King, Bella Abzug, and Betty Friedan march arm in arm with a diverse group of young women, one of whom holds aloft the torch that relay runners had carried from Seneca Falls, New York, to Houston. All are smiling. In the background, marchers hold large American flags. Women were staking their claim to represent American values, and they were doing it together, as part of a broad-based coalition irrespective of race, religion, sexual orientation, or generation. Women unite. Sisterhood is powerful.

Inside the convention, the story was quite different. Conflict erupted over several issues, especially the rights and roles of lesbians within the feminist movement and the politics of abortion. In the meantime, across town, anti-ERA activist Phyllis Schlafly led some fifteen thousand women in a counterrally, absorbing much of the media attention that the women's conference had hoped to garner for itself. Women were far from united.

Conflict had always rent the feminist movement, not only over strategies and goals but also, increasingly, over culture and identity. At the other end of the spectrum, conservative women like Schlafly had long feared that they stood to lose more than they stood to gain from feminism. Over the course of the 1970s, these two conflicts became stories as important as the very real gains women were making in many aspects of their lives. They are the subjects of the next two chapters.

NOTES

1. Alice Peurala, "People in the Plant Looked on Me as a Fighter," in O'Farrell and Kornbluh, *Rocking the Boat*, 268–69.

2. Not originally a traditional union, in 1981 9to5 become Service Employees International Union District 925.

3. National Organization for Women, "Hire him. He's got great legs," n.d. [ca. 1966–80], Library of Congress Prints and Photographs Division, Washington, DC, https://www.loc.gov/pictures/item/2015648079/.

4. Ruth Bader Ginsburg, quoted in Nancy MacLean, *Freedom Is Not Enough: The Opening of the American Workplace* (New York: Russell Sage Foundation, 2006), 134.

5. Shirley Chisholm, *Unbought and Unbossed* (1970; repr., Washington, DC: Take Root Media, 2009), 41.

6. Shirley Chisholm, "Presidential Candidacy Announcement," American Rhetoric Online Speech Bank, Jan. 25, 1972, https://www.americanrhetoric.com/speeches/shirleychisholmpresidentialcandidacyannouncement.htm.

7. Robert Gottlieb, quoted in Jackson Landers, "'Unbought and Unbossed': When a Black Woman Ran for the White House," *Smithsonian Magazine*, Apr. 25, 2016, https://www.smithsonianmag.com/smithsonian-institution/unbought-and-unbossed-when-black-woman-ran-for-the-white-house-180958699/.

8. Chisholm, quoted in Donna Brazile, "Foreword," in Chisholm, *Unbought and Unbossed*, xiii.

9. Mary Ziegenhagen, quoted in Sara Evans, *Tidal Wave: How Women Changed America at Century's End* (New York: Simon and Schuster, 2002), 73.

10. Toni Morrison, quoted in Evans, *Tidal Wave*, 75.

11. Bella Abzug, quoted in Evans, *Tidal Wave*, 67.

12. Bernice Sandler, quoted in Susan Ware, *Title IX: A Brief History with Documents* (Longview, IL: Waveland Press Inc., 2007), 36; Patsy Mink, quoted in Ware, *Title IX*, 3.

13. *Cohen v. Brown*, quoted in Ware, *Title IX*, 7.

14. Bil Gilbert and Nancy Williamson, quoted in Ware, *Title IX*, 44; Connecticut judge, quoted in Ware, *Title IX*, 8.

15. Quoted in Karen Blumenthal, *Jane against the World:* Roe v. Wade *and the Fight for Reproductive Rights* (New York: Roaring Brook Press, 2020), 64.

16. In *Bowers v. Hardwick* (1986), the Supreme Court upheld Georgia's antisodomy law, which was used to prosecute gay men there and in other states with similar laws. Harry Blackmun, who wrote for the majority in *Roe*, dissented in this case, arguing that the same standard of privacy should apply. The court adopted his position seventeen years later, in *Lawrence v. Texas* (2003).

17. Weddington went on to serve as a special assistant to the president in the Carter administration.

18. Bob Wilson, quoted in Rosen, *The World Split Open*, 183.

19. As one measure of how much feminism has changed in the past several decades, a similar protest established in 2011 called itself—in an attempt to challenge a derogatory term—SlutWalk.

CHAPTER 6

CONSERVATIVE WOMEN AND BACKLASH

INTRODUCTION

In September 2008, Republican vice presidential candidate Sarah Palin, only the second woman to appear on a major party's presidential ticket, caused a stir in an interview with CBS anchor Katie Couric. "Do you consider yourself a feminist?" Couric asked. Palin responded,

> I do. I'm a feminist who believes in equal rights and I believe that women certainly today have every opportunity that a man has to succeed and to try to do it all anyway. And I'm very, very thankful that I've been brought up in a family where gender hasn't been an issue. You know, I've been expected to do everything growing up that the boys were doing. We were out chopping wood and you're out hunting and fishing and filling our freezer with good wild Alaskan game to feed our family. So it kinda started with that. With just that expectation that the boys and the girls in my community were expected to do the same and accomplish the same. That's just been instilled in me. . . . [A feminist is] Someone who believes in equal rights. Someone who would not stand for oppression against women.[1]

Palin wavered on her use of this term in the years to follow, at times preferring to describe herself as a "mama grizzly" looking out for her children.

Palin's identification with feminism, even if inconsistent, rankled liberal and progressive women who also felt connected to this movement. Palin could not be a feminist, many argued, because she supported policies that would hurt most women, including restrictions on reproductive choice and the legal mechanisms that women could use to challenge workplace discrimination. But there is another way to understand Palin's engagement with the women's rights movement, one for which this chapter provides necessary background.

This chapter charts the rise of conservatism in postwar America, focusing on women's contributions to this movement. What did it mean, it asks, for women to take on prominent, public roles as political activists precisely so they could argue for maintaining women's traditional roles? In the 1970s, as today, political observers and historians have tried to make sense of this seeming contradiction. Were these women dupes or puppets of the patriarchy, acting out of a deeply rooted false consciousness? Were they simply hypocrites? Or were they earnest, committed activists who defined their interests as women differently from their feminist opponents?

THE EMERGENCE OF AMERICAN CONSERVATISM

As the postwar era began in 1945, there was no organized conservative movement in the United States. Instead, three groups of conservatives—libertarian conservatives, traditionalist conservatives, and southern Democrats—existed in pockets of academia, government, and culture. In the first group, a cadre of European-born intellectual émigrés and their allies, many of them tied to the University of Chicago, developed arguments for small government. Friedrich von Hayek, an Austrian-born economist who moved to Chicago in 1950, had argued in *The Road to Serfdom* that respect for private property and private profit were the only guarantees of political freedom. (He also believed, however, that the state should prevent companies from forming trusts and monopolies and provide socialized health care.) Milton Friedman, who worked with Hayek at Chicago, argued in his 1962 book *Capitalism and Freedom* that government was the greatest threat to freedom. He also assailed the income tax, urged privatization of government services, and challenged the Keynesian belief, practiced widely both before and after World War II, that government spending could stimulate the economy. In the cultural realm, Russian-born screenwriter and novelist Ayn Rand espoused the idea of "objectivism"—the idea that acting out of self-interest was the most ethical way to live one's life—in such novels as *The Fountainhead* (1943) and *Atlas*

Shrugged (1957). Rand created a community of similarly minded libertarians, and the popularity of her books continued to grow over the decades. Prominent conservatives, even those with whom Rand would disagree, continue to cite her work as influential. (Rand was an atheist who scored religion and called Christianity "the best kindergarten of communism possible.")

Traditionalist conservatives, by contrast, criticized the individualism of libertarianism and modernity more broadly, instead advocating stability, order, and the return to a society where each person knew their place and deferred to authority. They saw a world beset with moral decay and argued that a return to traditional values, especially religious values, was the only cure. In *The Conservative Mind* (1953), political theorist Russell Kirk included among his six tenets of conservative thought the "belief that a divine intent rules society as well as conscience" and the "conviction that civilized society requires order and classes."

The third group of postwar conservatives comprised southern Democrats. Mobilizing in opposition to postwar civil rights successes, in 1948, members of the group broke off from the Democratic Party in protest over the strong civil rights plank in its platform. They formed the States' Rights Democratic (Dixiecrat) Party and nominated hardline segregationist senator Strom Thurmond for president. Campaigning for states' rights and against integration, Thurmond took four southern states. After the *Brown v. Board* decision, members of its group pledged "massive resistance" to integration, attacking any civil rights legislation as communist-inspired violations of their freedom.

Even in the 1940s and '50s, these tendencies were not entirely discrete. William F. Buckley, the founder of the *National Review*, combined all three. A devoted Catholic, his 1951 book *God and Man at Yale* denounced his alma mater for turning away from Christianity. He also denounced "government paternalism inimical to the dignity of the individual." Finally, Buckley's early pieces in the *National Review* often sided with the white South on racial issues; he wrote, for example, that white supremacy was justified because "it [the white race] is the advanced race." From its founding in 1955, the *National Review* strengthened the conservative movement and brought more people under its fold, making Buckley a significant figure in popularizing a conservative ideology that brought together its various tendencies.

Still, these three groups—libertarian intellectuals sometimes scornful of religion, religiously motivated traditionalists, and southern segregationists—were not necessarily natural allies. The Cold War, however, gave them a common enemy. Each group in the emerging conservative movement had its own specific reasons to see the Soviet Union and all that it represented as a fundamental threat to the American way of life. For libertarians, it represented a violation of free enterprise. For traditionalists, "godless atheist communism" represented a turning away from religion, and its theoretical egalitarianism threatened orderly society. Segregationists also wanted to protect hierarchy, and they considered civil rights legislation a form of big government that encroached on their freedom. Different kinds of conservatives agreed, moreover, that liberalism promoted socialism and communism at home and weakened the military abroad. Though it was not yet a mass organized movement, this confluence represented the beginnings of modern conservatism.

In 1964, the tremendous grassroots mobilization for the Republican presidential candidate, Arizona senator Barry Goldwater, brought these and other groups together. Goldwater rose to prominence with his 1960 book, *The Conscience of a Conservative*, ghostwritten by L. Brent Bozell, William F. Buckley's brother-in-law. To win the nomination, Goldwater wrested control of the party from its liberal wing, represented by New York governor Nelson Rockefeller. Domestically, Goldwater focused on rolling back such civil rights legislation as the new Civil Rights Act, as well as Great Society expansions of the New Deal. Internationally, he pushed to conduct the Cold War more aggressively, up to and including the use of nuclear weapons. "Extremism in the defense of liberty is no vice," he argued at the Republican National Convention.

Goldwater's self-proclaimed extremism was too much for many Republicans, who actively campaigned for President Lyndon Johnson's reelection. But, in the beginnings of a mass grassroots conservative movement, new constituencies mobilized for Goldwater. On college campuses across the nation, Young Americans for Freedom (YAF), a conservative analog to SDS, rallied thousands of college students to the cause. In such places as Orange County, California, business elites, religious leaders, and most importantly, housewives mobilized for Goldwater, engaging in door-to-door campaigning, holding lunches and coffees, and urging support in the press.

Goldwater had long cultivated women's support. As many as nine thousand women spent three years working to ensure that an AFL-CIO campaign to unseat Goldwater in 1958 was unsuccessful. Unlike many politicians of either party, Goldwater frequently noted women's contributions to his success. Women were the ones willing to take on the "tough political chores." Indeed, he insisted, "if it were not for the National Federation of Republican Women, there would not be a Republican Party."[2]

Richard Nixon's 1960 presidential campaign disappointed conservatives, who almost immediately mobilized to win the nomination for Goldwater four years later. Women were essential to this effort. Goldwater's advisors knew that local party auxiliaries did much of the actual work of presidential nominating campaigns, and they considered it essential that their candidate's supporters control these groups. Through both a series of backstage maneuvers and genuine enthusiasm on the part of many women, the National Federation of Republican Women became a Goldwater stronghold.

First as a senator and then as a presidential candidate, Goldwater emphasized a message of morality, spirituality, and social order that especially appealed to women—and, not coincidentally, women-as-mothers. As Goldwater advisor F. Clifton White recalled in 1967, "The women of America have labored valiantly to help build this society, a society which, if preserved, promises an even brighter future for their children."[3] It certainly helped the candidate that just a year earlier the divorced Rockefeller had announced his marriage to Margaretta "Happy" Murphy, who was recently divorced herself. Rockefeller's support fell by 10 percent among women after the announcement, a Gallup poll showed. (His popularity among men remained unchanged.)

In 1964, a group of women founded Mothers for a Moral America (MFMA), a pro-Goldwater group focused on rooting out moral decay in society. While it is unclear exactly what role the campaign played in founding Mothers for a Moral America, Goldwater's advisors were in close contact with grassroots activists once the group was established. Within months, the organization existed in every major city in the nation.

As far as Goldwater's people were concerned, the main purpose of MFMA was to present the campaign-developed film *Choice*, specifically aimed at improving the senator's image among women. The controversial twenty-eight-minute production lay such problems as urban unrest (with racial overtones that were impossible to ignore), campus radicalism, rape, and pornography at President Lyndon Johnson's feet, implying that these developments were not a bug but a feature of liberalism's ultimate vision of America. In publicizing *Choice*, MFMA leaders were instructed to present the film as solely the creation of women; the campaign specifically prohibited them from associating the film with the candidate. Unfortunately for the campaign, journalists walked away from early screenings of the film horrified, and Goldwater himself disavowed it.

Goldwater's campaign had captured the attention of an enthusiastic and dedicated cohort of Republican women. When it came to actual voting, however, Goldwater's support was much higher among men than it was among women, and the election itself was a landslide. Johnson won 61 percent of the popular vote, and Democrats won two-to-one margins in both houses of Congress. Still, Goldwater's candidacy constituted a turning point in the growth of conservatism. In a trend that continues to this day, it was the first time that a majority of white southerners voted for the Republican candidate; Goldwater won five southern states. His campaign also featured a rising conservative star, Ronald Reagan, who spoke of the conservative cause as a divine mission. "You and I have a rendezvous with destiny," he argued in a televised speech that aired just days before the election. This speech catapulted Reagan to national prominence, helping to secure his election as governor of California two years later. The connection between Goldwater and Reagan was so powerful that the conservative columnist George Will once joked that Goldwater actually won the 1964 election—"it just took sixteen years to count the votes."

PHYLLIS SCHLAFLY AND THE EQUAL RIGHTS AMENDMENT

Goldwater's campaign also thrust a grassroots Cold Warrior, Phyllis Schlafly, into the spotlight. Born in Saint Louis, Missouri, to a family of modest means, Schlafly was a devout Catholic who dedicated the first part of her political career to educating the public about the dangers of communism. In 1952, she and her husband, Fred, supported Senator Robert A. Taft (of the Taft-Hartley Act) for president over the more liberal Dwight Eisenhower. Though unsuccessful, her efforts won her an invitation to deliver the keynote at the Illinois Republican State Convention

Conservative activist Phyllis Schlafly protests the Equal Rights Amendment. The visibility and successes of the feminist movement led to the emergence of a new kind of women's activism, as Schlafly and others became important leaders of a revitalized conservatism. (Library of Congress, Prints & Photographs Division, U.S. News & World Report Magazine Collection, LC-DIG-ds-00757)

that year, garnering a great deal of attention. For the remainder of the 1950s, most of her politics remained local, taking place through such organizations as the Daughters of the American Revolution (DAR) and the Illinois Federation of Republican Women. Still, she became plugged into the small network of conservatives that did exist, and she became a sought-after public speaker. Through the DAR, she secured a weekly, fifteen-minute radio spot on "America Wake Up," which she devoted to national security issues, and her prolific writing appeared in publications of all kinds. In 1957, she founded the Cardinal Mindszenty Foundation to educate Catholics about the dangers of communism, establishing a series of study groups and seminars to train average Americans to recognize communist propaganda. By 1961, the organization reached an audience of tens of thousands.

Though difficult to imagine today, for the first two decades after World War II, conservatives were a marginal minority within the Republican

Party. With some change over time and variation between parties, the liberal consensus—a term coined by British journalist Godfrey Hodgson—dominated the political landscape. The liberal consensus held that capitalism was the best economic system in the world, that capitalism and democracy were fundamentally intertwined, that the imperfections in American society could be fixed through incremental reforms rather than radical change, and that anti-communism and containment remained fundamental political commitments. As the postwar U.S. economy continued to grow, Americans felt that New Deal and subsequent reforms had done their job. By and large, this ideology held, society was working as it should, and all people were benefiting.

Though there were notable dissenters on both sides (southern Democrats on the one hand, Joseph McCarthy and his allies on the other), mainstream members of both parties embraced this ideology. As president, Eisenhower refused to dismantle, and in some cases expanded, New Deal programs, arguing that "should any political party attempt to abolish Social Security, unemployment insurance, and eliminate labor laws and farm programs, you would not hear of that party again in our political history." In 1956, the year that he successfully ran for reelection, the Republican Party platform called for expansion of social security; broader coverage in unemployment insurance; increased worker protection laws; strengthening unions; aid to workers with disabilities and minority and migrant workers; equal pay for equal work; an expanded minimum wage; and an end to employment discrimination based on race, creed, color, national origin, ancestry, and sex.

Coming just eight years later, Goldwater's nomination was thus a tremendous conservative coup, one to which Schlafly gave her full support. In her 1963 best seller intended to whip up grassroots support for the senator, *A Choice Not an Echo*, she accused moderate and liberal Republicans of betraying the party and the nation. Republican "kingmakers," she asserted, had for decades manipulated the political process to nominate liberals, with the ultimate goal of melding the two parties. Within two months, the book had gone through three printings. Schlafly received credit for helping Goldwater win the California primary and the nomination, going on to work full time for his campaign. After Goldwater's landslide defeat, however, party officials purged conservatives, including Schlafly, from leadership positions. Schlafly attributed this treatment to sexism: as historian Catherine Rymph explains, Schlafly believed that party leaders "preferred to keep women performing the housework of government and were determined not to let women choose their own leaders, express their own opinions, or exercise political power."[4] For the next several years, her influence waned.

Ironically, the growing strength of second-wave feminism thrust Schlafly back into the spotlight, ultimately making her one of the most important conservatives, and certainly the single most important conservative woman, of the twentieth century. Schlafly had not been much interested in feminism, or social issues more generally, before the end of 1971, as the Senate prepared to debate the ERA. A conservative forum in Connecticut invited her to participate in a debate, which she hoped would focus on national defense issues. Instead, the group wished to focus on the ERA. After studying the issue, Schlafly declared her opposition to the measure. Appearing in *The Phyllis Schlafly Report* in February 1972, "What's Wrong with 'Equal Rights' for Women?" became both a rallying cry and a political manifesto for anti-ERA forces.

As Schlafly saw it, the gendered division of labor was both natural and beneficial: women gave birth to babies and took care of children and the home, and men provided the financial support to make this possible. American women, she argued, benefited in particular from two aspects of the nation's culture: its reverence for motherhood and "the great American free enterprise system," which produced technology that freed them from all but a few hours' worth of childcare and household duties. The ERA would interfere with this arrangement, depriving women of their right to financial support from their husbands, alimony or widows' benefits, and the right to abstain from wage-earning. "Why should we lower ourselves to 'equal rights,'" she wondered, "when we already have the status of special privilege?"[5]

Herself a highly accomplished woman, Schlafly claimed that she had no problem with women taking on more public roles. She ran for Congress twice, and she entered law school in 1975, at age fifty-one. She cautioned, however, that "many women are under the mistaken impression that 'women's lib' means more job employment opportunities for women, equal pay for equal work, appointments of women to high positions, admitting more women to medical schools, and other desirable outcomes which all women favor. We support these purposes, as well as any necessary legislation which would bring them about."[6] She later argued that such legislation as the Equal Pay Act (1963), Title VII of the Civil Rights Act (1964), and Title IX of the Education Amendment Act (1972) already protected these rights. Recent court decisions, hard-won by feminists, had also shown a willingness to use the Fourteenth Amendment to combat gender discrimination, a strategy that Schlafly supported.

The real goal of the ERA and the women's liberation movement, Schlafly believed, was far more sinister. She first warned readers that the ERA would subject women to the draft, a particularly scary prospect in the midst of a divisive war. Beyond that, though, lay an even more terrifying reality. "The 'women's lib' movement," she reported, "is *not* an honest effort to secure better jobs for women who want or need to work outside the home. This is just the superficial sweet-talk to win broad support for a radical 'movement.' Women's lib is a total assault on the role of the American mother as wife and mother, and on the family as the basic unit of society." Her arguments rang hollow both to independent, well-educated white feminists and to those women—including many women of color, poor women, and single mothers—who never had male support in the first place. But they resonated deeply with middle-class, Christian housewives who feared they had more to lose than to gain from the feminist movement.[7]

In September Schlafly founded STOP ERA (Stop Taking Our Privileges), which provided the main political muscle behind the anti-ERA movement. Though many of the group's rank-and-file members were new to politics, almost all its early leaders had worked with Schlafly in the National Federation of Republican Women (NFRW) and elsewhere. They were politically savvy women with years of organizing experience behind them. By early the next year, women had organized STOP ERA chapters in twenty-six states, including many crucial to ratification. Schlafly founded the Eagle Forum, intended as an organizational counterweight to NOW, that same year.

Schlafly flummoxed her feminist opponents, who struggled to craft an effective response. As honed in the women's liberation movement, the style of feminist politics was deeply personal. While this approach worked in small consciousness-raising groups, in front of a broader audience it became a weakness for Schlafly to exploit. In a 1973 debate at Illinois State University, Betty Friedan accused Schlafly of being "a traitor to your sex, an Aunt Tom" and voiced her desire to burn Schlafly at the stake. "I'm glad you said that," the unflappable Schlafly replied, "because it just shows the intemperate nature of proponents of ERA." In the face of this "intemperance," Schlafly's star continued to rise. Feminist attempts to tie Schlafly to organizations in the radical and/or segregationist right also tended to backfire in the face of Schlafly's calm, unequivocal denials.[8]

Still, the anti-ERA movement faced an uphill fight. Celebrities, mainstream women's magazines, and both major political parties endorsed the ERA. First lady Betty Ford was an ardent pro-choice feminist and vocal ERA supporter, and she convinced her husband, President Gerald Ford (1974–77), to provide more active support as well. Ford's key advisor on women's issues, Jill Ruckelshaus, was a pro-ERA, pro-choice feminist. A founding member of the National Women's Political Caucus (NWPC) and its liaison to the 1972 Republican National Convention, Ruckelshaus had ensured the party's strong feminist platform that year. (Later, Reagan would try as a presidential candidate to assuage the concerns of Ruckelshaus and other Republican feminists over the party's rightward drift—and, in particular, its removal of support for the ERA—by agreeing to appoint a woman to the Supreme Court.)

The battle for the ERA, however, would be won or lost at the state level. In legislatures across the country, anti-ERA activists built on the arguments Schlafly had laid out in February 1972. Linking the ERA to homosexuality and "abortion on demand" proved to be especially effective. Pulitzer Prize–winning cartoonist Ben Sargent satirized these fears in his depiction of a husband and wife debating the ERA. The husband suggests that the measure is harmless, reading its brief text aloud. "No!" the wife exclaims, transforming into an outraged ogre, "Read th' part requiring homosexual bathrooms! An' th' part outlawing families!! Th' mandatory abortions!! . . . It's a trick! Another feminist trick! Ohhh, they're devious!"[9] The wife's portrayal is exaggerated (and more than a little elitist and misogynistic), but the real-life cousins of her concerns gained traction. Within two years of STOP ERA's emergence, seventeen states—including, due to energetic grassroots opposition, procedural obstacles, and behind-the-scenes political chicanery, Schlafly's home state of Illinois—had defeated the amendment.

Soon, changes in the political tenor of the nation at large would aid the anti-ERA fight. Ford and other moderate Republicans did not believe that conservatives within the party posed any real threat to their leadership. In 1976, however, Ford faced an ultimately unsuccessful but very real primary challenge from Reagan. Schlafly, unsurprisingly, supported Reagan. After Ford lost the general election to Jimmy Carter, Reagan, the former California governor and long a star of the conservative movement, became the face of the Republican Party itself. In 1980, with Schlafly's support, he won the Republican presidential nomination and then the presidency. For the first time, the Republican Party removed its support from the ERA, though at this point it hardly mattered. The amendment had lain largely moribund for years, finally expiring in 1982, three states short of ratification.

GENDER AND FAMILY IN THE CHRISTIAN RIGHT

This shift requires some explanation. How did a decade that cultivated a vital, diverse women's movement with enough power to effect real changes in people's lives also give birth to modern conservatism, of which anti-feminism was a key component? Simple backlash, in which conservative women and others saw their ways of life threatened, goes far in explaining this seeming contradiction. But importantly, this backlash took place against a growing sense of crisis in American politics and culture.

The post–World War II twentieth century in the United States can, in many ways, be divided in half, with 1973 serving as a fulcrum. People's faith in institutions eroded with such domestic crises as the Watergate scandal and the Johnson and Nixon administrations' dishonest prosecution of the Vietnam War. American defeat in Southeast Asia—along with, late in the decade, the Iran hostage crisis—seemed to threaten the place of the United States in the world. The period between 1945 and 1973, moreover, featured almost uninterrupted economic growth. Due to deindustrialization, growing trade deficits, post-Vietnam demobilization, and a series of oil crises, the United States thereafter found itself in a period of "stagflation"—the seemingly impossible combination of economic stagnation and monetary inflation. Commentators frequently described the nation as a family under attack, adding metaphorical heft to their fears about the literal family, while reuniting POWs with their actual families became a symbol of national healing. As consumers and managers of the family economy, women also tended to be blamed for the hardships brought on by oil crises. If a family were struggling to meet its expenses, the thinking went, it must be because wives were failing to manage money properly or spending it frivolously.[10]

At the same time, Americans began to think differently about the concept of rights. In the 1960s and early '70s, many Americans believed that rights could keep expanding indefinitely and that, as they did, all people would benefit. By the mid-1970s, people increasingly thought of rights as a zero-sum game: if one group was gaining rights, they must be taking them away from another group. A terrible historical coincidence emerged: women and minorities were gaining access to better-paid jobs and other opportunities just as all Americans' economic fortunes, for a variety of unrelated domestic and global reasons, were worsening. The people for whom these opportunities had traditionally been reserved did not always see the deeply rooted reasons for this economic contraction. Instead, they saw women and minorities taking "their" jobs. As a consequence, they blamed feminism and the civil rights movement for their own (real) hardships.

At the same time, a growing infrastructure ensured that conservative ideas were widely disseminated and well funded. The Heritage Foundation, a conservative think tank, was founded in 1973 by Joseph Coors of the Colorado Brewing Company and Richard Mellon Scaife, a former Goldwater supporter and heir to a Pittsburgh banking fortune. Connaught (Connie) Marshner, a YAF member who had organized a successful letter-writing campaign to convince President Nixon to veto the Comprehensive Childcare Development Act of 1971, soon became the most influential woman in the organization. David Koch, heir to an oil and gas fortune and son of a John Birch Society member, founded the libertarian Cato Institute. Such groups as the National Rifle Association (NRA) got involved in politics, hiring a staff of full-time lobbyists and embarking on a massive fundraising campaign. Business schools proliferated to train the next generation of conservative leaders, many of them at institutions that combined faith in free enterprise with religious conservatism. Goldwater veterans Richard Viguerie and Paul Weyrich (who had convinced Coors to start the Heritage Foundation) drew on the strategies developed by Marshner and other conservative women in direct-mail organizing, reaching out in particular to remote constituencies otherwise cut off from the growing national movement. Viguerie and Weyrich also convinced television preacher Jerry Falwell to found the Moral Majority, the most important organization within the emerging Religious Right.

Evangelical Christianity was on the rise in the 1970s, as the percentage of Americans who reported that they were "born again" increased from 24 percent in 1963 to nearly 40 percent by 1978. By the end of the decade, more than fifty million Americans self-identified as born again. Responding to what they saw as increasing intrusions by the secular state, this group turned its attention to influencing politics. Evangelicals looked with alarm at such court decisions as *Engel v. Vitale* (1962), which ruled school prayer unconstitutional, and a ruling the next year that banned compulsory Bible reading in schools. Then, in 1978, the IRS issued a mandate ordering religious schools to comply with desegregation law or risk losing their tax-exempt status. (These schools had grown over the course of the 1960s and '70s as parents hoping to escape desegregation orders flocked to them.) Well known for his show *The Old-Time Gospel Hour*, Jerry Falwell founded the Moral Majority in 1979 with the aim of fighting against these developments. Although most members were evangelicals, the new Religious Right was ecumenical in nature. Evangelicals including Falwell and Pat Robertson could work with Catholics like Schlafly to mobilize support for candidates who would fight abortion, defeat the ERA, wage war against homosexuality, and restore prayer to schools.

Historians have often argued that modern conservatism comprises an uneasy alliance of libertarians and social conservatives, and while this is sometimes true, these priorities were often deeply intertwined. The conservative discourse that emerged over the course of the 1970s combined antistatism with opposition to feminism, the gay rights movement, and other forms of activism. Its adherents feared that liberation movements and the state were conspiring to destroy the family and impose secular humanism. As economist George Gilder wrote in *Wealth and Poverty* (1981), a key text to the economic policy of the Reagan administration, people who wanted to expand the welfare state "want to ratify the female-headed family as the norm in America. They do not want to subsidize families; they want to subsidize feminism. . . . The female-headed households of today create an unending chain of burdens for tomorrow as their children disrupt classrooms, fill the jails, throng the welfare rolls, and gather as bitter petitioners and leftist agitators seeking to capture for themselves the bounty produced by stable families." He and other conservatives argued that the state, through the instrument of schools, was trying to brainwash children, undermine traditional family structure, and threaten parental authority. Reagan himself, in a 1983 speech before the National Association of Evangelicals, argued that challenges to conventional morality weakened the nation to the extent that it could not stave off communist threats either at home or abroad. This stripe of conservatism also singled out government programs aimed at the family—including Aid to Families with Dependent Children (AFDC) and childcare services—which, they argued, further stripped the family of its proper role at the center of society.[11]

Women, many but not all in Schlafly's orbit, played prominent roles in developing and supporting this discourse. Indeed, the new focus on women, gender, and the family—long a portion of women's purview—seemed to demand their leadership. It also staved off criticism: religious women could argue that they were not getting involved in politics but simply asserting their natural concerns as mothers. In Fort Worth, Texas, Church of Christ member Lottie Beth Hobbs, author of eight books of popular religion, founded Women Who Want to Be Women (WWWW). Before finding the ERA, evangelical women like Hobbs faced several obstacles to participation in politics. Many denominations, including the Church of Christ, staunchly adhered to both separation from politics and women's subordination within the home and the church. Hobbs, however, was able to reach out to women in such fundamentalist sects as the Assemblies of God, Bible Churches, and the Missionary Alliance, who justified their activism by citing the imminent threat to their way of life. As historian Marjorie J. Spruill puts it, "[D]efense of traditional women's roles seemed to require deviation from them, at least temporarily."[12]

Hobbs's flyer "Ladies! Have You Heard" (also known as "The Pink Sheet") functioned as a primer for women new to the movement (and likely to politics in general). God, she argued, had given women "a beautiful and exalted place to fill"—the care of home and family. But the ERA "strikes at the very foundation of family life, and the home is the foundation of our nation." Perhaps worse, feminism more broadly wished to turn over the care of children to the state. Under the ERA, "[Y]ou can be forced to put them [children] in a federal daycare center, if one is available. And to see that one is available is a major goal of the National Organization for Women (NOW)—leaders in the movement to ratify the Equal Rights

Amendment."[13] Like others, Hobbs saw feminists working through the federal government to achieve their aim of destroying the family.

A vice president in Schlafly's Eagle Forum, Hobbs first proposed the idea for the 1977 conservative counterrally against the International Woman's Year (IWY) conference in Houston. Though nonpartisan, the IWY was unmistakably a feminist gathering. As a recipient of federal funding, it was also a natural target for the new religious antistatism. Hobbs and her Pro-Family Forum (the renamed WWWW) cultivated connections across Texas for what ultimately became the Pro-Life, Pro-Family Rally. Under her leadership, the rally became a key event in linking the pro-life movement with the anti-ERA movement. Though Schlafly had argued since the Supreme Court issued its decision that the ERA would make it more difficult to repeal *Roe v. Wade*, before 1977, the two were separate movements, and most ERA opponents were single-issue activists.

In the aftermath of *Roe v. Wade*, polls consistently found that most Americans supported the decision. Even mainstream religious denominations supported it. In 1973, Protestant and Jewish leaders founded the Religious Coalition for Abortion Rights. Yet a small but growing opposition emerged, with Catholics at its core. In Washington, DC, Nellie Gray founded the March for Life, a yearly protest on the anniversary of *Roe v. Wade*. A devout Catholic, Gray left her position as an attorney in the Department of Labor to work full time on overturning the decision. In 1976, Dr. Mildred Jefferson, a Black physician, graduate of Harvard Medical School, and president of the National Right to Life Committee (NRLC), issued along with two other pro-life leaders a statement praising the GOP for including in their party platform a call for a constitutional amendment protecting the unborn. That same year, congressman Henry Hyde, a Republican from Illinois, introduced the Hyde Amendment, which made it illegal to use Medicaid funds for abortions except in cases of rape or incest. The Supreme Court upheld this restriction in *Maher v. Roe* the following January.

Still, before 1977, many women who opposed abortion identified as feminists and supported the ERA. In 1975, NRLC leaders easily defeated a proposal to condemn the ERA until "such a time as this ambiguity" about the amendment's effects on abortion "is removed." But as the feminist establishment—represented by the state-supported IWY—became more vocal about its support for abortion, pro-life feminists were brought into the anti-ERA fold. Ann O'Donnell, president of the Missouri chapter of the NRLC, a longtime pro-ERA feminist, and head of the Missouri delegation to the IWY, expressed these feelings amid the IWY debate over a pro–abortion rights resolution. "It is the antithesis of the feminist women's movement to oppress the less powerful," she told the crowd, and "it is therefore absolutely ridiculous for people to call themselves feminists to suggest that they kill their unborn children to solve our social problems. . . . You ask for reproductive freedom, but all freedom is based on recognition of the rights of those who are less powerful than you, and the unborn children are the least powerful and most helpless. You have more to offer this country, very positive things to offer, and the promise of the women's movement will be destroyed if you go on record in support of this unjust, destructive resolution" in support of abortion rights.[14] Despite O'Donnell's protestations, the resolution passed decisively. Later that year, the NRLC passed its condemnation of the ERA easily.

The alienation of pro-life women from the feminist movement was never complete, and some labored to carve out a distinct pro-life feminism. Inspired by Quaker teachings on nonviolence, Illinois native Rachel MacNair protested against the Vietnam War and nuclear proliferation while still a teenager. She was also an ardent pro-choice feminist. After reading a speech by influential pro-life feminist Juli Loesch Wiley, however, MacNair became convinced that abortion and nonviolence could not be reconciled. She threw herself into the pro-life movement, joining Prolifers for Survival and the NRLC. She was arrested five times for engaging in civil disobedience, once spending six weeks in jail. In 1984, MacNair became president of Feminists for Life, a position she held until founding the Susan B. Anthony List, which funds pro-life political candidates, in 1993.

MacNair was not alone in this approach. Feminists for Life itself had been founded in 1972 by Pat Goltz and Cathy Callaghan, NOW members whose anti-abortion stance put them at odds with most of the group's constituency. Establishing itself as a force within the National Right to Life Convention, Feminists for Life had a mailing list of fifteen hundred by 1983, and the group still exists today. Still, after 1977, being pro-life increasingly meant being anti-feminist and anti-ERA.

Conservative women also mobilized against the growing gay rights movement. Sexual orientation was not a protected category under the Civil

Rights Act, which meant that it was legal to fire or refuse to hire someone or to deny individuals equal access to public accommodations for being gay. For the next half century, states and localities were left on their own in this regard. In San Francisco, the assassinated politician Harvey Milk championed a nondiscrimination ordinance, and in late 1976, Dade County, Florida, passed a similar measure banning discrimination against gay men and lesbians in housing, employment, and public accommodations.

Almost immediately, singer, former Miss Oklahoma, and Florida Orange Juice spokesperson Anita Bryant, who had tried to stop the new law before it passed, began a campaign to repeal the measure by popular referendum. Since moving to Miami from Oklahoma in 1970, Bryant had seen her adopted hometown as a den of iniquity indicative of America's moral decline—an experience that many Americans of her generation shared as they moved from Middle America to Sunbelt centers. Born in the small, rural town of Barnsdall, Oklahoma, in 1940, Bryant grew up in a large religious family of modest means. She parlayed her singing and dancing talents into a third-place finish in the 1959 Miss America pageant, a recording contract, and several top-forty hits. Starting in 1960, she performed on USO tours to Vietnam with Bob Hope. Bryant and her husband-manager, Bob Green, cultivated an image associated with "God, country, [and] apple pie."[15] She represented several national brands, signing with the Florida Citrus Commission in 1969. In advertisements and later popular books for women, she presented herself as a happy mother and housewife who had learned to joyfully submit to her husband. She also increasingly linked her performing career to her religion, joining celebrity preacher Billy Graham on several of his crusades. At first concerned primarily with patriotism and religion, around 1972, Bryant turned her attention more explicitly to the family, and especially to supposedly God-ordained gender roles within it. On feminism, she wondered in 1976, "[A]s they fight for women's rights, who fights for children's rights? Who will keep our children from being devoured by evil forces we're too busy to recognize? . . . When we fight for our individual rights, our children are destroyed."[16] Far from the sudden politicization that Bryant usually described, her path to becoming a public leader of the New Christian Right in 1977 built on these experiences.

Polls found that most women voters in the county supported the non-discrimination ordinance, but Bryant thought she had a strategy to curdle their sympathy. Arguing that gay men and lesbians were child molesters, she insisted that the law would threaten innocent children. "I felt I had to take a stand against this ordinance because of the effect it would have on my children, and on all the children of Dade County," she wrote.[17] When voters went to the polls later that year, they overturned the measure by a two-to-one margin. Bryant's activism attracted national attention from such sympathetic conservatives as Schlafly, Jesse Helms, and Reagan, and similar campaigns sprang up around the country. With help from Bryant and her organization Save Our Children (later Protect America's Children), nondiscrimination ordinances were defeated in rapid succession in Saint Paul, Minnesota; Wichita, Kansas; and Eugene, Oregon. In all these cases, activists hewed to the logic of the new conservatism. First, opponents argued that laws against discrimination gave gay men and lesbians "special privileges" that "ordinary" Americans did not have (charges often levied against civil rights law, especially in its affirmative action phase). Second, as in Saint Paul, activists declared that these measures violated "the basic rights of parents and families," especially the right to "protect their children."[18] In 1978, she founded Anita Bryant Ministries (ABM), the stated goal of which was to help individuals "escape . . . from the homosexual life with the help of the Holy Spirit."[19]

Bryant soon became the target of a newly emboldened gay liberation movement. At a speaking engagement in Des Moines, Iowa, an activist threw a banana cream pie in her face. The National Gay Task Force's "We Are Your Children" campaign sought to educate Americans about homosexuality to counter the Christian Right's definition of family. Finally, activists embarked on a national boycott of Florida Orange Juice.

Bryant took a hit from this controversy, but the fame that made her a target also belied a more complicated truth about women in the Christian Right: their grasp on authority was always tenuous. For example, she was ABM's public face and its most important fundraiser, but the group's founders insisted on an all-male board, and Bryant herself always insisted that her activism did not take away from, but rather, reflected her roles as a wife and mother. This authority was contingent, however, on her continuing to play these roles correctly. After her 1980 divorce, her viability as a spokesperson for the movement waned.

As Mothers for a Moral America, Lottie Beth Hobbs, Anita Bryant, and others discovered, motherhood provided one strategy—albeit fraught—for women to claim authority within a cultural milieu that emphasized both women's subordination to men in the public realm and their continued authority in the home. Concerned Women for America (CWA) developed another: the idea that women were best positioned to speak out against the women's movement. Founded by Beverly LaHaye in San Diego in 1979 to combat the ERA, CWA represented the newly melded conservatism that emerged over the course of the decade: Christian, anti-feminist, anti-abortion, anti–gay and lesbian rights, anti-government, and pro-family (a particular vision thereof). At the same time, like Schlafly, LaHaye always insisted that she supported some feminist demands, including equal pay and professional opportunities.

Born into a working-class family in a suburb of Detroit in 1929, Beverly Jean Davenport entered Bob Jones University, an evangelical college in South Carolina, in 1946. There she met her future husband, Tim LaHaye, an air force veteran and pastor-in-training. Starting in 1956, he was the pastor of San Diego's Scott Memorial Baptist Church, which he nurtured into an early megachurch. Initially content to stay in the background of her husband's career, in the 1970s, Beverly joined Tim in a series of seminars related to marriage and family, which brought the couple national attention. Both LaHayes also authored several books, including a collaboration on sex and marriage. "Regardless of what the current trend towards 'Women's Lib' advocates," Beverly wrote in her first book, published in 1976, "anything which departs from God's design for women is not right."[20]

LaHaye told two different stories about the founding of CWA, both of which focused on the threat posed by feminism. As she wrote to supporters in the early 1980s, "I shall never forget the day when Tim (my husband) and I were watching Barbara Walters interview Betty Friedan on television. Something in me stirred to action as I realized Betty Friedan thought she was speaking for the women of America. I found myself saying verbally to Tim, 'They don't speak for me!! And I don't think they speak for the vast majority of women in America.'"[21] In the second story, LaHaye and five friends decided in the wake of the IWY conference to educate their friends and neighbors on the dangers of feminism through a series of coffee gatherings.

Neither story accounted for either the long history of conservative women's activism or the immediate circumstances in LaHaye's home state of California. In November 1978, voters narrowly declined to pass California Proposition 6, a ballot measure that would have made it illegal for gay men or lesbians to work in the state's public schools. Republican state senator John V. Briggs was inspired by Bryant to embark on his own "Save Our Children' campaign." Conservatives were deeply disappointed that the so-called Briggs Initiative, which they had worked hard to mobilize support for, failed to pass. Incorporated just two months later, CWA thus emerged at a moment when conservative activists were ready and eager to continue the fight.

LaHaye had grand visions for her new organization. Even when the group consisted of local, informal coffee gatherings, she called herself its national director. Within a few months, she released its first newsletter. Within a year, CWA began expanding nationally, boasting fifty-two prayer chapters in at least fourteen states by February 1980. Three years later, LaHaye began to hire paid staff members.

One of them was Michael Farris, a young attorney tasked with founding the group's Educational and Legal Defense Foundation (ELDF). While all areas of concern to the Religious Right fell under ELDF's remit, its most high-profile cases focused on parents' rights to control their children's schooling. By 1984, both Farris and the LaHayes had set up permanent shop in Washington, DC. Both the move and a new plan to train 535 women as lobbyists (one for each member of Congress) reflected a growing interest in influencing federal policy. With a sympathetic ally in the White House, the government emerged as a potential site for conservative reform. LaHaye testified before the Senate in support of Supreme Court nominees Antonin Scalia, Robert Bork, and (under George H. W. Bush), Clarence Thomas. CWA frequently praised Reagan, called for a constitutional amendment to protect parents' rights to educate and discipline their children as they saw fit, and praised as heroes the legislators who shepherded through the 1985 Protection of Pupil Rights Amendment (PPRA), which restricted schools' access to certain information about students. In theory, CWA and other conservatives maintained their anti-government position. In practice, however, activists were increasingly willing to work with the government in order to curb government power—a contradictory position at times, but not one limited to the Christian Right.

By the mid-1980s, CWA had emerged alongside Schlafly's Eagle Forum as one of the two largest conservative women's organizations in the nation, with over a thousand chapters in forty-nine states by 1986. Through grassroots organizing, legal initiatives, and lobbying, CWA led the movement through the culture wars of the 1980s and '90s and into the twenty-first century (see chapter 8). With the founding of the Beverly LaHaye Institute (BLI) in 1999, policy research became another priority.

Between 1979 and her retirement in 2006, LaHaye built an organization that came to closely resemble NOW and other feminist organizations in its structure and strategies. Women in the Christian Right, however, faced an obstacle to organizing that feminist women did not—the value placed on women's subordination in the church, the family, and politics. LaHaye cracked the code for doing so, developing a discourse that augmented women's authority without challenging patriarchal religious culture. This limitation does not mean, however, that LaHaye and other conservative women had been duped by evangelical leaders or that they experienced false consciousness, as feminists sometimes argued. Nor did conservative women see their activism on behalf of traditional gender roles as contradictory. Conservative religious women today—an important voting bloc and fixture in American politics—largely agree with LaHaye in this regard. Progressive and feminist historians and activists have often asked why conservatives—be they "Reagan Democrats" in 1980 or white women Trump supporters in 2016—have voted "against their own interests." This, however, is the wrong question. A better question, as the epilogue to this volume will explore, is how such women define their interests.

NOTES

1. Sarah Palin and John McCain interview with Katie Couric, Sept. 29, 2008, https://www.cbsnews.com/news/transcript-palin-and-mccain-interview/.

2. Barry Goldwater, quoted in Catherine Rymph, *Republican Women: Feminism and Conservatism from Suffrage through the Rise of the New Right* (Chapel Hill: University of North Carolina Press, 2006), 162.

3. F. Clifton White, quoted in Michelle M. Nickerson, *Mothers of Conservatism: Women and the Postwar Right* (Princeton, NJ: Princeton University Press, 2012), 150.

4. Rymph, *Republican Women*, 183.

5. Phyllis Schlafly, "What's Wrong with 'Equal Rights' for Women?" *The Phyllis Schlafly Report*, Feb. 1972.

6. Ibid.

7. Ibid.

8. Betty Friedan and Phyllis Schlafly, quoted in Marjorie Spruill, *Divided We Stand: The Battle over Women's Rights and Family Values That Polarized American Politics* (New York: Bloomsbury Publishing, 2017), 96. Historians have interpreted Schlafly's relationship to the radical and/or segregationist right differently. Donald Critchlow, who wrote his biography of Schlafly with her full support, argues that "while many of the anti-ERA activists held conservative beliefs that were anti-big government, anti-egalitarian, and fearful about moral disorder in society they never had contact with the segregationist Right—the Ku Klux Klan, the Minutemen, or white separatist groups." Donald Critchlow, *Phyllis Schlafly and Grassroots Conservatism: A Woman's Crusade* (Princeton, NJ: Princeton University Press, 2005), 222. More recently, however, Marjorie Spruill has found that many of Schlafly's lieutenants were members of the John Birch Society and Women for Constitutional Government (WCG), founded in Mississippi in 1962 to fight integration. Schlafly herself may have been unaware of these connections, but she did actively court former Alabama governor George Wallace's support for her movement. Spruill, *Divided We Stand*, 85.

9. Ben Sargent, "Mona, Darned If I Can See . . . ," in Jane J. Mansbridge, *Why We Lost the ERA* (Chicago: University of Chicago Press, 1986), 115.

10. See Natasha Zaretsky, *No Direction Home: The American Family and the Fear of National Decline, 1968–1980* (Chapel Hill: University of North Carolina Press, 2007).

11. See Robert O. Self, *All in the Family: The Realignment of American Democracy since the 1960s* (New York: Hill and Wang, 2012).

12. Spruill, *Divided We Stand*, 91.

13. Lottie Beth Hobbs, "Ladies! Have You Heard?" Kathryn Fink Dunaway Papers, Stuart A. Rose Manuscript, Archives, and Rare Book Library, Emory University.

14. Ann O'Donnell, quoted in Spruill, *Divided We Stand*, 247.

15. Bob Green, quoted in Emily Suzanne Johnson, "God, Country, and Anita Bryant: Women's Leadership and the Politics of the New Christian Right," *Religion and American Culture* 28, no. 2 (2018): 241.

16. Anita Bryant, quoted in Johnson, "God, Country, and Anita Bryant," 256–57.

17. Ibid., 256.

18. In June 2020, as of this writing the most recent word on the matter, the Supreme Court ruled six to three that Title VII's prohibition of sex discrimination applied to both sexual orientation and gender identity, adding new protections to about half of the states.

19. Protect America's Children Newsletter, quoted in Emily Suzanne Johnson, *This Is Our Message: Women's Leadership in the New Christian Right* (New York: Oxford University Press, 2019), 65.

20. Beverly LaHaye, quoted in Johnson, *This Is Our Message*, 93.

21. Ibid., 97.

CHAPTER 7

CULTURE AND CONFLICT IN THE SECOND WAVE

INTRODUCTION

Traditionally, holistic treatments of the second wave of feminism have moved from an account of how its various strands emerged to the ways in which race, class, sexuality, and other factors manifested themselves in the movement. This chapter addresses these same themes, but in a different way. Rather than devoting sections to different groups of women, I have organized this chapter in terms of issues—paid and unpaid labor, separatism, reproductive rights, and the debate over women's culture—in which different aspects of identity collide.

Those with a cursory knowledge of second-wave feminism may believe that its adherents were singularly focused on professional opportunities. As I have argued throughout this book, this was simply not the case. Feminists have articulated a wide range of positions *vis-à-vis* advancement within the capitalist economy, ranging from full-throated endorsement of its possibilities to revolutionary Marxist calls for its destruction. Moreover, to the extent that professional advancement has been an important feminist goal—and it certainly has been—it has more often than not reflected the interests of middle-class white women. As this chapter shows, poor Black women in the welfare rights movement developed a very different understanding of the role paid labor played in their lives.

Feminists also divided over the issue of separatism: should women establish new, separate communities in which they could live their politics as purely as possible? The Furies, a small lesbian-feminist collective in Washington, DC, took this path. While some feminists found freedom in a movement that did not put women's sexuality at the center of their identities, The Furies believed that lesbianism was the only true feminism, and the group regularly purged members who appeared beholden to heteronormative, patriarchal culture in any way. Unfortunately, this insistence on purity made it difficult to form coalitions and eventually to survive, and the group proved short-lived.

Understanding the role of reproductive rights in second-wave feminism requires looking beyond access to abortion and birth control. As the previous chapter showed, feminists who identified as pro-life felt increasingly alienated by these priorities. Additionally, for many women—particularly Black, Native American, and Latina women—forced sterilization was a far more urgent issue than abortion was. Like paid work, the issue of reproductive rights largely broke along fault lines of race and class; for many, the right to have children was just as important as the right to choose not to.

Finally, feminists were divided over perhaps the most fundamental question of all: what, exactly, was a woman? Stalwarts of the new cultural feminism postulated the existence of a female essence, which drew its power from the ability to bear children. Others balked at this theory, arguing that, in equating women once more with motherhood, it reified the tropes and stereotypes against which feminists fought. Positing a universal female essence or experience also elided differences among women. Equally damaging, this belief encouraged hostility toward trans individuals, especially trans women, a hostility that remains in certain feminist circles in the twenty-first century (note that some of the quotes in this chapter include misgendering and anti-trans language).

THE POLITICS OF PAID AND UNPAID LABOR

By the second half of the 1960s, financial exigencies, the changing kinds and character of work and employers' needs, and feminist pressure had increased the number of women who participated in paid labor throughout their adult lives. An unintended consequence of these developments was the stigmatization—even among some feminists—of women who received government aid, especially in the form of Aid to Families with Dependent Children (AFDC). Formerly Aid to Dependent Children

(ADC), this program was established in 1935 as part of the Social Security Act. It emulated nationally the mothers pensions enacted on the state level during the Progressive Era. It was one of several government-supported social welfare provisions included in the 1935 act, which also provided support for older Americans ("social security"), the unemployed, and individuals with disabilities. When Americans in the second half of the twentieth century referred to "welfare," however, they usually meant ADC and its successors. Its unusual stigmatization as one of a bundle of similar new rights derived in large part from the fact that it was the only program aimed specifically at women. White Americans also increasingly associated this form of aid with Black women, though whites have always been the majority of welfare recipients. By the 1950s, liberal reformers advocated changes aimed at getting people off of the program as quickly as possible, especially in the form of work requirements. Increasingly, employment became a prerequisite to receive a form of support initially established to recognize women's unequal burden in child-rearing and the difficulties of combining paid work and childcare.

Welfare recipients found these measures coercive, and the welfare rights movement officially kicked off in summer 1966. In New York City, fifteen hundred men and women activists gathered at city hall to demand welfare rights, insisting on both access to the resources they needed to support their families and their right to dignity as Americans. Specifically, they demanded higher grants, access to consumer goods, jobs and job training, day care for mothers who wanted it, and coverage of burial costs. A brand-new group, the City-Wide Coordinating Committee of Welfare Groups, planned the event. Following the summer 1966 protest, the City-Wide group staged a series of protests demanding access to warm clothes for their children. At this point, 30 percent of New York City women who received AFDC reported having to keep their children home from school due to a lack of clothes or shoes. They brought their message to city welfare offices, picketing, sitting in, and sometimes getting arrested.

Across the country, over six thousand people in over one hundred groups participated in similar protests. Several events were held in California, where the most important welfare rights activist was Johnnie Tillmon. Born in Arkansas, Tillmon moved to Los Angeles in 1960 with her five children. She worked in laundries, became the shop steward of her union, and was secretary of a local Democratic Party club. She also closely watched the civil rights movement. Sick and out of work in 1963, she heeded a friend's suggestion to apply for aid, quickly organizing a group of welfare mothers.

Tillmon became the welfare rights movement's most important theorist, connecting it in innovative ways to feminism. In "Welfare Is a Women's Issue," a now-classic article written in 1972 for *Ms.* magazine, Tillmon demonstrated how the logic of patriarchy informed both welfare policies and public perception of welfare. AFDC, she argued "is like a supersexist marriage." Like a cruel husband, the government controlled recipients' spending, sexuality, fertility, and more. It did not surprise Tillmon that welfare functioned as an extreme version of marriage between a woman and a man, because it reflected similar beliefs about women—primarily that they only mattered if attached to a male breadwinner. The real transgression of AFDC recipients, Tillmon argued, was their inability to marry a man who could support them financially. After all, politicians rarely if ever objected to middle-class white women who did not work for wages. But since women on welfare had failed to attach themselves to financially stable men, they had failed at their primary task as women and thus no longer mattered. "Society needs women on welfare as 'examples,'" Tillmon argued, "to let every woman, factory workers and housewife workers alike, know what will happen if she lets up, if she's laid off, if she tries to go it alone without a man."[1]

Americans espoused many myths about women on welfare: that they were lazy, dishonest, fecund, uneducated, and possible addicted to drugs or alcohol. "If people are willing to believe these lies," Tillmon argued, "it's partly because they're just special versions of the lies that society tells about all women." The insistence on welfare mothers' laziness, for example, drew on the larger myth that women did not belong to the paid labor force. In truth, most AFDC recipients deemed "employable" already worked for wages, but their wages were too low to support their families. More than perhaps any other Americans, mothers on welfare wished for work with dignity and a living wage.[2]

Over the course of 1966–67, Tillmon, and others began building a network of activists that in 1967 became the National Welfare Rights Organization (NWRO). George Wiley, a chemistry PhD and former associate national director of the Congress of Racial Equality (CORE), became its executive director. Members immediately targeted the federal government. After its founding convention, Tillmon led more than one thousand marchers to the Department of Health, Education, and Welfare (HEW). The NWRO, along with Martin Luther King Jr. and many others, called for a guaranteed minimum income, and they participated in planning the Poor People's March on Washington that took place shortly after King's assassination in 1968.

In the midst of this campaign, NWRO members testified before members of Congress in hearings on income maintenance programs. The issue at hand was a proposed Work Incentive program (WIN) that would empower the Labor Department to make welfare contingent on paid labor. As chair of the subcommittee on fiscal policy, Michigan representative Martha Griffiths played a prominent role in these hearings. Griffiths was a longtime supporter of the ERA and had advocated for the inclusion of "sex" in Title VII of the Civil Rights Act (see chapter 3). She was also, in her own words, "the most dedicated feminist we have in Congress."[3] A series of exchanges between Griffiths and NWRO members revealed fault lines between this group and mainstream white feminists.

As Griffiths saw it, the goal of welfare should be to get people off welfare. "Insofar as possible," she argued in her opening statement, "welfare programs should reinforce individual responsibility and human resources development programs. They should seek to move people into a dignified and rewarding participation in the economic life of the Nation."[4] To Griffiths, "dignified and rewarding participation" only came from one place: working for wages.

Beulah Sanders, who had moved to New York City from North Carolina in 1955 with her twin sons, was a cofounder of the City-Wide group and one of the NWRO's most prominent members. In her statement, Sanders laid out an opposing point of view. In addition to highlighting the daily financial hardships and intrusive surveillance that mothers on welfare faced, she emphasized three key aspects of the relationship between this constituency and paid work: first, contrary to what Griffiths believed, most women who received welfare already did work for wages. Second, these jobs did not provide the dignity that Griffiths and other white feminists insisted they did. Third, mothers on welfare often struggled to find affordable day-care facilities for their children.

Griffiths believed that she was looking out for women's best interests. "I am a woman," she told Wiley, "and I know the kinds of discriminations that have been used against women." She did not acknowledge Wiley's response noting that he "work[ed] for 5,000 or 6,000 women"—or the fact that these women may have interests that differed from hers.[5]

Ultimately, white feminists like Griffiths and welfare rights activists fell on opposite sides of a series of questions: when does a right to stay home become a requirement to stay home, and when does a requirement to work become coercive? Griffiths feared that, were the Labor Department not allowed to require work, welfare recipients would be forced out of the paid work force. Sanders, by contrast, knew that if they were required to work, they would be forced back into the most degrading sectors of the paid workforce, including domestic labor in white women's homes. Race and class differences meant that these women occupied very different positions in relation to paid work. Griffiths and other white professional women felt that they had for too long been restricted from remunerative, fulfilling careers. But Sanders and the women she represented did not have the same professional opportunities that Griffiths did. War on Poverty job training programs more often than not prepared people for jobs that did not exist, while training programs for jobs that did exist were not available.

NWRO reached the peak of its visibility in 1970, in a showdown with the Nixon administration. The year before, Nixon had unveiled his Family Assistance Plan (FAP), which essentially would have established a guaranteed minimum income. On the face of it, FAP seemed to meet the goals of the welfare rights movement. Activists, however, opposed the measure, which established support levels that were too low to live on and included a strict work requirement. To voice their disapproval, in May 1970, NWRO activists took over HEW headquarters.

From HEW and elsewhere, NWRO members criticized not only FAP but also the Vietnam War and its expansion into Cambodia. Why, they wondered, was the United States spending money to kill children abroad when it could be taking care of children at home—children whose slightly older brothers were disproportionately fighting and dying in the same war? The NWRO also devoted the May 1970 issue of its newspaper, the *Welfare Fighter*, to the subject of "Welfare and the War." Echoing the more famous anti-war statements of King, Muhammad Ali, and others, the Ohio Welfare Rights Organization (WRO) noted the "close relationships between the way human beings are being treated in Viet Nam and the way human beings are being treated in the United States. . . . Ohio's WRO members voice opposition to a system which forces their sons to fight for freedom in Viet Nam when there is a small chance for freedom in this country."[6] The guns-or-butter trap affected Black mothers on welfare more dramatically than perhaps any other group of Americans.

In the wake of the HEW sit-in, a few politicians offered limited support to NWRO. Senator Eugene McCarthy, for example, invited them to testify in a series of unofficial hearings. Ultimately, however, neither FAP nor NWRO alternatives progressed.

The welfare rights movement challenged one of the most cherished beliefs of Betty Friedan–style liberal feminism: that paid work was the key to liberation, especially from the prison of unpaid domestic and

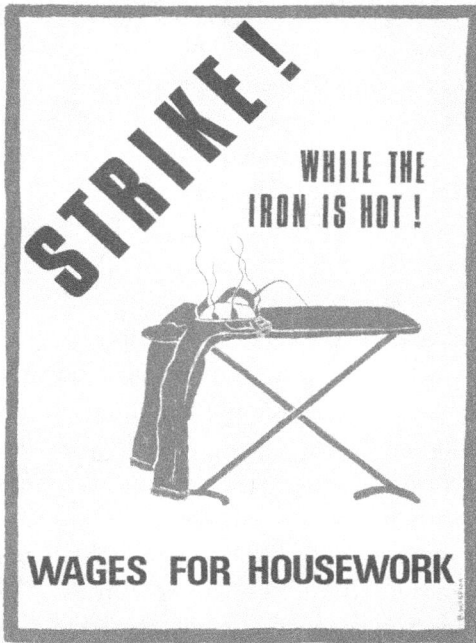

Betsy Warrior, "Strike! While the Iron Is Hot! Wages for Housework," n.d. Though the issue of paid work often divided the feminist movement, many activists recognized the value of unpaid domestic labor. Signs like this one were common at feminist rallies. (Library of Congress, Prints & Photographs Division, LC-DIG-ds-14907)

child-rearing responsibilities. In truth, mainstream feminists had developed a much more nuanced position on paid and unpaid labor, one that often demanded wages for housework. But the version of feminism that was transmitted to the public rarely recognized these subtleties. By the 1980s, mainstream feminism often equated it solely with success within the capitalist economy. These issues would reemerge in the welfare debates of the 1990s.

THE "WOMAN-IDENTIFIED WOMAN": FROM REFORM TO SEPARATISM

On the evening of May 1, 1970, three hundred women sat in a New York City school auditorium waiting for opening-night proceedings of the Second Congress to Unite Women to begin. A group of forty women, many of them sporting T-shirts emblazoned with the phrase "Lavender Menace," ran into the room and ascended to the stage. Members of the lesbian-feminist group Radicalesbians, for two hours they educated the NOW-sponsored crowd on their lives in a heterosexist culture. They also distributed to the audience a paper titled "The Woman-Identified Woman," primarily written by the event's main organizer, Rita Mae Brown.

"What is a lesbian?" the paper began. "[A] lesbian is the rage of all women condensed to the point of explosion." What followed theorized the relationship between gender and sexuality and assessed the way the term "lesbian" functioned as a rhetorical weapon against all women. As Radicalesbians saw it, by defining women in relation to men, systems of male supremacy created categories of sexual orientation. Straight women were those who adhered to these roles, while lesbians defied them. These categories, however, were cultural, not natural: "In a society in which men do not oppress women, and sexual expression is allowed to follow feelings, the categories of homosexuality and heterosexuality would disappear."[7]

In mainstream culture, Radicalesbians recognized, "lesbian" was often deployed against women who in any way challenged their second-class status. "Lesbian is a word, the label, the condition that holds women in line. When a woman hears this word, she knows she is stepping out of line. She knows she has crossed the terrible boundary of her sex role. . . . Lesbian is the label invented by the Man to throw at any woman who dares to be his equal, who dares to challenge his prerogatives . . . ."

Ultimately, this line of reason rested on the assumption that being a lesbian was incompatible with being a "real woman." "When you strip off all the packaging," *The Woman-Identified Woman* argued, "you must finally realize that the essence of being a 'woman' is to get f—d by men."[8]

Until recent decades, Americans frequently regarded the June 1969 Stonewall uprising, in which patrons at the Stonewall Inn fought back against a police raid, as the opening sally in the gay and lesbian rights movement. Stonewall has now come to represent a shift in LGBTQ activism toward more visible, public protests and a demand for acceptance—a shift that earlier protests, including one held in Philadelphia in 1964, had presaged. The Radicalesbians' protest of the Second Congress to Unite Women came less than a year after Stonewall, and the first pride parades were held in June 1970. More than fifty years later, Americans still recognize June as Pride Month.

The Stonewall uprising did not emerge from nowhere. Rather, it reflected the experiences of a generation of activists who had participated in the struggle for racial justice, the New Left, and second-wave feminism. These movements, however, were often unfriendly to their gay and lesbian members. Black Panther Eldridge Cleaver, for example, argued that homosexuality was anti-Black, while white, male New Leftists celebrated macho pride and heterosexual conquest. For women, as I will discuss in depth below, the issue was even more complicated: the gay rights movement was led by men, and the feminist movement was deeply homophobic. The Pride movement emerged, in other words, for the same reasons other social movements were proliferating and radicalizing in the 1960s and '70s: exposure to both activist training and discrimination in existing social movements.

Radicalesbians also owed a debt to an earlier generation of activists who urged acceptance for homosexuality and theorized the relationship between lesbianism and feminism. Activists founded the first organizations dedicated to fighting homophobia—shortly after World War II. In the early homophile movement, activists focused on educating the public about homosexuality, changing discriminatory laws, and making themselves more acceptable to the straight public. They demanded respectability in behavior and dress, including shirts and ties for men and skirts and heels for women. In Los Angeles, in 1950, a handful of white gay men founded the Mattachine Society, which argued that gay men and lesbians constituted a minority group. Then, in 1955, four lesbian couples founded the Daughters of Bilitis (DOB), which began as a social group. According to the organization's statement of purpose, it was "a women's organization for the purpose of promoting the integration of the homosexual into society." Its first priority was "education of the variant, . . . to enable her to understand herself and make adjustment to society in all its social, civic and economic implications." In addition to educating the public and pursuing legal changes, it advocated "a mode of behavior and dress acceptable to society."[9]

Over the course of the 1960s, DOB members recognized their common cause with feminists. As one of its founders, Del Martin, wrote in 1968,

> In speaking to public audiences about the Lesbian, DOB spokeswomen have often alluded to the fact that she is first a human being, a woman second, and incidentally a Lesbian. DOB's program over the years, however, has lent itself almost exclusively to the Lesbian role—the problems these women face in employment, for instance, as Lesbians. But don't they face employment discrimination just on the basis of being women? And wouldn't it serve the purpose of DOB to join with other women's organizations in fighting against sex discrimination as it relates to women?[10]

Unfortunately, the feminist movement of the 1960s and '70s reflected the homophobia of mainstream society. Betty Friedan felt that sexual politics in general were a distraction, and she famously referred to lesbians within the women's movement as a "lavender menace" (the inspiration for the Radicalesbians protest that opens this section). The New York chapter of NOW went through several purges in which lesbians were removed from high-profile leadership positions, and the national organization did not formally recognize the oppression of lesbians as a feminist concern until 1971. While some members of the women's liberation movement were more accepting, they were often befuddled at outsiders' attempts to link lesbianism and feminism. They feared that associating the movement with lesbians would discredit feminism in its entirety. Some felt that lesbianism and feminism were actually at odds, arguing that the former simply reduced women to their sexuality, exactly what the latter hoped to challenge. As Ellen DuBois put it, "I felt finally I had found a movement where I didn't have to worry about whether or not I was attractive or whether or not men liked me. . . . And just as I was beginning to feel here at last I could forget all of that, sex once again reared its ugly head."[11] Others assumed that lesbians wanted to be men and/or to re-create male and female roles in their own relationships, validating patriarchal, heteronormative power dynamics. A number of prominent feminists, including Gloria Steinem, Flo Kennedy, Aileen Hernandez, and Bella Abzug expressed solidarity with gay men and lesbians. Nonetheless, one of the goals of lesbian feminism was to challenge both the sexism of the gay liberation movement and the homophobia of the feminist movement.

Especially between 1970 and 1975, many women's liberationists framed lesbianism as a political choice and thus as the truest expression of their feminism. Marginalized within the broader feminist movement, some lesbian-feminists began to organize separately. Founded by twelve white lesbians in Washington, DC, in 1971, The Furies became the most famous of these groups, in part due to its influential, eponymous newspaper. In 1970, Joan E. Biren, a Mount Holyoke–educated DC native and veteran of Radicalesbians and the DC Women's Liberation Movement, began recruiting lesbians to the area. The group's first experiment with communal living, Amazing Grace, lasted for just a week. Shortly thereafter, Biren, Rita Mae Brown, Charlotte Bunch, and others founded the collective that became The Furies (for most of its existence, the group was known as "Those Women," after the dismissive way that many straight feminists discussed lesbians).

The group took its name from the Greek deities of vengeance. "The story of the Furies," Ginny Berson wrote in the first issue of its newspaper, "is the story of strong, powerful women, the 'Angry Ones,' the avengers of matricide, the protectors of women. Three Greek Goddesses, they were described (by men) as having snakes for hair, blood-shot eyes, and bats' wings; like Lesbians today, they were cursed and feared. . . . We call our paper The Furies because we are also angry."[12]

Ideologically, The Furies drew on the several movements in which its members had been involved. From the Black freedom movement, they learned that the most oppressed members of society should be the leaders of movements for social change, and from Black nationalism they learned to embrace separatism. Following radical groups within SDS, especially the Leninist Weathermen, they argued that a small cadre of committed individuals could foment revolution. Borrowing from women's liberationists the idea that "the personal is political," The Furies also insisted that "the political is personal"—that is, women should organize their personal lives in a way that reflected their politics. Little interested in changing laws and policies, The Furies sought to manifest their politics through communal living while strategizing other means to end women's oppression.

To this end, members learned martial arts, read Russian and Chinese revolutionary tracts, and studied women's history. They assembled a five-year plan to bring their message to women across the nation, the first step in what they imagined would be a fifty-year struggle. By 2021, Bunch envisioned, "women will have taken power in many regions in the U.S., [and] are governing and beginning to create a new feminist society." A lesbian-feminist political party would govern the new "Federation of Feminist States."[13] In concrete terms, they held skills workshops for local women, hosted film screenings, and organized theory workshops and poetry readings. But writing in and publishing *The Furies* remained the group's most important form of outreach.

More separatist and dogmatic than other lesbian-feminist groups, members insisted that "Lesbianism is not a matter of sexual preference, but rather one of political choice which every woman must make if she is to become woman-identified and thereby end male supremacy."[14] In theory, The Furies embraced sexuality, but largely as a manifestation of one's politics rather than one's desire. If one was not attracted to women, members sometimes argued, it meant that one was still beholden to patriarchy.

The Furies' insistence that lesbianism was a political choice may seem odd today, when many of those who see sexual orientation as a choice do so in the hopes of changing people's "deviant" behavior. In the early 1970s, however, framing one's sexual orientation this way functioned as a protest against dominant ideas about homosexuality, which the psychiatric community still defined as an illness. Biren learned while a college student that her desire for women had a name only because she looked it up in the Diagnostic and Statistical Manual (DSM), the American Psychiatric Association's (APA) encyclopedia of mental illness. Barbara Gittings, a Philadelphia lesbian-feminist activist, played a crucial role in convincing the APA to remove homosexuality from the DSM in 1973.

With both middle-class and working-class members, The Furies developed some of the most sophisticated class analysis to come out of the feminist movement but also hewed to a narrow ideological model. Private property was frowned upon, and members faced regular "criticism-self-criticism sessions" in which the collective criticized each woman's failings—with younger women, women from middle-class backgrounds, and women who had recently come out taken especially to task. "Basically what would happen would be you would be sitting up against the wall and everybody would criticize you and you couldn't talk back. You couldn't answer back. . . . So, we just had to listen, and it was really, really, hard, to sit there and not be able to talk and everybody tell you every single thing that you had done wrong," Biren recalled.[15] The group also knew that the FBI was monitoring it, which increased distrust among members.

Ultimately, a series of purges made The Furies' continued existence untenable. The first purge occurred over the issue of raising children. Male children had been banned from the collective from the beginning—one woman gave her son to his father when she joined—but the group had been collectively raising three girls, two of whom were the daughters of members and the third of whom was informally adopted when her mother had to go underground. Eventually, a faction led by Brown insisted that the girls could not stay either. The collective decided to return the girl to her mother, who placed her up for adoption. While Brown attributed this decision to concern for the children's safety, others attributed it to vanguardism. "We were purists almost to the point of being fascists about everything," Biren later admitted.[16] She and her partner, Sharon Deevey, opposed the decision. Brown convinced the collective to purge Biren and Deevey, only to find herself the victim of another purge shortly thereafter. The insular community quickly fell apart, but its contributions to lesbian-feminist theory remained influential.

REPRODUCTIVE POLITICS IN THE FEMINIST MOVEMENT

By the 1960s, state-sanctioned forced sterilizations had existed in the United States for several decades. In *Buck v. Bell* (1927), the U.S. Supreme Court upheld a Virginia law allowing the practice, leading many states to enact similar laws. (The decision was later cited by Nazi doctors to justify their atrocities.) In the 1930s, southern states established birth control clinics explicitly aimed at controlling Black population growth. Though subsequent court decisions chipped away at the legality of forced sterilization, the post–World War II population boom led several states to pass legislation aimed at curbing the growth of poor communities. In Mississippi, for example, a 1964 law made it a felony for a woman to have a second child outside of marriage, subjecting her to a prison sentence. Early in the next decade, funding provided by the Family Planning Act, HEW, and the Office of Economic Opportunity made sterilization cheaply and easily accessible (not to mention, profitable for hospitals). Doctors freely admitted that they routinely performed nonconsensual sterilizations on poor women for practice, for profit, and "for their own good."

Statistics bear these impressions out: poor women of color, especially those who received state benefits, were at a significantly higher risk for these procedures than were members of any other group. Civil rights activist Fannie Lou Hamer, who had been sterilized without her knowledge while in the hospital for the removal of a uterine tumor, reported to the Women's International League for Peace and Freedom (WILPF) that 60 percent of Black women admitted to her local hospital in Mississippi were sterilized. A 1970 study found that doctors sterilized Black women more than twice as frequently as they sterilized white women. In 1973, Black women were 43 percent of those sterilized in federally funded clinics. Latinas were also sterilized at higher rates, as were women whose education did not go beyond high school. Medicaid recipients were sterilized at rates between two and four times higher than nonrecipients. Many of these procedures took place without patients' knowledge or consent; consent, if received, was often coerced—under circumstances where true consent was impossible, as a requirement for state aid, or in a language or form women did not understand. In certain cases, doctors told patients that sterilization would wear off and that they would still be able to have children. In short, race and poverty left women vulnerable to a medical establishment and state welfare policies that often saw them as incapable or unworthy of making decisions about their own fertility.

In fact, white women often had difficulty securing sterilization even if they wanted it. Male doctors did not trust white women to make their own reproductive decisions either, but in this case, they encouraged women to have more children. They either simply refused to sterilize white women or adhered to arcane mathematical formulae to determine whether they would grant a white woman's request—for example, only if the number of children she had times her age equaled at least 120 (a thirty-year-old who had four children or a forty-year-old who had three children). As a result, in the early 1970s, white feminist activism focused more on expanding access to voluntary sterilization than on ending forced sterilization. A discourse developed that linked access to sterilization with access to abortion, making the two into key feminist demands.

Women of color thus led the way in challenging forced sterilization. In doing so, they broadened the definition of reproductive rights beyond access to birth control and abortion at a time when many white feminists did not see past these two issues. They also charted a course that differed from their male counterparts, some of whom insisted that birth control and abortion were forms of genocide against Black and brown populations (see chapter 5).

Within the Puerto Rican nationalist Young Lords Party (YLP), for example, men saw the popularity of sterilization on the island, as well as the exposure of Puerto Rican women to unsafe testing of the pill, as proof that birth control and abortion advocates wanted to eliminate the Puerto Rican population. In New York City, Puerto Rican women were sterilized at rates seven times higher than white women and twice as high as Black women. Even legal abortion was not necessarily safe for Puerto Rican women, as careless doctors sometimes neglected to administer lifesaving treatments. But the increasingly vocal and influential feminist contingent within the YLP pushed the organization to support such measures under control of the community, not the medical establishment, while still opposing forced sterilization. "We believe that abortions should be legal if they are community controlled, if they are safe, if our people are educated about the risks, and if doctors do not sterilize our sisters while performing abortions," a 1970 position paper asserted.[17]

In 1973, the case of Minnie Lee Relf, a twelve-year-old resident of Montgomery, Alabama, brought mainstream attention to the issue of forced sterilization. Welfare caseworkers had (with little evidence) diagnosed Minnie Lee with an intellectual disability, which according to Alabama law was enough to allow sterilization without consent from either the patient or her family. The law assumed that such patients were not competent to make decisions about their fertility and reproduction. Though nothing suggested that Minnie Lee was sexually active, the HEW-funded Montgomery Family Planning Clinic administered Depo-Provera, a contraceptive shot. When the clinic discontinued this treatment, it recommended sterilization.

The clinic presented Minnie Lee's mother with a consent form, which she signed with an "X." A sharecropper who could not read or write, she believed she was consenting to continued Depo-Provera shots, not sterilization. Minnie Lee herself did not understand the effects of the procedure. When lawyers party to a class-action lawsuit filed against HEW on her behalf asked her if she planned to have children in the future, she said yes.

In a case that attracted national attention, both NWRO and the Southern Poverty Law Center (SPLC) filed suit against HEW. Senator Edward Kennedy demanded that hearings be held on the issue. In March 1974, a U.S. District Court ruled in *NWRO v. Weinberger* that the HEW must no longer fund sterilizations of children or those deemed mentally incompetent. Judge Gerhard Arnold Gesell also ordered HEW to rewrite its policies for sterilizing welfare recipients. The new regulations, in place until 1978, required "uncoerced" consent.

In the years after the Relf case, several others made it clear that the forced sterilization of Black and brown women was a national, systemic issue. In 1971, the Los Angeles Medical Center of the University of Southern California allegedly sterilized eleven Chicanas without their consent. Four years later, the women brought suit, arguing that, though they had technically consented, they were asked to do so while in labor and under anesthesia. Moreover, the consent forms had been presented in English, and all the women were native Spanish speakers. Under those circumstances, the plaintiffs argued, it was impossible to give true consent. Two young Chicana women, Antonia Hernández, a recent graduate of the UCLA law school who worked at the Model Cities Center for Law and Justice, and Gloria Molina, president of the Comisión Feminil Mexicana, helped to research and publicize the case, which came before a judge in 1978. Unfortunately for the women, Judge Jesse W. Curtis ruled in *Madrigal v. Quilligan* that the doctors' actions resulted from miscommunication, not malice. However, the case did impel California to rewrite its sterilization guidelines to ensure informed consent.

In 1976, Dr. Constance Redbird Pinkerton-Uri, a Choctaw and Cherokee gynecologist in South Dakota, prompted a government investigation into sterilization abuse against Native American women when a twenty-six-year-old patient asked her for a womb transplant. Six years earlier, the woman's doctor had convinced her to consent to a hysterectomy because she suffered from alcoholism and already had two children. The woman believed that her womb was replaceable, and when her circumstances changed, she appealed to Pinkerton-Uri. The federal General Accounting Office (GAO) found that the Indian Health Service (IHS) and affiliated clinics in four metro regions had sterilized a total of 3,406 Native American women over the three-year period between 1973 and 1976. But since the procedures were technically consensual—and because the investigators did not speak to any hospital staff or sterilized women—the GAO found no evidence of abuse, though it did acknowledge less than robust compliance with HEW guidelines. In the wake of this report, Pinkerton-Uri left her medical practice, attended law school, and joined Indian Women United for Social Justice.

Interviews conducted elsewhere contradicted the GAO findings. Barbara Moore, a Lakota, was informed after a Caesarean that she had been sterilized without her knowledge or consent while under anesthesia. Norma Jean Serena, of Creek and Shawnee ancestry, had no recollection of signing a consent form, which had been presented to her during labor, as she came out from under anesthesia in August 1970. Just weeks earlier, child welfare services had taken away her two older children with dubious justification, continuing a long tradition of removing children from "unfit" Native parents. No one told Serena about the sterilization, which she discovered only a year later. Serena filed suit against the hospital and local government agencies over these twin civil rights violations, but separate juries found that her rights had been violated only by having her children removed, not by the sterilization, which was deemed consensual. Such experiences were common for Native American women. Working with Women of All Red Nations (WARN), a feminist offshoot of the American Indian Movement (AIM) founded in 1974, Pinkerton-Uri found in 1977 that up to 42 percent of Native American women of childbearing age had been sterilized. This number harkened to an ugly history between the U.S. government and Native American tribes. As the *American Indian Journal* commented, "They took our past with a sword and our land with a pen. Now they're trying to take our future with a scalpel."[18] Especially in this context, activists did not hesitate to call the forced sterilization of Native American women genocide.

In 1974–75, a group of women in New York City, many of them with experience in Puerto Rican nationalism, radical feminism, and legal

APR 9 1977

Who is Norma Jean Serena?

Women against Sterilization Abuse, "Who Is Norma Jean Serena," 1977. Serena was one of thousands of Native women sterilized without her knowledge or consent. When it came to reproductive rights, poor women of color could not afford to focus solely on access to birth control and abortion. (Women against Sterilization Abuse, "Who Is Norma Jean Serena," 1977. Indian Rights Association records [1523]. Historical Society of Pennsylvania. Reproduced with permission from the Historical Society of Pennsylvania.)

battles over reproductive rights, began meeting to discuss what became the Committee to End Sterilization Abuse (CESA). The group responded to a number of scandals, including the revelation that the Nixon administration had in 1972 refused to distribute HEW guidelines on sterilization to federally funded clinics across the country—including the one that sterilized Minnie Lee Relf. Had the clinic been informed of these guidelines, it is possible that she may not have been sterilized.

Like the YLP, CESA focused on links between sterilization abuse in Puerto Rico and New York City. In 1975, CESA sent representatives to the Advisory Committee on Sterilization, founded to help New York City hospitals craft new sterilization guidelines. Those proffered by HEW in the wake of the Relf case, CESA and the advisory committee felt, were still far too lax and far too easy too abuse. Their alternative guidelines, adopted by New York City hospitals, included a thirty-day waiting period and other measures to guarantee informed consent.

The new guidelines faced immediate opposition from doctors, who campaigned against the guidelines and tried to secure exceptions once they had been implemented, and, perhaps surprisingly, feminists. To such groups as Planned Parenthood, National NOW, and the National Association for the Repeal of Abortion Laws (NARAL), the waiting period was an unwelcome restriction on women's reproductive choice. But by 1978, New York City, New York State, and the HEW had adopted guidelines based on CESA's recommendations.

Despite CESA's disputes with NOW and NARAL, by the late 1970s, many white feminists understood that reproductive rights meant much more than access to abortion. In 1977, a mostly white group of women founded the Committee for Abortion Rights and against Sterilization Abuse (CARASA). Its goals reflected an agenda honed by women of color activists over the better part of a decade: not only access to safe, legal, affordable abortions and the end of forced and coerced sterilization—the new group's two priorities—but also welfare rights, childcare, and improved workplace conditions. Only with these other changes, CARASA members argued, would women truly be free to make decisions about their fertility.

CARASA's fight against the 1976 Hyde Amendment, which barred the use of Medicaid funds to pay for abortions, epitomized its belief that true reproductive freedom required not just the legal right but also the financial means to make decisions about fertility. Several reproductive rights groups joined together to fight the new law in court, and Rhonda Copelon, a CARASA lawyer, argued the case in the Supreme Court. But in *McRae v. Crawford* (1978), the Supreme Court upheld the law, and later that year, HEW announced strict new rules about the use of federal funds to pay for abortions. Together, these new restrictions meant that, though all women had the legal right to have an abortion, the poorest women could not afford to do so. By placing this option out of reach, the Hyde Amendment and other restrictions effectively encouraged poor women to "choose" sterilization if they wanted to ensure that they would not have more children.

In part because the erosion of abortion rights encouraged sterilization, CARASA continued to focus on the latter as well. Its sterilization committee pursued loopholes in New York City law; monitored hospitals for compliance with the 1978 local, state, and national guidelines; and opposed Planned Parenthood's casual approach to sterilization. In 1979, the American Cyanimid scandal drew the attention of CARASA's trade union/workplace committee, which investigated the intersections of reproductive rights and economic inequality.

American Cyanimid was a paint factory in Willow Island, West Virginia, that produced lead chromate, which had been linked to birth defects. In 1978, the company began requiring that female employees of childbearing age who were exposed to toxic substances be sterilized if they wished to keep their jobs. If they refused, they would be transferred to a lower-paying position. Of the seven women affected, five chose sterilization, and two chose to accept janitorial positions instead. A year later, the union representing American Cyanimid workers discovered the provision and filed a complaint with the Occupational Health and Safety Administration (OSHA). In response, the company shut down the factory and fired the five women who had been sterilized. Backed by the ACLU Women's Rights Project, the women successfully sued on the basis of gender discrimination. Shortly thereafter, CARASA and other women's and labor groups formed the Committee for the Reproductive Rights of Workers (CRRW).

CARASA's creative feminist vision lasted only for a short time. In part, this was because it was never able to build the coalition that it desired. Beyond its disputes with Planned Parenthood, National NOW, and NARAL, it had trouble attracting working-class women and women of color to the organization. White feminist rhetoric had changed over the course of the 1970s, but members of other groups were still understandably skeptical, and CARASA's broad-based agenda could appear scattershot. Lesbians also felt that the group did not put enough emphasis on securing their rights to bear and raise children. Finally, the growing strength of the pro-life movement in the 1980s increasingly meant that CARASA devoted most of its energies to defending abortion rights. The group disbanded in 1983, in the midst of impassioned attacks on its priorities.

FEMINIST CULTURE/CULTURAL FEMINISM

In certain ways, The Furies' separatist, lifestyle-based politics was prescient. By the early 1970s, cultural feminism, which nurtured women's values in women-only spaces, was on the rise. Cultural feminists espoused gender essentialism, asserting that certain traits (collaboration, compassion, creation, and often connection to the earth) were fundamentally female and others (competitiveness, aggression, acquisitiveness) were fundamentally male. A healthier society, cultural feminists claimed, would move away from valorizing these male qualities and toward embracing female qualities.

For a movement dedicated in part to breaking down stereotypes about women, this new focus seems surprising. Women's liberationists had long been skeptical of groups like Women Strike for Peace, which argued that women's role as mothers gave them a special role to play in the peace movement. In 1968, younger women openly protested the anti-war Jeannette Rankin Brigade for similar reasons. Two factors explain cultural feminism's ascendance especially over the course of 1973–75. First, feminism was by this time rent by differences among women. By asserting a universal femaleness, cultural feminism presented a way potentially to heal these wounds. Second, 1973 represented a turning point in the development of backlash against feminism from an increasingly powerful New Right. Cultural feminism held out the hope that a women's counter-culture could thrive even amid national political regression.

The first stirrings of cultural feminism emerged in the late 1960s. In 1974, Jane Alpert gathered many of its inchoate pieces together in her article *Mother Right: A New Feminist Theory*. A former Weatherman, Alpert had been arrested in 1969 for her involvement in the bombing of eight buildings, part of the group's plan to foment revolution against American imperialism. Alpert was tried along with Sam Melville, her lover, who pleaded guilty in exchange for a sentence of no more eighteen years in prison.[19] But Alpert balked at the deal, under which she could have spent up to five years in prison. Instead, she fled before sentencing, living underground for four years.

Alpert began writing *Mother Right* in her time as a fugitive, completing it in 1974. In it, she renounced the left as male dominated, argued that she had been a pawn of Melville and other charismatic men, and proclaimed her allegiance to feminism—a movement with which her contact had been minimal before going underground. Alpert had met and liked Robin Morgan, and her manifesto bore some similarities to Morgan's "Goodbye to All That," which had appeared four years earlier. Much had changed between 1970 and 1974, as Morgan's contributions to *Mother Right* make clear. She had moved much closer to Alpert's views.

Alpert identified a female consciousness or essence rooted in biological differences, arguing that "*female biology,*" specifically the ability to bear children, "*is the basis of women's powers.* Biology is hence the source and not the enemy of feminist revolution." Indeed, she believed that "the root of motherhood and the root of female consciousness are . . . one and the same." Alpert theorized the existence of ancient goddess-worshipping matriarchies that recognized women's creative power, only to be replaced by monotheistic patriarchies built on warlike aggression. She based these theories in part on Elizabeth Gould Davis's *The First Sex* (1971), which attempted to prove the existence of ancient matriarchies. In Alpert's view, "[T]he feminist revolution will be at its root a religious transformation of society, in which society-wide recognition of the creative principle as female will take the place of worship of the modern (male) God, and women will simultaneously gain not merely respect but true power." Feminism was not merely political; rather, it was "closely tied to theories of awakening consciousness, of creation and rebirth, and of the essential oneness of the universe—teachings which lie at the heart of all Goddess-worshipping religions. . . . Can our revolution mean anything else than the reversion of social and economic control to Her [the mother-goddess's] representatives among Womankind, and the resumption of Her worship on the face of the Earth?"[20]

Cultural feminism provoked a great deal of controversy within the movement. General criticism took two main forms. Many feminists took issue with its essentialism, arguing that it reified the female stereotypes they had long challenged. These critics espoused the idea that gender was a social construction, not innate and fundamental. Some longtime feminists also saw cultural feminism as an escape: from politics, from the tumult of the 1960s, from navigating differences among women, from fighting against patriarchy on a societal, not just personal, scale. Women learning automobile mechanics was fine, Meredith Tax observed in 1971, but she "worried about what else was going to happen. This wasn't going to be the whole thing, was it?" Unfortunately for Tax, historian Alice Echols notes, "[A]s the '70s wore on this was, if not the whole thing, then a large part of it."[21]

Another conflict arose over the place of race in gender essentialism, especially in the realm of feminist theology. A triple-doctorate with degrees in theology, philosophy, and religion, feminist theologian Mary Daly moved over the course of her career from attempting to reform the Catholic Church to wholesale rejection of its teachings, which she regarded as irredeemably patriarchal. In projecting original sin onto women, Daly concluded, Catholicism—and Christianity more generally—set the stage for patriarchy itself. Like Alpert and Gould Davis, she posited the existence of ancient gynocracies—societies ruled by women—and advocated a return to some of their precepts. The figures of the witch and the goddess became for Daly the most important symbols of women's power. Daly applied these beliefs to her academic career, in which she refused to admit male students to some of her women's studies classes at Boston College (ultimately leading to a lawsuit, out-of-court settlement, and Daly's retirement).

In 1978, Daly met Audre Lorde, Black feminist poet and theorist, when the two appeared together on a panel at a conference. The next year, Daly sent Lorde a copy of her most recent book, *Gyn/Ecology*. Lorde responded to the book in a letter, which she eventually published as "An Open Letter to Mary Daly." Though she admired many aspects of *Gyn/Ecology*, Lorde criticized the book on several related bases: its failure to recognize powerful women, be they actual or mythical; outside of western Europe; its misuse of contemporary Black women authors; and its implication that all women existed in a similar relationship to patriarchy. First, Lorde noted, Daly included only white women in her survey of goddesses, though many examples existed in African myth and religion. When Daly did discuss Black women—framed, in many cases, with the decontextualized words of contemporary Black women writers, including Lorde herself—it was only as victims of such processes as female genital mutilation. "Where was Afrekete, Y emanje, Oyo, and Mawulisa?" Lorde asked. "Where were the warrior goddesses of the Vodun, the Dahomeian Amazons and the warrior-women of Dan? . . . What you excluded from *Gyn/Ecology* dismissed my heritage and the heritage of all other noneuropean women, and denied the real connections that exist between all of us." Further, in equating all women's experience with white women's experience, this erasure dismissed the ways in which racism, classism, and homophobia shaped women's relationship to patriarchy. When white feminists failed to recognize this reality, they committed a grave error. "For then," Lorde concluded, "beyond sisterhood is still racism."[22]

Lorde's letter reached a large audience, and over the course of the 1980s, her stature—especially within the growing field of academic feminism—rose as Daly's fell. As literary scholar Elizabeth Hedrick notes, the women's studies departments that emerged in the early 1980s and grew over the course of the next two decades would reflect two key elements of Lorde's response to Daly: its anti-essentialism and its focus on intersectionality, concepts that by the 1990s had become nearly synonymous in academic feminism.[23]

Native American women also criticized cultural feminism's simultaneous appropriation and elision of Indigenous history. In her teaching and writing, Laguna Pueblo scholar Paula Gunn Allen advocated for the inclusion of Native voices in the American literary canon. As a graduate student, Allen was told that she could not write her dissertation on Native literature because no such literature existed. She transferred to the University of New Mexico, where she completed her doctorate in 1975. In her widely anthologized essay "Who Is Your Mother? Red Roots of White Feminism," Allen pointed out that cultural feminist values—including respect for the earth and its resources and the recognition of women's power—had long existed in many Indigenous nations. White American feminists failed to recognize this history, turning instead to esoteric, at least partially mythical, stories of goddesses and gynocracies. "Feminists too often believe that no one has ever experienced the kind of society that empowered women and made that empowerment the basis of its rules and civilization," Allen noted. "[T]he feminist idea of power as it ideally accrues to women stems from tribal sources." But cultural feminism and its offshoots, ecofeminism and feminist spiritualism, remained unmoored from these precedents.[24]

Finally, cultural feminism provoked conflict with individuals who did not identify with the gender assigned to them at birth, those who today may call themselves trans or transgender. The most notorious manifestation of this belief was Janice Raymond's 1979 book *The Transsexual Empire: The Making of the She-Male*, which began as a dissertation written under the supervision of Mary Daly, whose own views of trans individuals were no better. Trans women, Raymond argued, "rape women's bodies by reducing the real female form to an artifact, appropriating this body for themselves." This was especially true, Raymond insisted, of trans women who also identified as lesbians. "The transexually constructed lesbian-feminist," she wrote, "feeds off woman's true energy source, i.e., her woman-identified self. It is he who recognizes that if female spirit, mind, creativity, and sexuality exist anywhere in a powerful way, it is here, among lesbian-feminists." In this view, trans women who identified as lesbians could not abide and thus sought to reclaim spaces in which women devoted their attentions to other women. In Raymond's words, "[I]f men want to become women to obtain female creativity, then they will also want to assimilate those women who have withdrawn their energies from men at the most intimate and emotional levels." She continued, "[I]f feminists cannot agree on the boundaries of what constitutes femaleness, then what can we hope to agree on?"[25]

> We know that we are women who born with female chromosomes and anatomy, and that whether we were socialized to be so-called normal women, patriarchy has treated and will treat us like women. Transsexuals have not had this same history. No man can have the history of being born and located in this culture. He can have the history of *wishing* to be a woman and *acting* like a woman, but this gender experience is that of a transsexual, not of a woman. Surgery may confer the artifacts of outward and inward female organs but it cannot confer the history of being born a woman in this society.[26]

Ultimately, Raymond equated the category of woman with being born with female anatomy.

Cultural feminism never produced a wide-scale political movement—indeed, this was not usually its goal. From the mainstream to the avant-garde, women's attempts to produce culture that reflected their beliefs were more enduring. Founded by journalist and activist Gloria Steinem and others in 1972, Ms. magazine became the most popular and longest-lasting publication to emerge from second-wave feminism.[27] Steinem graduated from Smith College in 1956, after which she spent two years writing and observing political movements in India. Her 1963 *Show* magazine article "A Bunny's Tale," which detailed her time working under-cover in Hugh Hefner's Playboy Club, made her famous, but it also hurt her reputation among serious journalistic outlets and even led to a libel suit. Six years later, "After Black Power, Women's Liberation" brought her back into the public eye, and she spent the next several years covering the feminist movement, testifying on behalf of the ERA, cofounding the National Women's Political Caucus (NWPC), and more.

Feminist media was not new in 1972—some five hundred feminist publications circulated at the beginning of that decade—nor, of course, were glossy women's periodicals. But small magazines rarely reached a large audience, and mainstream women's magazines were hardly consistent bastions of feminism. In March 1970, over two hundred women took over the main office of the *Ladies' Home Journal*, protesting both the magazine's treatment of women employees and the stereotypical images of women found within its pages. The magazine responded with an eight-page supplement on the women's movement in its August 1970 issue—a good start, as far as activists were concerned, but hardly a satisfactory counterweight to the media's frequent dismissive and/or inaccurate coverage of feminism.

Steinem began planning her own feminist publication that same year, marshalling her contacts in both the feminist movement and the journalism world to secure seed money from Katherine Graham at the *Washington Post* and support for a preview issue from *New York* magazine, where Steinem was a staff writer. Borrowing the newly popular alternative to "Miss" or "Mrs.," the title of Ms. magazine reflected women's broader attempts to establish independent lives and identities for themselves. Ms. was based in New York City, and its staff came from that city's educated, progressive networks of cultural and political professionals. Yet its wide circulation ensured that feminist ideas reached far beyond the nation's urban centers. The magazine's preview issue sold three hundred thousand copies in eight days (and brought in twenty thousand reader letters) in April 1972, prompting a $1 million investment from Warner Communications. The first full-size issue appeared in July 1972 and featured Wonder Woman on the cover.

With a diverse readership, commercial backing, and reliance on advertisements, Ms. threaded the needle of feminist ideology. The April 1972 issue included both unapologetic calls for legalized abortion and an optimistic gloss on "sisterhood" as the key to overcoming women's differences. Borrowing from the successful model of mainstream women's magazines, Ms. positioned itself as a how-to publication. As cofounder Patricia Carbine explained,

> The strength of women's magazines in the past has been, in the most part, the how-to approach. They have dealt with the woman's life inside the home. For instance, how to prepare hamburger 101 ways. . . . Ms. is as well going to be a how-to magazine. The difference is that Ms. will address itself to the question of how a woman can change her life and what the ramifications of that change might be—in terms of one's self and one's relationship with husbands, lovers, children, other women, one's job and the community in which one lives.[28]

Much to the chagrin of many radical feminists, and despite Ms. editors' belief in sisterhood, this orientation aligned the magazine with the individualistic, self-help strand of liberal feminism—a contradiction that neither the magazine nor the movement ever resolved. But while Ms. was certainly not *The Furies*, it provided a pragmatic feminist lens on many issues, including in its first year alone articles on political candidates and elections, the ERA, wages for housework, the lives of women who received welfare, discrimination against lesbians, sex and marriage, mental health, rape and sexual assault, and unequal pay, along with fiction and poetry from well-known women writers. Ultimately, Ms. sought to smuggle in a feminist critique under the guise of a conventional women's magazine. Both its strengths and its weaknesses flowed from this decision.

Elsewhere in feminist culture, writers including Lorde, Gloria Anzaldua, and Adrienne Rich; visual artist Judy Chicago; and the theater artists in Spiderwoman Theater and Split Britches pushed the boundaries of genre. Women also challenged what counted as art, noting the frequent relegation of women's work to the less-respected category of "craft." In the 1980s, feminist art became a front in the culture wars, a battle over American identity and values that in this iteration pitted freedom of expression against "obscenity." But, as the final chapter will show, the sides did not always fall along expected political fault lines. Ultimately, the culture wars defined differences between not only liberals and conservatives but also second- and third-wave feminists.

NOTES

1. Johnnie Tillmon, "Welfare Is a Women's Issue," Ms. magazine, Spring 1972, 111, 112.

2. Ibid., 112.

3. Statement of Representative Griffiths, June 11, 1968, in Income Maintenance Programs Hearings, Ninetieth Congress, Second Session, vol. 1: Proceedings (Washington, DC: U.S. Government Printing Office, 1968), 77.

4. Statement of Representative Griffiths, 2.

5. Ibid., 78; Statement of Dr. George Wiley, in Income Maintenance Programs Hearings, 78.

6. Ohio Welfare Rights Organization, quoted in Wilson Sherwin and Frances Fox Piven, "The Radical Feminist Legacy of the National Welfare Rights Organization," Women's Studies Quarterly 47, no. 3–4 (2019): 147.

7. Radicalesbians, The Woman-Identified Woman (Pittsburgh, PA: Know Inc., 1970).

8. Ibid.

9. "Purpose of the Daughters of Bilitis," The Ladder, Dec. 1956.

10. Del Martin, "The Lesbian's Other Identity," in Baxandall and Gordon, Dear Sisters, 27.

11. Ellen DuBois, quoted in Alice Echols, Daring to Be Bad: Radical Feminism in America, 1967–1975 (Minneapolis: University of Minnesota Press, 1989), 217.

12. Ginny Berson, "The Furies," The Furies, Jan. 1972.

13. Charlotte Bunch, quoted in Anne M. Valk, Radical Sisters: Second-Wave Feminism and Black Liberation in Washington, DC (Urbana: University of Illinois Press, 2008), 145.

14. Berson, "The Furies."

15. Joan E. Biren oral history interview with Kelly Anderson, Voices of Feminism Oral History Project, Sophia Smith Collection, Smith College, Northampton, MA, Feb. 27, 2004, p. 56, https://www.smith.edu/libraries/libs/ssc/vof /transcripts/Biren.pdf.

16. Ibid., 53.

17. The Young Lords Party, Position Paper on Women, 1970, quoted in Jennifer Nelson, *Women of Color and the Reproductive Rights Movement* (New York: New York University Press, 2003), 128–29.

18. *American Indian Journal*, quoted in "Killing Our Future: Sterilization and Experiments," *Akwesasne Notes*, early spring 1977, 4.

19. Melville went on to be a leader in the 1971 Attica uprising. He was shot and killed by police as they retook the complex.

20. Jane Alpert, *Mother Right: A New Feminist Theory* (Pittsburgh, PA: Know Inc., 1974), 1, 7, 9, 10.

21. Meredith Tax, quoted in Echols, *Daring to Be Bad*, 5; Echols, *Daring to Be Bad*, 5.

22. Audre Lorde, "An Open Letter to Mary Daly," in *Sister Outsider: Essays and Speeches by Audre Lorde*, ed. Lorde (Berkeley, CA: Crossing Press, 1984), 67, 68, 70.

23. Elizabeth Hedrick, "The Early Career of Mary Daly: A Retrospective," *Feminist Studies* 39, no. 2 (2013): 457–83.

24. Paula Gunn Allen, "Who Is Your Mother? Red Roots of White Feminism," History Is a Weapon, 1986, https://www.historyisaweapon.com/defcon1/allenredrootsofwhitefeminism.html.

25. Janice G. Raymond, *The Transsexual Empire: The Making of the She-Male*, rev. ed. (New York: Teachers College Press, 1994), 104, 108, 110.

26. Ibid., 114, emphasis in original.

27. *Ms.* first appeared as an insert to *New York* magazine in December 1971.

28. Patricia Carbine, quoted in Amy Erdman Farrell, *Yours in Sisterhood: Ms. Magazine and the Promise of Popular Feminism* (Chapel Hill: University of North Carolina Press, 1998), 30.

CHAPTER 8

AMERICAN FEMINISM AT THE END OF THE TWENTIETH CENTURY

INTRODUCTION

"Is Feminism Dead?" asked the cover of *Time* magazine in June 1998. Against a solid black background, black-and-white images of Susan B. Anthony, Betty Friedan, and Gloria Steinem were juxtaposed against a color headshot of Calista Flockhart as Ally McBeal, the titular character of the television show that had premiered the previous fall. Below her image, red text brims with horror-film anticipation.

The visual language of the cover pulls a number of feints. By presenting three very different feminist figures in the same way, it implies a cohesive history of the women's movement dating from the 1840s to the 1970s, with recent developments marking an unprecedented interruption. But this, of course, is nonsensical: many of Steinem's priorities would have made no sense to Anthony, and even the two contemporaries pictured often disagreed. At the same time, anti-feminism was hardly a new innovation (and neither were pronouncements of the movement's death). The cover also contrasted three real women, whose lives were marked with all the complexities and inconsistencies of the human experience, with a fictional character—one who was, moreover, conceived of and written by David E. Kelley, a man with a reputation for sexist portrayals of female characters. "I don't know how anyone could mistake *Ally McBeal* for a 'women's show,'" wrote television critic Joyce Millman in *Salon*. "[I]t's purely a freewheeling, male workplace fantasy." Such portrayals were not an aberration. "It's a little frightening how sadistic Kelley can be toward his characters," Millman continued, "especially his women." Finally, by including a full-color image of Flockhart as McBeal, the cover reinforces one of the major feminist criticisms of the character: that she was overly concerned with her physical appearance. The accompanying article posited a similar then-versus-now dichotomy, with inserts comparing the "serious" feminist culture of the 1960s and '70s with the "flighty," "faux-feminist" celebrities of the '90s. "The personal is political," the rallying cry of earlier decades, had in this view transformed into the purely personal, individual self-expression untethered from an understanding of or hope for structural change.[1]

Feminism was not dead, but it faced wrenching conflicts, both internal and external, in the last two decades of the twentieth century. Feminists found themselves on opposing sides of a dizzying number of debates: on pornography, welfare reform, the meaning of consent, and the relationship of beauty culture to patriarchy, just to name a few. No cohesive feminist ideology defined the 1980s or '90s—but then, this had always been the case.

THE CULTURE WARS

Feminism's opponents, by contrast, entered the 1980s unified and empowered. The anti-abortion movement, a crucial factor in unifying the New Right in the '70s, gained strength in the '80s and '90s, pushing back against *Roe v. Wade* through grassroots activism, the court system, state and local legislation, and sometimes, violence. Though many conservatives did indeed wish to overturn *Roe*, the movement was more successful in its attempts to chip away at the ruling through such restrictions as waiting periods, restrictions on where and by whom abortions could be performed, and mandates that doctors share with patients sometimes erroneous information about the dangers and/or immorality of abortion.

As governor of California, Ronald Reagan had supported liberalization of that state's abortion laws. As president, however, he openly opposed the procedure, calling in 1983 for an end to "abortion on demand."[2] Rather than making it a priority in his legislative agenda, Reagan primarily sought to reach this goal through court appointments. Abortion became a key issue in the confirmation of Sandra Day O'Connor, whose views on the issue were largely unknown. As in many areas, O'Connor was a moderate on abortion, though her early decisions showed a willingness to restrict access to the procedure. In 1983, she dissented from the court's decision to strike down a series of abortion restrictions enacted in Akron, Ohio (which mirrored laws passed elsewhere).

By 1988, Reagan had appointed two more Supreme Court justices—Antonin Scalia and Anthony Kennedy—both of whom were expected to be reliable anti-abortion votes. Early the next year, shortly before the inauguration of George H. W. Bush—who along with his family had long supported Planned Parenthood—the president-elect asked this new court to overturn *Roe* in the upcoming case of *Webster v. Reproductive Health Services*, which considered a series of restrictions enacted in Missouri. Chief Justice William Rehnquist hoped to use this case to assert a new standard for abortion restrictions, one that considered the state's interest in the fetus but not, as *Roe* had done, the privacy rights of the woman. However, the majority, again including O'Connor, would only go so far as to uphold the new restrictions. Unlike 1983, the restrictions stood; like the earlier decision, so did the general framework of *Roe*.

The final abortion-related Supreme Court case of the Reagan-Bush years was *Planned Parenthood of Southeastern Pennsylvania v. Casey* (1992). By then, the conservative Clarence Thomas had replaced the liberal Thurgood Marshall on the court (see below). Centering on the constitutionality of a Pennsylvania law, *Casey* gave the court the opportunity to reconsider several restrictions it had rejected in 1983: a twenty-four-hour waiting period, a required lecture on the dangers of and alternatives to abortion, spousal notification, and parental consent. The court also had the option of striking down *Roe* entirely, which the Bush administration again asked it to do. Overturning *Roe* was also Rehnquist's wish. Instead, five justices—O'Connor, Blackmun, Kennedy, David Souter (a Bush appointee), and John Paul Stevens (a Ford appointee)—crafted a compromise: first, with the exception of spousal notification, the Pennsylvania restrictions could stand. Second, viability would replace *Roe's* trimester framework. Before viability, the state could not impose restrictions that placed an "undue burden" (O'Connor's concept) on the woman; restrictions were allowed after this point as long as they included exceptions for the woman's life or health. Third, *Roe* would remain in place.

Roe survived twelve years of Republican presidents who would have preferred to see it overturned, and Bill Clinton, elected president in 1992, supported protecting women's access to abortion. As legislative and judicial avenues narrowed, however, anti-abortion activists increasingly took matters into their own hands, sometimes violently. By the end of the 1970s, anti-abortion activists had set more than a dozen abortion clinics on fire. In 1984, alone, they bombed or burned twice this number. A group of four men from Maryland and Virginia committed ten of these acts. Harry Blackmun, who had written the original Roe decision, regularly faced death threats and picketers.

In 1986, Randall Terry and other activists founded Operation Rescue, which organized protests to block clinic entrances and disrupt their activities. (Terry also opposed most forms of birth control.) Other individuals took it further. In 1993, Michael Griffin shot and killed Dr. David Gunn as he walked from his car to one of his clinics in Florida. That same year, Dr. George Tiller was shot and wounded in Kansas. Congress attempted to stem the tide of violence with the Freedom of Access to Clinic Entrances (FACE) Act in 1994, but anti-abortion activists killed six more people over the course of the decade. Operation Rescue protests were generally peaceful, but Terry and others did not condemn the violence committed in their name. In 2009, Tiller was shot again, this time fatally, while serving as an usher in his church. Terry responded with a video arguing that Tiller got what he deserved.

Another front in the culture wars coalesced around the concept of "obscenity." Conservatives were dismayed by a proliferation of cultural products—movies, television shows, and music—that featured sex, disrespect for authority, violence, the occult, and challenges to the gender binary—not only because this culture existed but also because they were convinced it was going to lead to moral breakdown in real life. In 1990, two Nevada parents sued the band Judas Priest because they claimed its subliminal messages had led their teenage son to attempt suicide. Conservative commentator George Will argued that the popularity of rock music was evidence that the American people were incapable of self-government, and that this form of expression had to be reined in to preserve the democratic process. At the very end of the century, many cultural commentators attributed the Columbine massacre in Colorado and other school shootings across the nation to violent video games. (A decade earlier, this perspective was satirized in the film *Heathers*, in which a priest nonsensically blamed a rash of suicides among high school students on "the MTV video games.")

In 1985, so-called porn rock became the subject of congressional hearings. Tipper Gore, wife of then-senator Al Gore, became upset with the music industry after catching her eleven-year-old daughter listening to a Prince song that included lyrics about a woman masturbating. She and others founded the Parents' Music Resource Center (PMRC), which convinced record companies to put labels on "filthy" music. Music videos, shown on the new channel Music Television (MTV) were particularly concerning; PMRC screened Twisted Sister's "We're Not Gonna Take It" in the Senate. Gore always insisted that she was interested in education, not censorship, but PMRC's campaign against heavy metal unintentionally paved the way for intense criticism of rap and hip-hop music, not coincidentally a campaign that targeted Black music rather than white music.

While by the 1980s the abortion debates largely fell along predictable political lines—feminists on one side, conservatives on the other—the obscenity debates sometimes made for strange bedfellows. Feminists in the 1980s and '90s were divided among themselves in a series of battles over sex in general and pornography in particular, with some of them forming alliances with the Christian Right.

In 1969, the Supreme Court in *Stanley v. Georgia* had invalidated state laws banning possession of obscene materials. In part due to this decision, pornography had become widespread over the course of the 1970s and into the '80s. The resulting feminist anti-pornography movement emerged from a broader campaign targeting violence against women in the media. By the 1980s, self-identified anti-pornography feminists argued that pornography reflected and perpetuated men's domination of women. Some feminists, however, argued that pornography offered validation of female sexual pleasure and thus countered the sexual double standard. Members of this cohort called themselves pro-sex or anticensorship.

Three groups—Women against Violence against Women (WAVAW), Women against Violence in Pornography and Media (WAVPM), and Women against Pornography (WAP)—led the feminist movement against media violence. The first, WAVAW, was founded in response to the 1975 film *Snuff*, which purported to show a real young woman's murder, and the

Rolling Stones album *Black and Blue*. Gloria Steinem and other feminists demanded an investigation into *Snuff*. The Manhattan district attorney found that, in fact, the murder had been staged, and the actress was alive and well. Still, feminists felt that the film would inure viewers to violence against women in real life, and they asked the DA to ban it ahead of its opening in New York City. The controversy, however, had increased the film's notoriety, and *Snuff* stood to make a large amount of money for theater owners.

WAVAW was founded by women in the Los Angeles and Orange County Feminist Women's Health Centers (FWHC) ahead of the film's arrival in California. When they failed to prevent the film's opening, they protested outside the theater. The protest drew enough attention that WAVAW members eventually won a court order declaring the film obscene. The Los Angeles WAVAW's successful protest became a model for feminist groups across the nation, who successfully mobilized against *Snuff* in such cities as Buffalo; San Jose; Denver; and Rochester, New York. Soon thereafter, WAVAW became a national organization with United Farm Workers (UFW) veteran Julia London as national chairperson.

In June 1976, the group took on the ad campaign for the Rolling Stones album *Black and Blue*, which featured a bruised and bound woman in the throes of sexual ecstasy. The accompanying text read, "I'm Black and Blue from the Rolling Stones and I Love It!" In response to WAVAW protests, the record company rolled back the ad campaign, but executives refused to get rid of it. Band members, too, dismissed the complaints, insisting that they had done more to liberate women than feminism had. WAVAW members persisted, quickly realizing that the violence in the Rolling Stones ads was endemic to the music industry. London's experience with the UFW, which had led a five-year boycott of table grapes in support of workers' demands for a fair contract, proved crucial for what happened next: a boycott of Warner Records, which had released *Black and Blue* and many other popular albums. After nearly three years of letter-writing campaigns, street performances, and constant pressure on executives, Warner capitulated.

WAVAW differed from later organizations in three important ways: first, its Warner boycott determinedly called for consumer action, not government censorship. Next, it focused on violence against women in all forms of media, not just pornography. Finally, WAVAW did not argue that violence against women in media caused violence against women in real life, but rather, that it normalized and downplayed the seriousness of such treatment. WAVPM and WAP took a different tack on all three issues, calling for government intervention, narrowing their focus to one form of media, and identifying a causal relationship between media violence and real-life violence. As Robin Morgan famously and succinctly put it, "[P] ornography is the theory; and rape the practice."[3]

Growing out of a 1976 Bay Area Conference on Violence against Women, WAVPM was formally founded early in 1977. Among its founders were several prominent feminist intellectuals, including sociologists Diana Russell and Kathleen Barry, authors, respectively, of *The Politics of Rape* (1975) and *Sexual Slavery* (1979), and poet and playwright Susan Griffin, later editor of *Take Back the Night*, a 1980 collection of feminist anti-pornography writing.

WAVPM's campaign against sadomasochism (S/M) ignited an early skirmish in the feminist sex wars. The organization's first public protest was against the Ultra Room, a San Francisco theater in which patrons paid to watch women perform S/M-themed live sex acts on another. To WAVPM, the implication was that women found violence erotic. The protest caught the attention of San Francisco sex radicals, including feminist anthropologist Gayle Rubin, who became a central antagonist to anti-pornography feminists. Finding WAVPM's views on sexuality repressive, Rubin and others founded Samois, a lesbian-feminist S/M rights group. Samois members believed that lesbian S/M provided a safe way for disempowered women to play with and learn about how power functioned and thus constituted a feminist act.

Later that year, WAVPM members in New York City mobilized against a Max Factor campaign that likened skincare to a form of self-defense. The campaign had the misfortune of premiering at the same time that the "Son of Sam," wanted for the brutal murders of six young women, terrorized the city. In this context, the ads seemed to trivialize the real fear in which women lived. Under the leadership of national coordinator Laura Lederer, WAVPM organized a letter-writing campaign to Max Factor, boycotted the brand, picketed stores that carried the self-defense line, and raised awareness through media interviews, a newsletter, and a press conference. Under pressure, Max Factor eventually agreed to cancel the campaign, and WAVPM went on to spearhead many similar actions.

In 1978, the group took on *Hustler* magazine. More explicit in its portrayal of sexually exploitative scenes than *Playboy* or *Penthouse*, *Hustler* raised feminist ire through such features as *Chester the Molester*, a cartoon about a middle-aged man who liked to rape young girls. In June 1978, the magazine appeared on newsstands with a still-infamous cover of a naked woman going through a meat grinder, half of her already ground up and sitting on a plate nearby. WAVPM picketed outside stores that sold *Hustler*, resulting in the magazine's temporary removal from many of them.

That same summer, WAVPM began planning the first national feminist conference on pornography, held in San Francisco in November. Members hoped that the conference would lead to a more systematic feminist analysis of pornography and its effects, as well as the best strategies for tackling it. In addition to Russell, Barry, and Griffin, speakers included Susan Brownmiller, author of *Against Our Will: Men, Women, and Rape* (1975); Andrea Dworkin, who would go on to write *Pornography: Men Possessing Women* (1981) and *Intercourse* (1987); and Audre Lorde. Indeed, the conference crystallized many of the tenets of the anti-pornography feminism of the next decade: notably, a distinction between pornography and erotica (one of Lorde's contributions to the conference) and a call for government intervention premised on the idea that sexual violence, whether on-screen or in life, deprived women of their First Amendment and equal protection rights by instilling fear. In this light, calls for censorship seemed to promise the *restoration* of both free speech rights and equality before the law. Yet such calls remained controversial, even within the conference: what constituted pornography, and who got to decide? If a small group of feminists could not agree on the kind of material that should be restricted, what hope was there that courts and legislators could agree? Could they, in fact, use anti-pornography measures against feminist culture? As Ellen Willis put it, "Though I share the impulse behind them [legal restrictions], I think these appeals for an official crackdown are mistaken and dangerous. Feminists who support censorship are offering the state a weapon that will inevitably be used against us." Increasingly, the perspectives of WAVAW and WAVPM were diverging, and differences between the nascent pro-sex and anti-pornography camps were crystallizing.[4]

In 1977, a group of feminist luminaries including Gloria Steinem, Robin Morgan, Adrienne Rich, Andrea Dworkin, and Susan Brownmiller began organizing an East Coast–based anti–media violence group, Women against Pornography (WAP), which was formally founded in 1979. From the beginning, the new group's willingness to support government restrictions locked its members in conflict with liberal feminists and civil libertarians, to whom free speech was sacred and censorship anathema. For the entirety of its existence, WAP was forced to play defense on this issue, making it impossible for it to develop a multifaceted feminist critique. In truth, its members' theories were much more nuanced than their opponents painted them. Building on the theories shared at the 1978 WAVPM conference, WAP members hoped that the state would see media representations of sexual violence to be a form of discrimination against women and thus an appropriate place for the government to intervene. It wasn't so different, feminist attorneys argued, from what the Supreme Court had done in *Brown v. Board of Education*. As historian Carolyn Brownstein articulates this theory, "[I]t was impossible for women living in such a culture to claim equal rights before the law, knowing that men would not only threaten women who challenged male power, but would back up their threats with the use of terrible sexual violence. . . . pornography was not a form of protected speech, but an act of sex discrimination that robbed women of their right to speak and to be heard." To civil libertarians, however, the difference between this kind of discrimination and that addressed in *Brown v. Board* was clear: *Brown v. Board* had dealt with discriminatory *acts*, while media violence dealt with discriminatory *images*—and regulating images was a bridge too far for many, even among those sympathetic to feminist political goals.

WAP became a media sensation, with members making appearances on the talk show *Donahue*, in *Newsday* magazine, and elsewhere and eclipsing WAVAW and WAVPM in public notice. The organization set up shop in New York City's Times Square, determined to take on that area's sex industry and mounting high-profile protests against *Playboy*, *Hustler*, the popular pornographic film *Deep Throat*, and a Broadway adaptation of *Lolita*. In doing so, it courted resistance from three sectors, starting with other feminists, who continued to see the organization as conservative and paternalistic, reminiscent of nineteenth-century moral crusaders and Comstock laws. Pro-sex feminists also feared that advocating legal restrictions was inviting disaster, especially as courts and legislatures became more conservative in the early 1980s. Sex workers, too, were concerned that WAP posed a threat to their often already precarious living. (For their part, WAP members sympathized with sex workers—after fleeing an abusive husband and becoming homeless, Dworkin herself turned to sex work—but they did not believe that such work could be freely chosen.) Finally, WAP's decision to accept funding from pro-gentrification groups determined to "clean up" Times Square worried progressives.

WAP did have allies, but some of them came from a surprising place—the Christian Right. For such activists as Anita Bryant, Beverly LaHaye, and Jerry Falwell, the spread of pornography was an affront to family values and evidence of moral decay. Certainly, the two anti-pornography camps differed. Feminists attempted to draw a distinction between feminism and erotica, while Christian Right activists wished to eradicate all sexually explicit materials. The latter group also argued that homosexuality was just as threatening as pornography. Each group, however, believed pornography should be banned, and over the course of the early 1980s, some of their discourse grew closer together. In 1983, Dworkin and Catharine MacKinnon drafted anti-pornography statutes for the Minneapolis and Indianapolis city councils, codifying the idea that pornography constituted a form of discrimination against women. Though the Minneapolis measure failed (the mayor vetoed it), the Indianapolis ordinance became law, in part thanks to the support of Christian conservatives including Falwell and Phyllis Schlafly. The same unlikely coalition supported and testified at hearings called by U.S. attorney general Edwin Meese's commission on pornography, founded in 1985.

In 1986, the Supreme Court declared the Indiana ordinance unconstitutional, a ruling that proved the death knell for the feminist anti-pornography movement. Further legal measures gained no traction, and it was increasingly obvious that the forms of legal restrictions on sexual expression that did pass muster in the courts had nothing to do with media violence against women. Rather, moral panics over AIDS, homosexuality, obscenity, and family values reflected the ascendancy of the Right in that decade.

One final front in the culture wars illustrates this point. In the late 1980s, conservatives looked with increasing concern at the work being funded by the National Endowment for the Arts (NEA). Two artists in particular, Andres Serrano and Robert Mapplethorpe, both of whom had received NEA grants, galvanized the Right. Serrano's photograph "Piss

Christ," which depicted a plastic crucifix submerged in the artist's urine, convinced many Christian conservatives that their religion was under attack. At the same time, Mapplethorpe's erotic, often sadomasochistic, photographs of male bodies offended such politicians as U.S. senator Jesse Helms of North Carolina, who had once called homosexuality "a battle against American values." Mapplethorpe had recently died from complications of HIV/AIDS.

When the NEA budget was reauthorized in 1990, it included a new decency clause (this was in place of the proposed Helms amendment, which would have specifically prohibited depictions of homoeroticism, among other "obscene" subjects). Now, in order to receive grants, artists would have to pledge not to create certain kinds of art. When four artists, among them feminist performance artists Holly Hughes and Karen Finley, were denied grants on this basis, they sued. The case of the "NEA Four" made it all the way to the Supreme Court, which sided with the NEA in ruling that the artists' freedom of expression had not been violated. The message was clear: if the government was going to censor cultural and artistic expression, which it was indeed willing to do, it was not going to do so in a way that reflected feminist values. In recognizing this truth early on, the pro-sex contingent of the movement was undoubtedly correct.

ANITA HILL, CLARENCE THOMAS, AND THE YEAR OF THE WOMAN

In 1991, the civil rights legend Thurgood Marshall retired from the Supreme Court, and George H. W. Bush nominated circuit court judge Clarence Thomas to replace him. Thomas had replaced Eleanor Holmes Norton as head of the Equal Employment Opportunity Commission, where he served as a staunch opponent of affirmative action and comparable worth. Liberals disliked Thomas, but they did not expect to mobilize a concerted opposition. Then, however, National Public Radio's Nina Totenberg reported that the judiciary committee had suppressed evidence from Anita Hill, a lawyer and EEOC staffer who alleged that Thomas had sexually harassed her. Four other women were prepared to corroborate her allegations, but the committee did not call them to testify.

Responses to the story broke along racial and gender lines. Many white men (including the fourteen on the all-white, all-male judiciary

Lawyer Anita Hill testifies in front of the Senate Judiciary Committee about Supreme Court nominee Clarence Thomas's alleged sexual harassment, 1991. Hill's testimony met bipartisan skepticism and mockery from the all-male committee, but it also inspired many women to run for office and contributed to the emergence of new forms of feminist activism. (Library of Congress, Prints & Photographs Division, CQ Roll Call Photograph Collection, LC-DIG-ppmsca-65032)

committee) saw a nonissue. Some Black men charged racism; Thomas himself called the allegations a "high-tech lynching." Women's responses varied by race too, but the majority were angry that Hill's testimony had been suppressed. "They just don't get it, do they?" became a common refrain among women. Men's obliviousness became even more apparent when the committee reversed course and allowed public testimony from Hill, proceeding to alternate between grilling the witness and mocking the allegations.

In the end, the Senate confirmed Thomas to the Supreme Court by a margin of fifty-two to forty-eight. Yet the process angered and galvanized many women. Twenty-two women ran for the Senate in 1992; for comparison, only eight had done so two years earlier. Carol Moseley-Braun successfully challenged a Thomas supporter, becoming the first Black woman elected to the Senate. In Pennsylvania, Lynn Yeakel nearly unseated powerful judiciary committee member Arlen Specter with ads featuring clips of him questioning Hill. Women's presence in the Senate grew from two in 1992 to a record five in 1993. Organizations that supported women's candidates, including NWPC, the Women's Campaign Fund, and Emily's List, were flooded with donations and new members. And at least some men on the judiciary committee recognized that they had erred. As the committee's ranking Democratic member, Senator Joe Biden actively participated in the decision to suppress Hill's testimony. In the years that followed, Biden committed himself to advocating for women's issues, including as cosponsor of the 1994 Violence against Women Act.

ENTER THE CLINTONS

The 1992 election proved a reckoning over gender, feminism, and women's roles in other ways as well. In the midst of the campaign, Dan Quayle, George H. W. Bush's vice president, criticized the television character Murphy Brown, a single mother. According to Quayle, the plot line represented a "poverty of values" that "mocked the importance of fathers" and portrayed single motherhood as "just another lifestyle choice." Liberals mocked Quayle, but conservatives rallied to his defense.

At the same time, the emergence of Bill Clinton and Hillary Rodham Clinton onto the national stage galvanized public opinion over a polarizing figure: the professional feminist woman who refused to subsume her own career to her husband's. In Arkansas, conservatives had glommed onto the fact that Hillary used her birth name, Rodham, as part of her professional identity, making it a campaign issue in one of her husband's reelection campaigns. In 1992, Hillary carefully distanced herself from the term "feminist," but the press constantly grilled her about her decision to continue her professional activities while Bill was governor. Frustrated with this treatment, she at one point retorted that she supposed she could have "stayed home, baked cookies, and had teas." The press exploded, claiming that she was attacking homemakers. Under attack, Hillary felt compelled to engage in a cookie baking contest with Barbara Bush, the incumbent's wife. Yet Hillary found that she could not win, as her attempts to adopt a more traditional style and demeanor also invited attacks. She continued to face similar scrutiny as First Lady (1993–2001), senator from New York (2001–9), secretary of state (2009–13), and, indeed, as the nominee of the Democratic Party in the 2016 presidential election (see epilogue).

In his speech at the 1992 Republican National Convention, conservative political commentator Pat Buchanan, who had challenged the sitting president in that year's primaries, gave full voice to the Christian Right's concerns over Hillary Clinton's feminism. In what historians often dub the "culture war" speech, Buchanan asserted that the election was about more than economic or foreign policy. It was, rather, "about who we are. It is about what we believe, and what we stand for as Americans. There is a religious war going on in this country. It is a cultural war, as critical to the kind of nation we shall be as was the Cold War itself, for this war is for the soul of America. And in that struggle for the soul of America, Clinton & Clinton are on the other side, and George Bush is on our side."

Buchanan's repeated references to "Clinton & Clinton"—which implied not only that Hillary had insinuated herself as Bill's equal in the campaign but also that in voting for Bill, who presented himself as a moderate, Americans were also voting for his "radical" wife—were only one indication that perceived gender transgressions were a large part of this war for the soul of America. The Democratic National Convention one month earlier, Buchanan claimed, was nothing less than "the greatest single exhibition of cross-dressing in American political history." Buchanan spoke of radicals pretending to be moderates, but the sly implication was clear: Democrats did not respect what he saw as God-given gender roles. Under Hillary's influence, Buchanan argued, Bill would pursue policies that reflected his wife's "radical feminism":

> Elect me, and you get two for the price of one, Mr. Clinton says of his lawyer-spouse. And what does Hillary believe? . . . The agenda that Clinton & Clinton would impose on America—abortion on demand, a litmus test for the Supreme Court, homosexual rights, discrimination against religious schools, women in combat units—that's change, all right. But it is not the kind of change America needs. It is not the kind of change America wants. And it is not the kind of change we can abide in a nation that we still call God's country.[5]

Buchanan failed to convince a majority of the nation's women voters, and Clinton carried the day with a plurality of the electorate.[6] As noted above, the new president was more sympathetic to women's concerns than Reagan or George H. W. Bush had been. Just weeks into his presidency, Clinton signed into law the Family and Medical Leave Act (1993), which guaranteed some employees up to twelve weeks of unpaid leave per year to care for an infant, other family member, or themselves. His first appointment to the Supreme Court, Ruth Bader Ginsburg, was a longtime feminist activist on her way to becoming an icon. Yet other of the president's policies, along with his personal conduct, troubled feminists (or at least should have).

As the previous chapter showed, women who received welfare have long been stigmatized. This stigma increased in the 1980s, especially among conservatives. In his 1976 battle to unseat President Gerald Ford, Reagan had used the racist and sexist term "welfare queen" to raise the specter of supposedly rampant welfare fraud, under which recipients wore fur coats and drove Cadillacs. A related accusation held that recipients used their money for drugs and had more children to receive more money and avoid work. But it was Clinton, a Democrat, who vowed in 1991 to "end welfare as we know it." Five years later, facing a Republican Congress that had made the end of welfare a priority of its 1994 Contract with America, Clinton signed into law the Personal Responsibility and Work Opportunity Reconciliation Act (PRWORA). This legislation eliminated the sixty-one-year-old AFDC and replaced it with Temporary Aid to Needy Families (TANF).

Under the PRWORA, states received block grants from the federal government and were allowed to design their own programs, as long as they met several basic requirements, the most important of which was a five-year lifetime limit on support. In order to maintain full benefits, women were also required to identify and cooperate in locating a child's father so that he could be compelled to pay child support, thus forcing women to be involved with men whom they may have very good reasons to stay away from (granting exceptions in cases of abuse was entirely at the discretion of welfare workers). Single women who received TANF support were required to work for wages, but married women were not. States were also allowed under the new legislation to provide incentives, including cash payments, to recipients who pursued marriage or stayed married (the federal government also rewarded states that increased marriage rates among welfare participants).

At first glance, it seems strange for a piece of economic policy to focus so much attention on marriage. But debates about welfare have never been just about economic need; rather, they have always rested on several assumptions about women, work, sexuality, and family. Much of the debate over welfare reform centered on the supposed pathology of single-parent households (assumed to be those headed by poor Black women). Welfare reformers and opponents alike voiced concern over the morality of these women, but they voiced two seemingly incompatible desires. The more liberal position held that, by incentivizing women to work for wages, welfare reform would reduce out-of-wedlock births and thus interrupt the cycle of poverty. But for many conservatives, this was not the real goal. Explaining Republican opposition to childcare funding, Missouri representative James Talent observed that "if you restore the two-parent family, then you don't *need* child care." Political scientist Gwendolyn Mink explains this logic: "Under the Personal Responsibility Act of 1996, marriage constitutes an alternative to—or perhaps a form of—employment for mothers, immunizing them from the obligation to work outside the home." Mink continues, "[T]he TANF regime treats wage work as the alternative to marriage, not to welfare—as punishment for mothers' independence." As Johnnie Tillmon had argued over two decades earlier, the real threat that women on welfare posed derived from the fact that they were women who remained unattached to men. Only this fear could explain why, since the 1960s, politicians and reformers had tried to push poor, single women into the paid labor force while encouraging married, middle-class women to remain at home. Buried beneath this distinction was an even older assumption that assigned white women the role of wives and Black women the role of workers.[7]

By and large, white, middle-class feminists raised few concerns about the effects of welfare reform on poor Black women, instead continuing to conflate the right to work for wages with the requirement to work for wages and heralding the legislation's promise to "make fathers pay." This position made some feminist sense—since the 1960s, men had enjoyed many of the benefits and borne few of the responsibilities of the sexual revolution—but it came at the expense of poor women's sexual autonomy, privacy, and perhaps safety.

Two years later, in January 1998, news broke that President Bill Clinton had engaged in a sexual relationship with Monica Lewinsky, a former White House intern. Testifying under oath in an unrelated investigation, Clinton initially denied the affair. But evidence—including taped conversations between Lewinsky and a confidante and even a sample of Clinton's DNA—mounted, and on August 17, the president acknowledged their "inappropriate" relationship. The House of Representatives proceeded to impeach Clinton on charges of perjury and obstruction of justice, though he was acquitted by the Senate early the next year.

Remarkably, prominent feminists rallied to Clinton's defense. In March, Gloria Steinem published an op-ed in the *New York Times* titled "Why Feminists Support Clinton," citing two reasons for her support. First, she argued, Clinton's relationship with Lewinsky was consensual, and thus, it was nobody's business. Its consensual nature also differentiated Clinton from, for example, Clarence Thomas. But Steinem was also pragmatic, and she recognized that Clinton was feminists' best hope for preserving reproductive rights.[8]

Bill Clinton's relationship with Lewinsky took place in a decidedly pre-#MeToo era, when it was difficult for many to fathom that Lewinsky, an adult, had entered into the relationship with anything less than full consent. Certainly, the intellectual tools to evaluate the relationship through a different lens existed at the time—Andrea Dworkin's *Intercourse*, which argued that power differentials between men and women made true consent difficult if not impossible, had come out in 1987—but Dworkin's ideas were decidedly out of fashion in the late 1990s. A full-scale reevaluation of the Clinton-Lewinsky affair would not take place until twenty years later, when a president who had openly bragged about his ability to "grab them [women] by the pussy" nominated an alleged sexual assailant to the Supreme Court. Feminist definitions of consent changed greatly in the intervening years.

THIRD-WAVE FEMINISM

Twenty-two-year-old Rebecca Walker, the daughter of author and feminist Alice Walker, tied the Clarence Thomas hearings to yet another development: the emergence of a feminist "Third Wave," a term she has been credited with coining. Alice Walker's own contributions to feminist culture and theory included coining the term "womanist," which she defined as

A black feminist or feminist of color. From the black folk expression of mothers to female children, "You acting womanish," i.e., like a woman.

Usually referring to outrageous, audacious, courageous or willful behavior. Wanting to know more and in greater depth than is considered "good" for one. Interested in grown-up doings. Acting grown up. Being grown up. Interchangeable with another black folk expression: "You trying to be grown." Responsible. In charge. Serious. . . . A woman who loves other women, sexually and/or nonsexually. Appreciates and prefers women's culture, women's emotional flexibility (values tears as natural counterbalance of laughter), and women's strength. Sometimes loves individual men, sexually and/or nonsexually. Committed to survival and wholeness of entire people, male and female.[9]

In the wake of Thomas's confirmation a decade later, Rebecca Walker wrote in a 1992 article for Ms. Magazine, "I have uncovered and unleashed more repressed anger than I thought possible. For the umpteenth time in my 22 years, I have been radicalized, politicized, shaken awake." To Walker, the real affront was not Thomas's alleged harassment of Hill, but rather, the grilling she received from senators in her public testimony. The message, Walker felt, was clear: men would not listen to or believe anything women had to say about their own experiences, especially if it threatened male prerogative (in this case, a Supreme Court seat). After Thomas's confirmation and, a week later, an incident with a group of men loudly discussing their sexual conquests on a train, Walker became determined to figure out what it meant to be a feminist in the 1990s. "To be a feminist," she concluded, "is to integrate an ideology of equality and female empowerment into the very fiber of my life. It is to search for personal clarity in the midst of systemic destruction, to join in sisterhood with women when often we are divided, to understand power structures with the intention of changing them."[10]

In the 1980s and '90s, Baby Boomer women who had been active in the feminist movements of the '60s and '70s bemoaned the fact that younger women did not seem to care about feminism (see, for example, the Time magazine cover story discussed at the beginning of this chapter). In large part, this perception was a creation of the media, which pronounced with not a little schadenfreude that it was a "postfeminist" age or an era of "I'm not a feminist, but . . . ." This insistence on young women's apathy was overblown, however. Women born after 1970 fashioned a third-wave feminism that intentionally defined itself in opposition to both second-wave feminism and the conservative cultural milieu in which they were raised. As Walker put it, "I am not a postfeminist feminist. I am the Third Wave."[11]

Girls and women who came of age after the gains of second-wave feminism grew up receiving mixed messages: they were told that, like Sally Ride (the first American woman in space), Sandra Day O'Connor (the first woman on the Supreme Court), or Geraldine Ferraro (the first woman to appear on a major party's presidential ticket), they could accomplish anything they wanted, with gender as no impediment. At the same time, they inherited ugly stereotypes about the movement—feminism—that made these impressive firsts possible: that its adherents were bitter, man-hating "feminazis," a term popularized by conservative radio host Rush Limbaugh, and, perhaps worst of all, that the movement was no longer necessary. As college student Linn Thomas told *Time* magazine in 1992, "I picture a feminist as someone who is masculine and who doesn't shave her legs and is doing everything she can to deny that she is feminine."[12] Third-wave feminists developed their ideology in part from these conflicting messages: they placed a great deal of emphasis on personal, individual choice, agency, and autonomy; they were decidedly pro-sex; and they were often unafraid of using beauty culture to create their own self-image. As musician India Arie put it in her 2000 debut single, "Video,"

> Sometimes I shave my legs and sometimes I don't Sometimes I comb my hair and sometimes I won't Depend on how the wind blows I might even paint my toes It really just depends on whatever feels good in my soul[13]

At first glance, these lyrics, which celebrate women's freedom to make even those choices that seem to conflict with a structural critique of patriarchy, appear to represent a clear division between the feminism of the 1960s and '70s and that of the turn of the twenty-first century. Yet the break between second- and third-wave feminism was never as stark nor as total as the media, early memoirs, treatises, and some histories have painted it.

Following such scholars as Kimberlé Crenshaw and Patricia Hill Collins, third-wave feminists placed a great deal of emphasis on the concept of intersectionality—the ways in which race, class, gender, sexuality, and other factors interacted to shape women's lives. While feminists had long recognized that women's experiences varied, previous generations of white women were inclined to do so in comparative or additive ways—for example, they understood gender as *similar to* race, and race as an *additional* burden that Black and brown women faced. But theories of intersectionality went further than this to explore the ways in which these characteristics fundamentally shaped and were shaped by one another. Describing what she calls "interlocking systems," Hill Collins argues that

> viewing relations of domination for Black women for any given socio-historical context as being structured via a system of interlocking race, class, and gender oppression expands the focus of analysis from merely describing the similarities and differences distinguishing these systems of oppression and focuses greater attention on how they interconnect. Assuming that each system needs the others in order to function creates a distinct theoretical stance that stimulates the rethinking of basic social science concepts.[14]

Crenshaw and Hill Collins consciously drew on decades of Black feminist thought. Yet in making their heightened consciousness of intersectionality into a breaking point between second- and third-wave feminism, third wavers unintentionally reified the whiteness of the earlier movement. In practice, moreover, white third-wavers' intersectionality often manifested itself as calls for diversity and inclusion—not so different from their second-wave forebears.

Third-wave feminist mobilization did differ from its predecessors in some important ways. Young women, some of them still in high school, were just as angry about anti-feminist backlash—manifested in the Thomas hearings, the erosion of reproductive rights and the social safety net, and virulent cultural stereotypes—as were older women. But while established feminist professionals in such groups as NOW and NARAL were able to mount expansive voter education campaigns and lobby and educate politicians, some third-wave women were too young even to vote. They could not vote out George H. W. Bush or the senators who confirmed Thomas, and nor were politicians likely to listen to teen girls, whom they were loath to take seriously. At the same time, growing out of the long-term centrality of "the personal is political" to American feminism, many young women had concerns that legislation could not fix. As journalist Sara Marcus put it in her book on Riot Grrrls,

When you're a teenage girl who's trying with all your might not to hate yourself, trying not to get harassed or raped, trying not to let bikini blondes in beer ads crush your self-image, trying not to be discouraged from join-ing a sports team or math club or shop class, trying not to let your family's crippling dysfunction (and the confounding irony of enduring domestic cruelty in an age of Family Values) make you want to fucking *die*, a feminist movement that's mostly about electing new Senators might not be all that compelling to you.[15]

For these and other reasons, third-wave feminism manifested itself most visibly in the cultural realm. Newly available technologies, too, contrib-uted; 1990s feminists, for example, were the first generation of women's rights activists to have the internet at their disposal as a platform and organizing tool. As just one of many tools—including video technology, indie record labels, and cheap and accessible printing and photocopying—that put the means of cultural production and distribution in the hands of young women, the internet democratized (to an extent) the dissemina-tion of feminist ideas and also dramatically expanded its geographical and generational reach.

New magazines, especially the beloved but short-lived (1988–94) *Sassy*, shook up the publishing world. Founded as an alternative to such standard teen fare as *Seventeen*, *Sassy* was unabashed in its coverage of sexuality and other issues relevant to teen girls. The magazine shared office space with *Ms.*, and though they remained entirely separate, the kinship between the two publications was clear. But when the Moral Majority subjected the magazine to a boycott, advertisers fled, and the magazine was sold. In its later years, *Sassy* toned down its content. The magazine's original tone, however, inspired hundreds—if not thousands—of personal zines, as well as a new crop of feminist magazines for adults. *Bitch* (1996–) cofounders Andi Zeisler and Lisa Jervis began as interns at *Sassy*, while *Bust* (1993–) cofounders Debbie Stoller and Marcelle Karp began their magazine with inspiration from both *Sassy* and their extensive educations in women's studies. Both magazines continue to exist as of this writing.

In another corner of publishing, cartoonist Alison Bechdel produced one of the earliest ongoing cultural representations of lesbians with her long-running comic strip *Dykes to Watch Out For*, which ran from 1983 to 2008 in independent and gay and lesbian newspapers. Bechdel, who later published the graphic novel *Fun Home* (2006), also gifted culture with the enduring Bechdel-Wallace test, which measures women's representation in films and other media. In a 1985 *Dykes to Watch Out For* strip titled "The Rule," two friends discuss the three criteria a piece of popular culture must meet in order to pass: it must include at least two women, the two women must talk to each other, and the conversation must be about something other than a man. Though never intended as a measure of a film's feminism—critics have pointed out, for example, that Sir Mix-a-Lot's "Baby Got Back" technically passes—the test's ubiquity suggests the long way these tenets have traveled from alternative newspapers to the mainstream.[16]

Third-wave feminism also manifested itself in music. In 1989, Kathleen Hanna, a student at Evergreen State College in Olympia, Washington, traveled to Seattle to meet her idol, feminist writer Kathy Acker. Raised by a mother who volunteered with survivors of domestic violence, subscribed to Ms., and had taken her young daughter to hear Gloria Steinem speak, Hanna well understood the crucial contributions of second-wave feminism. But the most visible feminist strain of the 1980s, anti-porn feminism, did not speak to her. Hanna had worked as a stripper and felt that she had freely chosen to do so. (Just a few years later, she would sing, in 1992's "Jigsaw Youth," "Can sell my body if I wanna / God knows you already sold your mind." But at nineteen, she was a budding writer of spoken-word poetry. "I feel like my whole life no one's ever listened to me," Hanna told Acker. "I want people to listen." But in discouraging Hanna from pursuing this vocation, Acker inadvertently set the younger woman on her life course: "If you want people to hear what you're doing," she counseled, "don't do spoken word, because nobody likes spoken word, nobody goes to spoken word. There's more of a community for musicians than for writers. You should be in a band."[17]

Joining a band was a natural move in Olympia, which hummed with punk and grunge activity. This scene was not necessarily friendly to women, however. As Riot Grrrl convention participant Melissa Klein later put it, "I see punk, like the antiwar and civil rights movements before it, as a place where young women learned or solidified radical means of analyzing the world and then applied these powers of analysis to their own lives, only to realize that, as girls, they felt disenfranchised within their own supposedly 'alternative' community." When Hanna met Olympia drummer Tobi Vail, whose own feminism was deeply influenced by the theories of Angela Davis, bell hooks, and Judith Butler, she knew she had found a kindred spirit. Along with friends Billy Karren and Kathi Wilcox, Hanna and Vail founded Bikini Kill in 1990, determined to challenge the sexism in punk and culture at large. Soon, Bikini Kill was joined by Bratmobile (1991) and Sleater-Kinney (1994) in the vanguard of feminist punk. Soon, members of this movement started a zine, *Riot Grrrl*, giving a name to a new kind of feminism. These young women assailed "the general lack of girl power in society as a whole, and in the punk rock underground specifically"; in this new vision, girls and women would insist that their voices be heard, and they would use the punk idiom to do it. "When she talks, I hear the revolution," sang Bikini Kill in "Rebel Girl," first performed in 1991. Riot grrrl discussion groups, DIY merchandise, conventions, and even a press sprang up.[18]

Eventually, riot grrrls became a media sensation that reporters at best found unintelligible and at worst demeaned, consumer culture tried to commodify, and movement founders distanced themselves from. It suffered, too, from an inability to expand beyond its white, middle-class core constituency. The widespread adoption of the internet facilitated riot grrrl email lists and America Online message boards, prolonging the movement's relevance into the mid-1990s. By that point, however, the call to action in the first issue of *Riot Grrrl*—increasing "girl power"—had softened into the more easily digestible messages of the British pop band the Spice Girls.

Within rap and hip-hop music, artists including MC Lyte, Queen Latifah, and Missy Elliot challenged the misogyny of mainstream music of all genres with strong female-centered lyrics. While such groups as N—Wit Attitude (NWA) mounted a potent challenge to systemic racism and police brutality, they also evinced hostility to women and feminism. "This so-called women's lib / I'll retire it" claimed one song. At the same time, the marketability of hip-hop often depended on artists conforming to white stereotypes of Black men and women. But in feminist hip-hop, historian Sara Evans argues, "Afrocentric racial consciousness and progressive gender politics joined hands." Black women who listened to the genre, like Elisa Davis, gained "a language that made my black womanhood coherent to myself and the world."[19] More broadly, scholars have identified not only feminist hip-hop but also a particular hip-hop feminism, which discards the sexism of the former and the racism of the latter to claim a new Black "womanist" consciousness. Hip-hop feminists, many of them college educated and up-wardly mobile, hoped to empower Black girls and young women through education and institution-building. As historian Whitney A. Peoples puts it, the goal of hip-hop feminists was "providing a political education and tools of critical analysis . . . to critique the social, political, and economic structures that govern their [Black girls and women's] lives and that gave rise to the conditions that produce some of the violent and misogynist lyrics that dominate much of mainstream rap music." It was not enough simply to critique the misogyny of hip-hop music, as second-wave Black feminists had done. Under hip-hop feminism, the more problematic as-pects of hip-hop became a fruitful site from which to explore the socio-political realities of Black women and men. According to Gwendolyn D. Pough, author of *Check It While I Wreck It: Black Womanhood, Hip-Hop Culture, and the Public Sphere* (2004), "Rap music provides a new direction for Black feminist criticism. It is not just about counting the bitches and hoes in each rap song. It is about exploring the nature of Black male and female relationships."[20]

In television, *Buffy the Vampire Slayer* (1997–2003) turned the camp film of the same name (1992) into a parable of 1990s feminism, exposing both its strengths and weaknesses. A normal teenage girl who is mysteri-ously chosen to receive super powers, Buffy is equally invested in owning her sexuality and "kicking ass," in serving the cause to which she has been called and maintaining her own individuality. Often, the supernatural foes Buffy must defeat take the form of ordinary male authority figures, including her vampire ex-boyfriend, the town mayor, and a misogynis-tic preacher. (Yet one of the show's most terrifying villains is an ordi-nary aggrieved teen boy who resents the women who will not date him.) Over the course of the series, Buffy also chafes against the authority of her watcher, Giles, who guides her training. The show concludes by giving all girls around the world the power of the slayer—symbolically, the power to fight patriarchy.

Yet the show's feminism is almost exclusively white. For most of its run, *Buffy*'s characters of color appear only as tokens, and often tinged with primitivism. The nameless "First Slayer," played by a Black actress, is wild and untamable, and she has no voice. The show's final season featured a new, multiracial crop of potential slayers, but their cultural differences were often played for laughs.

Buffy thus dramatized the dilemmas of third-wave feminism—the individual and the collective, the white savior and global sisterhood, feminism and femininity—providing viewers with possibilities for reconciling these conflicts (or living with ambiguity and contradiction). It is unsurprising, then, that "Buffy studies" remains a vibrant academic field nearly twenty years later, especially among the Generation X and older Millennial women who formed its fan base. At the same time, revelations about creator Joss Whedon's treatment of women have placed the show within ongoing discussions about #MeToo, the relationship of artists to their work, and the ethics of consuming culture made by problematic creators.

CONCLUSION

In the year 2000, Jennifer Baumgardner and Amy Richards, both born in 1970, published *Manifesta: Young Women, Feminism, and the Future*. Both an assessment of feminist movements past and present and a call to action, *Manifesta* quickly established itself as a core text of the third-wave canon. Beyond their wide-ranging and meticulous research, Baumgardner and Richards impress with their tone, which balances earnestness with snark and wit.[21]

Chapter three, "Feminists Want to Know: Is the Media Dead?" is characteristic in this regard. In it, the authors turn the "Is Feminism Dead?" question on its head: if journalists could not see the feminism that surrounded them, it was because there was something wrong with the media, not with feminism. Third-wave feminism was not just the Spice Girls or Courtney Love, and Courtney Love was not only Kurt Cobain's widow or a gallivanting party girl. Indeed, further research showed that, by focusing on celebrities, the *Time* article discussed at the beginning of this chapter cherry-picked evidence to serve its point.[22] It could have discussed the United Nation's Fourth World Conference on Women, which in 1995 endorsed a comprehensive plan to achieve global gender equality. It could have traced Mia Hamm's ongoing attempts to establish a professional women's soccer league and to win respect for her sport. It could have recognized the thousands of young women who participated in pro-choice organizations on their college campuses or volunteered with Planned Parenthood or other organizations. At the turn of the twenty-first century, Baumgardner and Richards believed, a new movement was just beginning. The possibilities for feminism seemed endless.

NOTES

1. "Is Feminism Dead?" (cover image), *Time* magazine, June 29, 1998; Joyce Millman, "Kelleyvision," *Salon*, Sept. 20, 1999, https://web.archive.org /web/20060618215629/http://salon.com/ent/col/mill/1999/09/20/kelley/index .html. As Kelley himself put it, "She's [McBeal] not a hard, strident feminist out of the '60s and '70s. She's all for women's rights, but she doesn't want to lead the charge at her own emotional expense." David E. Kelley, quoted in Ginia Bellafonte, "Feminism: It's All about Me!" *Time* magazine, June 29, 1998, 58.

2. Ronald Reagan, quoted in Blumenthal, *Jane against the World*, 279.

3. Robin Morgan, quoted in Carolyn Brownstein, *Battling Pornography: The American Feminist Anti-Pornography Movement, 1976–1986* (New York: Cambridge University Press, 2011), 131.

4. Ellen Willis, quoted in Brownstein, *Battling Pornography*, 171.

5. Patrick Joseph Buchanan, "Culture War Speech: Address to the Republican National Convention," Voices of Democracy: The U.S. Oratory Project, Aug. 17, 1992, https://voicesofdemocracy.umd.edu/buchanan-culture-war-speech-speech -text/.

6. No candidate won a majority in the three-way race among Bush, Clinton, and Ross Perot. In 1992, women voted overall 45–37 percent for Clinton. White women were evenly split between the two major candidates, 41–41 percent. Four years later, 54 percent of women voted for Clinton, and 38 percent voted for Bob Dole. Clinton carried 48 percent of white women, compared to 43 percent for Dole. Black women overwhelmingly supported Clinton in both 1992 (87 percent) and 1996 (89 percent). "Portrait of the Electorate: Gender," Portrait of the 1996 Electorate, *New York Times*, https://archive.nytimes.com/www.nytimes. com/library/politics/elect-port-gender.html.

7. James Talent, quoted in Gwendolyn Mink, *Welfare's End* (Ithaca, NY: Cornell University Press, 1998), 23; Mink, *Welfare's End*, 39, 134.

8. Gloria Steinem, "Why Feminists Support Clinton," *New York Times*, Mar. 22, 1998.

9. Alice Walker, "Preface," in Walker, *In Search of Our Mothers' Gardens: Womanist Prose* (New York: Harcourt Brace Company, 1983), xi.

10. Rebecca Walker, "Becoming the Third Wave," *Ms.* magazine, Jan./Feb. 1992, 86, 87.

11. Ibid., 87. On "postfeminism" and "I'm not a feminist, but . . . ," see Susan Faludi, *Backlash: The Undeclared War against American Women* (New York: Anchor Press, 1991); Susan J. Douglas, *Where the Girls Are: Growing up Female with the Mass Media* (New York: Three Rivers Press, 1994); and Tania Modleski, *Feminism without Women: Culture and Criticism in a "Postfeminist" Age* (New York: Routledge, 1991).

12. Linn Thomas, quoted in Claudia Wallis, "Onward, Women!" *Time* magazine, Dec. 4, 1989, 81.

13. India Arie, "Video," on *Acoustic Soul*, Motown, 2001.

14. Patricia Hill Collins, *Black Feminist Thought: Knowledge, Consciousness, and the Politics of Empowerment* (New York: Routledge, 1990), 222.

15. Sara Marcus, *Girls to the Front: The True Story of the Riot Grrrl Revolution* (New York: HarperCollins, 2010), 26.

16. Though these criteria are more commonly known as the Bechdel test, Bechdel herself prefers the more inclusive title, which acknowledges the inspiration of her friend Liz Wallace.

17. Kathleen Hanna and Kathy Acker, quoted in Marcus, *Girls to the Front*, 34.

18. Melissa Klein, quoted in Evans, *Tidal Wave*, 216; *Riot Grrrl*, quoted in Marcus, *Girls to the Front*, 77.

19. NWA, quoted in Evans, *Tidal Wave*, 216; Elisa Davis, quoted in Evans, *Tidal Wave*, 216.

20. Whitney A. Peoples, "'Under Construction': Identifying Foundations of Hip-Hop Feminisms and Exploring Bridges between Black Second Wave and Hip-Hop Feminisms," in *No Permanent Waves: Recasting Histories of U.S. Feminism*, ed. Nancy A. Hewitt (New Brunswick, NJ: Rutgers University Press, 2010), 411; Gwendolyn D. Pough, quoted in Peoples, "Under Construction," 417–18.

21. Jennifer Baumgardner and Amy Richards, *Manifesta: Young Women, Feminism, and the Future* (New York: Farrar, Straus and Giroux, 2000).

22. These omissions likely reflected not malice but rather the reality of *Time's* leadership structure: writer Ginia Bellafonte was one of only two women among the magazine's complement of senior writers. The magazine's editors had at first assigned Bellafonte to write a piece on women's views of Monica Lewinsky.

EPILOGUE

M ore than two decades in, the history of gender and feminism
in the twenty-first century remains difficult to parse, a dizzying array of conflicting tendencies. What were the overarching
themes and patterns in early twenty-first-century feminism and reactions
against it? When future historians attempt to answer this question, they
will look to some of the following events as evidence.

On September 11, 2001, members of the Islamist terrorist group Al-
Qaeda hijacked four commercial airplanes, two bound for the World
Trade Center in New York City; one for the Pentagon in Arlington, Virginia; and one for Washington, DC (eventually diverted to near Shanks-
ville, Pennsylvania, after passengers seized control). The original attacks
killed 2,977 victims, most of them at the World Trade Center. A thorough
analysis of post–9/11 politics lies well outside the scope of this volume.
One discourse, however, stands out.

Approximately two months after the attacks and one month after the
official launch of the U.S. war against Al-Qaeda, called Operation Enduring Freedom, in Afghanistan, First Lady Laura Bush gave the White
House's weekly radio address. It was a rare moment for Bush, a former
educator for whom politics held little allure, who at that point rarely
spoke publicly on policy issues. Later, the subjects of her address—cruelty
against women and children—became signature issues of her tenure as
First Lady.

In Bush's estimation, the War on Terror was not just about rooting
out the perpetrators of the 9/11 attacks. Rather, it was about mitigating
the brutal oppression of Afghani society's vulnerable members. Under the

Taliban, the fundamentalist religious-political sect that Al-Qaeda supported, women were denied an education, the right to earn a living, and the right to exercise personal agency and autonomy. Children were malnourished and often had little access to health care. Bush did not mention the practice in her speech, but Westerners often blanched at the burqas that some Muslim women wore. Perhaps learning of this treatment for the first time, "civilized people throughout the world are speaking out in horror—not only because our hearts break for the women and children in Afghanistan, but also because in Afghanistan we see the world the terrorists would like to impose on the rest of us."[1] Preventing the spread of this culture, then, provided justification for George W. Bush's foreign policy:

> All of us have an obligation to speak out. We may come from different backgrounds and faiths—but parents the world over love our children. We respect our mothers, our sisters and daughters. Fighting brutality against women and children is not the expression of a specific culture; it is the acceptance of our common humanity—a commitment shared by people of good will on every continent. Because of our recent military gains in much of Afghanistan, women are no longer imprisoned in their homes. They can listen to music and teach their daughters without fear of punishment. Yet the terrorists who helped rule that country now plot and plan in many countries. And they must be stopped. *The fight against terrorism is also a fight for the rights and dignity of women.*[2]

Bush no doubt spoke sincerely, and her concerns reflected grave limitations on the lives of women and children under the Taliban. As just one example, the fifteen-year-old educational activist Malala Yousafzai was shot in the head and nearly killed by a Taliban gunman in Pakistan in 2012. Some mainstream feminists, including Eleanor Smeal of the Feminist Majority, praised Bush's speech and the broader goal it represented. Feminist and novelist Jane Smiley recognized that the focus on women's rights was likely political, but she welcomed it nonetheless: when "the Afghan women took off their burkas," she wrote, "I put my doubts [about the war] away, for the time being."[3]

Other commentators questioned the Bush administration's commitment to international women's rights. After all, U.S. diplomats and oil executives had eagerly wooed the Taliban as recently as 1997; the group's views and policies on women had not changed in the past four years. How could it be, moreover, that equally repressive policies in such nations as Saudi Arabia and Kuwait, which remained strategically and economically important to the United States, were allowed to remain? How did attacking a nation's civilian population, infrastructure, and resources improve the lives of regular women?[4]

Finally, as anthropologist Lila Abu-Lughod asked, "Do Muslim women really need saving?" The Bush administration's fascination with Muslim

Nobel Peace Prize recipient Malala Yousafzai. In the early decades of the twenty-first century, U.S. foreign policy goals sometimes obscured the actual lives of Muslim women. Though Yousafzai faced violent retribution for her activism on behalf of women and girls in her home country of Pakistan, she was much more than a victim in need of a Western savior. (Simon Davis/DFID licensed under CC BY 2.0 <https://creativecommons.org/licenses/by/2.0>)

women, Abu-Lughod argued, both reflected the long history of Western colonialist discourse and disavowed any role that colonialism played in the way such cultures developed. It also reduced Muslim women to a homogenous, oppressed "other," denying Muslim women agency in determining, for example, what face and body coverings meant to them as individuals—or, more broadly, what liberation would look like *to Muslim women*. Abu-Lughod noted, for example, that the Revolutionary Association of the Women of Afghanistan (RAWA), which since the 1970s had fought for women's rights in that nation, opposed the U.S. military effort.[5]

Twenty years later, as the United States prepared to mark the twentieth anniversary of the events of September 11, 2001, President Joe Biden removed the nation's remaining troops from Afghanistan, citing the untenable monetary and human cost of the "forever war." Within days, the Taliban had retaken the nation, reigniting fears about women's lives and freedom there.

Critics found it ironic that President George W. Bush had positioned himself as Muslim women's savior. Early in his presidency, Bush had reintroduced the Reagan-era gag rule, which denied U.S. funding to any global family-planning organization that mentioned abortion as an option. In 2003, Bush signed a ban on late-term abortions (often called "partial birth abortions" by abortion opponents), which the administration termed an "abhorrent practice . . . that offends human dignity."[6] The Supreme Court upheld the ban in 2007. Bush also increased funding for abstinence-only education and introduced a set of "conscience clauses," most commonly invoked in matters pertaining to reproduction, that allowed medical practitioners to decline to provide treatments to which they objected.

During the Obama administration (2009–17), the issues of birth control and abortion manifested themselves most visibly in debates over the Affordable Care Act (ACA). Among other provisions, the 2010 law required insurance policies to include coverage for birth control. Despite repeated, factually incorrect claims to the contrary, ACA did not overturn the decades-old ban on using taxpayer money to fund most abortions. Still, this misperception informed much of the opposition to the ACA, which coalesced in the 2010s with a movement to defund Planned Parenthood. In one notorious exchange in 2011, Senator John Kyl (R-AZ) incorrectly argued on the Senate floor that abortions constituted "well over

90 percent of what Planned Parenthood does." When critics pointed out that the actual number was under 3 percent, Kyl's spokesperson claimed that the senator's assertion "was not intended to be a factual statement."[7]

Religious organizations were exempt from the ACA's birth control requirement, but other employers (including religiously affiliated colleges and universities) were not. Almost as soon as the law was passed, opponents began a campaign to widen this exemption, and in February 2012, the Republican-led House Oversight and Government Reform Committee held hearings on the matter. As reproductive rights advocates quickly noted, the only experts invited to testify were male clergy and theologians.

In response, congressional Democrats invited Sandra Fluke, a thirty-year-old Georgetown Law student, to testify. Because of its affiliation with the Catholic Church, Georgetown did not provide coverage for birth control in its student health plans. As Fluke testified, this policy caused financial difficulty for many of her classmates, who relied on birth control not only to prevent pregnancy but also to regulate such conditions as polycystic ovary syndrome (PCOS).

Fluke was prepared to receive criticism for her testimony, but she did not expect the vicious personal attacks levied against her, especially by conservative radio host Rush Limbaugh. Apparently unaware that birth control costs the same amount no matter how much sex a person is or is not having, Limbaugh claimed that Fluke "essentially says that she must be paid to have sex—what does that make her? It makes her a slut, right? It makes her a prostitute. She wants to be paid to have sex. She's having so much sex she can't afford the contraception. She wants you and me and the taxpayers to pay her to have sex."[8] Limbaugh later apologized for his choice of words, but not for the content of his attack.

Shortly thereafter, the Obama administration instituted new regulations that would allow employees of religiously affiliated institutions to receive birth control coverage directly from their insurer, allowing the employer itself to opt out of the original mandate. This exemption, however, satisfied neither religious institutions nor nonreligious companies owned by individuals who personally opposed birth control. The Supreme Court upheld these objections in the five-to-four *Burwell v. Hobby Lobby Stores, Inc.* decision (2014), which exempted "closely held" companies from the birth control mandate if their owners objected to it on religious grounds.

More recently, the issue of abortion helped to ensure evangelical loyalty to Donald Trump. Trump's personal life may have violated many of their most important tenets about gender and family, but he promised to appoint anti-abortion judges—and as president, he delivered. The additions of Neil Gorsuch, Brett Kavanaugh, and Amy Coney Barrett to the court gave conservatives a six-to-three majority. As states continued to enact restrictions—Texas Senate Bill 8 (2021), for example, banned almost all abortions after about six weeks, when many women do not yet know they are pregnant, and deputized civilians to enforce the law—a showdown became imminent. On June 24, 2022, as this book headed to press, the court decided in *Dobbs v. Jackson Women's Health Organization* to uphold a Mississippi law that severely limited abortion rights and to overturn *Roe v. Wade* itself, despite the fact that a majority of Americans believe abortion should be legal in at least some cases. As of this writing, thirteen states have banned the procedure entirely, and such conservatives as former vice president Mike Pence have called for a national ban. The effects of this decision will be tremendous, especially for women with limited financial resources.

In 2013, Facebook chief operating officer Sheryl Sandberg published *Lean In: Women, Work, and the Will to Lead*. In it, she documented her travails in corporate America: inadequate accommodations for pregnant women, lack of access to childcare and parental leave, tokenism, the absence of mentors, and more. At the same time, she argued, "[W]omen are hindered by barriers that exist within ourselves. We hold ourselves back in ways both big and small, by lacking self-confidence, by not raising our hands, and by pulling back when we should be leaning in. We internalize the negative messages we get throughout our lives—the messages that say it's wrong to be outspoken, aggressive, more powerful than men. We lower our expectations of what we can achieve. We continue to do the majority of the housework and childcare. We compromise our career goals to make room for partners and children who may not even exist yet. Compared to our male colleagues, fewer of us aspire to senior positions." Sandberg recognized the importance of addressing structural inequalities, and she admitted that her book would be less relevant to the many women struggling to take care of their families. Still, she insisted "that getting rid of these internal barriers is crucial to [women] gaining power," and this was the subject on which her book focused. "I believe that if more women lean in," she wrote, "we can change the power structure of our world and expand opportunities for all. More female leadership will lead to fairer treatment for *all* women."⁹

The problems, Sandberg believed, began in childhood, when girls learned that they should be docile and polite. These learned behaviors persisted into the workplace, where women's insecurities—about likeability, about competence, about the near impossibility of appearing to be both at the same time—made it difficult for them to claim, as Sandberg put it, "a seat at the table." Women were often reluctant to negotiate their salaries, speak up in meetings, or apply for leadership positions. In planning their lives and careers, they sometimes passed up opportunities that may make it more difficult to combine paid work and family responsibilities. Change would come, Sandberg argued, when women said yes to more opportunities, challenged their partners to take on more responsibilities in the world, and were unafraid to speak about gender bias in the workplace—a particular challenge to women of Sandberg's generation, who were raised to expect that any lingering inequality in the workplace could be overcome through sheer hard work.

Responses to *Lean In* ran the gamut. Many professional women responded with joy and relief, feeling that Sandberg's manifesto had vocalized their own feelings. Lean In circles sprang up in the corporate, technology, and government sectors of Washington, DC, New York City, and elsewhere—the same powerful circles in which Sandberg herself had worked. But criticism, too, poured in, some of it from fellow professionals. In a widely circulated article for *The Atlantic*, Princeton academic and former State Department advisor Anne-Marie Slaughter questioned the seeming ease with which Sandberg achieved work-life balance, or "having it all." "I still strongly believe that women can 'have it all,'" Slaughter wrote, "(and that men can too). I believe that we can 'have it all at the same time.' But not today, not with the way America's economy and society are currently structured." Even former first lady Michelle Obama, while on tour in 2018 for her own book, *Becoming*, entered the fray: "It's not always enough to lean in," she admitted, "because that s— doesn't work." Entering the workforce in the years just before or during the Great Recession of the previous decade, many Millennial feminists also found Sandberg's largely individualistic solutions unhelpful.¹⁰

The most powerful and important critiques focused on the women for whom the book would never reflect reality: working-class and poor women, including the disproportionate numbers of women of color in those groups. Though Michelle Obama spoke in 2018 from a place of tremendous privilege, she came from a working-class background that her overwhelmingly white, elite Princeton classmates, and law firm colleagues did not always understand. Combined with very real structural barriers, cultural mismatches made it difficult for women from similar backgrounds to advance in corporate America. Moreover, as workplace justice activist Ellen Bravo argued in *The Atlantic*, working-class women had always leaned in. Sandberg would do well, according to Bravo, to follow the example of women in the National Domestic Workers Alliance and the Fight for $15, groups that were fighting for collective, not individual, advancement. In the past decade, historians have begun to study precedents for this activism, including the poor Black women who responded to Reagan-era cuts to social welfare programs by founding their own anti-poverty groups and the some 1.5 million women who attempted to sue Walmart for sex-based employment discrimination. (In 2011, the Supreme Court decided in a 5–4 decision that the plaintiffs could not constitute a class.)[11]

Along with workplace challenges, women continue to shoulder an unequal caregiving burden. In 2020 and 2021, the COVID-19 pandemic shone a bright light on this reality. When schools suddenly shut down in March 2020, parents became responsible for monitoring and supplementing their children's digital education. Some chose to homeschool entirely—all while trying to maintain productivity while working from home, as kitchens and couches became makeshift schools and offices. Many Gen-X and Millennial women also found themselves newly responsible for the care of aging relatives, the group most susceptible to COVID-19. Yet balancing remote work and caregiving was among the better-case scenarios during the pandemic. As health care workers, warehouse employees, grocery store clerks, and more, women on the front lines put their lives at risk to support themselves and their families. At the same time, millions of Americans lost their jobs. Many women have not returned to the paid workforce, either unable to find employment or recognizing the impossibility of balancing all their responsibilities. Increased recognition of these issues has ignited a necessary public discussion on caregiving, burnout, and the possibility of government aid for caregivers.

Sandberg's "Why aren't there more female CEOs?" version of feminism also depended on, and assumed the inevitability of, an economy structured around CEOs. More recent revelations about Sandberg's participation in Facebook's less savory activities—including the erosion of user privacy and the failure to quell disinformation ahead of the 2016 election—have damaged her personal reputation. *Lean In*, however, was only one example of the corporate, consumerist feminism that became popular in the early twenty-first century, as feminism became a trendy commodity.

"As I started to write this book," *Bitch* cofounder Andi Zeisler wrote in the introduction to her 2016 book *We Were Feminists Once*, "[S]omething weird happened: feminism got *cool*." Zeisler traces this development to 2014, when billionaire pop star Beyoncé appeared at MTV Video Music Awards with "FEMINIST" emblazoned on the wall behind her. From there, a growing number of female celebrities, including actresses Emma Watson and Lena Dunham, singers Taylor Swift and Katy Perry, and Muppet Miss Piggy, publicly embraced feminism. Corporate marketing teams glommed onto the trend, using feminism to sell products from shampoo to cell phones. This "empowertising" did not emerge whole cloth after Beyoncé's bold proclamation—Dove's "Campaign for Real Beauty" and Nike's iconic "Like a Girl" campaign had debuted earlier—but it certainly intensified in the mid-2010s. T-shirts, mugs, jewelry, and other mass-produced merchandise proclaimed "feminist as fuck" and "I Blame the Patriarchy" as companies tried to replicate the success of the Feminist Majority Foundation's "This Is What a Feminist Looks Like" T-shirt. According to Zeisler, this "marketplace feminism," as she calls it, is "decontextualized. It's depoliticized. And it's probably feminism's most popular iteration ever."[12]

It feels good to proclaim one's politics in this way (indeed, "feel-good feminism" is used synonymously with Zeisler's "marketplace feminism"). But consuming such products often aligns with the goals of global neoliberalism, as women's choices are severed from the cultural and political context in which they make these choices and anything a woman chooses must be empowering. Purchasing cute T-shirts also fuels the search for cheaper and cheaper workers to make these products, leading to deadly results. In 2013, a garment factory in Bangladesh collapsed, killing 1,134 workers, many of them women. Reducing feminism to any choice a (white, middle-class, or elite American) woman makes elides this reality.

Finally, T-shirts hold little efficacy against predatory men or institutional-ized misogyny, as the second half of the 2010s made clear.

When the dust settled from the 2016 election, one statistic fired the public imagination more than any other: according to exit polls, 52 per-cent of white women had voted for Republican Donald Trump, compared to 43 percent for Hillary Clinton, his Democratic opponent.[13] In and of itself, this behavior is not that striking, as white women supported Re-publicans Mitt Romney in 2012 and John McCain in 2008 by similar margins. The political gender gap between men's and women's voting behavior was well known, but now the general public was beginning to understand what social scientists had long known: it was women of color, not white women, who more consistently backed Democratic candidates. Thus, in 2016, hand-wringing and think pieces analyzing white women's behavior proliferated as never before.

To a large extent, this reckoning centered on the singular figure of Trump himself. A well-known womanizer, Trump made no attempt during the campaign to hide his disdain for women. "What a nasty woman," he derided his opponent on the debate stage. At rallies, he often led his fol-lowers in chants to "lock her up." Many women came forward with allega-tions of sexual assault, which Trump sometimes dismissed by implying that his accusers were not attractive enough for him to have assaulted them.

Perhaps most remarkably, Trump himself seemed to confirm the allega-tions against him. On October 7, 2016, reports emerged of a decade-old recorded conversation between Trump and *Access Hollywood* host Billy Bush (cousin to George W. Bush). In it, Trump warned Bush of how he might approach the woman they were about to meet: "I better use some Tic Tacs just in case I start kissing her. You know I'm automatically at-tracted to beautiful—I just start kissing them. It's like a magnet. Just kiss. I don't even wait. And when you're a star, they let you do it. You can do anything. Grab 'em by the pussy. You can do anything." In the wake of these new revelations, prominent Republicans—most notably, Arizona senator and 2008 presidential nominee John McCain—withdrew their support from the candidate. Mitt Romney, the party's 2012 nominee, had never endorsed Trump, and now Romney took to Twitter to condemn Trump's "vile degradations." Trump was already trailing in the polls, and experts predicted that this latest revelation would doom his campaign. Certainly, the reasoning went, no women could vote for him now.[14]

Trump's appeal to white women was all the more bewildering because of whom he faced: not only one of the nation's best-known, most experienced politicians but also the first woman ever to become a major party's presidential nominee. Former first lady Hillary Clinton—a lawyer, former senator, and former secretary of state—seemed to embody the promise of liberal feminism. But to some, therein lay the problem: Clinton represented the educated technocratic elite, a group that had weathered the twenty-first century's wrenching shift to an information economy more successfully than the working class. Clinton alienated members of the latter group when she termed Trump supporters "deplorables" who were "racist, sexist, homophobic, xenophobic, Islamaphobic—you name it."[15] Trump's campaign, by contrast, wooed this group with his promise to "Make America Great Again." As many commentators have pointed out, this slogan hearkened to an era before the successes of the civil rights movement, before second-wave feminism, and before the new immigrant waves of the late twentieth century. Journalist Sarah Jaffe notes that "it is also a nostalgia for a period of time when a white couple could raise children on one income, when union jobs in factories provided steady work and regular vacations." For working-class women, this vision—unencumbered through selective memory by the less pleasant aspects of the era—offered a sense of security. By contrast, "telling women to find liberation through work—the implicit and at times explicit (think welfare reform) message of Hillary Clinton—is not that great an offer when that work is McDonald's."[16]

The importance of class resentment to the 2016 election should not be overstated. While much commentary in its aftermath focused on the white working class, Trump's victory depended heavily on the country's wealthiest voters, a reliably Republican demographic. Yet the culture wars surely factored into his ascension. Like the Catholic and evangelical Protestant women politicized in the 1970s, conservative women in 2016 saw Clinton's candidacy and potential presidency as an attack on their way of life. Some hewed to white Christian patriarchy, which reserved leadership roles for men. Others were single-issue voters focused on abortion above all else. This group influences U.S. elections out of proportion to its numbers; though roughly 15 percent of the population, white evangelicals make up approximately a quarter of the electorate, and in 2016 they preferred Trump over Clinton at a margin of nearly eight to two. (By contrast, 62 percent of evangelicals of color voted for Clinton.)[17]

Trump's racism also galvanized some voters. Trump's screeds against immigrants, Muslims, and others often included the false claim that men in these groups posed a special threat of sexual violence. Announcing his candidacy in July 2015, Trump denounced Mexican immigrants: "They're bringing drugs. They're bringing crime. They're rapists. And some, I assume, are good people." White women had long seen themselves as the embodiment of the nation's morality and purity, and so many of them saw a special role for themselves in the effort to stem the tide of demographic change.

Equally important, Trump's election engendered a new feminist resistance. On January 21, 2017, the day after the new president's inauguration, over 470,000 people descended on Washington, DC, for the inaugural Women's March on Washington, inspired by the need to resist both Trump's personal deportment and proposed policies, which included repealing the Affordable Care Act and restricting reproductive choice. Across the country, as many as five million people participated; worldwide participation was approximately seven million. It was the largest single-day protest in U.S. history. Many participants donned pink, handmade "pussy hats," reclaiming Trump's infamous "grab them by the pussy" comment. "Pussy grabs back," declared signs and chants, as celebrities and politicians argued passionately for women's rights.

The wounds from the 2016 election had not healed, of course. People of color were understandably skeptical of white women's political engagement. In Los Angeles, actor Amir Talai held a sign that read, "I'll see you nice white ladies at the next #blacklivesmatter march right?" In Washington, DC, Angela Peoples, codirector of GetEqual, an LGBTQ advocacy group, wore a hat that said "Stop Killing Black People" and carried a sign with the message, "Don't forget: White women voted for Trump." Kevin Banatte, Peoples's boyfriend, captured a photograph in which three white women stand behind Peoples with their cell phones, one of them taking a selfie. According to Peoples, the photo "tells the story of white women in this moment wanting to just show up in a very superficial way and not wanting to do the hard work of making change, of challenging their own privilege. You're here protesting, but don't forget: The folks that you live with every single day—and probably some of the women that decided to come to the march—voted for Trump, made the decision to vote against self-interests to maintain their white supremacist way of life."[18]

By 2019, amid accusations of anti-Semitism, exclusivity, and financial mismanagement, the Women's March was no longer on the cutting edge of feminist activism. By then, however, grassroots political campaigns, many of them founded and staffed by women of color, had begun to bear real fruit. Even as Trump carried the state of Arizona in 2016, a coalition of Latina activists in Maricopa County led the successful campaign to unseat Sheriff Joe Arpaio, an anti-immigrant hardliner facing prosecution for racial profiling. In 2017, Black women–run organizations such as the Black Voters Matter Fund and BlackPAC funneled resources into the special election for an Alabama Senate seat. Ordinary Black women turned out in droves, paving the way for a surprise defeat of far-right candidate Roy Moore.

The movement to defeat Moore, whose past was littered with allegations of sexual misconduct toward underage girls, also benefited from timing: the election came just one month after widespread accusations of sexual abuse against film producer Harvey Weinstein, which began a domino effect of similar allegations against powerful men in sports (USA Gymnastics doctor Larry Nassar), media (comedian Louis C. K.), and law (Supreme Court nominee and later justice Brett Kavanaugh), as well as institutions such as the military. The movement to hold these men accountable coalesced around the Twitter hashtag #MeToo. Over ten years earlier, in 2006, Black activist Tarana Burke had founded the Me Too movement, which grew out of her work with young girls. Burke's MySpace page attracted national attention, and the movement started to receive donations and grants. But it was not until 2017, when white actress Alyssa Milano used the hashtag to encourage women to share their stories, that the movement became a national phenomenon. In the intervening years, national media attention had focused, too, on rape culture in college and university settings. Columbia University senior Emma Sulkowicz spent the 2014–15 school year carrying a mattress around campus to protest her alleged rapist's continued presence at the school. In 2016, University of California, Santa Barbara, student Chanel Miller prepared an anonymous victim impact statement, which was read at the trial of her convicted sexual assailant, Stanford University student Brock Turner. Later released online, Miller's searing testimony went viral, sparking further outrage at Turner's lenient sentence and its "boys will be boys" apologism.

It was in this context that the nomination of Brett Kavanaugh to replace retiring Supreme Court justice Anthony Kennedy in the summer of 2018 became a national referendum on when and whether to believe women. In September that year, the *Washington Post* made public allegations from Christine Blasey Ford that Kavanaugh and a friend had sexually assaulted her at a party while both were in high school. The Republican-controlled Senate judiciary committee invited both to testify publicly. While Ford drew on both personal experience and her expertise as a psychologist to emphasize the lifelong trauma such attacks cause, Kavanaugh fumed about damage to his reputation. But a short FBI investigation failed to convince Republicans of the veracity of Ford's accusations, and the full Senate confirmed Kavanaugh 51–49, almost entirely along party lines.

Like Clarence Thomas's appointment to the court twenty-seven years earlier, Kavanaugh's confirmation galvanized feminist and other liberal and progressive women. A younger, more progressive, and more diverse cohort of women ran for public office in the 2018 midterm election. In New York and Boston, respectively, Alexandria Ocasio-Cortez and Ayanna Pressley upset long-serving white male members of their own party before prevailing in the general election. LaTosha Brown, one of the organizers behind Roy Moore's 2017 defeat in Alabama, threw her resources into races across the South, most notably in Georgia with Stacey Abrams's quest to become the nation's first Black female governor. Abrams's narrow loss occurred amid widespread accusations of voter suppression, and she has since become an influential power broker within the Democratic Party. Finally, Kamala Harris parlayed her high-profile performance in the Kavanaugh hearings into a run for president in 2020, which failed to win the nomination but won her such respect that the Democratic presidential nominee selected her as his vice presidential running mate. With her election, she became the first woman and the first woman of color to ascend to the position.

The contours of this new feminist movement are still emerging, but one aspect of it is very clear: it will need to grapple with intersectionality in ways that previous women's movements have not been able to do. This task will fall not only to adult women in formal positions of leadership, but also and perhaps especially to members of Gen-Z and beyond, who have already taught their elders much about feminism and gender. By them and by our generational predecessors, let us all be inspired to, as the late poet Maya Angelou put it, "Take up the battle, take it up! It's yours, this is your life. This is your world."[19] The battle to protect women's rights is going to take all of us.

NOTES

1. "Radio Address by Mrs. Bush," President George W. Bush Archives, the White House, Nov. 17, 2001, https://georgewbush-whitehouse.archives.gov/news/releases/2001/11/20011117.html.

2. Ibid., emphasis added.

3. Jane Smiley, "Women's Crusade," *New York Times*, Dec. 2, 2001.

4. See, for example, Sharon Smith, "Using Women's Rights to Sell Washington's War," *International Socialist Review*, Jan.–Feb. 2002, http://www.isreview.org/issues/21/afghan_women.shtml.

5. Lila Abu-Lughod, "Do Muslim Women Really Need Saving? Anthropological Reflections on Cultural Relativism and Its Others," *American Anthropologist* 104, no. 3 (2002): 783–90. See also Abu-Lughod, *Do Muslim Women Need Saving?* (Cambridge, MA: Harvard University Press, 2013).

6. "Fact Sheet: 2003: A Year of Accomplishment for the American People," American Presidency Project, Dec. 13, 2003, https://www.presidency.ucsb.edu/node/280142.

7. Gail Collins, "Behind the Abortion War," *New York Times*, Apr. 13, 2011.

8. Brian Stelter, "Limbaugh Apologizes for Attack on Student in Birth Control Furor," *New York Times*, Mar. 3, 2012.

9. Sheryl Sandberg, *Lean In: Women, Work, and the Will to Lead* (New York: Alfred A. Knopf, 2013), introduction, chap. 11.

10. Anne-Marie Slaughter, "Why Women Still Can't Have It All," *The Atlantic*, Jul./Aug. 2012; "Michelle Obama Got Especially Comfortable during Her Book-Tour Stop in Brooklyn," *Vanity Fair*, Dec. 2, 2018. Slaughter based her criticism on two of Sandberg's speeches given in the years leading up to the publication of *Lean In*.

11. Ellen Bravo, "Many Working-Class Women Are Already Leaning In," *The Atlantic*, Mar. 12, 2013.

12. Andi Zeisler, *We Were Feminists Once: From Riot Girl to Cover Girl, the Buying and Selling of a Political Movement* (New York: PublicAffairs, 2016), intro.

13. The actual numbers—47 percent for Trump, as compared to 45 percent for Clinton—differed, though they still indicated that a plurality of white women voters supported Trump. "An Examination of the 2016 Electorate, Based on Validated Voters," Pew Research Center, Aug. 9, 2018, https://www.pewresearch.org/politics/2018/08/09/an-examination-of-the-2016-electorate-based-on-validated

-voters/. Many older adults, including white women, feel a particular antipathy toward Clinton, but these feelings do not entirely explain their support of Trump, who increased his share of white women voters in the 2020 election, which otherwise lies outside the scope of this study.

14. David A. Fahrenthold, "Trump Recorded Having Extremely Lewd Conversation about Women in 2005," *Washington Post*, Oct. 8, 2016; Madeline Conway, "Romney: Trump's Comments 'Demean Our Wives and Daughters and Corrupt America' Face to the World," *Politico*, Oct. 7, 2016, https://www.politico .com/story/2016/10/mitt-romney-donald-trump-comments-women-229325.

15. Amy Chozick, "Hillary Clinton Calls Many Trump Backers 'Deplorables,' and G.O.P. Pounces," *New York Times*, Sept. 10, 2016.

16. Sarah Jaffe, "Why Did a Majority of White Women Vote for Trump?" *New Labor Forum* 27, no. 1 (2018): 23–24.

17. "An Examination of the 2016 Electorate, Based on Validated Voters."

18. Angela Peoples, quoted in Brooke Obie, "Woman in Viral Photo from Women's March to White Female Allies: 'Listen to a Black Woman,'" *The Root*, Jan. 23, 2017, https://www.theroot.com/woman-in-viral-photo-from-women-s -march-to-white-female-1791524613.

19. Dr. Maya Angelou, "Just Do Right," YouTube video, 2013, https://www .youtube.com/watch?v=bxrV2J_OjGo.

BIOGRAPHICAL ESSAYS

The following is not intended to provide a comprehensive "who's who" of the women's rights movement. Rather, the figures discussed here meet at least one of three criteria: (1) they represent the diversity of those who engaged with the women's rights movement, including by race, sexuality, generation, politics, and area of focus/principal mode of activism; (2) their presence in the text thus far is not commensurate with their importance; and/or (3) they deserve to be better known. The one partial exception to this model is Ruth Bader Ginsburg, whose death as I prepared these essays compelled me to include her.

YET-SI-BLUE (JANET RENECKER MCCLOUD, 1934–2003)

A member of the Tulalip and Nisqually tribes, a fishing rights activist, and a founder of the feminist group Women of All Red Nations (WARN). Born on the Tulalip Reservation in Washington state, she survived an abusive father and stepfather. In fact, the very first manifestation of her activism was to organize her cousins to defend themselves against their assailants. Blue and her siblings were eventually placed in foster care, but her early life left a permanent mark, and she tried to commit suicide at age twelve. Around the same time, Blue dropped out of school. By the mid-1960s, she and Don McCloud, her second husband, had purchased a farm near Tacoma, Washington. There, the couple became involved in the ultimately successful movement to restore Native American fishing rights, guaranteed by treaties with the federal government but threatened by state law and rampant hooliganism. Both of them were arrested several times for their participation in fish-ins. Blue then joined the American Indian Movement (AIM), advocating for the religious rights of imprisoned Native Americans and for Native sovereignty. Frustrated by sexism within the AIM, she cofounded WARN in 1974. WARN focused its attention on issues, including the lingering, gendered effects of colonialism, domestic violence, forced sterilization of Native women, the health and welfare of Native women and children, and environmental protection. Blue continued this activism in 1985, when she hosted the founding conference of the Indigenous Women's Network. That same year she served as a delegate to the United Nations World Conference on Women. Blue died at age sixty-nine of complications from diabetes.

ANDREA DWORKIN (1946–2005)

Andrea Dworkin was a radical feminist and anti-pornography activist born in Camden, New Jersey, to progressive, social justice–minded Jewish parents. When she was nine years old, a stranger sexually assaulted her in a movie theater, and her parents moved the family to Cherry Hill, New Jersey. Later, as a teenager, she was beaten and raped. Dworkin turned to protest at an early age: in grade school, she refused to sing "Silent Night" because her family was Jewish (she was punished for her refusal). In middle school, she boycotted atomic bomb drills. Enrolling in Bennington College in 1965, Dworkin joined protests against the war in Vietnam, leading in one instance to her arrest and mistreatment in the Women's House of Detention in Lower Manhattan. Her testimony about the incident for the first time brought her national attention. After a short stint in Crete, she returned to Bennington, where her priorities soon encompassed access to birth control and legalized abortion. She graduated in 1969. Dworkin then traveled to Amsterdam to interview and write about members of that city's counterculture, marrying one of them. Unfortunately, the marriage was abusive, and Dworkin left her husband in 1971. Homeless, alone in a foreign country, and without any other prospects for income, Dworkin supported herself through sex work. Back in the United States, Dworkin threw herself into the burgeoning feminist movement as a writer, organizer, and speaker. In her personal life, she began a long-term domestic partnership and eventual marriage with cultural critic John Stoltenberg, though both identified as gay. Dworkin became well known for her war against pornography, arguing that the medium encouraged violence against women and constituted a violation of women's civil rights. In 1979, she cofounded Women against Pornography and published *Pornography: Men Possessing Women*. In the early 1980s, Dworkin and lawyer Catherine MacKinnon drafted anti-pornography legislation for Minneapolis and Indianapolis; the former was vetoed by the mayor, and the latter was found unconstitutional. Dworkin also found unlikely allies in conservatives, including U.S. attorney general Edwin Meese, testifying in his 1986 commission on pornography. Her best-known work, *Intercourse*, which argued that true consent between women and men was impossible under patriarchy, was published the following year. Always controversial within the feminist movement, Dworkin continued to oppose all forms of violence against women until her early death at age fifty-eight.

RUTH BADER GINSBURG (1933–2020)

Ruth Bader Ginsburg was a feminist legal strategist appointed to the Supreme Court by President Bill Clinton in 1993, making her the second woman to serve on that body. Born in Brooklyn to a working-class Russian Jewish family, Ginsburg attended Cornell University on scholarship, graduating in 1954. At Harvard Law School, where she began her legal studies, discrimination was rampant; on one occasion, dean Erwin Griswold demanded that Ginsburg and the other eight women in the program explain why they were justified in taking a "man's place." She eventually transferred to Columbia University, graduating in 1959 in a tie for first in her class. Nonetheless, she struggled to find work, eventually taking a summer position with a Columbia-based project on international civil law. She spent six weeks in Sweden, where feminism was flourishing and women were demanding policies that would help them balance paid work and family life. Ginsburg applied these insights to her teaching, first at Rutgers University Law School and then back at Columbia, and in her work as director of the American Civil Liberties Union (ACLU) Women's Rights Project. Through the ACLU, she worked to convince courts that the Fourteenth Amendment guarantee of equal protection applied to sex as well as race discrimination. In the six cases she argued before the Supreme Court, Ginsburg methodically chipped away at laws that treated women and men differently, often by revealing how they hurt members of both groups. In *Reed v. Reed* (1971), she successfully challenged an Idaho law that, based on the assumption that women lacked business acumen and experience, granted men preference in estate administration. In *Weinberger v. Wiesenfeld* (1975), she represented a widower who had been denied access to survivor benefits, a practice based on the assumption that women's contributions to the family economy were incidental. Once on the court herself, she authored several significant opinions, including the majority opinion in a case that overturned the Virginia Military Institute's male-only admissions policy (1996) and dissents in cases related to the 2000 election, abortion, pay discrimination, campaign finance, and voting rights. In the last decade of her life, Ginsburg became a different kind of feminist icon after law student Shana Knizhnik dubbed her the "Notorious RBG." Her workout regimen and frilly lace collars soon attracted almost as much attention as her scathing dissents, delighting and comforting progressives as the conservative majority consolidated its grip on the Supreme Court. In her personal life, Ginsburg was well known for her long, remarkably egalitarian relationship with husband and fellow lawyer Martin Ginsburg, as well as for her unlikely friendship with conservative Supreme Court justice Antonin Scalia. After her death in 2020, Ginsburg became the first woman and the first Jewish American to lie in state at the Capitol.

BARBARA GITTINGS (1932–2007)

Barbara Gittings, a lesbian and gay rights activist, was born in Vienna, Austria, to Elizabeth and John Sterett Gittings, who served in the U.S. Diplomatic Corps. After an international childhood, Gittings and her family settled in Wilmington, Delaware, where she graduated from Ursuline Academy in 1948. After she was denied admission to the National Honor Society due to "homosexual tendencies," she began a quest to find accurate information about homosexuality—not an easy task in an era that often treated same-sex desire as a perversion, disease, or crime. After an unsuccessful stint at Northwestern University and a falling out with her family, Gittings moved to Philadelphia in 1950. There, she began to read about, and eventually participate in, the organizations that made up the new lesbian and gay rights movement, most importantly the Daughters of Bilitis (DOB). Gittings founded the group's New York branch. She also met her longtime partner, Kay Tobin Lahusen, through DOB. From 1963 to 1966 she served as editor of *The Ladder*, the organization's publication. She was fired from this position for pushing for lesbians and gay men to participate in more public protests, a controversial strategy at the time. One of her most important allies in this regard was Frank Kameny, who had founded the Washington, DC, branch of the Mattachine Society. Along with psychiatrist John Fryer, Gittings and Kameny spoke at the 1972 conference of the American Psychiatric Association (APA), which classified homosexuality as a mental illness. In response to pressure from Gittings and others, the APA changed this classification the next year. Gittings also served as longtime head of the American Library Association's Gay Task Force, where she strove to make literature by and about lesbians and gay men accessible to young people—a lifelong passion that dated back to her own attempts to find such resources.

DOROTHY HAENER (1917–2001)

Dorothy Haener was the sixth of seven children born to working-class parents in Detroit, Michigan. As a teenager in the Great Depression, Haener watched her siblings enter the automobile industry just as the United Auto Workers (UAW) was embarking on an ambitious organizing drive. Her brothers worked at the Ford River Rouge plant, and her older sister worked at Ternstedt, a General Motors plant, where she participated in a 1937 sit-down strike. After becoming the first person in her family to graduate from high school, Haener found employment as a welder at Wayne Wire Cloth Company. There, poor safety standards, inadequate rest periods, unequal pay for women, and rampant sexual harassment pushed Haener to speak to her coworkers about the benefits of unionizing; she was fired for her efforts. During World War II, Haener became one of thousands of women to find work in the defense industries, as a department clerk at Ford's Willow Run bomber plant. She felt, however, that she had been barred from more lucrative positions, and she petitioned the UAW, which represented workers at the plant, to file a grievance on her behalf. The grievance was successful, and Haener moved to a new position as an inspector in the small parts department. When the war ended and servicemen returned, the factory converted to automobile production. Haener lost her position, despite an agreement with the UAW local that was supposed to protect women's positions. She was eventually hired back as a department clerk, a low-paying, nonunionized job. Haener pressured the management to respect its agreement with the UAW to rehire women into the positions they held during the war, and eventually she was promoted to a prestigious position in statistical quality control. Haener then served the union in a number of roles (sometimes to the chagrin of male unionists), including as a member of the local's collective bargaining unit and as a delegate to the union's constitutional convention. She also advised women who were frustrated with their meager employment prospects to use the union to secure better jobs, as she had done.

Despite the intransigence of some men, the UAW had made tremendous strides toward gender equality. At the behest of UAW president Walter Reuther, who had recently issued new directives for combatting sex discrimination within the union, Haener became a UAW national organizer. In 1944, the UAW had established a women's bureau, which in 1955 became a full-fledged women's department. As a member of the department committee, Haener worked alongside Director Caroline Davis to secure equal workplace rights for women. The two also worked together between 1961 and 1963 on the President's Commission on the Status of Women, where their opposition to protective legislation placed them in a distinct minority. Unsurprisingly, Haener strongly supported the 1963 Equal Pay Act, the inclusion of "sex" in Title VII of the Civil Rights Act, and the robust pursuit of violations of the latter. In 1966, she and Davis broke away from their labor colleagues to become founding members of the National Organization for Women. However, though both personally supported the Equal Rights Amendment, they temporarily resigned from NOW when its endorsement of the measure conflicted with UAW policy.

In the 1970s and beyond, Haener served on the National Women's Task Force on Women and Employment, the Michigan Civil Rights Commission, and the International Women's Year Commission, among other responsibilities. She retired from the UAW in 1982 but remained politically active into the 1990s, when she lobbied on behalf of health care reform.

FANNIE LOU TOWNSEND HAMER (1917–1977)

Fannie Lou Townsend Hamer was born into a family of sharecroppers in Montgomery County, Mississippi, the youngest of twenty children. By the age of six, she had joined her parents and older siblings picking cotton, though she continued to attend school through sixth grade. A childhood bout with polio left her with a slight lifelong limp. Hamer married Perry "Pap" Hamer, a sharecropper in Ruleville, Mississippi, in 1944. The Hamers were unable to have biological children—after two stillbirths, doctors performed an involuntary hysterectomy on Fannie Lou—but the couple raised two daughters whose biological families could not care for them.

Hamer did not actively participate in the civil rights movement until she was in her forties. In 1962, she attended a mass meeting hosted by the Student Nonviolent Coordinating Committee (SNCC), which was in Ruleville to register Black voters. Unaware until then that she had a constitutional right to vote, Hamer became the first to volunteer. But local registrars had the power to require some—meaning Black—applicants to pass a test interpreting the state constitution before they were allowed to register. Unable to do so, Hamer was forbidden from registering. On the way back to Ruleville, police officers stopped the bus and detained all passengers. Though Hamer and the others were eventually released, her employer learned of what had happened and threatened to fire her if she did not give up her quest to vote. Hamer would not do so, and she left her job and, for a short time, her family. She received multiple threats against her life, and one night, white vigilantes fired sixteen shots into the house where she was staying with friends.

Hamer began teaching voter education classes with SNCC, and in December 1962, she successfully registered to vote. She also became a speaker at SNCC rallies. In June 1963, she was arrested at a bus station in Winona, Mississippi. In her cell at the Montgomery County Jail, three white police officers ordered two incarcerated Black men to beat her with a blackjack. Her injuries were so severe that she never fully recovered from them. Nonetheless, she was involved later that year in founding the Council of Federated Organizations (COFO), an umbrella voting rights group, and in 1964 became a fierce advocate of the Freedom Summer voter registration drive. At the same time, she attended the Democratic National Convention as a delegate of the Mississippi Freedom Democratic Party (MFDP). Her speech to the credentials committee garnered national attention, but in the end, the committee would not instate the MFDP.

After 1964, Hamer continued to fight against segregation, ran for elected office, and threw herself into anti-poverty and anti-hunger work.

She also joined the National Organization for Women (NOW) shortly after its founding, and as the Democratic Party reckoned with its history of exclusion, she became a staple at conventions. Yet by the 1970s, her health began to fail, possibly as a consequence of the beating she received in the Montgomery County Jail. Hamer died in 1977 at age fifty-nine.

DOLORES CLARA FERNÁNDEZ HUERTA (1930–)

Dolores Clara Fernández Huerta was born in the small mining town of Dawson, New Mexico. Her mother's family had been in New Mexico for generations, and her father was the son of Mexican immigrants. Her parents divorced in 1935, and Huerta, her mother, and her two brothers moved to Stockton, California. Stockton's diversity provided Huerta with a rich multicultural experience, but it was not without inequality. As a student, Huerta was once accused by a teacher of copying her work because the teacher did not believe she had written a series of essays on her own. After graduating from high school, Huerta married her first husband, which relationship turned out to be short-lived. She returned to school at Delta Community College to receive her associate's degree in education, becoming the first person in her family to receive a postsecondary degree, and began teaching elementary school. She also became involved in such organizations as the Catholic Relief Services and Club Azul y Oro (Blue and Gold Club). In 1955, she helped found the Stockton branch of the Community Service Organization (CSO), which sought to organize and empower the poor, tackle discrimination against Mexican Americans, and register voters. Many of her students were the children of migrant farmworkers, and she wanted to do something to ameliorate the poverty she witnessed in the classroom. Often, her students came to school hungry and without adequate clothing.

Through the CSO, Huerta met and married her second husband, Ventura Huerta, and began working alongside César Chávez, who had been pushing the CSO unsuccessfully to organize farmworkers. Huerta shared this commitment, and she and Chávez worked together in the CSO, the Agricultural Workers Organizing Committee (AWOC). She served the CSO as a lobbyist, advocating for bills to extend Social Security and disability insurance to farmworkers and to end the bracero program, among other issues. In 1962, she moved to Delano, California, and joined Chávez in founding the organization that became the United Farm Workers (UFW). Huerta served the UFW as its vice president and chief contract negotiator, placing her at the center of a series of strikes and boycotts starting in the 1960s. When local grape pickers first struck in 1965, Huerta oversaw negotiations of the first successful collective bargaining in the industry; over the next five years, she negotiated as many as two hundred contracts. At the same time, she oversaw the nationwide UFW grape boycott, which resulted in a three-year collective bargaining agreement signed by the entire California table grape industry. She reprised her leadership role in another grape boycott in the 1970s, which contributed to the passage of the 1975 Agricultural Relations Act, which officially recognized farmworkers' right to organize. Huerta was also deeply committed to using the UFW to secure better wages, safer working conditions, and a higher standard of living for farmworkers. In doing so, she was carefully attuned to gender issues. As the mother of eleven children (her third husband was César Chávez's brother Richard), Huerta knew the challenges that inhered in combining wage work and family responsibilities. She also knew that women often decided whether a family would support the union, and so she focused on winning over housewives. She also worked to end sexual harassment of female farmworkers.

In 1988, Huerta was beaten by a police officer during a nonviolent protest of presidential candidate George H. W. Bush, resulting in broken ribs and a ruptured spleen. She used the money she received as settlement from the city of San Francisco to found the Dolores Huerta Foundation, which trains the next generation of organizers. She took a leave of absence from the UFW and focused more explicitly on women's issues, working with the Feminist Majority's Feminization of Power campaign, which encouraged women to pursue elected office. In the decades since, she has continued to advocate for economic justice and women's issues, as well as health care reform, amnesty for undocumented workers, environmental justice, and other issues. Now in her nineties, she remains politically active.

MILDRED JEFFERSON (1927–2010)

Mildred Jefferson was a physician and activist born in Pittsburg, Texas, to a Methodist minister father and a schoolteacher mother. She graduated summa cum laude from Texas College, a historically Black school in Tyler, Texas; earned a master's degree from Tufts University; and in 1951, became the first Black woman to graduate from Harvard Medical School. She hoped to pursue a career in surgery, but at the time, the American Board of Surgery had never certified a Black woman. Jefferson finally received her certification in 1972, after which she became assistant clinical professor of surgery at Boston University Medical Center.

Jefferson's activist career began in 1970, when the American Medical Association voted to relax its rules for when members were allowed to perform abortions. Jefferson opposed this resolution, founding the Value of Life Committee, an educational group, and the Massachusetts Citizens for Life. *Roe v. Wade* (1973) propelled Jefferson further into leadership of the pro-life movement. She became board chair of the National Right to Life Committee (NRLC), which sought to ban abortion, in 1974 and president of the organization in 1975. That same year, she served as an expert witness in the trial of Boston doctor Kenneth Edelin, who faced manslaughter charges for performing a third trimester abortion; her testimony played a key role in securing a conviction (later overturned by the Massachusetts Supreme Judicial Court). Under Jefferson's leadership, the NRLC contributed to the passage of the 1976 Hyde Amendment, which banned the use of federal funds for abortions; made abortion a major issue in the 1976 presidential election; embarked on a campaign to add a human life amendment to the U.S. Constitution; and established a fund for legal challenges to *Roe v. Wade*.

The pro-life movement was predominantly white, but Jefferson, who opposed abortion under all circumstances, felt that the procedure constituted a form of Black genocide. As she told *Ebony* magazine in 1978, "I would guess that the abortionists have done more to get rid of generations and cripple others than all of the years of slavery and lynchings." In certain cases, her arguments aligned with those seeking to broaden women's reproductive freedom. Recognizing how forced sterilization had been used as a weapon against poor women of color, she feared that state officials would force Black women to have abortions as a condition for receiving welfare. Overall, however, she shared the conservative outlook of her white, Catholic colleagues, opposing state aid for mothers, federally funded day care, and laws against gender and racial discrimination in the workplace, and though her views on abortion as Black genocide echoed the era's Black nationalists, she was reluctant to acknowledge the racism and sexism she herself had faced.

By 1978, internal dissent had pushed Jefferson out of the NRLC, but she continued to participate in the pro-life movement. She established the Right to Life Crusade and remained active in several other organizations, and she ran for Congress unsuccessfully four times between 1982 and 1990. In the 1990s, she established a career as a public speaker, staking out positions in favor of moral education and abstinence and against feminism, physician-assisted suicide, and secular humanism.

Jefferson married real estate agent and fellow pro-life activist Shane Cunningham in 1963. The two had no children and divorced in 1981. Jefferson died in Cambridge, Massachusetts, at the age of eighty-four.

MARY YURIKO (YURI) NAKAHARA KOCHIYAMA (1921–2014)

Mary Yuriko (Yuri) Nakahara Kochiyama was born in San Pedro, California, the daughter of a merchant father and a piano teacher mother, both Japanese immigrants. Though many Issei (first generation) parents socialized their Nisei (second generation) children into traditional gender roles, Kochiyama's parents gave her a great deal of freedom to pursue her interests.

In December 1941, while a college student, Kochiyama witnessed FBI agents arrest her father, who was recovering from surgery, under suspicions that he was a security threat. Detained and interrogated for six weeks, he died the day after being returned home. Kochiyama, her mother, and her two brothers were then among the more than 120,000 Japanese American interned by the U.S. government during World War II. On her way to the Jerome War Relocation Center in Arkansas, she witnessed southern racial segregation and realized the different forms racism could take. While in Arkansas, she also met her future husband, Bill Kochiyama, then among the first group of Japanese Americans authorized to leave the camps to serve in the army.

In 1960, the Kochiyamas moved to Harlem, where all the members of the family became involved in activism. Kochiyama met and began a friendship with Malcolm X in 1963, each deepening the other's understanding of how racism functioned in U.S. society. In a photograph that appeared in newspapers and magazines around the world after his assassination in 1965, Kochiyama appears holding Malcolm X's head after he was shot. Kochiyama's activism intensified after this point, as she participated in protests against the Vietnam War and for Black civil rights and women's rights. After its founding in 1966, Kochiyama supported the Black Panther Party (BPP) and its calls for Black separatism.

Kochiyama did not self-identify as a feminist, a term that she equated with white, bourgeois concerns or with radical separatism. She also did not feel it was her place to challenge sexism within the BPP, and thus, she did not participate in the growing Black feminist movement. She did focus her attention on some issues that primarily affected women—specifically, the military rape of Asian women. As her biographer, Diane C. Fujino, concludes, Kochiyama's life of activism, which challenged many of the tenets of Asian American womanhood, stood as a powerful call for gender equality.

In the 1980s, both Yuri and Bill were leaders of the ultimately successful campaign to secure reparations for Japanese American internees. Following Bill's death and her own health problems in the 1990s, Yuri Kochiyama returned to California, where most of her children lived. She remained politically active into the twenty-first century, protesting, for example, indefinite detainment of suspected terrorists and racial profiling after September 11, 2001. In 2005, she was nominated for the Nobel Peace Prize. Kochiyama died in 2014 at age ninety-three.

Primary Documents

1. The House Committee on Un-American Activities Reports on the Congress of American Women, 1950

Founded in 1946, the Congress of American Women (CAW) promoted international peace, child welfare, women's advancement, and anti-racism. Because of its left politics and its open ties to the Communist Party, CAW attracted the scrutiny of anti-communists in government, including the House Un-American Activities Committee (HUAC). In this document, an excerpt from a 119-page report, HUAC presented the results of its investigation, concluding that CAW was a communist front. Forced to register with the Department of Justice as a "subversive" organization, CAW disbanded in 1950. Its fate reflects the broader connection between anti-communism and anti-feminism, as well as the ways in which conservatives used the former to enact the latter.

The Congress of American Women is an affiliate of the Women's International Democratic Federation, which was founded and supported at all times by the international Communist movement. The purpose of these organizations is not to deal primarily with women's problems, as such, but rather to serve as a specialized arm of Soviet political warfare in the current "peace" campaign to demobilize the United States and democratic nations generally, in order to render them helpless in the face of the Communist drive for world conquest. While professedly American in name, the Congress of American Women has been anti-American and pro-Soviet since its inception. In fact, the Congress of American Women, as well as its parent body, the Women's International Democratic Federation, has consistently denounced and opposed all recognized non-Communist women's organizations both here and abroad.

It would indeed be unfortunate if any significant body of American women were persuaded to join or lend themselves to the purposes of the organization simply because it has adopted so deceptive a name as the Congress of American Women. It is the purpose of this report to offset any such eventuality. . . .

Proclaimed originally as the "first women's political-action organization since the suffrage movement," the Congress of American Women is just another hoax specifically designed to ensnare idealistically minded but politically gullible women. . . . The chief purpose of the Congress of American Women is to act as part of a world-wide pressure mechanism among women, in support of Soviet foreign and domestic policy. From its inception this group has displayed a marked anti-American bias. Its real aims are discreetly hidden behind a smoke screen of such attractive idealistic bait as equal rights for women "in all aspects of political, economic, legal, cultural, and social life," the extension of educational and health benefits, child care, "defeat of the maneuvers of the Fascists," and unity for world peace. The Congress of American Women and its international parent body assume that these purposes have reached their fruition in the Soviet Union and that the United States is chiefly derelict along these lines. The memberships of both organizations have been exaggerated to tremendous proportions.

Under no circumstances does the committee wish to leave the impression that it is critical toward any women's organization sincerely interested in social reform, in promoting world peace or honestly critical of our foreign policy. However, the organization with which we are dealing is definitely not of that character.

Source: House Committee on Un-American Activities, *Report on the Congress of American Women* (Washington, DC: U.S. Government Printing Office, 1950), 1–3.

2. Katharine St. George, Patricia Harris, and Mary Anderson Debate the Equal Rights Amendment, 1956

In 1956, the Senate Judiciary Committee held hearings on the Equal Rights Amendment (ERA). Among the witnesses were many women's rights activists, who ap-

peared on both sides of the issue. This document presents excerpts from the testimony of three of them: Katharine St. George, Patricia Harris, and Mary Anderson. St. George was a congressional representative from New York, a chief sponsor of the ERA in the House of Representatives, and later a champion of the 1963 Equal Pay Act. Contrast her testimony in support of the amendment with the opposition voiced by the National Council of Negro Women (NCNW), represented by legislative committee chair Patricia Harris, and Mary Anderson, longtime head of the Women's Bureau within the Department of Labor. At the time, the ERA was among the most controversial issues within the women's rights movement.

KATHARINE ST. GEORGE: A great deal has been made of this amendment which, in reality, seems to me to be a very simple one, indeed, one that should be easily understood. . . .

What is taken away by these words, because we are constantly being told that there are certain rights that will be taken away? It seems to me, absolutely nothing. All it does is bring the Constitution up to date by adding the word "sex" to the original "race, creed, or color," that appears elsewhere in our much-vaunted laws against discrimination.

Now, someone will say, "Why do we need this amendment?"

Because the Constitution's provisions are framed in the language of English common law, and under that common law which, as we all know, is very ancient indeed, women have no citizens' rights whatsoever. The 14th and 15th amendments give equal protection and political rights to all persons, citizens, regardless of race; yet the effect of court decisions has been to exempt women in certain of their applications.

The 19th amendment in 1920 gave women the right to vote, but did not alleviate the legal results of the denials of their other citizens' rights and responsibilities.

Laws in many of the States prohibit women from engaging in business without their husbands' consent, grant the father preference in children's guardianship, provide different bases for divorce, discriminate against widows, capriciously protect some workingwomen, relegate women to inferior roles despite the responsibilities they must assume in the modern world.

In the absence of a constitutional amendment, what the State legislature gives this year it can take away next year.

Jury service is still denied women in some States, and there are separate provisions for qualifying women jurors in several States.

Court sanction, and in some cases the husband's written consent, are necessary before a wife may go into independent business in some of our States.

Married women are treated unequally in all community-property States, while provisions vary in general the husband may will one-half the property, the wife may not. Management and control of property are vested in the husband, and the husband—but not the wife—may contract against it.

Husbands may spend or dispose of community property, while the wife has no redress. . . .

Widows' rights are inferior to widowers' in many States, including that of title to real estate, personal property, and the right to real property. . . .

We hear a great deal about this protective legislation.

One of these great protections is that women are not permitted to run elevators after the hour of 11 o'clock or midnight. That is supposed to protect them. Nevertheless, as you gentlemen well know, and ladies, too, there is no protection for women who work in offices cleaning and so forth, at all hours of the night and in the early morning, so it is simply discriminating against women for good jobs and putting them in a rather inferior position in the labor market.

The amendment will preserve States rights. States may still legislate under their police powers on health, welfare, and civil matters.

The only proviso is that the laws shall apply to citizens, without regard to sex.

PATRICIA HARRIS: The National Council of Negro Women wishes to go on record as opposed to the so-called equal rights amendment to the Constitution of the United States as embodied in Senate Joint Resolution 15 and Senate Joint Resolution 39.

The National Council of Negro Women, founded in 1935 by that distinguished American, the late Mary McLeod Bethune, has 21 national affiliates and 90 local councils capable of reaching 850,000 women. The majority of these women are employed full time and provide a necessary part of a family income, for they are also wives and mothers. In convention after convention these women have gone on record in opposition to the so-called equal rights amendment because in their view it simply confirms rights they already possess and places in jeopardy protections won only after years of hard work.

We are not unmindful of the fact that certain legal disabilities are still suffered by women in certain jurisdictions. However, these disabilities are rapidly disappearing through repeal in consistent disuse. On the other hand, there is greater social acceptance than ever before of the need to grant the protection of the society to women as they fulfill their roles as wives and mothers, the touchstone of the all-important family unit.

We agree that women must enjoy the unimpeded right to manage their lives and personal property. There can be no doubt that they are equal to males in their ability to exercise these rights.

However, the demand of women for equal rights must not be taken to mean that men and women have identical needs. As stated before, it is only after long years of public education and legislative petition that women have won understanding of their need for special health and welfare protection. These protections, by and large, are directly related to the special concerns of women who by reason of physical structure are not capable of the same activity as men.

A further social judgment has been made that the community will facilitate the assumption of the role of mother by women by extending special protection in this area.

As we look at Senate Joint Resolutions 15 and 39, we are convinced that the primary result of the adoption thereof would be to make every legal protection of women a constitutional issue and to obstruct the securing of protection where they do not now exist.

The members of the National Council of Negro Women labor under the double handicap of race and sex and they have always stood at the forefront of movements to remove all vestiges of discrimination, the basis of racial origins or sex. Were the so-called equal rights amendment capable of extending one right to improve the lot of women, no voice would be louder than ours in demanding its passage.

However, we are convinced that the adoption of this amendment would worsen the position of all women and we therefore have no alternative to opposing its adoption.

MARY ANDERSON: We have appeared here for the last 33 years on this amendment. And it is really laughable to think that we are still opposing and still affirming the amendment. I don't know what the amendment would do. I know that the amendment in itself will do nothing.

It is an enabling act, and it says that you can do something in the States. The States are permitted to pass laws, the States right now are permitted to pass laws. The States have States rights, and they permit—if you want to appeal a law, or if you want to affirm a law, the States have a perfect right to do so.

And some of these laws that are not equality for women are being done away with in the States; a good many have already been done away with. And I daresay if all the friends on the other side had worked as hard for doing away with the State laws that are against the women, or equality for women, I think that they would have been done away with long ago.

In regard to the women in industry, I would say that the laws that were passed for the improvement of women in industry were passed because people realized in the States, and in the Federal Government also, that the women in industry had worked long hours, with low pay and poor conditions at work. And for that reason, some of those laws were passed. They are still necessary, the minimum wage particularly.

This equal-rights amendment, it doesn't make any difference how much they say it won't touch them—it will. There are many employers right now that will go to the court immediately if this amendment is passed, and ratified, and sak [sic] that this law not be enforced, and the judge can't do anything else but say they are right.

And so, it is almost impossible to tell all the ramifications and all the intricacies that this amendment would involve in the States. And it would be a lawyer's paradise.

I don't think I want to say any more. But we oppose this amendment, and we will oppose it all the time.

Source: Hearings before a Subcommittee of the Committee on the Judiciary, United States Senate, Eighty-Fourth Congress, Second Session, on S. J. Res. 39, Proposing an Amendment to the Constitution of the United States Relative to Equal Rights for Men and Women, April 11 and 13, 1956 (Washington, DC: U.S. Government Printing Office, 1956), 15–17, 52–53, 54–55.

3. The President's Commission on the Status of Women Calls for Expanded Child Care, 1963

In 1961, President John F. Kennedy established the President's Commission on the Status of Women (PCSW) and appointed his longtime advisor and friend Esther Peterson, then head of the Women's Bureau, as its executive vice president. The PCSW's 1963 report, American Woman, *provides a link between the labor feminism of the 1940s and '50s and the liberal feminism of the 1960s. The report called for more educational, professional, and political opportunities for women, but it also reinforced their status as caregivers.*

Child care services are needed in all communities, for children of all kinds of families who may require day care, afterschool care, or intermittent care. In putting major emphasis on this need, the Commission affirms that child care facilities are essential for women in many different circumstances, whether they work outside the home or not. It is regrettable when women with children are forced by economic necessity or by the regulations of welfare agencies to seek employment while their children are young. On the other hand, those who decide to work should have child care services available.

The gross inadequacy of present child care facilities is apparent. Across the country, licensed day care is available to some 185,000 children only. In nearly half a million families with children under 6 years, the mother is frequently the sole support. There are 117,000 families with children under 6 with only a father in the home. Almost 3 million mothers of children under 6 work outside the home although there is a husband present. Other mothers, though not at work, may be ill, living in overcrowded slum conditions with no play opportunities for children, responsible for mentally retarded or emotionally handicapped children, or confronting family crises. Migrant families have no fixed homes.

In the absence of adequate child care facilities, many of these mothers are forced to resort to makeshift arrangements or to leave their children without care. A 1958 survey disclosed no less than 400,000 children under 12 whose mothers worked full time and for whose supervision no arrangements whatsoever had been made. Suitable afterschool supervision is especially crucial for children whom discrimination in housing forces into crowded neighborhoods.

Plans for housing developments, community centers, urban renewal projects, and migratory labor camps should provide space for child care centers under licensing procedures insuring adequate standards.

Localities should institute afterschool and vacation activities, in properly supervised places, for schoolage children whose mothers must be away from home during hours when children are not in school.

Failure to assure such services reflects primarily a lack of community awareness of the realities of modern life. Recent Federal legislation offering assistance to communities establishing day care is a first step in raising its provision to the level of national policy. As a number of localities have discovered, child care can be provided in many ways as long as proper standards are assured: cooperatively by groups of parents; by public or private agencies with fees on a sliding scale according to ability to pay; or as a public undertaking.

Where group programs serve children from a cross section of a city, they provide training grounds for democratic social development. Their educational possibilities range from preparing underprivileged children for school, to providing constructive activities for normal youngsters, to offering especially gifted children additional means of development.

For the benefit of children, mothers, and society, child care services should be available for children of families at all economic levels.

Source: American Woman: Report of the President's Commission on the Status of Women (Washington, DC: U.S. Government Printing Office, 1963), 19–20.

4. Martha Griffiths, Beulah Sanders, and George Wiley Debate Welfare Rights, 1968

In 1968, the Joint Economic Committee of the U.S. Senate and House of Representatives held hearings on the efficacy and viability of current welfare programs. At the time, conservatives and some liberals, represented here by Martha Griffiths, feared that welfare cost too much and bred dependency. The first woman elected to Congress from the state of Michigan and a longtime ERA supporter, Griffiths described herself as "the most dedicated feminist we have in Congress." Her 1968 exchange with Beulah Sanders and George Wiley, both of the National Welfare Rights Organization (NWRO), reveals the ways in which feminists were often divided by race and class.

MARTHA GRIFFITHS: Now I would like to ask you what I think is the $64 question. Did the welfare department ever attempt to find a job for you?

BEULAH SANDERS: No.

GRIFFITHS: Did the Department of Labor ever contact you?

SANDERS: No. I had a job.

GRIFFITHS: And what happened?

SANDERS: I will tell you about it. They set up the poverty program about 3 years ago and they said that they were setting them up for poor people, they wanted total participation of the poor. They also had written in some of their requirements that one-third of the poor should sit on their boards of directors and they would oversee the program to see that the poor people benefited from them. I could sit here and tell you today, I worked in a poverty program for 1 whole year. I learned nothing because they could not teach me anything. I was hired on my own experience and knowledge, working in the community free, helping my neighbors. I was hired on that experience and that background. I was one of the key persons that helped that program to get off to a very good start. The minute the program got on its feet, there were 35 of us poor people who were just phased out of the program, for no reason whatsoever that we thought was valid.

We had no one to turn to. We even took it to the department of welfare and asked them to fight for us so we could keep our jobs, and they could do nothing.

The poverty program has only created hostility among people instead of creating jobs. I worked as a community worker for a whole year and I was phased out of the program. That was a year ago. I have only been unemployed for 1 year.

GRIFFITHS: But neither the welfare nor the Labor Department has ever attempted to find a job for you?

SANDERS: I have been to the Labor Department. There are no jobs.

GRIFFITHS: To your knowledge, do you know anybody on welfare who was ever contacted by the Labor Department?

SANDERS: No.

GEORGE WILEY: Mrs. Griffiths, may I turn that around for a minute? . . . I have some figures from Miss Orshansky's study of poverty which show that of the female-headed family, 69 percent in 1966 were not in the labor force. Our feeling is that a good number, in fact the vast majority, of the welfare recipients and many of the other people who need income support legitimately should not be in the labor force because they have other important responsibilities at home, to take care of their families. And in some cases, they are disabled or aged, and what not.

It is an important question for many people, that they find jobs. But the important thing is that the men, that the people who are able to be heads of households or ought to be legitimate heads of households be the ones to get those jobs.

GRIFFITHS: Let me ask you one other question. In the State of New York a family can draw ADC with the father at home?

WILEY: Yes.

GRIFFITHS: Now, I regret to say, Mr. Wiley, you are speaking to the most dedicated feminist we have in Congress. I want to point out to you what I think the welfare program does.

In the first place, we discovered in Ways and Means that the welfare department and the Labor Department were not really attempting to find jobs for people on welfare at all, that if they had their choice between a person who was on welfare and a person who was just out of a job and both were equally qualified, they would simply put on the people who were just out of a job. If you are going to do it this way, you are going to have forever in this country a group of people who are on welfare. Maybe that is all right for the country, but it is not all right for the people on welfare. Those people have a right to participate in the economy of this country. They have just as much right to have a job as anybody else has.

You say that this work incentive program [will] be used to force mothers to work. Well, they will have a choice as to which mothers work and which do not. But if you do not say anything about mothers working, then they are going to see to it that none work. They are not going to be given any chance to work. And in my opinion, this is wrong.

After we went through all of this in the Ways and Means Committee, Mr. Cohen called me and told me that they were quite surprised. They had run a survey in New York City and they had discovered that 70 percent of the women drawing welfare in New York City who had families, 70 percent of them wanted to work if they had a place to put their children.

And I said to him, well, Mr. Cohen, the other 30 percent did not understand the question or they would have wanted to work, too. Who would not prefer to have a job?

But if you give the welfare officials a chance, and the Labor Department, you are going to consign the women to welfare. I just do not think that is fair. I am a woman, Mr. Wiley, and I know the kinds of discriminations that have been used against women.

WILEY: I work for 5,000 or 6,000 women.

GRIFFITHS: I know the discriminations that have been used against women. I am not for just consigning poor women forever to welfare. . . .

SANDERS: Could I say one thing before you go, woman to woman? . . . The fact is, Mrs. Griffiths, that most of us—if this 12,080 goes into effect—are very concerned about it, because, take for example, me. I have qualifications that can hold down a number of jobs.

GRIFFITHS: I'm sure you have.

SANDERS: But the thing is that there is still something lacking, because the Labor Department tells me that: you do not have a college degree. I only have a high school diploma. I was unfortunate. I was not able to go to college. This is what I have against me. This is what a lot of mothers are going to face.

One of the things we are concerned about is being forced into these nonexisting positions which might be going out and cleaning Mrs. A's kitchen. I am not going to do that because I feel I am more valuable and can do something else. This is one of the things these people are worrying about, that they are going to be pushed into housework when they can be much more valuable doing something else. But they do not have the training, they do not have the experience, they do not have the college degree. But what they do have that is going for them is the nitty-gritty stuff and that is out in the community, mixing with the people, finding out what their problems are, and trying to help solve those problems.

Because we all have the same common problem, we are women who are heads of households. We have children, small children that we have no day care facilities for. We have nobody to leave our kids with that we can feel that if we go to work, our kids are going to be taken care of properly. These are the things that we are worried about. . . .

The fact that they are talking about giving us counseling, I say to you, Mrs. Griffiths, I don't need anyone to give me counseling. Our people do not need it. We need concrete programs that if you have to put the people to work, why can't you give them something that they will be able to get off the welfare completely, but you are not doing it with 12,080, because they have no jobs.

Source: Income Maintenance Programs: Hearings before the Subcommittee on Fiscal Policy of the Joint Economic Committee, Congress of the United States, Ninetieth Congress, Second Session, June 11, 12, 13, 18, 19, 20, 25, 26, and 27, 1968 (Washington, DC: U.S. Government Printing Office, 1968), 76–79.

5. Harry Blackmun Delivers the Opinion of the Supreme Court in *Roe v. Wade*, 1973

In 1971 and 1972, lawyer Sarah Weddington argued in front of the Supreme Court that a Texas anti-abortion law was unconstitutional. She represented a class of litigants headed up by Jane Roe, the pseudonym of Norma McCorvey. Justice Harry Blackmun wrote for the court's seven-to-two majority, which voted to overturn state bans on abortion. In his opinion, Blackmun laid out two countervailing interests: women's right to privacy and the fetus's right to survive. During the first trimester, he argued, the former outweighed the latter; after the point of viability—the point at which the fetus could potentially survive outside the womb—their positions reversed. As technology improved over the remainder of the twentieth century and into the twenty-first, viability became a sticking point in many of the debates over the morality and legality of abortion. In 2022, conservatives attained a long-sought goal: the Supreme Court overturned Roe, allowing states to restrict or eliminate access to legal abortion.

V

The principal thrust of appellant's attack on the Texas statutes is that they improperly invade a right, said to be possessed by the pregnant woman, to choose to terminate her pregnancy. Appellant would discover this right in the concept of personal "liberty" embodied in the Fourteenth Amendment's Due Process Clause; or in personal, marital, familial, and sexual privacy said to be protected under the Bill of Rights. . . . Before addressing this claim, we feel it desirable briefly to survey, in several aspects, the history of abortion, for such insight as that history may afford us, and then to examine the state purposes and interests behind the criminal abortion laws.

VI

It perhaps is not generally appreciated that the restrictive criminal abortion laws in effect in a majority of States today are of relatively recent vintage. Those laws, generally proscribing abortion or its attempt at any time during pregnancy except when necessary to preserve the pregnant woman's life, are not of ancient or even of common-law origin. Instead, they derive from statutory changes effected, for the most part, in the latter half of the 19th century. . . .

By 1840, . . . only eight American States had statutes dealing with abortion. It was not until after the War Between the States that legislation began generally to replace the common law. . . .

It is thus apparent that at common law, at the time of the adoption of our Constitution, and throughout the major portion of the 19th century, abortion was viewed with less disfavor than under most American statutes currently in effect. Phrasing it another way, a woman enjoyed a substantially broader right to terminate a pregnancy than she does in most States today. At least with respect to the early stages of pregnancy, and very possibly without such a limitation, the opportunity to make this choice was present in this country well into the 19th century. Even later, the law continued for some time to treat less punitively an abortion procured in early pregnancy. . . .

VII

Three reasons have been advanced to explain historically the enactment of criminal abortion laws in the 19th century and to justify their continued existence.

It has been argued occasionally that these laws were the product of a Victorian social concern to discourage illicit sexual conduct. Texas, however, does not advance this justification in the present case, and it appears that no court or commentator has taken the argument seriously. The appellants and *amici* contend, moreover, that this is not a proper state purpose at all and suggest that, if it were, the Texas statutes are overbroad in protecting it since the law fails to distinguish between married and unwed mothers.

A second reason is concerned with abortion as a medical procedure. When most criminal abortion laws were first enacted, the procedure was a hazardous one for the woman. This was particularly true prior to the development of antisepsis. Antiseptic techniques, of course, were based on discoveries by Lister, Pasteur, and others first announced in 1867, but were not generally accepted and employed until about the turn of the century. Abortion mortality was high. Even after 1900, and perhaps until as late as the development of antibiotics in the 1940s, standard modern techniques such as dilation and curettage were not nearly so safe as they are today.

Thus, it has been argued that a State's real concern in enacting a criminal abortion law was to protect the pregnant woman, that is, to restrain her from submitting to a procedure that placed her life in serious jeopardy.

Modern medical techniques have altered this situation. Appellants and various *amici* refer to medical data indication that abortion in early pregnancy, that is, prior to the end of the first trimester, although not without its risk, is now relatively safe. Mortality rates for women undergoing early abortions, where the procedure is legal, appear to be as low or lower than the rates for normal childbirth. Consequently, any interest of the State in protecting the woman from an inherently hazardous procedure, except when it would be equally dangerous for her to forgo it, has largely disappeared. Of course, important state interests in the areas of health and medical standards do remain.

The State has a legitimate interest in seeing to it that abortion, like any other medical procedure, is performed under circumstances that insure maximum safety for the patient. This interest obviously extends at least to the performing physician and his [sic] staff, to the facilities involved, to the availability of after-care, and to adequate provision for any complication or emergency that might arise. The prevalence of high mortality rates at illegal "abortion mills" strengthens, rather than weakens, the State's interest in regulating the conditions under which abortions are performed. Moreover, the risk to the woman increases as her pregnancy continues. Thus, the state retains a definite interest in protecting the woman's own health and safety when an abortion is proposed at a late stage of pregnancy.

The third reason is the State's interest—some phrase it in terms of duty—in protecting prenatal life. Some of the argument for this justification rests on the theory that a new human life is present from the moment of conception. The State's interest and general obligation to protect life then extends, it is argued, to prenatal life. Only when the life of the pregnant mother herself is at stake, balanced against the life she carries within her, should the interest of the embryo or fetus not prevail. Logically, of course, a legitimate state interest in this area need not stand or fall on acceptance of the belief that life begins at conception or at some other point prior to live birth. In assessing the State's interest, recognition may be given to the less rigid claim that as long as at least *potential* life is involved, the State may assert interests beyond the protection of the pregnant woman alone.

Parties challenging state abortion laws have sharply disputed in some courts the contention that a purpose of these laws, when enacted, was to protect prenatal life. Pointing to the absence of legislative history to support the contention, they claim that most state laws were designed solely to protect the woman. Because medical advances have lessened this concern, at least in early pregnancy, they argue that with respect to abortions the laws can no longer be justified by any state interest. There is some scholarly support for this view of original purpose. The few state courts called upon to interpret their laws in the late 19th and early 20th centuries did focus on the State's interest in protecting the woman's health rather than in preserving the embryo ad fetus. . . .

It is with these interests, and the weight to be attached to them, that this case is concerned.

VIII

The Constitution does not explicitly mention any right of privacy. In a line of decisions, however, . . . the Court has recognized that a right of personal privacy, or a guarantee of certain areas or zones of privacy, does exist under the Constitution. . . .

This right of privacy, whether it be founded in the Fourteenth Amendment's concept of personal liberty and restrictions upon state action, as we feel it is, or, as the District Court determined, in the Ninth Amendment's reservation of rights to the people, is broad enough to encompass a woman's decision whether or not to terminate her pregnancy. The detriment that the State would impose upon the pregnant woman by denying this choice altogether is apparent. Specific and direct harm medically diagnosable even in early pregnancy may be involved. Maternity, or additional offspring, may force upon the woman a distressful life and future. Psychological harm may be imminent. Mental and physical health may be taxed by child care. There is also the distress, for all concerned, associated with the unwanted child, and there is the problem of bringing a child into a family already unable, psychologically and otherwise, to care for it. In other cases, as in this one, the additional difficulties and continuing stigma of unwed motherhood may be involved. All these are factors the woman and her responsible physician necessarily will consider in consultation.

On the basis of elements such as these, appellant and some *amici* argue that the woman's right is absolute and that she is entitled to terminate her pregnancy at whatever time, in whatever way, and for whatever reason she alone chooses. With this we do not agree. . . . The Court's decisions recognizing a right of privacy also acknowledge that some state regulation in areas protected by that right is appropriate. As noted above, a State may properly assert important interests in safeguarding health, in maintaining medical standards, and in protecting potential life. At some point in pregnancy, these respective interests become sufficiently compelling to sustain regulation of the factors that govern the abortion decision. The privacy right involved, therefore, cannot be said to be absolute. . . .

X

. . . These interests are separate and distinct. Each grows in substantiality as the woman approaches term and, at a point during pregnancy, each becomes "compelling."

With respect to the State's important and legitimate interest in the health of the mother, the "compelling" point, in the light of present medical knowledge, is at approximately the end of the first trimester. . . .

This means, on the other hand, that, for the period of pregnancy prior to this "compelling" point, the attending physician, in consultation with his [sic] patient, is free to determine, without regulation by the State, that, in his [sic] medical judgment, the patient's pregnancy should be terminated. If that decision is reached, the judgment may be effectuated by an abortion free of interference by the State.

With respect to the State's important and legitimate interest in potential life, the "compelling" point is at viability. This is so because the fetus then presumably has the capability of meaningful life outside the mother's womb. State regulation protective of fetal life after viability thus has both logical and biological justifications. If the State is interested in protecting fetal life after viability, it may go so far as to proscribe abortion during that period, except when it is necessary to preserve the life or health of the mother. . . .

XI

To summarize and to repeat:

1. A state criminal abortion statute of the current Texas type, that excepts from criminality only a *life-saving* procedure on behalf of the mother, without regard to pregnancy stage and without recognition of the other interests involved, is violative of the Due Process Clause of the Fourteenth Amendment.

   a. For the stage prior to approximately the end of the first trimester, the abortion decision and its effectuation must be left to the medical judgment of the pregnant woman's attending physician.

   b. For the stage subsequent to approximately the end of the first trimester, the State, in promoting its interest in the health of the mother may, if it chooses, regulate the abortion procedure in ways that are reasonably related to maternal health.

   c. For the stage subsequent to viability, the State in promoting its interest in the potentiality of human life may, if it chooses, regulate, and even proscribe, abortion except where it is necessary, in appropriate medical judgment, for the preservation of the life or health of the mother. . . .

XII

Our conclusion that Art. 1196 is unconstitutional means, of course, that the Texas abortion statutes, as a unit, must fall.

Source: Roe v. Wade, 410 U.S. 113 (1973).

6. Consuelo Nieto Describes the Need for Chicana Feminism, 1974

In 1974, Civil Rights Digest, *a publication of the U.S. Commission on Civil Rights, devoted an issue to the feminist movement. As in this excerpt from an article by Consuelo Nieto, pieces focused on the needs of women from different*

*racial and ethnic backgrounds, revealing the breadth of second-wave feminist or-
ganizing, as well as its deep-seated connections to other social movements. Consuelo Nieto was a member of the Comision Feminil Mexicana, a Chicana feminist organization, and of the National Education Association Women's Rights
Task Force. She later received her PhD from Claremont Graduate University
and taught for several decades at California State University–Long Beach.*

Like the Adelitas who fought with their men in the Mexican Revolution, Chicanas have joined their brothers to fight for social justice. The
Chicana cannot forget the oppression of her people, her *raza*—male and
female alike. She fights to preserve her culture and demands the right
to be unique in America. Her vision is one of a multicultural society in
which one need not surrender to a filtering process and thus melt away to
nothingness. . . .

How does the women's rights movement affect a Chicana's life? The Chicana shares with all women the universal victimhood of sexism. Yet the
Chicana's struggle for personhood must be analyzed with care and sensitivity. Hers is a struggle against sexism within the context of a racist society. Ignore this factor and it is impossible to understand the Chicana's struggle. . . .

The Chicana shares with all women basic needs that cut across ethnic
lines. Yet she has distinctive priorities and approaches, for the Chicana is
distinct from the Anglo woman. The Chicana's world, culture, and values
do not always parallel those of the Anglo woman.

Many Chicanas support the women's movement as it relates to equity
in pay and job opportunities, for instance. Yet for some, particularly the
non-activists, the closer the movement comes to their personal lives, the
more difficult it becomes to tear themselves away from the kinds of roles
they have filled. . . .

Traditionally, the Chicana's strength has been exercised in the home
where she has been the pillar of family life. It is just this role that has
brought her leadership and her abilities to the larger community. . . .

Because life in the poorer barrios is a struggle for survival, the man cannot
always participate in such community activities unless they pay a salary.
He must provide the material support for his family. This is the tradition.
It is in his heart, his conscience. . . .

It's not that they [Chicana women] . . . [don't] view change as personally attractive, but that to demand it would place their family and their home in too much jeopardy. It would mean pulling away from their husbands in a manner that could not be reconciled. And they will not pay that price. . . .

Similarly, some Chicano men will state that they are fighting for their women, but not for that kind of status and position that would give women equal footing. They are fighting to be able to provide for their women the social and economic status and position that Anglo men have been able to give Anglo women. . . .

Chicanas find that to advocate feminist positions frowned upon by the Church often evokes family criticism and pressure. Thus some compromise personal values and feign conformity for the sake of peace within the family. . . .

Chicanos often question the goals of the women's movement. Some see it as an "Anglo women's trip," divisive to the cause of *el movimiento*. These men assert the need to respect women, but women's liberation . . . ? "That deals with trivia, minutiae—we all must concentrate on the battle for social justice."

Many of our brothers see the women's movement as another force which will divert support from *la causa*. On a list of priorities, many Chicanos fail to see how the plight of *la mujer* can be of major concern within the context of la raza's problems. They see the women's movement as a vehicle to entrench and strengthen the majority culture's dominance. They are concerned that their sister may be deceived and manipulated. They warn her never to be used as a pawn against her own people.

Yet the Chicana may sometimes ask, "Is it your real fear, my brother, that I be used against our movement? Or is it that I will assume a position, a stance, that you are neither prepared nor willing to deal with?"

Other Chicanos may be more sensitive and try to help their sisters achieve a higher status, but the fact that they too usually limit the aspirations of their sisters is soon evident. They would open the doors to new roles and new alternatives, but on a selective basis. Some support upward mobility for their sisters in the professions, but renege when it comes to equality at home.

A good number of Chicanos fear that in embracing the women's movement their sisters will negate the very heritage they both seek to preserve. The Chicana would ask her brother, "To be a Chicana—proud and strong in my culture—must I be a static being? Does not the role of women change as life changes?" . . .

Participation within organizations of the women's rights movement can bring to the Chicana a painful sense of alienation from some women of the majority culture. The Chicana may often feel like a marginal figure. Her Anglo sisters may assure her that their struggle unequivocally includes her within its folds.

Yet if she listens carefully, certain contradictions will soon emerge. The Anglo women will help the Chicana by providing a model, a system to emulate. The Anglo will help the Chicana erase those "differences" which separate them. Hence, "We will all be united under the banner of Woman. This will be our first and primary source of identity."

For a Chicana allied with the struggle of her people, such a simplistic solution is not acceptable. Furthermore, it is difficult for the Chicana to forget that some Anglo women have oppressed her people within this society, and are still not sensitive to minorities or their needs. With Anglo women the Chicana may share a commitment to equality, yet it is very seldom that she will find with them the camaraderie, the understanding, the sensitivity that she finds with her own people. . . .

Source: Consuelo Nieto, "The Chicana and the Women's Rights Movement: A Perspective," *Civil Rights Digest* 6, no. 3 (1974): 36–42.

7. Nan D. Hunter and Andrea Dworkin Debate Pornography, 1985–86

In 1985–86, U.S. attorney general Edwin Meese convened a series of hearings on the effects of pornography. This issue divided feminists, some of whom worked to ban the medium. In 1983, Indianapolis enacted such an ordinance, drafted by anti-pornography feminists Andrea Dworkin and Catharine MacKinnon of Women Against Pornography (WAP). The law became a particularly contentious issue at the hearings, including in this excerpt from Nan D. Hunter's testimony. Hunter represented the Feminist Anti-Censorship Taskforce, which opposed anti-pornography laws. On the other side, Dworkin argued that pornography's damaging nature justified laws against its dissemination.

Content warning: the following contains graphic descriptions of sexual violence.

HUNTER: . . . The problem with pornography, in our view, lies in the extent to which it reflects, validates and glorifies male supremacy. Unfortunately, the indicia of male supremacy are found throughout the society, not just in pornography. Pornography is not the cause of the oppression of women nor is it even the primary channel in which that supremacy is reflected, validated and glorified. Other, much more powerful, established and legitimate institutions contribute far more than does the pornography industry to the second-class status of women. Thus we and many other feminists believe that targeting pornography in a civil rights law, as has been attempted by the ordinance in question, is a fundamentally misguided attempt to get at the root causes of an ideology which tells us that women are inferior and incompetent.

Moreover, such an approach holds real dangers for women which we believe far outweigh the possible benefits from this particular piece of legislation. . . .

First, the definitional problem is central. The ordinance seeks to carve out a new exception to the First Amendment for all texts and images which constitute the "sexually explicit subordination" of women. The subcategories of the definition, assertedly meant in part to explicate the meaning of that term, fail to contain the scope of the ordinance even to material which is sexist or contemptuous of women, much less delineate which material could be said to actively subordinate human beings. . . . Even among feminists, strong disagreement results from attempts to specify which graphic sexual portrayals are "postures . . . of submission" and which are depictions of women actively initiating sexual intercourse or other activities. Unquestionably, some sexually explicit materials produced by women for consumption by women could be removed from public availability pursuant to the trafficking cause of action in this ordinance.

Second, the proposed ordinance commits the interpretation of this highly subjective language to the judicial system, which would be required to render judgment on the meanaing [*sic*] [of] whatever sexually explicit material arguably falls within the definition. We believe that such materials are far too contextual, coded and layered in their meaning to justify the literalistic interpretation which this proposal demands. Frankly, we also do not believe that the judicial system is, especially for women, an advantageous or appropriate forum in which to resolve disputes over which sexually explicit images or texts should be declared "subordinating" or "degrading." Represenetation [*sic*] of the diverse sexual cultures, activities and styles present in our society have often been vulnerable to efforts of suppression. We oppose giving the state yet another tool with which to regulate and restrict expressions of sexuality.

Third, the ordinance itself reinforces sex-based classifications and stereotypes. It goes far beyond recognizing the differences in life experiences which are produced by social structures of gender inequality. It defines pornography in specifically sex-based terms, including men only when they are "use[d] . . . in place of women." The ordinance thus reflects the assumption that in sexuality, degradation is a condition which attaches only to women or to female surrogates. . . . Further, the positing of such uncontrollable male "natural physiologic response[s]" [to sexually explicit materials] invites displacement of the responsibility for the acts of sexual abuse and violence which do occur. We believe the efforts of the state should be directed against the perpetrators of those acts, not against imagery which is itself mostly non-violent.

Last, we believe that sexually explicit speech as a category should receive greater, not less, protection under the First Amendment. The disfavoring of sexually explicit speech beyond the bounds of "obscene" and already unprotected speech is a necessary ingredient for the success of this ordinance. We oppose such a development. Speech describing sexual conduct communicates ideas, suggests varying possibilities and potentials of human experience, affirms core parts of our perceived self-identities, and provides a forum for advocacy.

In summary with respect to the proposed ordinance, we believe that what its supporters describe as a clash between freedom of expression and equality for women is a false conflict. Properly understood, the ordinance fails the test of constitutionality both because it suppresses protected speech, often with content of particular political significance to women, and because it creates sex-based classifications which are not tailored to remedy the conditions of sexual violence and abuse which do exist. . . .

We therefore urge this Commission: to conclude that while sexually explicit materials are not generally a problem in our society, a far greater problem is the demeaning portrayal of women in all media; to recommend that obscenity laws be repealed and prostitution decriminalized; and to recommend the adoption of laws which will seek to remedy significant problems which do exist by conferring greater economic and social power on women.

DWORKIN: My name is Andrea Dworkin. I am citizen of the United States, and in this country where I live, every year millions of pictures are being made of women with our legs spread. We are called beaver, we are called pussy, our genitals are tied up, they are pasted, makeup is put on them to make them pop out of a page at a male viewer. Millions and millions of pictures are made of us in postures of submission and sexual access so that our vaginas are exposed for penetration, our anuses are exposed for penetration, our throats are used as if they are genitals for penetration. In this country where I live as a citizen real rapes are on film and are being sold in the marketplace. And the major motif of pornography as a form of entertainment is that women are raped and violated and humiliated until we discover that we like it and at that point we ask for more.

In this country where I live as a citizen, women are penetrated by animals and objects for public entertainment, women are urinated on and defecated on, women and girls are used interchangeably so that grown women are made up to look like five- or six-year-old children surrounded by toys, presented in mainstream pornographic publications for anal penetration. There are magazines in which adult women are presented with their pubic areas shaved so that they resemble children.

In this country where I live, there is a trafficking in pornography that exploits mentally and physically disabled women, women who are maimed;

there is amputee pornography, a trade in women who have been maimed in that way, as if that is a sexual fetish for men. In this country where I live, there is a trade in racism as a form of sexual pleasure, so that the plantation is presented as a form of sexual gratification for the black woman slave who asks please to be abused, please to be raped, please to be hurt. Black skin is presented as if it is a female genital, and all the violence and the abuse and the humiliation that is in general directed against female genitals is directed against the black skin of women in pornography.

Asian women in this country where I live are tied from trees and hung from ceilings and hung from doorways as a form of public entertainment. There is a concentration camp pornography in this country where I live, where the concentration camp and the atrocities that occurred there are presented as existing for the sexual pleasure of the victim, of the woman, who orgasms to the real abuses that occurred, not very long ago in history.

In the country where I live as a citizen, there is a pornography of the humiliation of women where every single way of humiliating a human being is taken to be a form of sexual pleasure for the viewer and for the victim; where women are covered in filth, including feces, including mud, including paint, including blood, including semen; where women are tortured for the sexual pleasure of those who watch and those who do the torture, where women are murdered for the sexual pleasure of murdering women, and this material exists because it is fun, because it is entertainment, because it is a form of pleasure, and there are those who say it is a form of freedom.

Certainly it is freedom for those who do it. Certainly it is a freedom for those who use it as entertainment, but we are also asked to believe that it is freedom for those to whom it is done. . . .

The women in the pornography, sixty-five to seventy percent of them we believe are victims of incest or child sexual abuse. They are poor women; they are not women who have opportunities in this society. The[y] are frequent runaways who are picked up by pimps and exploited. . . .

Pornography is used in rape—to plan it, to execute it, to choreograph it, to engender the excitement to commit the act. . . .

We see pornography in the harassment of women on jobs, especially in nontraditional jobs, in the harassment of women in education, to create terror and compliance in the home, which as you know is the most dangerous place for women in this society, where more violence is committed against women than anywhere else. . . .

We see pornography having introduced a profit motive into rape. We see that filmed rapes are protected speech. We see the centrality of pornography in serial murders. There *are* snuff films. We see boys imitating pornography. . . .

We see a major trade in women, we see the torture of women as a form of entertainment, and we see women also suffering the injury of objectification—that is to say we are dehumanized. We are treated as if we are subhuman, and that is a precondition for violence against us.

I live in a country where if you film any act of humiliation or torture, and if the victim is a woman, the film is both entertainment and it is protected speech. Now that tells me something about what it means to be a woman citizen in this country, and the meaning of being second class.

When your rape is entertainment, your worthlessness is absolute. You have reached the nadir of social worthlessness. The civil impact of pornography on women is staggering. It keeps us socially silent, it keeps us socially compliant, it keeps us afraid in neighborhoods; and it creates a vast hopelessness for women, a vast despair. One lives inside a nightmare of sexual abuse that is both actual and potential, and you have the great joy of knowing that your nightmare is someone else's freedom and someone else's fun. . . .

I am . . . asking you to acknowledge the international reality of this—this is a human rights issue—for a very personal reason, which is that my grandparents came here, Jews fleeing from Russia, Jews fleeing from Hungary. Those who did not come to this country were all killed, either in pogroms or by the Nazis. They came here for me. I live here, and I live in a country where women are tortured as a form of public entertainment and for profit, and that torture is upheld as a state-protected right. Now, that is unbearable.

I am asking you to help the exploited, not the exploiters. You have a tremendous opportunity here. I am asking you as individuals to have the courage, because I think it's what you will need, to actually be willing yourselves to go and cut that woman down and untie her hands and take the gag out of her mouth, and to do something, for her freedom.

Sources: Testimony of Nan D. Hunter on Behalf of the Feminist Anti-Censorship Task Force (FACT) before the Attorney General's Commission on Pornography, July 25, 1986; U.S. Department of Justice, *Attorney General's Commission on Pornography: Final Report* (Washington, DC: U.S. Government Printing Office, 1986), 770–72.

8. Anita Hill Describes Alleged Sexual Harassment, 1991

In 1991, attorney Anita Hill testified that Clarence Thomas, her former boss at the Department of Education and Equal Employment Opportunity Commission and a nominee to the Supreme Court, had sexually harassed her. During her testimony, the white, male senators on the Senate Judiciary Committee questioned her professional qualifications, her decision to follow Thomas to the EEOC, and her motivations in coming forward. In this excerpt, she is questioned by Senator Howell Heflin, a Democrat from Alabama. Thomas was confirmed, but anger over Hill's treatment both emboldened a record number of women to run for office in 1992 and fueled the rise of a self-identified third-wave feminism.

SEN. HEFLIN: Professor Hill, we heard Judge Thomas deny that he had ever asked you to go out with him socially, dating, and deny all allegations relative to statements that allegedly he had made to you that involved sex, sex organs, pornographic films and materials and this type of thing.

You have testified that this occurred, and that he asked you to date and go out socially. You have testified here today concerning statements that he had made to you about pornographic films and materials and other things.

I, and I suppose every member of this committee, have to come down to the ultimate question of who is telling the truth. My experience as a lawyer and a judge is that you listen to all the testimony and then you try to determine the motivation for the one that is not telling the truth.

Now, in trying to determine whether you are telling falsehoods or not, I have got to determine what your motivations might be. Are you a scorned woman?

MS. HILL: No.

SEN. HEFLIN: Are you a zealoting civil rights believer that progress will be turned back, if Clarence Thomas goes on the Court?

MS. HILL: No, I don't—I think that—I have my opinion, but I don't think that progress will be turned back. I think that civil rights will prevail, no matter what happens with the Court.

SEN. HEFLIN: Do you have a militant attitude relative to the area of civil rights?

MS. HILL: No, I don't have a militant attitude.

SEN. HEFLIN: Do you have a martyr complex?

MS. HILL: No, I don't. [Laughter.]

SEN. HEFLIN: Well, do you see that, coming out of this, you can be a hero in the civil rights movement?

MS. HILL: I do not have that kind of complex. I don't like all of the attention that I am getting, I don't—even if I liked the attention, I would not lie to get attention.

SEN. HEFLIN: Well, the issue of fantasy has arisen. You have a degree in psychology from the University of Oklahoma State University.

MS. HILL: Yes.

SEN. HEFLIN: Have you studied in your psychological studies, the question of fantasies? Have you ever studied that from a psychology basis?

MS. HILL: To some extent, yes.

SEN. HEFLIN: What are the traits of fantasy that you studied and as you remember?

MS. HILL: As I remember, it would require some other indication of loss of touch with reality other than one instance. There is no indication that I am an individual who is not in touch with reality on a regular basis and would be subject to fantasy.

SEN. HEFLIN: The reality of where you are today is rather dramatic. Did you take, as Senator Biden asked you, all steps that you knew how to take to prevent being in that chair today?

MS. HILL: Yes, I did. Everything that I knew how to do, I did.

SEN. HEFLIN: There may be other motivations. I just listed some that you usually look to relative to these. Are you interested in writing a book? [Laughter.]

MS. HILL: No, I'm not interested in writing a book.

Source: Anita Miller, ed., *The Complete Transcripts of the Clarence Thomas–Anita Hill Hearings, October 11, 12, 13, 1991* (Chicago: Academy Chicago Publishers, 1994), 65–66.

9. Laura Bush Addresses the Nation on the Status of Afghan Women, 2001

In the wake of the attacks of September 11, 2001, the George W. Bush administration linked its War on Terror to a defense of women's rights. This speech by First Lady Laura Bush was among the first to make this connection, which left many feminists conflicted.

Good morning. I'm Laura Bush, and I'm delivering this week's radio address to kick off a world-wide effort to focus on the brutality against women and children by the al-Qaida terrorist network and the regime it supports in Afghanistan, the Taliban. That regime is now in retreat across much of the country, and the people of Afghanistan—especially women—are rejoicing. Afghan women know, through hard experience, what the rest of the world is discovering: The brutal oppression of women is a central goal of the terrorists. Long before the current war began, the Taliban and its terrorist allies were making the lives of children and women in Afghanistan miserable. Seventy percent of the Afghan people are malnourished. One in every four children won't live past the age of five because health care is not available. Women have been denied access to doctors when they're sick. Life under the Taliban is so hard and repressive, even small displays of joy are outlawed—children aren't allowed to fly kites; their mothers face beatings for laughing out loud. Women cannot work outside the home, or even leave their homes by themselves.

The severe repression and brutality against women in Afghanistan is not a matter of legitimate religious practice. Muslims around the world have condemned the brutal degradation of women and children by the Taliban regime. The poverty, poor health, and illiteracy that the terrorists and the Taliban have imposed on women in Afghanistan do not conform with the treatment of women in most of the Islamic world, where women make important contributions in their societies. Only the terrorists and the Taliban forbid education to women. Only the terrorists and the Taliban threaten to pull out women's fingernails for wearing nail polish. The plight of women and children in Afghanistan is a matter of deliberate human cruelty, carried out by those who seek to intimidate and control.

Civilized people throughout the world are speaking out in horror—not only because our hearts break for the women and children in Afghanistan, but also because in Afghanistan, we see the world the terrorists would like to impose on the rest of us.

All of us have an obligation to speak out. We may come from different backgrounds and faiths—but parents the world over love our children. We respect our mothers, our sisters and daughters. Fighting brutality against women and children is not the expression of a specific culture; it is the acceptance of our common humanity—a commitment shared by people of good will on every continent. Because of our recent military gains in much of Afghanistan, women are no longer imprisoned in their homes. They can listen to music and teach their daughters without fear of punishment. Yet the terrorists who helped rule that country now plot and plan in many countries. And they must be stopped. The fight against terrorism is also a fight for the rights and dignity of women.

In America, next week brings Thanksgiving. After the events of the last few months, we'll be holding our families even closer. And we will be especially thankful for all the blessings of American life. I hope Americans will join our family in working to insure that dignity and opportunity will be secured for all the women and children of Afghanistan.

Have a wonderful holiday, and thank you for listening.

Source: Radio Address by Laura Bush to the Nation, November 17, 2001, U.S. Department of State Archive, https://2001-2009.state.gov/g/wi/7192.htm.

10. Sandra Fluke Describes the Importance of Affordable Birth Control, 2012

The 2010 Affordable Care Act (ACA) for the first time required insurance poli-
cies to include coverage for birth control (with an exemption for religious organi-
zations). Despite the exemption, legal challenges to the mandate emerged almost
immediately; in 2010, Republicans won control of the House of Representatives
and set their sights on overturning the ACA in general and the birth control man-
date in particular. When the House organized hearings on the matter in 2012,
only men were called to testify. In response, Democrats invited Sandra Fluke, a
law student at Georgetown University, to speak. The following excerpt comes
from her testimony, which provoked personal attacks on Fluke by conservative
radio personality Rush Limbaugh.

Leader Pelosi, Members of Congress, good morning, and thank you for calling this hearing on women's health and allowing me to testify on behalf of the women who will benefit from the Affordable Care Act contraceptive coverage regulation. My name is Sandra Fluke, and I'm a third-year student at Georgetown Law, a Jesuit school. I'm also a past president of Georgetown Law Students for Reproductive Justice or LSRJ. I'd like to acknowledge my fellow LSRJ members and allies and all of the student activists with us and thank them for being here today.

Georgetown LSRJ is here today because we're so grateful that this regulation implements the nonpartisan, medical advice of the Institute of Medicine. I attend a Jesuit law school that does not provide contraception coverage in its student health plan. Just as we students have faced financial, emotional, and medical burdens as a result, employees at religiously affiliated hospitals and universities across the country have suffered similar burdens. We are all grateful for the new regulation that will meet the critical health care needs of so many women. Simultaneously, the recently announced adjustment addresses any potential conflict with the religious identity of Catholic and Jesuit institutions.

When I look around my campus, I see the faces of the women affected, and I have heard more and more of their stories. On a daily basis, I hear from yet another woman from Georgetown or other schools or who works for a religiously affiliated employer who has suffered financial, emotional, and medical burdens because of this lack of contraceptive coverage. And so, I am here to share their voices, and I thank you for allowing them to be heard.

Without insurance coverage, contraception can cost a woman over $3,000 during law school. For a lot of students who, like me, are on public interest scholarships, that's practically an entire summer's salary. Forty percent of female students at Georgetown Law report struggling financially as a result of this policy. One told us of how embarrassed and powerless she felt when she was standing at the pharmacy counter, learning for the first time that contraception wasn't covered, and had to walk away because she couldn't afford it. Women like her have no choice but to go without contraception. Just last week, a married female student told me she had to stop using contraception because she couldn't afford it any longer. Women employed in low wage jobs without contraceptive coverage face the same choice.

You might respond that contraception is accessible in lots of other ways. Unfortunately, that's not true. Women's health clinics provide vital medical services, but as the Guttmacher Institute has documented, clinics are unable to meet the crushing demand for these services. Clinics are closing, and women are being forced to go without. How can Congress consider the Fortenberry, Rubio, and Blunt legislation that would allow even more employers and institutions to refuse contraceptive coverage and then respond that the nonprofit clinics should step up to take care of the resulting medical crisis, particularly when so many legislators are attempting to defund those very same clinics?

These denials of contraceptive coverage impact real people. In the worst cases, women who need this medication for other medical reasons suffer dire consequences. A friend of mine, for example, has polycystic ovarian syndrome and has to take prescription birth control to stop cysts from growing on her ovaries. Her prescription is technically covered by Georgetown insurance because it's not intended to prevent pregnancy. Under many religious institutions' insurance plans, it wouldn't be, and under Senator Blunt's amendment, Senator Rubio's bill, or Representative Fortenberry's bill, there's no requirement that an exception be made for such medical needs. When they do exist, these exceptions don't accomplish their well-intended goals because when you let university administrators or other employers, rather than women and their doctors, dictate whose medical needs are legitimate and whose aren't, a woman's health takes a back seat to a bureaucracy focused on policing her body.

In 65 percent of cases, our female students were interrogated by insurance representatives and university medical staff about why they needed these prescriptions and whether they were lying about their symptoms. For my friend, and 20 percent of women in her situation, she never got the insurance company to cover her prescription, despite verification of her illness from her doctor. Her claim was denied repeatedly on the assumption that she really wanted the birth control to prevent pregnancy. She's gay, so clearly polycystic ovarian syndrome was a much more urgent concern than accidental pregnancy. After months of paying over $100 out of pocket, she just couldn't afford her medication anymore and had to stop taking it. I learned about all of this when I walked out of a test and got a message from her that in the middle of her final exam period she'd been in the emergency room all night in excruciating pain. She wrote, "It was so painful, I woke up thinking I'd been shot." Without her taking the birth control, a massive cyst the size of a tennis ball had grown on her ovary. She had to have surgery to remove her entire ovary. On the morning I was originally scheduled to give this testimony, she sat in a doctor's office. Since last year's surgery, she's been experiencing night sweats, weight gain, and other symptoms of early menopause as a result of the removal of her ovary. She's thirty-two years old. As she put it: "If my body indeed does enter early menopause, no fertility specialist in the world will be able to help me have my own children. I will have no chance at giving my mother her desperately desired grandbabies, simply because the insurance policy that I paid for totally unsubsidized by my school wouldn't cover my prescription for birth control when I needed it." Now, in addition to potentially facing the health complications that come with having menopause at an early age—increased risk of cancer, heart disease, and osteoporosis, she may never be able to conceive a child.

Perhaps you think my friend's tragic story is rare. It's not. One woman told us doctors believe she has endometriosis, but it can't be proven without surgery, so the insurance hasn't been willing to cover her medication. Recently, another friend of mine told me that she also has polycystic ovarian syndrome. She's struggling to pay for her medication and is terrified to not have access to it. Due to the barriers erected by Georgetown's policy, she hasn't been reimbursed for her medication since last August. I sincerely pray that we don't have to wait until she loses an ovary or is diagnosed with cancer before her needs and the needs of all of these women are taken seriously.

This is the message that not requiring coverage of contraception sends. A woman's reproductive healthcare isn't a necessity, isn't a priority. One student told us that she knew birth control wasn't covered, and she assumed that's how Georgetown's insurance handled all of women's sexual healthcare, so when she was raped, she didn't go to the doctor even to be examined or tested for sexually transmitted infections because she thought insurance wasn't going to cover something like that, something that was related to a woman's reproductive health. As one student put it, "this policy communicates to female students that our school doesn't understand our needs." These are not feelings that male fellow students experience. And they're not burdens that male students must shoulder.

In the media lately, conservative Catholic organizations have been asking: what did we expect when we enrolled at a Catholic school? We can only answer that we expected women to be treated equally, to not have our school create untenable burdens that impede our academic success. We expected that our schools would live up to the Jesuit creed of *cura personalis*, to care for the whole person, by meeting all of our medical needs. We expected that when we told our universities of the problems this policy created for students, they would help us. We expected that when 94 percent of students opposed the policy, the university would respect our choices regarding insurance students pay for completely unsubsidized by the university. We did not expect that women would be told in the national media that if we wanted comprehensive insurance that met our needs, not just those of men, we should have gone to school elsewhere, even if that meant a less prestigious university. We refuse to pick between a quality education and our health, and we resent that, in the twenty-first century, anyone thinks it's acceptable to ask us to make this choice simply because we are women.

Many of the women whose stories I've shared are Catholic women, so ours is not a war against the church. It is a struggle for access to the healthcare we need. The president of the Association of Jesuit Colleges has shared that Jesuit colleges and universities appreciate the modification to the rule announced last week. Religious concerns are addressed and women get the healthcare they need. That is something we can all agree on. Thank you.

Source: 158 Cong. Rec. S1135 (daily ed. February 29, 2012) (statement of Sandra Fluke).

ANNOTATED
BIBLIOGRAPHY

OVERVIEWS

No single monograph captures the scope of the women's rights movement since 1945. Ruth Rosen, *The World Split Open: How the Modern Women's Movement Changed America* (New York: Penguin Books, 2000), and Sara Evans, *Tidal Wave: How Women Changed America at Century's End* (New York: Simon and Schuster, 2002), provide able narratives, though Nancy MacLean, *The American Women's Movement, 1945–2000: A Brief History with Documents* (Boston, MA: Bedford/St. Martin's, 2008), reflects more insights from recent literature.

LABOR AND WORKPLACE RIGHTS

Some of the earliest books to explore feminism in the era between the Nineteenth Amendment and the 1960s focused on the National Woman's Party (NWP). See, for example, Christine Lunardini, *From Equal Suffrage to Equal Rights: Alice Paul and the National Woman's Party, 1912–1928* (New York: New York University Press, 1986); and Leila J. Rupp and Verta Taylor, *Survival in the Doldrums: The American Women's Rights Movement, 1945 to the 1960s* (New York: Oxford University Press, 1987). In the past twenty-five years, however, historians have turned away from this cohort of self-identified feminists and instead focused on the robust movement for women's rights in other sectors.

Two essential texts, for example, discuss women's participation in the labor movement and the connection between this activism and feminism over the course of several decades of the twentieth century:

Annelise Orleck, *Common Sense and a Little Fire: Women and Working-Class Politics in the United States, 1900–1965* (Chapel Hill: University of North Carolina Press, 1995), focused in but not exclusively about the pre–World War II era, is a joint biography of four women activists. Dorothy Sue Cobble, *The Other Women's Movement: Workplace Justice and Social Rights in Modern America* (Princeton, NJ: Princeton University Press, 2005), follows the next generation of labor activists as its members influenced unions, government policy, and the shape of modern feminism. See also on this subject Kathleen A. Laughlin, *Women's Work and Public Policy: A History of the Women's Bureau, U.S. Department of Labor, 1945–1970* (Boston: Northeastern University Press, 2000). Important primary sources on this topic include *American Women: Report of the President's Commission on the Status of Women* (Washington, DC: U.S. Government Printing Office, 1963), and Brigid O'Farrell and Felicia L. Kornbluh, *Rocking the Boat: Union Women's Voices, 1915–1975* (New Brunswick, NJ: Rutgers University Press, 1996), especially, interviews with Esther Peterson.

The standard narrative holds that the power of organized labor declined starting in the 1970s. However, recent books have convincingly shown that this assertion is not necessarily true if one looks at the experiences of women and minorities; see, for example, Lane Windham, *Knocking on Labor's Door: Union Organizing in the 1970s and the Roots of a New Economic Justice* (Chapel Hill: University of North Carolina Press, 2019). Robyn Muncy, *Relentless Reformer: Josephine Roche and Progressivism in Twentieth-Century America* (Princeton, NJ: Princeton University Press, 2015), uses one woman's experiences to demonstrate continuity within the twentieth-century labor movement. The now classic book by Nancy MacLean, *Freedom Is Not Enough: The Opening of the American Workplace* (New York: Russell Sage Foundation, 2006), charts the movements that demanded workplace equity, the sometimes ironic ways in which these demands made their way into law, and the ways in which certain groups were excluded from the benefits of new policies. Finally, a growing body of work addresses the persistence of labor activism in the era of neoliberalism, focusing on such topics as the Fight for $15 and the legal battle over pay equity at the retail giant Walmart. See, respectively, Annelise Orleck, *"We Are All Fast-Food Workers Now": The Global Uprising against Poverty Wages* (Boston: Beacon Press, 2018); and Liza Featherstone, *Selling*

Women Short: The Landmark Battle for Workers' Rights at Wal-Mart (New York: Basic Books, 2009).

For some women, workplace rights also included the right *not* to work for wages. Felicia Kornbluh, *The Battle for Welfare Rights: Politics and Poverty in Modern America* (Philadelphia: University of Pennsylvania Press, 2007); Premilla Nadasen, *Welfare Warriors: The Welfare Rights Movement in the United States* (New York: Routledge, 2004); and Wilson Sherwin and Frances Fox Piven, "The Radical Feminist Legacy of the National Welfare Rights Organization," *Women's Studies Quarterly* 47, no. 3–4 (2019): 135–53, all detail the founding, development, and major personalities of the National Welfare Rights Organization (NWRO). Jennifer Mittlestadt, *From Welfare to Workfare: The Unintended Consequences of Liberal Reform* (Chapel Hill: University of North Carolina Press, 2006), and Gwendolyn Mink, *Welfare's End* (Ithaca, NY: Cornell University Press, 1998), trace the policy changes that eventually led to the disestablishment of Aid to Families with Dependent Children (AFDC) in 1997.

WOMEN, THE COLD WAR, AND THE POLITICS OF DOMESTICITY

For an overview of this era, see Ellen Schrecker, *Many Are the Crimes: McCarthyism in America* (Princeton, NJ: Princeton University Press, 1998). Of the historians who have looked at this era, two have most thoroughly documented the connections between anti-communism and anti-feminism: Elaine Tyler May, *Homeward Bound: American Families in the Cold War Era* (New York: Basic Books, 1988), and Landon Storrs, *The Second Red Scare and the Unmaking of the New Deal Left* (Princeton, NJ: Princeton University Press, 2012). Recent historians, including Storrs, have criticized May's characterization of the era, challenging the idea of the period between 1945 and 1963 as a time of unquestioned conformity and heteronormative stability. See also Stephanie Coontz, *The Way We Never Were: American Families and the Nostalgia Trap* (New York: Basic Books, 1992); Coontz, *A Strange Stirring: The Feminine Mystique and American Women at the Dawn of the 1960s* (New York: Basic Books, 2011); Daniel Horowitz, *Betty Friedan and the Making of* The Feminine Mystique: *The American Left, the Cold War, and Modern Feminism* (Amherst: University of Massachusetts Press, 1998); and Joanne Meyerowitz, ed., *Not June Cleaver:*

Women and Gender in Postwar America, 1945–1960 (Philadelphia: Temple University Press, 1994). Others have identified a full-fledged left feminism that emerged in these years before being tamped down. See Kate Weigand, *Red Feminism: American Communism and the Making of Women's Liberation* (Baltimore: The John Hopkins University Press, 2001). For a biography of the most important activist of this cohort, see Carol Boyce Davies, *Left of Karl Marx: The Political Life of Black Communist Claudia Jones* (Durham, NC: Duke University Press, 2007).

WOMEN IN THE CIVIL RIGHTS MOVEMENT

This book benefited from a number of excellent overviews of Black women's activism, including Deborah Gray White, *Too Heavy a Load: Black Women in Defense of Themselves, 1894–1994* (New York: W. W. Norton, 1999), and Dana Ramey Berry and Kali Nicole Gross, *A Black Women's History of the United States* (Boston: Beacon Press, 2020). For works that connect women's work in the postwar civil rights movement to earlier movements, such as economic nationalism, labor activism, and radical left activism, see Darlene Clark Hine, "The Housewives' League of Detroit: Black Women and Economic Nationalism," in *Visible Women: New Essays on American Activism*, ed. Nancy A. Hewitt and Suzanne Lebsock (Urbana: University of Illinois Press, 1993), 223–42; Eric S. McDuffie, "A 'New Movement of Negro Women': Sojourning for Truth, Justice, and Human Rights during the Early Cold War," *Radical History Review* 101 (2008): 81–106; McDuffie, *Sojourning for Freedom: Black Women, American Communism, and the Making of Black Left Feminism* (Durham, NC: Duke University Press, 2011); and Premilla Nadasen, *Household Workers Unite: The Untold Story of African American Women Who Built a Movement* (Boston: Beacon Press, 2015).

The literature on women's participation in the post–World War II civil rights movement more specifically is vast. Though not just about women, Charles M. Payne's *I've Got the Light of Freedom: The Organizing Tradition and the Mississippi Freedom Struggle* (Berkeley, CA: University of California Press, 1995) is an excellent source of information. On women and desegregation efforts, see Rachel Devlin, *A Girl Stands at the Door: The Generation of Women Who Desegregated America's Schools* (New York: Basic Books, 2018); Jo Ann Gibson Robinson, *The Montgomery Bus Boycott and* the *Women Who Started It: The Memoir of Jo Ann Gibson Robinson*, ed. David J. Garrow (Knoxville: University of Tennessee Press, 1987); Rosalind Rosenberg, *Jane Crow: The Life of Pauli Murray* (New York: Oxford University Press, 2017); and Jeanne Theoharis, *The Rebellious Life of Mrs. Rosa Parks* (Boston: Beacon Press, 2013). On the Student Nonviolent Coordinating Committee (SNCC), see Faith Holsaert et al., eds., *Hands on the Freedom Plow: Personal Accounts by Women in SNCC* (Urbana: University of Illinois Press, 2012); Anne Moody, *Coming of Age in Mississippi: The Classic Autobiography of Growing up Poor and Black in the Rural South* (New York: Doubleday, 1968); and Barbara Ransby, *Ella Baker and the Black Freedom Movement: A Radical Democratic Vision* (Chapel Hill: University of North Carolina Press, 2003). Shirley Chisholm, *Unbought and Unbossed* (1970; repr., Washington, DC: Take Root Media, 2009), provides a first-person account of women in politics. See also generally Belinda Robnett, *How Long? How Long? African-American Women in the Struggle for Civil Rights* (New York: Oxford University Press, 1997). On the relationship between the civil rights movement and the emergence of second-wave feminism, see Sara Evans, *Personal Politics: The Roots of Women's Liberation in the Civil Rights Movement and the New Left* (New York: Vintage Books, 1979), and more recent books that take a different approach: Wini Breines, *The Trouble between Us: An Uneasy History of White and Black Women in the Feminist Movement* (New York: Oxford University Press, 2006); Danielle McGuire, *At the Dark End of the Street: Black Women, Rape, and Resistance—A New History of the Civil Rights Movement from Rosa Parks to the Rise of Black Power* (New York: Vintage Books, 2010); Benita Roth, *Separate Roads to Feminism: Black, Chicana, and White Feminist Movements in America's Second Wave* (New York: Cambridge University Press, 2004); and Anne M. Valk, *Radical Sisters: Second-Wave Feminism and Black Liberation in Washington, DC* (Urbana: University of Illinois Press, 2008).

THE WOMEN'S LIBERATION MOVEMENT

Conventional narratives of the (white) women's liberation movement have recognized its debt to the Black civil rights movement but not necessarily centered the experiences of minority women within the women's liberation movement itself. See, for example, Alice Echols, *Daring to Be*

Bad: Radical Feminism in America, 1967–1975 (Minneapolis: University of Minnesota Press, 1989); Rosalyn Baxandall and Linda Gordon, eds., *Dear Sisters: Dispatches from the Women's Liberation Movement* (New York: Basic Books, 2000); and Robin Morgan, ed., *Sisterhood Is Powerful: An Anthology of Writings from the Women's Liberation Movement* (New York: Vintage Books, 1970); see also Evans, *Personal Politics*.

In this book, I have drawn on the literature that centers self-identified third-world feminists. As many activists and contemporary historians have noted, the Black Power movement was not always receptive to Black women's concerns; see, for example, Frances M. Beal, *Double Jeopardy: To Be Black and Female*, 1969, http://www.hartford-hwp.com/archives/45a/196.html. Yet Black feminists carved out their own niche both within and outside this movement; see Angela Davis, *An Autobiography* (New York: Random House, 1974); Ashley D. Farmer, *Remaking Black Power: How Black Women Transformed an Era* (Chapel Hill: University of North Carolina Press, 2017); Mary Phillips, "The Feminist Leadership of Ericka Huggins in the Black Panther Party," *Black Diaspora Review* 4, no. 1 (2014): 187–221; Kimberly Springer, *Living for the Revolution: Black Feminist Organizations, 1968–1980* (Durham, NC: Duke University Press, 2005); and Keeanga-Yamahtta Taylor, ed., *How We Get Free: Black Feminism and the Combahee River Collective* (Chicago: Haymarket Books, 2017).

This activism also took place against the backdrop of the Vietnam War, which granted Asian and Asian American women a higher degree of visibility that sometimes made interracial feminist activism possible. See Dionne Espinoza, "'La Raza en Canada': San Diego Chicana Activists, the Indochinese Women's Conference of 1971, and Third World Womanism," in *Chicana Movidas: New Narratives of Activism and Feminism in the Movement Era*, ed. Dionne Espinoza, María Eugenia Cotera, and Maylei Blackwell (Austin: University of Texas Press, 2018), 261–75; Diane C. Fujino, *Heartbeat of a Struggle: The Revolutionary Life of Yuri Kochiyama* (Minneapolis: University of Minnesota Press, 2005); Judy Wu, *Radicals on the Road: Internationalism, Orientalism, and Feminism during the Vietnam Era* (Ithaca, NY: Cornell University Press, 2013); and Wu, "Asian American Feminisms and Women of Color Feminisms: Radicalism, Liberalism, and Invisibility," in *Asian American Feminisms and Women of Color Politics*, ed. Lynn Fujiwara and Shireen Roshanravan (Seattle: University of Washington Press, 2018), 43–68; see also more generally Fujiwara and Roshanravan, *Asian American Feminisms and Women of Color Politics.*

On the development of Chicana feminism, see more generally Espinoza, Cotera, and Blackwell, *Chicana Movidas*; and Roth, *Separate Roads to Feminism.* On Native American women and feminism, see Devon Abbott Mihesuah, *Indigenous American Women: Decolonization, Empowerment, Activism* (Lincoln: University of Nebraska Press, 2003); and Cheryl Suzack et al., eds., *Indigenous Women and Feminism: Politics, Activism, Culture* (Vancouver: UBC Press, 2010).

Of the issues that divided the women's liberation movement, those related to sex, sexuality, and reproduction were among the most contentious. On the history of the lesbian rights movement and lesbian feminism, see Lillian Faderman, *The Gay Revolution: The Story of the Struggle* (New York: Simon & Schuster, 2015); Faderman, *Odd Girls and Twilight Lovers: A History of Lesbian Life in Twentieth-Century America* (New York: Columbia University Press, 1991); Marcia M. Gallo, *Different Daughters: A History of the Daughters of Bilitis and the Rise of the Lesbian Rights Movement* (Emeryville, CA: Seal Press, 2007); Radicalesbians, *The Woman-Identified Woman* (Pittsburgh, PA: Know Inc., 1970); and Valk, *Radical Sisters.* Though some feminists (often white) put access to birth control and safe, legal abortion at the center of their activism, women of color were often more concerned with ending forced sterilization and maintaining the right to take care of their children. See Karen Blumenthal, *Jane against the World:* Roe v. Wade *and the Fight for Reproductive Rights* (New York: Roaring Brook Press, 2020); Jennifer Nelson, *Women of Color and the Reproductive Rights Movement* (New York: New York University Press, 2003); and Jael Silliman et al., *Undivided Rights: Women of Color Organize for Reproductive Justice* (Chicago: Haymarket Books, 2004). In the 1980s, feminists were divided into "pro-sex" and "anti-porn" camps; see Carolyn Brownstein, *Battling Pornography: The American Feminist Anti-Pornography Movement, 1976–1986* (New York: Cambridge University Press, 2011).

CONSERVATIVE WOMEN

One of the most rapidly growing, and most exciting, literatures in American historiography over the course of the past two decades focuses on the growth of conservatism, particularly conservative women. Books on the broader conservative movement, including its discourses of gender and family, include Lisa McGirr, *Suburban Warriors: The Origins of the New American Right* (Princeton, NJ: Princeton University Press, 2001); Bethany Moreton, *To Serve God and Wal-Mart: The Making of Christian Free Enterprise* (Cambridge, MA: Harvard University Press, 2010); Robert O. Self, *All in the Family: The Realignment of American Democracy since the 1960s* (New York: Hill and Wang, 2012); and Natasha Zaretsky, *No Direction Home: The American Family and the Fear of National Decline, 1968–1980* (Chapel Hill: University of North Carolina Press, 2007).

Several works provide in-depth looks at specific women within this movement. The most important book in this vein is Donald Critchlow, *Phyllis Schlafly and Grassroots Conservatism: A Woman's Crusade* (Princeton, NJ: Princeton University Press, 2005), which, due to Schlafly's prominence and centrality, also documents the broader right; see also Emily Suzanne Johnson, "God, Country, and Anita Bryant: Women's Leadership and the Politics of the New Christian Right," *Religion and American Culture* 28, no. 2 (2018): 238–68; and Johnson, *This Is Our Message: Women's Leadership in the New Christian Right* (New York: Oxford University Press, 2019).

For broader works on women and conservatism, see Michelle M. Nickerson, *Mothers of Conservatism: Women and the Postwar Right* (Princeton, NJ: Princeton University Press, 2012); Catherine Rymph, *Republican Women: Feminism and Conservatism from Suffrage through the Rise of the New Right* (Chapel Hill: University of North Carolina Press, 2006); and Stacie Taranto, *Kitchen Table Politics: Conservative Women and Family Values in New York* (Philadelphia: University of Pennsylvania Press, 2017).

All the books mentioned in this section address the relationship between feminists and conservatives, but two in particular focus on it: Jane J. Mansbridge's classic, *Why We Lost the ERA* (Chicago: University of Chicago Press, 1986), and, more recently, Marjorie Spruill, *Divided We Stand: The Battle over Women's Rights and Family Values That Polarized American Politics* (New York: Bloomsbury Publishing, 2017).

THIRD-WAVE AND TWENTY-FIRST-CENTURY FEMINISM

In the 1980s and '90s, many longtime activists bemoaned younger women's supposed lack of interest in feminism. On "postfeminism" and "I'm not a feminist, but . . . ," see Susan Faludi, *Backlash: The Undeclared War against American Women* (New York: Anchor Press, 1991); Susan J. Douglas, *Where the Girls Are: Growing up Female with the Mass Media* (New York: Three Rivers Press, 1994); and Tania Modleski, *Feminism without Women: Culture and Criticism in a "Postfeminist" Age* (New York: Routledge, 1991). At the same time, however, a self-identified third-wave feminist movement was emerging. For overviews of this movement, see Jennifer Baumgardner and Amy Richards, *Manifesta: Young Women, Feminism, and the Future* (New York: Farrar, Straus and Giroux, 2000), and Lisa Levenstein, *They Didn't See Us Coming: The Hidden History of Feminism in the Nineties* (New York: Basic Books, 2020). Culture played an important role in third-wave feminism; see Sara Marcus, *Girls to the Front: The True Story of the Riot Grrrl Revolution* (New York: HarperCollins, 2010); Patricia Pender, *I'm Buffy and You're History*: Buffy the Vampire Slayer *and Contemporary Feminism* (London: I. B. Tauris, 2016); and Whitney A. Peoples, "'Under Construction': Identifying Foundations of Hip-Hop Feminisms and Exploring Bridges between Black Second Wave and Hip-Hop Feminisms," in *No Permanent Waves: Recasting Histories of U.S. Feminism*, ed. Nancy A. Hewitt (New Brunswick, NJ: Rutgers University Press, 2010), 403–30, among other essays in this collection, several of which bridge the twentieth and twenty-first centuries. On two early (pre-2016) twenty-first-century manifestations of feminism—"Lean In" and marketplace or feel-good feminism—see Sheryl Sandberg, *Lean In: Women, Work, and the Will to Lead* (New York: Alfred A. Knopf, 2013), and Andi Zeisler, *We Were Feminists Once: From Riot Girl to Cover Girl, the Buying and Selling of a Political Movement* (New York: PublicAffairs, 2016); see also books on the twenty-first-century labor movement cited above.

INDEX

Page numbers in *italics* indicate photos.

About the Author

Christina G. Larocco received her PhD from the department of history at the University of Maryland, College Park. A historian of women and social movements, she is editor of the *Pennsylvania Magazine of History and Biography* and scholarly programs manager at the Historical Society of Pennsylvania. She is writing a biography of nineteenth-century abolitionist and feminist Martha Schofield.